BEYOND *the* BOUNDARIES

the BEYOND BOUNDARIES

A NEW STRUCTURE OF AMBITION IN AFRICAN AMERICAN POLITICS

The National Political Science Review, Volume 12

Georgia A. Persons, *editor*

A Publication of the National Conference of Black Political Scientists

Transaction Publishers
New Brunswick (U.S.A.) and London (U.K.)

This book is printed on acid-free paper that meets the American National Standard for Permanence of Paper for Printed Library Materials.

Library of Congress Catalog Number: 2008051231
ISBN: 978-1-4128-1048-7
Printed in the United States of America

Library of Congress Cataloging-in-Publication Data

Beyond the boundaries : a new structure of ambition in African American politics / Georgia A. Persons, editor.
p. cm. -- (National political science review ; v. 12)
Papers from a symposium.
Includes bibliographical references and index.
ISBN 978-1-4128-1048-7 (alk. paper)
1. African Americans--Politics and government--21st century--Congresses. 2. Ambition--Political aspects--United States--Congresses. 3. African American politicians--Congresses. 4. Political candidates--United States--Congresses. 5. Political campaigns--United States--Congresses. 6. Elections--United States--Congresses. 7. United States--Politics and government--2001---Congresses. 8. United States--Race relations--Political aspects--Congresses. I. Persons, Georgia Anne.

E185.615.B49 2009
323.1196'073--dc22

2008051231

Contents

Part II: The Evolving Developmental Context of Black Politics and Praxis

Part III: Book Forum

Acknowledgments

The Editor extends special thanks to all of the contributors whose work is included in this volume of the *National Political Science Review*. Deepest gratitude to Associate Editor Robert C. Smith for organizing and managing the anchoring symposium for this volume, and to colleagues in the discipline who served as reviewers and made completion of this volume possible.

Thanks to Stephen Henderson, Ivan Allen College of Georgia Tech, whose small but frequent favors and consideration provided support and encouragement in ways that engender deepest appreciation.

The Editor extends deep gratitude to all of the members of the Editorial Board, and a special welcome to new members who have agreed to lend their assistance in furthering the goals of this journal.

Editor's Note

It has long been a well established truism that African American politics was a politics of low resources defined by an insurgent, black liberationist ideological thrust, bounded by the opportunities and restrictions of a relatively small and spatially concentrated primary support base of black voters, and limited by the persistent resistance of many white voters to support black candidates. The results have been the presumption and reality of black electoral gains being disproportionately restricted to areas of sizeable black population bases, and the subsequent inability of black candidates to be successful in statewide electoral contests in all but a handful of cases. Presumably, the aspirations of black candidates for national office were just a dream.

Analysts of African American politics had arrived at a conventional wisdom that conceded a virtual cap on both the possible number of black elected officials and the level of elective office to which they could ascend. Yet in the fall of 2008 as this volume went to press, we found ourselves poised between the astonishing breakout, statewide campaigns of some half dozen black candidates in 2006, and the even more astonishing emergence of Barack Obama as the Democratic nominee for United States president.

The anchoring symposium of this volume of the National Political Science Review was planned before the emergence of Obama as a strong contender for the Democratic Party's nomination. Rather, the early focus then was to attempt to capture the dynamics of a newly emergent episode of ongoing social change; a new spate of statewide campaigns for high-level offices in the evolution of that which we call black politics. When we focus just on the 2006 statewide races, we see what appears to be, in the words of Symposium Editor, Robert Smith, a new structure of ambition in African American politics. We see the ways in which individual ambition operates at the core of a set of strategic variables that hold the promises of expanding the boundaries of African American electoral politics. Or do we? Are we really seeing merely a new structure of ambition, or did the 2006 races presage an emergent dynamic of complexity that requires a more nuanced framing and analysis?

As the reader looks beyond the anchoring symposium and across the totality of this volume, she will notice something of a mix of ways the contributors use to frame the evolving state of black political activity against the broader context of social change that black politics helps both to illuminate and to define significantly. We see the use of the notion of a new structure of ambition in African American politics as essentially an overlay upon the more conventional, though still relatively new, frame of a deracialized black politics—the latter framing having always harbored the seeds of its own internal contradictions. The analyses also show that successful black politics remains hugely disproportionately Democratic Party politics and that black Republican candidates cannot easily obtain successful political lift, nor electoral victory. Indeed, the analyses clearly reveal the persistence of a strongly issue-based black politics that is nestled within the larger context of Democratic Party philosophy and issue positions. Perhaps not surprisingly, contributors reveal that despite the widespread adoption of deracialized campaigns, black candidates remain uniquely vulnerable to the use of racial stereotypes and racist symbolism by their white opponents.

We also see that some analysts continue to frame contemporary black politics as "post civil-rights era black politics"—which is a bluntly accurate framing—though it somewhat erringly suggests the continuing utility of a dichotomous conceptualization of the current state of social change and group relations in America. Of course, any analysis of the black reparations movement is a reminder of the persistence of enormous ideological diversity within the black community, though perhaps now more than ever, that diversity resides mainly at the margins.

As we gauge the thinking of our political science colleagues as presented in the contributions to this volume, perhaps what we find particularly missing are compelling discussions and analyses of the changing nature of race in American politics. The confounding and chameleonic nature of race makes this omission substantially understandable. Indeed, some dimensions of this change are yet quite new.

What we do see when we look at this volume of essays in full, is that within that vortex of social change that engulfs black politics, many things are likely happening at the same time. Thus, what will likely be required to facilitate a truly fulsome understanding of the present-day incarnation of black politics is a highly nuanced analysis yet to be developed. Yet one can readily conclude that the contributions to this volume move us much closer to development of that new analytic framing. As we develop that new analytic framing, we must not be afraid to ask the hard questions, some of which are suggested by the analyses in this volume. Questions such as: What is it that black politics should be about? What goals should black politics aspire to in early twenty-first-century America? Equally compelling is the question of in what ways is race a continuing useful context for framing the interests of black Americans in ways that will most effectively advance those interests? Let the reflection begin; and let it begin with this volume. Or should we more accurately say, let the reflection continue?

Georgia A. Persons

Part I

A New Structure of Ambition in African American Politics: A Symposium

Beyond the Boundaries: A New Structure of Ambition in African American Politics

Robert C. Smith
Symposium Editor
San Francisco State University

The last volume of this review was anchored by a symposium on the expanding boundaries in the study of African American politics.[1] This volume's symposium focuses on the expanding boundaries of African Americans in the quest for elective office. The ambitions of the first and second waves or generations of blacks elected in the 1960s through the 1980s were limited to Congress, big city mayoralties and lower-level state executive offices, such as lieutenant governor, secretary of state, or commissioner of education (Stone, 1968).[2] In the face of these perceived boundaries, only two black members of the U.S. House of Representatives have left to seek statewide office (Alan Wheat of Missouri, who left in 1994 to run unsuccessfully for a U.S. Senate seat, and Denise Majette of Georgia, who did the same thing in 2004). White congressmen, however, frequently follow such a career path.

Gerber summarized the character of this black structure of ambition as follows.

> African American members of Congress rarely seek higher office. Prospects for winning statewide are discouraging. No African American has moved from the House to the Senate or to the governor's mansion. The liberal voting record that African American representatives typically compile does not provide a strong foundation for winning statewide elections and there remains some resistance to voting for African Americans for higher office (Gerber 1996).

And when blacks have run, they have tended to lose. Since the 1960s, there have been twenty-one African American major party nominees for the Senate (eleven Democrats, ten Republicans) and ten for governor (nine Democrats, one Republican).[3]

Only four of the Senate nominees were successful (Edward Brooke twice in Massachusetts and Carol Mosley Braun and Barack Obama once each in Illinois). Of the ten nominees for governor, only Douglas Wilder was successful. Los Angeles Mayor Tom Bradley ran a very competitive race for governor in California in 1982 and Harvey Gantt for Senate from North Carolina in 1990.[4] Otherwise, the African American nominees ran largely symbolic campaigns with little realistic chance of winning.

Despite these seemingly daunting odds, in 2006 a relatively large number of blacks ran for either the Democratic or Republic nominations for governor or Senate. In the Maryland Senate race, Michael Steele, the lieutenant governor, was the Republican nominee and Kwesi Mfume, the former congressman and head of the NAACP, ran for the Democratic nomination. In Tennessee, Harold Ford left the House to become the Democratic Senate nominee and Keith Butler, a former Detroit City Councilman and pastor of one of the city's largest churches, sought the Republican Senate nomination in Michigan. Meanwhile, two African American Republicans won their party's nomination for governor; Lynn Swann, the former Pittsburgh Steelers star football player, in Pennsylvania and Ken Blackwell, Ohio's controversial secretary of state (controversial because many African Americans allege that he played a key role in suppressing the Ohio black vote in 2004 and thereby facilitated Bush's victory) won the Republican nomination for governor. Finally, in Massachusetts, Deval Patrick, the former assistant attorney general for civil rights in the Clinton administration, won the Democratic gubernatorial nomination.

The most extensive study of blacks running for higher office in the United States finds that the presence of a black Democrat on the ballot increases black turnout, (the presence of a black Republican has no effect on black turnout), while the presence of a black of either party increases white turnout (Washington, 2006). Although the percentage increases are about the same for both races, the actual increase is much greater for whites given the larger size of the white population. And both white Democrats and Republicans are less likely to vote for their party's nominee when she or he is black. Thus, the barriers are considerable for African American candidates seeking to expand the boundaries of race to become governors or senators.

Nevertheless, the 2006 elections suggest that among ambitious black politicians the perceptions of these racial and ideological boundaries to higher office may be diminishing. That is, it appears that this third wave of black politicians see an America where they can aspire to the highest offices in the land, including president.[5]

This symposium examines this new structure of ambition for black politicians, with five case studies of African Americans who won major party nominations for governor and U.S. Senate in 2006.[6] In terms of the racial boundaries all of the states, of course, have white majorities, ranging from a black population in Massachusetts of 5 percent to 36 percent in Mississippi. Ideologically, Maryland and Massachusetts are relatively liberal and reliably Democratic; Pennsylvania and Ohio are generally partisan and ideological swing states and Mississippi and Tennessee are conservative and Republican.

Except for Mississippi, in each of the states the African American nominees were credible candidates, with adequate financing and each ran with the full support of their state and national party organizations. Indeed, the three Republican nominees—Steele, Swann, and Blackwell—were virtually anointed by the Republican National Committee as part of its ongoing strategy to build a base of support for the party in the African American community (see Fauntroy, 2007; Smith and Seltzer, 2007).

After the election of the second wave of black elected officials in 1989 (which included the election of Douglas Wilder as governor of Virginia and David Dinkins as the mayor of New York City), African American political scientists employed the concept of deracialization to explain what some saw as a new phenomenon in black politics. McCormick and Jones' seminal paper (1993) identified four defining elements of a deracialized campaign. First, the candidate employs a political style that is "non-threatening" to the white majority. Second, the candidate avoids explicit appeals to blacks. Third, the candidate avoids the use of race in mobilizing the black vote. Finally, the candidate emphasizes racially transcendent issues in order to mobilize the vote of whites.

Critics of deracialization argued to some extent that there was nothing new about this style of campaigning by blacks; and to the extent it was a new phenomenon it was an unsettling development. As McCormick and Jones wrote "If deracialization as a successful electoral strategy leads it practitioners to ignore the policy-oriented concerns of African Americans, then we should rightly dismiss their political behavior as non-legitimate expressions of black politics" (1993: 76). (See also Starks, 1991; Smith, 1990; Walters, 1992, and more generally Orey and Ricks, 2007.)

All of the 2006 candidates ran deracialized campaigns, with the exception of Steele in Maryland. In an ironic twist, Steele sought to radicalize his campaign in order to attract black voters, while taking the vote of his conservative, white Republican base for granted. In Tennessee, Ford, who began planning to run for the Senate as soon as he was elected to the House in 1996, ran a textbook deracialized campaign. But, alas, the Tennessee campaign was the most racialized of the six, contributing in a major way to his defeat.

Although only one of the six candidates won—Patrick in Massachusetts—the 2006 election and the Obama presidential campaign suggest that a new structure of ambition is emergent among black politicians,[7] who perceive, perhaps correctly, that the white electorate in the twenty-first century is willing to vote for an ideologically and culturally mainstream black candidate for any office.[8] This is certainly a sign of growth and development in American politics, but it also may mean the continued decay of black politics.

Notes

1. Shaw, the editor of the symposium on the expanding boundaries in the study of black politics, divides the work into three generations of research, which parallels generational shifts in the election of blacks to office (Shaw, 2007).
2. Andra Gillespie (2007) uses "third wave" in her study of post civil rights era black elected officials.
3. Source "Political Report", *Focus*, May/June, 2006, p. 6.
4. On the Bradley campaign, see Henry, 1987 and on Gantt's, see Wilson, 1993.
5. Friends and associates of Obama report that he began talking about running for senate, governor, and president while he was in law school. See Mundy, 2007.
6. A paper on Swann's Pennsylvania campaign was commissioned, but its author was unable to complete the work.
7. The appointments of Colin Powell and Condoleezza Rice to the arguably second most visible position in the American government may have helped to adjust the mind of white America to seeing blacks exercise power "responsibly" in behalf of the nation generally or whites specifically (Lusane, 2006).
8. The Republican candidates, whatever else might account for their defeats, faced significant barriers to election in 2006, because of the unpopularity of the war, the Republican Party and President Bush. In the context of this intense dissatisfaction with the status quo, it was difficult for Republican candidates to win, except in the most secure partisan places.

References

Fauntroy, Michael. 2007. *Republicans and the Black Vote*. Boulder, CO: Lynne Rienner.

Gerber, Alan. 1996. "African American Careers and the House Delegation." *Journal of Politics* 58: 831-45.

Gillespie, Andra. 2007. "The Third Wave: A Theoretical Introduction to the Post Civil Rights Era Cohort of Black Elected Leadership." Paper presented at the annual meeting of the National Conference of Black Political Scientists, March 22-24, 2007, San Francisco.

Lusane, Clarence. 2006. *Colin Powell, Condoleezza Rice and the New American Century*. New York: Praeger.

McCormick, Joseph and Charles Jones. 1993. "The Conceptualization of Deracialization: Thinking Through the Dilemma" in Georgia Persons (ed.) *Dilemmas of Black Politics*. New York: HarperCollins.

Mundy, Lize. 2007. "A Series of Fortunate Events". *Washington Post Magazine,* August 12, 2007.

Orey, Byron and Boris Ricks. 2007. "A Systematic Analysis of the Deracialization Concept." *National Political Science Review* 11: 325-34.

Shaw, Todd. 2007. "The Expanding Boundaries of Black Politics." *National Political Science Review* 11: 3-16.

Smith, Robert C. 1990. "Recent Elections: The Maturation or Death of Black Politics." *PS* 2: 160-62.

——— and R. Seltzer. 2007. "The Deck and the Sea: The African American Vote in the Presidential Elections of 2000 and 2004." *National Political Science Review* 11: 253-69.

Starks, Robert. 1991. "A Commentary and Response to Exploring the Meaning of Deracialization." *Urban Affairs Quarterly* 27: 216-22.

Stone, Pauline. 1980. "Ambition Theory and Black Politicians." *Western Political Quarterly* 32: 94-107.

Walters, Ronald. 1992. "Two Political Traditions: Black Politics in the 1990s." *National Political Science Review* 3: 198-208.

Washington, Eboyna. 2006. "How Black Candidates Affect Turnout." Cambridge, MA: Bureau of Economic Research, Working Paper #11915.

Wilson, Zaphon. 1993. *"Gantt vs. Helms: Deracialization Confronts Southern Traditionalism"* in Georgia Persons (ed.) *Dilemmas of Black Politics.* New York: HarperCollins.

Making History, Again, So Soon? The Massachusetts Gubernatorial Election

Angela K. Lewis
University of Alabama at Birmingham

Introduction

On November 6, 2006, the voters of Massachusetts made history—for only the second time in the United States, voters elected a black governor. It was seventeen years earlier when Douglas Wilder became the nation's first elected black governor. Deval Patrick, a political novice virtually unknown before the election, states he did not campaign as the black candidate, in fact he comments "If all I was offering was to be the first black governor of Massachusetts, I wouldn't have won" (Pierce, 2006). Running a grass-roots campaign rejecting large monetary donations from supporters, for two years Patrick visited neighborhoods and spoke to voters across their kitchen tables about restoring hope back into politics and how to make Massachusetts better. What he offered was an approach that transcended race.

The purpose of this chapter is to provide an in-depth analysis of the 2006 Massachusetts gubernatorial election where Deval Patrick ran against Kerry Healey. First, this chapter provides a history of Massachusetts politics, followed by information about the candidates and the campaign. The chapter concludes with an analysis of how Patrick, unlike so many past black candidates in other states, successfully navigated the campaign trail to attain a high-level statewide office as a governor or U.S. senator.

Massachusetts Politics

"Massachusetts is the most liberal and Democratic state in national elections" (Sonenshein, 1990). Known as the home of the Kennedys and John Kerry, the Democratic nominee for president in 2004, Massachusetts is also the first state to recognize and make legal same-sex marriages. For some time, Massachusetts was under one-party control. Voters last elected a Democrat to the office of governor in 1986 with the election of Michael Dukakis. It was 1990 when Republicans took the governor's office, with William Weld beating John Silber. Voters were angry over the state's economy, the budget, and one-party leadership and they wanted change. Although Massachusetts is a blue state, after the 1990 Republican takeover, Republicans held it up as an example, "that they could win even in the bluest state" (Mehren, 2006).

Similar to the 1990 Republican takeover, voters in the 2006 election also wanted change after an increase in the cost of living in the state and the state's steady population decline.

Voters were also displeased about how their incumbent governor, Mitt Romney, made fun of the state, for being too liberal and being the first to allow same-sex marriage, while he traveled the country campaigning for president. In addition, state funding for education had decreased tremendously, causing it to fall behind Alabama and Mississippi in higher education funding (Mehren, 2006). In the end, voters were upset and wanted change. "Many are considering a vote for Patrick because they are upset by the Big Dig, the high cost of living, and the negative tone of the Healey campaign" (Mooney and Wangsness, 2006). Whichever way the election would have gone, Massachusetts would make history by electing the state's first black or female governor.

The Candidates

Both candidates were self-made millionaires. Although Patrick's story is more revealing of his character, both candidates have a mix of experiences that would have made them qualified governors.

A single-mother that was briefly on welfare raised Deval Patrick in his grandparent's South Side Chicago apartment. Although Patrick grew up around crime and gangs, he avoided them. At age 14 he received a scholarship from A Better Chance program to attend Milton Academy in Massachusetts, a move that would change his life forever.

The first in his family to attend college, he graduated from Harvard College with honors, and later Harvard Law School. Before attending law school, he traveled overseas to Sudan and South Africa on a youth training project funded by a Rockefeller Foundation grant.

At fifty years old, Patrick had a variety of work experiences, which included work as a law clerk to a federal appellate judge, work at the NAACP Legal Defense and Education Fund, at Day, Berry & Howard, and as a partner at Hill & Barlow, two leading law firms. Patrick also served as a federal prosecutor and as the assistant attorney general for civil rights under President Clinton.

In the private sector, two multi-national companies, Texaco and Coca-Cola, hired Patrick as vice president and general counsel. He also served on numerous corporate and charitable boards. He has been married to Diane Patrick for over twenty years and they have two children in college.

The Republican candidate, Kerry Healey, then current lieutenant governor, grew up in Daytona Beach, Florida. Her mother was a public school teacher and her father served 27 years in the US Army and Army Reserves. Healey graduated Harvard with a degree in government in the early '80s. She later received a Ph.D. from Trinity College in Dublin, Ireland.

Healey had two unsuccessful bids at political office, both for state representative in 1998 and 2000. In 2002, she ran successfully in the primary for lieutenant governor beating Jim Rappaport. She later became lieutenant governor as the running mate of Mitt Romney. She was active in numerous community organizations. Her work experience includes work as a law and public safety consultant at Abt Associates and as an adjunct faculty member at Endicott College and the University of Massachusetts at Lowell where she taught social policy and criminal justice. She has two school-aged children with her husband Sean Healy. They have been married for twenty years.

The Primaries

The Democratic Party's rule in Massachusetts is that in order for a candidate's name to appear on the primary ballot, they must receive at least 15 percent of the delegate's votes at the State Convention. Two other Democratic candidates besides Deval Patrick vied for the governor's office, Attorney General Tom Reilly, and millionaire Chris Gabrieli. Even in early March, Patrick was well ahead of his contenders in gaining the Democratic Party's nomination for governor. In his first run for elective office, Patrick received his party's nomination with 58 percent of the convention delegates' votes, while Reilly received 27 percent and Gabriela received 15 percent. Therefore, all three candidates received positions on the ballot. There was some speculation that Reilly and Gabrieli swapped votes to ensure they both had a spot on the ballot although both denied it (Johnson, 2006).

By August, Patrick continued his lead over Reilly and Gabrieli. Polls showed Patrick at 35 percent, Gabrieli at 30 percent and Reilly at 27 percent (O'Sullivan, 2006). Before the primary election, in preparation for one of the debates, Patrick spoke of the problems with school districts charging fees for extracurricular activities and transportation. He argued that the activities are part of a child's education and the parent's ability to pay should not determine a child's participation. He wanted to create a fund to help schools with these programs so parents will not have to pay fees. Gabrieli focused on transportation, more specifically how to make commuting easier for workers. Reilly focused on how his opponents were millionaires who did not understand the significance of a state income tax rollback because they were rich. As a result, Reilly released both he and his wife's tax returns hoping other candidates would do the same, although they did not. This move earned Reilly the endorsements of 15 mayors across the state.

Both Gabriela and Patrick attacked Reilly about two critical issues during his tenure as attorney general—his lack of supervision of the Big Dig Project and how he handled the gay marriage ballot question. The Big Dig is a massive tunnel and bridge road project in Boston that ended up costing much more than forecasted. Moreover, the finished parts of the project were plagued with defects. The project caused outrage because of overspending and the failure of the Romney administration to be accountable for its failure. They both stated that Reilly could have done more to hold elected officials and contractors accountable for the Big Dig's massive cost overruns and defects. They also argued that Reilly should have blocked attempts to put the gay marriage question on the ballots because the issue was already decided by the courts.

Although both Reilly and Gabrieli criticized Patrick for his work with Texaco and Coca-Cola, as well as his board membership with Ameriquest, Patrick won the Democratic primary election in September by nearly a 30 percentage-point margin. Patrick's victory in the primary is related to Reilly's poor performance as attorney general and Gabrieli's lack of a broad spectrum of support. Most of Gabrieli's campaign was self-funded. Although, he counted on support from the 50 percent or more of voters who were unregistered as Democrats or Republicans, in the end, independent voters were more likely to support Patrick.

Other candidates in the general election for governor included Christy Mihos and Green Rainbow Party candidate Grace Ross. Mihos, who some hoped would run against Healey in the Republican primary, decided to run as an independent, a move that would challenged Healey because it took away her ability to garner votes from independents.

The Campaign

Patrick's candidacy gave voters a comfortable candidate that offered an opportunity for change. A *Boston Globe*/CBS 4 Poll found that a large percentage of respondents had unfavorable views of Healey. In fact, 42 percent of respondents had unfavorable views of Healy, compared to Patrick's 16 percent although voters agreed with Healey on many issues. What damaged Healey during the campaign was her past association with Governor Romney, who was very unpopular at the time (Moynihan, 2006). Voters were unhappy with the previous four years of the Romney-Healey administration and they wanted change. The fact that Patrick had no prior experience as an officeholder did not matter much to voters because he emphasized that his corporate experience was just the experience needed to run a state government and to make it more fiscally responsible.

Healey's unfavorable ratings were likely associated with her negative campaign ads. She consistently attacked Patrick for his work as an attorney involved with rape and death penalty cases. She even went as far as to state that Patrick's experience as a lawyer should disqualify him for running for governor. For example, in one televised debate, Healey suggested that Patrick was soft on crime because of his support of Benjamin LaGuer, a man convicted of raping a 59-year-old woman who was his neighbor.[1] Patrick responded by pointing out that Healey did not care about crime because during her tenure as lieutenant governor the Romney/Healey administration cut police resources to local communities.

Voters believed Patrick was a promising leader often rising above the negative attack ads ran by Healey. He refused to respond with his own negative ads. Former Governor Michael Dukakis honed in on the negative campaigning and remarked, "This has been the dirtiest campaign in the history of the commonwealth" (Mehren, 2006). The ads ran by Healey reminded some of the Willie Horton ads George W. Bush ran against Michael Dukakis in his bid for the presidency. There were two particularly negative ads by Healy. One was of an elderly white woman in a garage at night. It shows Patrick complimenting the man convicted of the crime while in the background stating that Patrick should not be governor because he spoke of a convicted rapist highly and he contributed money to the man's cause. The second set of ads criticized Patrick as an NAACP defense attorney for successfully minimizing a death sentence for a man convicted of killing a state trooper. Even though initially the ads narrowed the margin between the candidates, they eventually worked against Healey giving Patrick the advantage (Anderson, 2006).

Other attacks by the Healey camp included the leaking of information about Patrick's brother-in-law, referring to him as a convicted rapist. Patrick responded by clarifying the situation between his sister and husband and stated that their marriage had problems in the past, but they recently celebrated their twenty-fifth wedding anniversary through a rededication ceremony and that their children had no knowledge of their past before the press leaked the story. Although Healey denied leaking the story, Patrick's response was that the negative campaigning had to end. His specific response "We are going to ask the people to choose whether the politics of fear, division, and personal destruction is what they want, or whether we're better than that, and are ready to finally throw out those who dump this trash in the public square" (Monahan, 2006).

Despite Healey's attacks, Patrick, continued to work on his grass-roots campaign by holding town hall meetings. Polls immediately following the leak showed Patrick 25 points ahead of Healey (Anderson, 2006). Instead of launching his own negative ads, Patrick's response was to focus exclusively on Healey's record during the Romney administration. Patrick argued that Healey utilized negative ads to keep voters off track and off her record. Patrick went on to state that her campaign was nasty and she had set a negative tone for Massachusetts that politics in the state was toxic. Healey's negative campaign did more to hurt her credibility than to move voters over to her side. In fact, polls indicated that 45 percent of voters stated that her negative ads made them less likely to vote for her for (Anderson, 2006).

Both candidates raised a large amount of money for the campaign. Healey received nearly $12 million in donations compared to Patrick's nearly $7.5 million. However, Healey outspent Patrick by a 2:1 margin in advertising (Mooney, 2006).

The Issues

Several issues featured as part of newspaper reports and in the debates were important to voters in the election. Among them were the candidate's positions on fiscal issues such as taxes, the state's economy and the cost of living, healthcare, education, crime, and immigration, and social issues such as abortion and gay marriage. Most important to a large percentage of voters was the cost of living. According to voters, one solution was to lower the state income tax, passed in 2000. Healey supported rolling back the state income tax from 5.3 percent to 5 percent while at the same time increasing aid to local communities. Patrick opposed rolling back the state income tax, arguing that it would be fiscally irresponsible and it would shift the burden to local communities, which would result in higher property taxes. He instead wanted to reduce property taxes and provide more funding to local communities by proposing a local-options or meal tax to help ease their tax burden.

In one televised debate, the moderator questioned the candidates about the cost of living and the problem of residents relocating out of state, Patrick's responses were to propose increasing the minimum wage, building more affordable housing, and making transportation easier for citizens who work in Boston but cannot afford to live there. Healey focused on reducing the cost of unemployment insurance for employers and creating a tax-free savings account for workers saving to purchase their first home.

Related to the cost of living is the cost of health insurance. Massachusetts is ahead of the nation, recently passing legislation requiring all residents to have health insurance. The new administration will shoulder most of responsibility for executing the law, specifically how much businesses and lower income residents will have to pay. The new law expands the state's Medicaid program by covering uninsured adults and children. Adults with incomes 300 percent below the federal poverty level will be subsidized and those greater than the 300 percent threshold are required to purchase an affordable health plan developed by insurance companies. The major difference between the candidates was the fee per worker charged to employers who cannot afford to offer health care benefits to employees. Healey opposed the fee and Patrick supported it.

Patrick and Healey both have criminal justice backgrounds; Patrick as an assistant attorney general for civil rights under Clinton and Healey as a professor of criminal justice. Two major issues in the area of public safety separated the candidates; the death penalty and how the state issues gun licenses. Healey was supportive of the death penalty and Patrick opposed it. Late in the campaign, Healey changed positions on how the state issues gun-licenses. The current policy allows local police chiefs to issue licenses. Worcester Police Chief Gary J. Gemme came out against Healey after she spoke before the Massachusetts Major City Chiefs Association. Healey's proposal for a uniform policy in issuing gun permits, took power away from local police. The proposal included a statewide panel of police chiefs who would decide if an individual receives a permit to carry a gun. Gemme had recently started a new gun issuing policy in Worcester that was more restrictive than the state's. His policy denied permits to anyone who was arrested for drugs, driving-under-the-influence, affiliated with gangs, or any misdemeanor that was punishable by more than two years in jail. Gemme argued that neither the state nor other police chiefs knew what was happening in a community enough to be able to determine whether a person should receive a permit. Moreover, the move for one overarching statewide policy seems antithetical to the Republican view of decentralization of power (Croteau, 2006). On the other side of the issue was the Gun Owners Action League, which believed police chiefs had too much authority in deciding who should receive gun licenses. The League believed local police chiefs would eventually abuse this power. Patrick supported the decentralized policy and adding more police officers to local communities.

Although both candidates' children went to private schools and both wanted to improve public education, they had different approaches. Healey desired to change the age that a student can drop out from 16 to 18. Patrick did not have a position on this proposal. While both candidates supported charter schools, Patrick wanted a cap on how much local governments spend on charter schools. He was also supportive of a bond measure to help fund higher education. The major disagreement in education between the candidates was whether illegal aliens should receive in-state tuition rates. Patrick supports this proposal and like many voters, Healey opposes it.

On the issue of gay marriage, Patrick was supportive of and believed the courts had resolved the issue. Patrick argued that people should stand before the law equally although black ministers criticized him for his stance. Healey opposed same sex marriage, but supported civil unions. She also supported the proposed constitutional amendment banning same sex marriage.

Other issues important in the campaign supported by Patrick included giving driver's licenses to illegal immigrants and limiting employers' access to criminal records. Healey and most voters disagreed with Patrick's positions on these issues.

The position each candidate took on abortion was also important to voters. Both candidates were pro-choice but there was speculation as to where Healey stood on this issue because of her association with Romney who changed positions on abortion frequently.

Endorsements

Because of this speculation, three notable women's groups, the Massachusetts chapter of the National Organization for Women, the Planned Parenthood Advocacy Fund, and NARAL Pro-Choice Massachusetts endorsed Patrick over Healey who would have been the state's first female governor (Wangsness and Simpson, 2006). Healey refused to respond to a survey about her stance on abortion, prompting these groups to support Patrick.

Patrick also received support from a myriad of black political leaders and raised more money from out-of-state contributors than any other candidate in the early days of the campaign. Among the notables who may have had appeal to whites were former National

Urban League president Vernon Jordan, former labor secretary Alexis Herman, and Illinois state senator, Barack Obama. Reports suggest that 24 percent of Patrick's funding were from grass-roots sources, black voters who would like to increase the number of black victories for statewide offices, particularly the office of governor and senator (Williams, 2006). Even former President Bill Clinton stomped for Patrick at a rally. The fundraiser in which Clinton appeared raised $2 million for the campaign. Clinton's major appeal to voters was a message that was very similar to Patrick's theme throughout the entire campaign. Clinton urged supporters to speak with their neighbors about Patrick regardless of their political leanings. He stated that Americans were tired of "politics as usual." Voters want, Clinton said, a civil and calm discussion about the issues. His message was one of taking the moral high ground and of bringing out the best in people to make the world better, the foundation of Patrick's campaign. Others in attendance at this rally included Senators Edward M. Kennedy and John F. Kerry.

As common in most political campaigns, major newspapers in Massachusetts also weighed in by endorsing candidates. Among those supporting Patrick were the *Boston Globe*, *Worchester Telegram & Gazette*, *MetroWest Daily News*, *Providence Journal*, *Berkshire Eagle*, *Boston Phoenix*, *Newton Tab*, and the *West Roxbury & Rosindale Transcript*. Major newspapers supporting Healey included the *Boston Herald*, *The Eagle-Tribune*, *Sentinel & Enterprise*, *Lowell Sun*, and *Cape Cod Times*. The most common themes in the newspaper endorsements were the fact that those who supported Patrick believed in his campaign rhetoric of restoring hope back into politics and a desire to make Massachusetts better. They also complimented Patrick on running a campaign that was free of negative advertisements. In the end, Patrick's campaign was one of consensus building and compromise. Those supporting Healey pointed out that the bulk of voters in Massachusetts had the same issue positions as Healey. They also pointed out that Healey agreed to uphold the tax rebate voters supported in 2000.

Other endorsements for Patrick included the Massachusetts Teachers Association and the Service Employees International Union Local 119. The Teachers Association supported Patrick's education policies, pointing to the failure of the Romney administration, which included Healey. The union supported Patrick's promise to make healthcare more affordable.

The Gun Owners Action League endorsed Healey because of her position on creating a state board to issue gun licenses. However, Chief Gemme of Worcester endorsed Patrick (Croteau, 2006).

Depoliticizing Race

In today's political climate, it is often the norm for black candidates to depoliticize race in order to appeal to white voters. It is very unlikely for white voters to elect a passionate civil rights activist to a statewide office. Depoliticizing race is tempting to black candidates who must garner white votes to win.

Most blacks who have won statewide office take race off the table as a part of the dialogue while others have such impeccable credentials that most reasonable Whites do not consider their race while casting their vote. This approach certainly helped Patrick in this campaign. Part of his appeal is that he has had access to an Ivy League university education, experience in the top levels of corporate America, and had a broader political agenda than previous black candidates. Patrick's resume and campaign style was an integral part of this election.

In a state that is nearly 90 percent white and approximately 7 percent black, it was necessary for Patrick to appeal to whites just as Edward Brooke did in his bid for the United States Senate in 1966. Brooke was the nation's first popularly elected black United States senator. He represented Massachusetts from 1967-1979. Since then, only two other blacks have held this prestigious position—Carol Mosely Braun representing Illinois from 1993 to 1999 and, most recently, Barack Obama also representing Illinois (2005-2008). Brooke, however, did extensive research before launching his candidacy for the Senate. According to Becker and Heaton (1967), Brooke's research was part of one of the largest research programs carried out for a statewide election. This intensive research program proved quite beneficial in helping Brooke win the election.

Almost forty years later, Patrick's campaign for governor has some strong similarities to Brooke's campaign. Both had opponents that the public viewed as unfavorable based on their record of service while in office and their previous unsuccessful campaigns. For example, Brooke's opponent, Endicott Peabody, was a former governor who was defeated in his reelection bid in the Democratic gubernatorial primary by Francis X. Bellotti in 1964. Healey had previously run for state representative twice unsuccessfully and was part of a past administration that was unpopular. Brooke's popularity and favorability ratings never slipped in the polls, neither did Patrick's. However, both of their opponents had unpopular records with voters, Peabody as governor and Healey as lieutenant governor. Peabody had a blemished record because voters did not believe he accomplished much in office as governor. Healey's popularity plummeted because of her negative ads and her affiliation with Romney. Brooke had a record of honesty in pubic office. As attorney general, he was part of the investigation that uncovered corruption that indicted many state officials. Voters knew Patrick as a United States assistant attorney general in the civil rights division of the federal government who worked for underrepresented groups. Voters also appreciated the positive tone of his candidacy despite the negative ads run by his opponent, which served to lower her popularity throughout the course of the campaign.

All of these circumstances as well as others that are discussed below, factor into both Brooke's and Patrick's success in Massachusetts. Research suggests there are a variety of conditions necessary for blacks to win statewide office. Sonenshein (1990) notes the following factors that influence a candidates chances of winning; the candidate's campaign strategy, the political leaning of voters in the state, and the viability of the party. Jeffries (1998) agrees with this assessment but adds and stresses that the black candidates must have an appropriate apprenticeship. For both authors, an ideal political situation for black candidates is a state with a large enough black population to help the candidate win in the general election so that the party will not publicly oppose their candidacy. The voters in the state should also have liberal attitudes. There is, however, a point of departure between Sonenshein (1990) and Jeffries (1998) pertaining to this condition. The latter argues that blacks should not limit their choices to states with liberal attitudes; doing so would severely limit choices where blacks could run for office. Patrick's candidacy in Massachusetts met one of these conditions, having voters with liberal attitudes.

Secondly, black candidates must work within the party structure and have as much party support as their opponent. Support from the party legitimizes the black candidate's campaign and provides him with a myriad of resources. Black candidates should also have extensive previous political experience. Being a former mayor,[2] representing an area that is majority black, or losing their last election is a liability to the black candidate. Beyond the black candidate's control is the quality of the opponent. When the opponent has major flaws, it strengthens the black candidate. Nevertheless, the black candidate must keep their liabilities to a minimum. Patrick had the support of the Democratic Party, which provided him with the vast resources of the party. Former President Clinton and Senators Ted Kennedy and John Kerry both made public appearances to support Patrick. However, he did not have previous experience in elected office. His work as a United States assistant attorney general and the experiences as vice president and general counsel at two of the country's largest corporations, he argued, gave him just the experience need to run a state government responsibly.

Finally, most appealing to whites is a black candidate that is middle class, highly qualified, and one that has a deracialized political strategy. The candidate should have a conciliatory style that "attempts to defuse the divisive effects of race by avoiding references to ethnic or racially construed issues, while at the same time emphasizing those issues that appeal to a wide community" (Jeffries, 1998: 167). The candidate should transcend race and focus on issues that appeal to all voters regardless of race, issues like education, healthcare, and transportation. However, the black candidate must delicately balance their deracialized approach while at the same time utilizing race as an asset. In short, they must appeal to blacks without alienating whites.

Patrick did not have to appeal to blacks as much as others candidates do because of the small number of blacks in the state. Moreover, according to some reports, the fact that Patrick was black did not register with the electorate. At a meeting with the local Chamber of Commerce, Patrick's race did not come up. In fact, one business owner commented, "I don't even see him as black. It looks like to me that he has a deep tan" (Page, 2006). In addition, at the same meeting, Patrick never mentioned his race or any potentially racially divisive issues. Instead, he talked about public education and the state's economy. Unfortunately, the fact that some voters looked at Patrick as having a "deep tan" may lend some credibility to Strickland and Whicker's (1992) assertion that in order for black candidates to win statewide office, they must look white.

Despite Patrick's success, historically, black candidates do not win statewide elections because a proportion of whites will not vote for a black candidate (Williams, 1989; Jeffries, 1998; Jeffries and Jones, 2006). In fact, Hutchings states that "There remains a non-trivial faction of white voters who will not vote for a candidate simply because (the candidate is) black. We are kidding ourselves if we argue these people have disappeared from the landscape" (Page, 2006). If the candidate is a strong advocate for civil rights for blacks or if the candidate makes this issue prominent during the campaign, this phenomenon is exaggerated. The candidate will likely alienate whites and prompt them to cast a vote for the other candidate. What helped both Brooke and Patrick is their failure to place civil rights on the agenda of their campaign. Becker and Heaton (1967) stated that even though voters knew Brooke was black, they did not associate him with the civil rights movement. Similar to Brooke's campaign, race was not an integral part of Patrick's dialogue while campaigning.

What helped Patrick win the election was voters dislike for Healey. When pollsters asked voters why they were supporting Patrick, many suggested because they disliked Healey and because of her negative ads. On the other hand, when voters mentioned why they supported Healey, a larger percentage said they disliked Patrick. This dislike for Patrick could be related to his race or to the fact that Healey made light of Patrick's support of LaGuer who turned out to be guilty. This in fact made quite a few voters upset with Patrick. However, Patrick said he sincerely believed the justice system mistreated LaGuer. In the end however, Healey's missteps helped Patrick win the election. The fact that this was an open seat also helped Patrick.

Data Analysis

Although the data in Table 1 cannot yield rigorous statistical analysis, I do observe patterns in how the voters of Massachusetts made their decisions in the gubernatorial election. First, neither candidate made much crossover appeal to independents or to voters identifying with the opposing party. Exactly the same percentage of Republicans voted for Patrick as Democrats voted for Healey. This is one area where a larger percentage of voters voted for Healey over Patrick. Furthermore, only a four-percentage point difference separates the candidates' support from Independents. It appears that Patrick had more crossover appeal to conservatives than Healey had with liberals. Only 9 percent of liberal leaning voters cast their ballots for Healey while Patrick was able to garner a fifth of conservative voters.

The data on community size indicates that Patrick had more support from voters in urban and rural communities than in the suburbs. He also garnered more votes from large cities and the Boston area. In North and South Shore Massachusetts, there is an even split between voters.

Looking at the data on gender and vote choice, no patterns emerge. There was no gender gap in this election. Conversely, upon examining the data dissected by race and gender two facts emerge. First, white women gave more support to Patrick than white men. While only 45 percent of white men voted for Patrick, 57 percent of white women voted for him. What is also clear is that white women preferred Patrick almost by a 2 to 1 margin; only 35 percent voted for Healey while 57 percent voted for Patrick. The strong support white women showed for Patrick could be the result of the endorsements from three major women's groups, the Massachusetts chapter of the National Organization for Women, the Planned Parenthood Advocacy Fund, and NARAL Pro-Choice Massachusetts and that Healey's position on abortion was ambiguous. Although during the campaign Healey stated she was pro-choice, she was part of an administration that was pro-life.[3] Moreover, when directly asked about her position in a survey from women's groups, she refused therefore a majority of white women opted for Patrick in the election.

When examining the data by race, it is clear that a large percentage of African Americans, 89 percent, voted for Patrick and 11 percent voted for Healey. These numbers are congruent with nationwide data, which indicate that blacks overwhelmingly vote for Democrats, but a small percentage, usually between 5-10 percent, votes Republican.

Table 1
Exit Poll Data

Vote by Gender			
	Healey	Patrick	Mihos
Male (46%)	38%	51%	9%
Female (54%)	32%	61%	5%
Vote by Race			
	Healey	Patrick	Mihos
White (83%)	39%	51%	8%
Black (9%)	11%	89%	*
Latino (6%)	*	*	*
Asian (0%)	*	*	*
Other (2%)	*	*	*
Vote by Race and Gender			
	Healey	Patrick	Mihos
White Men (37%)	42%	45%	11%
White Women (45%)	35%	57%	7%
Non-White Men (9%)	13%	78%	1%
Non-White Women (9%)	21%	78%	*
Vote by Party ID			
	Healey	Patrick	Mihos
Democrat (41%)	9%	85%	5%
Republican (19%)	85%	9%	6%
Independent (39%)	41%	45%	10%
Vote by Ideology			
	Healey	Patrick	Mihos
Liberal (26%)	9%	83%	6%
Moderate (51%)	36%	55%	8%
Conservative (23%)	72%	20%	6%
Vote by Age			
	Healey	Patrick	Mihos
18-29 (11%)	22%	66%	10%
30-44 (23%)	35%	57%	7%
45-59 (35%)	34%	55%	8%
60 and older (32%)	41%	53%	5%

Table 1 (cont.)

Vote by Income			
	Healey	**Patrick**	**Mihos**
Under $15,000 (3%)	*	*	*
$15-30,000 (9%)	37%	51%	7%
$30-50,000 (20%)	34%	51%	11%
$50-75,000 (20%)	31%	57%	9%
$75-100,000 (20%)	34%	62%	4%
$100-150,000 (19%)	40%	56%	4%
$150-200,000 (5%)	*	*	*
$200,000 or More (4%)	*	*	*
Would Romney Make a Good President?			
	Healey	**Patrick**	**Mihos**
Yes (31%)	76%	18%	6%
No (65%)	20%	69%	8%
Would Kerry Make a Good President?			
	Healey	**Patrick**	**Mihos**
Yes (25%)	8%	85%	5%
No (71%)	49%	40%	8%
Vote by Size of Community			
	Healey	**Patrick**	**Mihos**
Urban (22%)	29%	63%	7%
Suburban (67%)	38%	52%	8%
Rural (11%)	30%	65%	2%
Vote by Region			
	Healey	**Patrick**	**Mihos**
Boston Area (25%)	28%	65%	6%
Other Large Cities (12%)	31%	59%	7%
N. Shore/S. Shore (17%)	44%	46%	8%
Eastern Mass (35%)	40%	50%	8%
Western Mass (11%)	30%	65%	2%

Source: http://edition.cnn.com/ELECTION/2006/pages/results/states/MA/G/00/epolls.0.html. n=655

Because Patrick was a black candidate, he should have garnered more support from blacks, especially considering the fact that the state has such a small black population and he would be the first black governor elected. Notwithstanding blacks who identify with the Republican Party, Patrick outraged some black ministers and voters because he supported gay marriage. It seems that Patrick made a strong appeal to blacks to overlook his stance on gay marriage because issues that are more serious should be their focus like unemployment and crime. It may be, however, that some blacks withheld their votes from him because of his position on gay marriage.

More than half of whites voted for Patrick. While neither candidate made race part of the campaign, it is clear that for some whites, Patrick's race did matter. It is also clear that a generation gap exists. There is a forty-point difference between 18-29 year olds who voted for Patrick over Healey. Becker and Heaton's (1967) study of the Brooke campaign revealed that the most prejudiced group in Massachusetts were older people and this group had the lowest percentage of individuals who favored Brooke in the 1966 election. They concluded that race had an impact on candidate preference in that election, and this appears true today.

Whatever the case, it is clear that the hopeful campaign Patrick ran appealed to younger voters. In an article the Sunday before the election, candidates sent messages directly to voters. Patrick's comments were simple and straightforward in that it asked voters how they are doing. He then goes on to asks voters if they are tired of the way things are, particularly with the cost of living, school fees, and friends and family leaving the state because of the cost of living. Patrick's message was one of hope, one that inspired voters to work with him to bring Massachusetts back to its glory. His message was color-blind and it resonated with most voters. As Mooney and Wangsness (2006) point out, most voters just wanted a change from the Romney administration. They wanted to be able to afford to live in Massachusetts. Walker (2006) makes the point painfully clear by speaking to a couple who are residents at a teaching hospital in Boston. The couple commented, "Even on our salaries, we can't afford it here," and they were pediatric dental surgeons. Thus if a family of surgeons find it difficult to live in Massachusetts, one could only imagine how a blue-collar worker would feel pinched. In the end, Patrick's candidacy appealed to all types of people in Massachusetts regardless of race and income.

Healey's message in the same article did not have the same positive appeal as Patrick's. Her words were reminiscent of the same vibe that she put off in her campaign. Instead of primarily focusing on her plans if she became governor, within the first sentence of her statement, she refers to Patrick's promises and feel good message. One voter, registered as an independent stated that she considered voting for Healey, but instead would vote for Patrick. She commented: "Enough is enough. More than voting for Deval Patrick, I'd be voting against Kerry Healey.' 'I don't believe her and don't like the way she is running her campaign. She should be answering the question: What are you going to do for us?" (Mooney and Wangsness, 2006). Other voters in the same article made comments about Healey's negative ads. One made this comment about the campaign, "It's very, very negative, particularly Kerry Healey." "Her ads are totally negative.... If she had things to stand on, she wouldn't have to do these ads" (Mooney and Wangsness, 2006).

Conclusion

Although Patrick's candidacy proved to be successful, there remains a cloud of doubt about whether whites are ready for a black candidate who does not depoliticize race. Patrick always overlooked race. After winning the election he said, "never raised (the race) question. People voted for him because they have confidence in his ability" (Atkins and Sweet, 2006). The odds were with Patrick in that Healey's association with Romney and the failure of his administration in addition to her negative campaigning turned most voters off. Healey's campaign provided Patrick the ideal circumstances for a black candidate to win statewide election. If the conditions were different, would Patrick be the first black governor of Massachusetts? Only time will tell if he decides to run for reelection, different circumstances and a different candidate. In the meantime, the fact that one of the states with the smallest black population was able to elect a black governor should show promise for the future of the black candidate for statewide office in states with larger black populations.

Acknowledgments

This chapter is dedicated to my son Aiden Lewis Wilson.You are my inspiration. I also thank his cousins Jazmin Nikole Welch and Jessica Victoria Welch who provided him with love and care while I worked on this chapter. I also send a special thanks to my sister, Regina Warren, and my parents Joseph and Cynthia Lewis. And a final thanks to my graduate assistant, Yvonne Simms.

Notes

1. Deval Patrick was supportive of a Latino man convicted of rape. Various other individuals supported the man while in prison because they believed he was mistreated by the criminal justice system and was a victim of juror misconduct. Evidence of several letters written by Patrick to LaGuer surfaced. DNA evidence later proved LaGuer was guilty of the crime.
2. Judson and Jones (2006) find that several unsuccessful statewide black candidates were former mayors (Thomas Bradley, Ron Kirk, Harvey Gantt, and Andrew Young). They go on to state that historically the office of mayor has not been a stepping-stone to a higher elected office.
3. It is clear those voters who support a Romney candidacy for president supported Healey more by nearly 60 percentage points. Although her affiliation with Romney as lieutenant governor may have cost the election, she does have a base of support, albeit small. The total percentage of those supporting a Romney candidacy for president was only 31 percent. An equally important fact to note is that an even smaller percentage supports a Kerry candidacy for president. They split their support between Healey and Patrick evenly.

References

Anderson, Lisa. Massachusetts gubernatorial candidates wage brutal campaigns. (October 27, 2006). Chicago Tribune. Retrieved from http://web.lexis-nexis.com.fetch.mhsl.uab.edu: Lexis Nexis.

Atkins, Kimberly. Battle for Governor; Deval turns up heat on Healey. (October 20, 2006). The Boston Herald, 005. Retrieved April 19, 2007, from http://web.lexis-nexis.com.fetch.mhsl.uab.edu: Lexis Nexis.

Atkins, Kimberly and Sweet, Laurel J. The vote is in 2006; Leaders say 1st black gov a 'bookend' for Mass. Race woes. November 9, 2006). The Boston Herald, 006. Retrieved April 19, 2007, from http://web.lexis-nexis.com.fetch.mhsl.uab.edu: Lexis Nexis.

Becker, John F. and Heaton Jr., Eugene E. 1967. The Election of Senator Edward W. Brooke. *The Public Opinion Quarterly*, 31, 346-358.

Canellos, Peter S. Voters' anger erupts; and the message is a towering no; Primary '90. (September 19, 1990). The Boston Globe, 34p. Retrieved May 25, 2007, from http://web.lexis-nexis.com.fetch.mhsl.uab.edu: Lexis Nexis.

————. Weld staffers celebrate, but then comes the shock: Silber's the foe. The Boston Globe, 38p. Retrieved May 25, 2007, from http://web.lexis-nexis.com.fetch.mhsl.uab.edu: Lexis Nexis.

CNN Exit Poll Data. http://edition.cnn.com/ELECTION/2006/pages/results/states/MA/G/00/epolls.0.html. Retrieved April 1, 2007.

Croteau, Scott J. Police chiefs blast Healey on gun permits; Gun group endorses proposal. (October 19, 2006). Telegram & Gazette, A1. Retrieved May 25, 2007, from http://web.lexis-nexis.com.mhsl.uab.edu: Lexis Nexis.

Helman, Scott. Patrick at pulpit, lists his priorities. (February 27, 2006). The Boston Globe, B1. Retrieved May 25, 2007 from http://web.lexis-nexis.com.mhsl.uab.edu: Lexis Nexis.

Jeffries, Judson. 1998. Blacks and High Profile Statewide Office: 1966-1996. The *Western Journal of Black Studies*, 22, 164-173.

Jeffries, Judson L. and Jones, Charles E. 2006. Blacks who run for governor and the U.S. Senate: An examination of their candidacies. *The Negro Educational Review*, 57, 243-261.

Jones, Charles and Clemons, Michael. 1993. A model of racial crossover voting: An assessment of the Wilder victory. In Georgia Persons (Ed), Dilemmas of Black Politics (pp. 128-147). New York: Harper Collins.

Johnson, Glen. Patrick garners most votes; Reilly touts success at convention. (June 3, 2006). Associated Press State and Local Wire. Retrieved May 25, 2007, from http://web.lexis-nexis.com.fetch.mhsl.uab.edu: Lexis Nexis.

Kalke, Rushmie. Patrick, Mihos trade praise, push local aid; Candidates for governor campaign in Central Mass. (September 29, 2006). Telegram & Gazette , A6. Retrieved May 25, 2007, from http://web.lexis-nexis.com.mhsl.uab.edu: Lexis Nexis.

Kiely, Kathy. These are America's governors. No blacks. No Hispanics. (January 21, 2002). USA Today, 1A. Retrieved May 25, 2007, from http://web.lexis-nexis.com.mhsl.uab.edu: Lexis Nexis.

Kush, Bronislaus. Muslims drawn to Patrick; Local community also working against Question 1.. (October 25, 2006). Telegram & Gazette, B5. Retrieved May 25, 2007, from http://web.lexis-nexis.com.fetch.mhsl.uab.edu: Lexis Nexis.

Lehigh, Scot and Phillips, Frank. Poll finds Weld leading Silber; CLT petition support seen as soft; Politics and Government. The Boston Globe, 24. Retrieved May 25, 2007, from http://web.lexis-nexis.com.fetch.mhsl.uab.edu: Lexis Nexis.

Loth, Renee. Liberal voters struggle with field of irreconcilables; For some, neither candidate is comfortable ideological fit; Campaign '90. The Boston Globe, 1p. Retrieved May 25, 2007, from http://web.lexis-nexis.com.fetch.mhsl.uab.edu: Lexis Nexis.

McNamara, Eileen. Women's Questions. (September 27, 2006). The Boston Globe, B1. Retrieved June 18, 2007, from http://web.lexis-nexis.com.fetch.mhsl.uab.edu: Lexis Nexis.

Mehren, Elizabeth. The Nation; Blue for Beacon Hill?; The man who might be Massachusets' first Democratic governor in 20 years is far from a standard-issue liberal. (October 31, 2006). Los Angeles Times. Retrieved April 19, 2007, from http://web.lexis-nexis.com.fetch.mhsl.uab.edu: Lexis Nexis.

Monahan, John J. Attack ads skew gubernatorial campaign. (October 15, 2006). Telegram & Gazette, A1. Retrieved May 25, 2007, from http://web.lexis-nexis.com.fetch.mhsl.uab.edu: Lexis Nexis.

————. Gubernatorial candidates do battle in third debate; Patrick, Gabrieli spar with Reilly on gay marriage. (May 25, 2006). Telegram & Gazette, A9. Retrieved May 25, 2007, from http://web.lexis-nexis.com.mhsl.uab.edu: Lexis Nexis.

————. Democratic gubernatorial debate is tonight. (September 7, 2006). Telegram & Gazette, B1. Retrieved May 25, 2007, from http://web.lexis-nexis.com.mhsl.uab.edu: Lexis Nexis.

Mohl, Bruce and Howe, Peter J. Election becomes battleground in car insurance war. (October 25, 2006). The Boston Globe, C1. Retrieved May 25, 2007, from http://web.lexis-nexis.com.fetch.mhsl.uab.edu: Lexis Nexis.

Mooney, Brian C. Patrick gets help in ad battle with Healey. (October 18, 2006). The Boston Globe, A1. Retrieved May 25, 2007, from http://web.lexis-nexis.com.fetch.mhsl.uab.edu: Lexis Nexis.

————. Gabrieli readies run for governor; Hires operatives, cites positive polling. (March 22, 2006). The Boston Globe, B1. Retrieved May 25, 2007, from http://web.lexis-nexis.com.fetch.mhsl.uab.edu: Lexis Nexis.

————. Patrick's path from courtroom to boardroom. (August 13, 2006). The Boston Globe, A1. Retrieved May 25, 2007, from http://web.lexis-nexis.com.fetch.mhsl.uab.edu: Lexis Nexis.

Moynihan, Kenneth. Kerry Healey has work cut out to catch up with Deval Patrick. (October 4, 2006). Telegram & Gazette, A11. Retrieved May 25, 2007, from http://web.lexis-nexis.com.fetch.mhsl.uab.edu: Lexis Nexis.

Nealon, Patricia. Turnout for gubernatorial races set record; crisis in middle east. (November 7, 1990). The Boston Globe, 36p. Retrieved May 25, 2007, from http://web.lexis-nexis.com.fetch.mhsl.uab.edu: Lexis Nexis.

O'Sullivan, Jim. Patrick critic heading for Mass., intending to dog candidate. (August 8, 2006). State House News Service.

Page, Susan. Election test how much race matters; African-American candidates for major state offices try to break some 'old barriers'. (2006). USA Today, 1A. Retrieved November 1, 2006, from http://web.lexis-nexis.com.fetch.mhsl.uab.edu: Lexis Nexis.

Phillips, Frank. Patrick outpaces two rivals in new poll; Democrat surges to a 21-point lead as vote nears. (September 17, 2006). The Boston Globe, A1. Retrieved May 25, 2007, from http://web.lexis-nexis.com.fetch.mhsl.uab.edu: Lexis Nexis.

Phillips, Frank and Samuels, Adrienne. Healey calls for stripping police chiefs of gun-licensing role. (October 18, 2006). The Boston Globe, B4. Retrieved May 25, 2007, from http://web.lexis-nexis.com.fetch.mhsl.uab.edu: Lexis Nexis.

Pierce, Charles. The Optimist 'I wasn't campaigning as the black candidate.' And because he didn't, because he ran a hopeful, grass-roots campaign that ended with his election as governor, Deval Patrick is our 2006 Bostonian of the Year. (December 31, 2006). The Boston Globe, 28. Retrieved April 15, 2007, from http://web.lexis-nexis.com.fetch.mhsl.uab.edu: Lexis Nexis.

Sonenshein, Raphael J. (1995). Can Black Candidates Win Statewide Elections? *Public Opinion Quarterly*, 105, 219-241.

Strickland, R. and Whicker, M. 1992. Comparing the Wilder and Gantt campaigns: A model for Black statewide success in state wide elections. *Political Science & Politics*, 25, 204-212.

Vennochi, Joan. For Reilly, things go better with Coke. (August 11, 2006). The Boston Globe, A17. Retrieved May 25, 2007, from http://web.lexis-nexis.com.fetch.mhsl.uab.edu: Lexis Nexis.

Wangsness, Lisa. A hushed Clinton speaks proudly of Patrick: Says the electorate wants to be lifted up. (October 17, 2006). The Boston Globe, B1. Retrieved April 19, 2007, from http://web.lexis-nexis.com.fetch.mhsl.uab.edu: Lexis Nexis.

——————. At rally, Patrick tries to turn Healey's ads back at her. (October 16, 2006). The Boston Globe, B4. Retrieved April 19, 2007, from http://web.lexis-nexis.com.fetch.mhsl.uab.edu: Lexis Nexis.

——————. Healey will sign antitax pledge; 3 in4candidates support rollback. (September 4, 2006). The Boston Globe, B1. Retrieved May 25, 2007, from http://web.lexis-nexis.com.mhsl.uab.edu: Lexis Nexis.

Wangsness, Lisa. and Simpson, A. 3 women's group to endorse Patrick. (October 12, 2006). The Boston Globe, B4. Retrieved April 19, 2007, from http://web.lexis-nexis.com.fetch.mhsl.uab.edu: Lexis Nexis.

Williams, Joseph. Black political figures rally around Patrick. (April 18, 2006). The Boston Globe, A1. Retrieved April 19, 2007, from http://web.lexis-nexis.com.fetch.mhsl.uab.edu: Lexis Nexis.

Williams, Linda F. 1989. White/Black perceptions of the electability of Black political candidates. *National Political Science Review*, 1, 45.

Williamson, Dianne. Patrick caught in cross hairs; Support of LaGuer preceded DNA test. (October 5, 2006). Telegram & Gazette, B1. Retrieved May 25, 2007, from http://web.lexis-nexis.com.mhsl.uab.edu: Lexis Nexis.

Running on Race and Against Convention: Michael Steele, Kweisi Mfume, and Maryland's 2006 Senate Contest

Tyson D. King-Meadows
University of Maryland Baltimore County

Introduction

The 2006 campaign for Maryland's open U.S. Senate seat challenged convention, providing an excellent counterfactual to deracialization theory. On one side was conservative one-term Republican Lieutenant Governor Michael Steele, the state's first black to win statewide elected office in 2002. On the other side, fighting for the Democratic primary win were, among others, ten-year incumbent Democratic U.S. House Representative Ben Cardin in a tight contest against former five-term Democratic U.S. House Representative and former national NAACP president Kweisi Mfume. There were historical, attitudinal, and pragmatic reasons for blacks *not* to have supported Steele. Yet both Mfume and Steele defied expectations by running on race. Steele specifically defied the odds by making the 2006 senate contest competitive in a decidedly blue state and by picking up 25 percent of the black vote despite high national anti-Republican sentiment.[1]

This chapter explains how Steele defied these expectations. It pays particular attention to how Steele spoke about black empowerment, black racial consciousness, and Republican partisanship, and synergies between the three constructs, in ways that were unanticipated by the Democrats. In addition, the chapter addresses how Steele capitalized on black angst over the substantive and descriptive dividends received from Democratic allegiance—including resentment over Cardin's primary defeat of Kweisi Mfume—despite the 2006 Democratic lieutenant governor-nominee being a black State Delegate from Prince George's County. More importantly, this chapter situates the 2006 Senate campaign as a counterfactual to the deracialization construct. While the conventional wisdom of the deracialization construct suggests running away from race, here was a case in which a black Democrat seeking statewide office did emphasize racial issues and in which a black Republican seeking the same office did emphasize race over partisanship. Furthermore, while deracialization largely precludes the possibility that either would occur in the same statewide election cycle, the political context of the 2006 Maryland Senate campaign allowed Mfume and Steele to break convention and to run on race.[2] The conclusion addresses what this campaign may portend about the construct and about the future relationship between blacks and the two parties.

Deracialization Theory

There continues to be a love-hate relationship with the deracialization construct in the literature on black electoral behavior and black political attitudes.[3] The construct refers to a combined rhetorical, electoral, and governance strategy in which black candidates deemphasize "racially-specific issues." In remarking on the distinctions between the agenda setting and the electoral strategy dimensions of the construct, McCormick and Jones define the latter in the following manner:

> Conducting a campaign in a stylistic fashion that defuses the polarizing effects of race by avoiding explicit reference to race-specific issues, while at the same time emphasizing those issues that are perceived as racially transcendent, thus mobilizing a broad segment of the electorate for purposes of capturing and maintaining public office.[4]

Moving further into the analysis, McCormick and Jones assert three components that will enable one to certify the existence of a deracialized campaign. First, the black candidate will employ a political style that seems "non-threatening" to whites. Second, the black candidate will avoid "racial appeals in organizing the black community." Third, the black candidate will avoid a specific racial agenda. At its base, the deracialization construct emerged to explain the value of electoral victories in the 1990s by black candidates in white jurisdictions, the "second wave" of black politics where biracial coalition building replaced direct confrontation as a means of achieving policy goals and elected office.[5]

In offering deracialization as an expression of black politics, McCormick and Jones follow an analytical framework that defines black politics as actions done for the "expressed purpose of improving the material conditions of African Americans" in a way "sensitive to the historical role and continuing impact of white racism in American political life."[6] As such, black candidates who attempt to capture public office for this "express purpose" are working within the analytical parameters of black politics. These authors then conclude with a tacit warning, "If deracialization as a successful electoral strategy lends its practitioners to ignore the policy-oriented concerns of African-Americans, then we should rightly dismiss their political behavior as nonlegitimate expressions of black politics."[7]

The 2006 Maryland Senate Race

In March 2005, Senator Paul S. Sarbanes announced his retirement. This made the 2006 senatorial race the first open seat contest since 1986 when Democratic Representative Barbara Mikulski ran for the seat vacated by Republican Charles McCurdy "Mac" Mathias (1969-1989). Three days later, Kweisi Mfume announced his candidacy. His candidacy seemed inevitable—Mfume was a former Baltimore City council member (1979-1986), former five-term congressman and Congressional Black Caucus (CBC) chair, former national NAACP president (1996-2004), and alumnus of historically black Morgan State University. Yet, his announcement surprised Maryland Democrats, including the state's black federal legislators and CBC members Representatives Elijah Cummings (Seventh District) and Albert Wynn (Fourth District).[8] It also generated both jubilation and consternation. On the one hand, Mfume had expanded the NAACP's membership, had retired organizational debt, and had remained a spokesperson for race-related causes. On the other hand, Mfume's personal and political stories—from gang life, out of wedlock children, and accusations of nepotism and sexual improprieties at the NAACP—produced one tapestry of questions about his judgment.

Even so, black elites saw Mfume's candidacy as an opportunity to break Maryland's glass ceiling of black electoral politics. Mfume characterized it this way: "It's time for the Democratic Party to make a bold statement in a blue state where blacks have always been willing to support white Democrats for office."[9] Without this statement Mfume feared a possible "seismic change in terms of voter loyalty (to the Democratic Party) because the black community will feel betrayed."[10] When other prominent politicians decided against running for the seat, black Democrats hoped the party's leadership would clear the field.

However, the Democratic Party leadership had other plans. Five weeks later Representative Ben Cardin of the Third District announced his candidacy. In fact, one journalist remarked that party leaders "scoured the field for a viable alternative to Mfume" in between the announcement by the former NAACP president and that of the ten-year incumbent from the Third District.[11] Cardin was a relatively unknown commodity outside of his district (representing parts of Anne Arundel, Baltimore, and Howard Counties, and Baltimore City). Cardin, however, secured a host of high-profile endorsements from the "neutral" party leadership (including that of House Minority Whip Steny Hoyer), severely outpaced Mfume's financial backing, made sure that neither Wynn nor Cummings endorsed Mfume until right before the September primary, and paraded out a string of endorsements by black leaders.[12] Despite the genteel nature of the Mfume-Cardin debates, Mfume made it a point to rail publicly against the Democratic leadership who had seemingly "anointed" Cardin as Sarbanes' successor.[13] Mfume surrogates and other blacks echoed these points.

The Cardin team and Democratic operatives took Mfume's candidacy seriously, but not for the reasons one would suspect.[14] Referred to as the "Kweisi Problem," Democrats feared that an Mfume victory in the September Democratic primary was a lost Democratic Senate seat.[15] To win they had to (a) dismiss the Mfume candidacy; (b) heal wounds from the 2002 gubernatorial race; and (c) attack Steele (who had officially announced in October 2005). All the above was inevitable: This was the first statewide election since the gubernatorial race and wounds from it had festered for four years.

Old Wounds: The 2002 Governor's Race

The 2006 battle for black votes began when Republican Representative Robert Ehrlich chose Steele as a gubernatorial running mate in a campaign against two-term Democratic Lt. Governor Kathleen Kennedy Townsend (daughter of the late Sen. Robert F. Kennedy) serving under two-term Democratic Governor Parris N. Glendening.[16] Ehrlich capitalized on a misstep made by Townsend who, after long speculation, shocked black activists with a late June 2002 choice of retired U.S. Naval Academy superintendent Admiral Charles Larson—a white Republican who had recently switched parties. Townsend's decision negatively resounded on racial and political dimensions: The Democrats held the majority of elected office positions and blacks enjoyed high levels of political incorporation across the state.

A few days later, Ehrlich announced Michael S. Steele as the lieutenant governor-nominee. Steele was two-years into his leadership of the Maryland Republican Party and was a long-term resident of Prince George's County—a predominately black jurisdiction wielding increasing political and economic influence across the state. As the first black elected chair of any state's Republican caucus, the Catholic pro-life, anti-gun control, and pro-school reform candidate had a natural partisan base. He extended it by securing endorsements from disgruntled black Democrats and marketing a black vote for Ehrlich-Steele as payback for the Democrats' disrespect of black interests and as history in the making.[17] Other blacks criticized Republicans for tokenism, playing the race card, and suggesting that Democrats were unwilling to advance black elected office seeking.

The 2002 Ehrlich-Steele victory rippled through national politics. First, Townsend lost by three percentage points. Second, Ehrlich became Maryland's first Republican governor since Spiro T. Agnew (1967-1969). Third, the ticket did well in competitive and minority jurisdictions. Fourth, Steele became Maryland's first black statewide elected officer and the most prominent elected black Republican. Fifth, Ehrlich's victory was attributable to political context: Governor Glendening's approval was low; Townsend's campaign was poorly organized; the election occurred in a midterm year; and black voters were demobilized.

The 2006 Democratic Primary

The 2002 Ehrlich-Steele victory spread speculation about Democratic support of future black statewide office seekers. This speculation turned to consternation when Maryland's Democratic leadership responded unenthusiastically to Mfume's candidacy. However, problems besieged the Mfume campaign from the beginning. It lacked support beyond black circles and experienced fundraising problems. Mfume characterized Cardin as a Democratic insider—beholden to Washington-centered interests rather than state constituents—and as a politician whose votes (e.g., authorizations for military activities in Iraq and the Patriot Act) and campaign contributors (e.g., pharmaceutical companies) placed him out of step with most Marylanders. Mfume's tag lines were that he could not "be bought" and that Maryland could "make history." Cardin countered with his longevity in Maryland politics, widespread backing, and his ability to build coalitions.

Mfume's conundrum was clear: pitch his candidacy beyond black circles without alienating black voters who valued descriptive representation. *The Washington Post's* Marc Fisher put it this way: "But despite his efforts to make white audiences comfortable with him, Mfume has not been shy about mentioning race as one justification for his candidacy...."[18] As detractors of the deracialization construct understood, black candidates had to balance both black voter aspirations and white fear. Fisher then concludes his article with these words, "Race, of course, is the trickiest of weapons in a political campaign. When Mfume uses his prodigious rhetorical skills to neutralize the issue, he is masterful. When he wields race as a threat, he risks losing the advantage he has so carefully gained."[19] Undaunted, Mfume pressed on as Cardin's black gadfly.

Cardin, on the other hand, continued to assail Steele. For example, playing up President Bush's support for Steele; highlighting the endorsement of the MD-Washington Minority Contractors Association for his (Cardin's) candidacy; contrasting his vote to override President Bush's veto on stem cell research with what Senator Steele would do; and criticizing the Bush prescription drug plan. Prior to the September primary, Cardin's press releases mentioned Steele twelve times in the title compared to mentioning Mfume only once. These late 2006 words by Mfume best encapsulate his feelings about Cardin's dismissal: "As I've run this campaign for almost a year and a half, we've always been considered the underdog. We didn't have the same amount of money or the blessing of the party. We're still trying to reach the ears of the voters."[20] By early 2006 Cardin had become a financial juggernaut. His response to Mfume and black discord—"I have not been anointed.... I have a record"—seemed dismissive.

It was politically expedient for Cardin to marginalize the campaign of Mfume and to attack Steele. Polls consistently revealed that an Mfume primary victory could create a competitive general election. For example, an April 2006 survey, suggested that the outcome of the Senate race could turn on who won the Democratic nomination.[21] This poll showed an eight-point Cardin lead over Mfume offset by a large percentage (22 percent) of likely primary voters remaining undecided. According to the poll, if Cardin faced Steele, he would lead by double digits but with an equal number of undecided voters. If Steele faced Mfume, the latter's lead would only be five percentage points with a huge number of undecided voters (17 percent). In either scenario, Steele would pick up between 16 and 21 percent of the African American vote. An August 2006 poll showed Steele picking up 23 percent of this electorate against Cardin but only 8 percent of this electorate against Mfume. The August poll also showed Cardin with a lead of three percentage points over Steele, with 16 percent of voters undecided. Cardin bounced on this news with the only release mentioning Mfume in the title. In the end, Mfume lost the primary election to Cardin, 40.5 to 43.7 percent.

This jockeying for the black vote affected all involved. Cardin's electability forced Mfume into campaigning to *neutralize* race (so that he would not alienate white Democrats) and campaigning to *exploit* race (so that he could mobilize angry black Democrats). Steele's prominence, Mfume's discontent, and the possibility of black defection forced Cardin into obfuscating on issues of race, presenting his candidacy as non-threatening to black interests, and portraying party as more important than race. Along the way, while both Democrats tried to deescalate talk of race and to run a genteel campaign, Steele did neither. Steele, like Mfume, portrayed race as more important than party allegiance: The "Kweisi Problem" had become the "Steele Problem."[22]

The 2006 Steele Campaign

Steele did not run a deracialized campaign. He consistently expressed issues related to race and racism, and made reference to how Democrats responded to his race and party identification before and after he became the lieutenant governor-nominee. For example, Steele often intonated about the 2001 incident where white Democrat and Maryland Senate President Thomas V. Mike Miller called him an "Uncle Tom" because Steele complained about minority vote dilution in the redistricting process. He also referenced a September 2002 "Oreo Cookie" incident, where allegedly some in the crowd "pelted" him with the snacks at Morgan State University during a gubernatorial campaign debate.[23] Although some challenged the veracity of the "Oreo" incident, Steele and others pressed on with the story. He also reiterated the story during an appearance on *Hannity and Colmes*.[24]

Using these incidents as a thematic backdrop, Steele presented his official entrée into the Senate contest as an evolution of independent black politics. "For too long, one party worried more about prices in the stock market than prices in the corner market.... And too many in the other party preached reconciliation at the same time they practiced division," he remarked. Later he said, "As a young man I realized that the front lines in the New Civil Rights Struggle would be different ... instead of the right to sit at the lunch counter ... the New Civil Rights Struggle would be a struggle for the right to own the diner and to create legacy wealth for our children."[25] During the speech Steele criticized both parties and refrained from mentioning his Republican affiliation, proclaiming that he would be "A bridge that not only brings both parties together, but, more importantly, brings all of us closer to one another."

Furthermore, Steele tried to conjoin black racial consciousness with partisanship, and, like Mfume, to present his candidacy an evolution in black perseverance against racism. He brought up the federal investigation of two Democratic Senatorial Campaign Committee staffers for illegally obtaining Steele's credit report. (One pleaded guilty and avoided jail time, the other resigned.) Steele called this a "low point" in the campaign, remarking that the media did not react to the story as it would have if the Republican Senatorial Campaign Committee employed such a tactic against Illinois Senator Barack Obama.[26] Steele also reminded blacks that New Yorker Steve Gilliard, a liberal black Democratic operative, had depicted him as a minstrel in black face.[27] The picture, titled "I's Simple Sambo and I's Running for the Big House," was decried by Democratic Virginia gubernatorial candidate Timothy M. Kaine and was eventually pulled—to the dismay of liberal bloggers. Reportedly, Gilliard defended the picture by saying "Steele invited the portrayal by failing to criticize Gov. Robert L. Ehrlich Jr.'s (R) decision to hold a fundraiser at an all-white country club."[28] Steele also brought up House Minority Leader Hoyer's remark that the lieutenant governor had "a career of slavishly supporting the Republican Party." For Steele, reaction to Hoyer's remark underscored the problem he faced: Steele calls the term racist; Hoyer apologizes but sticks to the underlying sentiment; Cardin calls Steele's reaction an attempt to "change the subject"; the divided response of black elites make headlines; and black Democrats remain sidelined.

It was easy for Steele to connect these above incidents to a controversial strategy memo prepared for the Democratic National Committee and leaked to *The Washington Post* in April 2006. The 37-page internal document, prepared by DNC pollster Cornel Belcher and reportedly in consultation with the Democratic Senatorial Campaign Committee (DSCC), advised the party to "knock Steele down" by identifying Steele as the "hand-picked candidate" of President Bush. The memo hoped Democrats would capitalize on high anti-Bush sentiment amongst black voters. The memo also specifically urged the party to "turn Steele into a typical Republican in the eyes of voters, as opposed to an African American candidate." Why? Because, according to the *Post*, "a sizable segment of likely black voters—as much as 44 percent—would readily abandon their historic Democratic allegiances 'after hearing Steele's messaging.'"[29] The memo also carried a warning, picked up by another news organization, that Democrats might not press Steele about his relationship with President Bush. According to this news report, Belcher warned, "Democrats must be aggressive, Steele is a unique challenge." Part of that unique challenge, according to the memo, stemmed from "Steele's messaging to the African American community [which] clearly had a positive effect—with many voters reciting his campaign slogans and his advertising."[30]

Steele's response to the memo was immediate and direct, labeling the strategy instructive of how Democrats valued black voters: "They're afraid of what I represent. They're afraid of the fact that African American voters have options, and I'm one of them."[31] Steele surrogates labeled the memo another example of race baiting. Others decried the proposed strategy to discredit and "knock down" Steele's candidacy and objected to depicting Steele as a guaranteed, rather than swing or likely, vote for Bush policies on Medicare reform and Social Security privatization.[32]

While prominent black Democrats remained silent about these practices, they did respond to Steele's use of black colloquialisms. In July 2006, blacks chastised Steele for employing the "homeboy" colloquialism in reference to President Bush during a radio interview. It never became clear as to whether black angst centered on the term, the reference point, or belief that Steele was using the term to ingratiate himself with blacks or with Republicans. Either way when pressed, Steele explained it this way, "I've been quoted before as calling the president my homeboy, you know, and that's how I feel."[33] Steele also invoked another colloquialism when discussing prior critical comments about the Republican Party and President Bush:

> "I'm not trying to dis the president ... I'm not trying to distance myself from the president. I'm trying to show those lines where I have a different perspective and a different point of view. If I'm not free to share that as a candidate for the U.S. Senate, how can people expect me to share that and express that as a United States senator?"[34]

These comments came in response to the revelation that Steele was the anonymous Republican whose critiques of the party went public in a July *Washington Post* article, "For One Senate Candidate, the 'R' is a 'Scarlet Letter'." The then-anonymous candidate challenged the president's war policy, the federal response to Katrina, and stated that he would "probably not" want President Bush to campaign for him in the state.[35] The title of the article was derived from Steele's comment, "For me to pretend I'm not a Republican would be a lie ... [to run as a proud Republican is] going to be tough, it's going to be tough to do.... If this race is about Republicans and Democrats, I lose."[36] For Steele and supporters, the campaign was about black political independence.[37]

Unwilling to confront Steele on race, Cardin hammered him as a Bush Republican. A Cardin television commercial even featured President Bush's comments that "Michael Steele is the right man for the United States Senate." Cardin's move was both easy and difficult. It was easy because Republican star power fueled Steele's candidacy. Bush headlined a November 2005 fundraiser and appeared on the same stage with Steele at Baltimore's M&T Bank Stadium. White House insider Karl Rove, President Bush, Vice President Cheney, and Arizona Senator John McCain hosted or appeared at fundraisers for Steele in Washington and Maryland. White House Chief of Staff Andrew H. Card Jr. headlined a fundraiser in New York, and Bush "Ranger" Mallory Factor (head of the Free Enterprise Fund in D.C.) spearheaded a private fundraiser.[38]

Steele's commercials and campaign zingers also made Cardin's job easy. For example, in television commercials Steele said the following: "politicians in Washington say one thing but do another"; it was time to "show [politicians] the door"; "real change" meant thinking differently about the vote; and, appearing with trash containers that it was time to take "out the trash." In another commercial, Steele appeared with a puppy, that reportedly was not his own. He intonated that Democrats would call him anything other than a "child of God" and say that he "hated puppies." These commercials were edgy, confrontational, and elusive about his stances on the issues. Cardin surrogates pointed out that President Bush, like Steele, was recalcitrant on Iraq, was confrontational to those with dissimilar views, was allusive about solutions, and employed discourse on the edge of acceptable political debate.

Despite this, Cardin surrogates faced a difficult time in rallying blacks to denounce Steele as a black Republican or as an individual. Some notable non-Marylanders with racial and partisan cache failed to campaign for Cardin inside the state. Only Illinois Senator Barack Obama and former President Clinton ventured into Maryland, with Al Sharpton, Jesse Jackson, and John Conyers appearing outside.[39]

To counter the label as a *Bush* Republican, Steele offered a new twist to the "Reagan Democrat" moniker: "Steele *Democrats*." The former label, firmly ensconced in America's political lexicon, explains both process and outcome. The outcome being a vote cast for Reagan by loyal Democrats (e.g., middle class, low-income, blue-collar, and union workers) who had grown increasingly disconcerted about their party's approach to cultural issues, economic policy, and foreign affairs. Envisioning similar success, Steele believed his personal appeal and public policy vision would win over black Democrats whose racial consciousness, religious convictions, and belief in economic empowerment could trump partisan affinity. Unlike the Reagan campaign however, there was never a clear message as to which political orientations differentiated segments of the party. The "Steele Democrat" slogan left constituents wondering about the similarities between a Reagan Democrat (who valued a strong military defense and conservative values) and a Steele Democrat (who valued racial consciousness and conservative values). The ambiguity was an especially strategic error for a campaign targeting young people born after the presidency of George H.W. Bush (1989-1993).[40]

Nonetheless, many Democrats with racial and partisan cache were nervous about the message and visual presentation of the "Steele Democrat" moniker. Presented in white letters against a light blue background, some believed the "Steele Democrat" moniker to be deceptive (akin to partisan identity theft); a position exaggerated by news of filmmaker Michael Mfume, a child of the primary contender, proudly sporting the moniker. Yet the Republican pressed on with its message and its display. For example, in the first debate between Cardin, Steele, and independent Kevin Zeese, Steele chastised Cardin for not learning to "look around the room and shut up and listen." This was, in part, a response to Cardin's attack on Steele for supporting the Bush administration's policies on health care, Iraq, and Social Security. Steele later remarked, "Stop the noise. Stop the race baiting, stop the fear mongering, and deal with me as a man." Steele's hyperbolic comments were strategic. The debate was at the headquarters of the Greater Baltimore Urban League headquarters, notable for being both a former church and a stop on the Underground Railroad. Steele, in effect, charged Cardin with racism, myopic partisanship, and indifference to black voices; charged he hoped would motivate blacks to think of themselves as Steele Democrats.

Finally dealing with the issue of race, Cardin stated, "Voters in the African-American community want change, and if they vote for me, they will get change." He went on, "I voted against [President] Bush's budget because Bush's budget is leading America in the wrong direction, and the people in the African-American community know that." Steele responded, "I appreciate your message of change, but it is an outdated message.... How can you be a change agent if you vote with your party 95 percent of the time?"[41] For Steele, Cardin's loyalty to party trumped loyalty to Maryland, and a citizen's loyalty to his/her economic, social, geographic, or racial interests should then trump (what Steele believed was) atavistic partisan attachment.

During other debates Steele tried again to depict Democrats, and Cardin, as out of touch with non-elite (or black) concerns. The second debate, held in October, occurred on WJLA's *News Talk Live*. At one point during the debate Steele asked Cardin about the beginning and ending of the proposed Metro Purple Line—a point of contention in Maryland's suburbs of Prince George's and Montgomery Counties. For many residents, the state's failure to ameliorate traffic congestion, and the state's federal elected officials refrain from directing traffic funds to solve the problem, was unacceptable. Flustered by Steele's aggressiveness and the unexpected question, Cardin stumbled to answer the question and then refused to answer it. In response Steele uttered "This gentleman has no clue about Metro traffic, congestion in this region ... I know exactly what the needs are because I live here." Steele's words were a not-so-thinly veiled nod to descriptive politics—both racially and geographically; Maryland had yet to elect a senator from the Washington suburbs (a place of growing minority presence).[42] News accounts of the debate characterized Steele as aggressive and Cardin as a policy-wonk unaware of problems outside the Baltimore City/County corridor.

Steele would make another such nod to descriptive politics during a third debate with Cardin in late October on Tim Russert's *Meet the Press*. Steele characterized himself more as a Reagan Republican or Lincoln Republican than a Bush Republican.[43] He also affirmed that Justice Clarence Thomas was his hero, but couched it this way: "In this sense, that, as an African-American, and the only African-American on the bench. You know, I've disagreed with Clarence Thomas on a number of issues." Steele then went on to explain his support for affirmative action. After this, Cardin began to pick up steam with black voters.[44]

It was easy to see why blacks were skeptical of Steele. He vacillated between running a racialized campaign and running a partisan campaign. For example, in a change of tactics, in mid-2006 Steele missed a fundraiser with Bush held at the Baltimore-Washington International Airport Marriott—choosing instead to appear at a fundraiser in Las Vegas. He cited scheduling conflicts. Ehrlich did not miss the fundraiser.[45] When asked about missing the fundraiser, Steele again employed black colloquialisms: "The reality of it is: Friends agree [and] friends disagree.... Where I agree with him, I say, 'Yo, Mr. President. I've got your back.' Where I disagree with him, I'm like, 'Yo, hold up. Let's talk about this.'"[46] These comments reminded voters of Steele's earlier support for the president's position against embryonic stem cell research; a position poorly articulated by horrific turn-of-the-year remarks linking stem cell research to experimentation done on imprisoned Jews and enslaved blacks. Although Steele's later apologies to the Jewish community were accepted, onlookers continued to question the veracity of Steele's moderate image.[47] His attempts to run against the party line—by distancing himself from the Republican president, from the pro-stem cell research Republican Governor Ehrlich, and by presenting himself as an independent thinker—were unpersuasive.

Running back to race, Steele publicized an endorsement by Russell Simmons—hip-hop cultural icon (e.g., founder of Def Jam Records and Phat Farm Clothing) and founder of the Hip Hop Summit Action Network—who hosted an August 2006 Baltimore fundraiser.[48] The Steele-Simmons relationship was below the radar. They had previously hosted financial empowerment summits in the state, and the Senate candidate had addressed Simmons' Hip Hop Summit in Detroit.[49] With the theme of "Change the Game" to mark his senatorial candidacy, Steele employed hip-hop phraseology to connect with young voters and Simmons' endorsement video went viral. Political analyst Donna Brazile characterized Simmon's entrée into the Steele camp as "a major endorsement for Lieutenant Governor Steele that will help him attract young people, as well as black voters." Brazile also noted, "Once again, this should serve as a wake-up call to Democrats not to take their most loyal constituents and voters for granted."[50] David Bositis, of the Joint Center for Political and Economic Studies, however downplayed the endorsement, claiming that Steele would no longer pursue black voters if Mfume won the primary.[51] Steele also secured the endorsement of Cathy Hughes, founder and chair of Radio One. The Simmons and Hughes endorsement videos were marketed throughout minority communities. Steele's former brother-in-law and former heavyweight boxing champion Mike Tyson (who was previously married to Steele's sister, physician Monica Turner) also advocated for Steele, as did Don King who had endorsed Bush in 2004.[52] Understandably, Tyson's pro-Steele campaign activities were not endorsed by the Steele campaign. While Mfume stated that the Hughes and Simmons endorsements were "lost on him,"[53]others saw potential precursors to an avalanche of weighty endorsements.

While not an avalanche, a flurry of later endorsements did affect how the two party nominees jockeyed for the black vote. In October 2006, early Mfume supporter, and former Prince George's County executive, Wayne K. Curry endorsed Steele. As the county's first black executive and a vocal Democrat, Curry's endorsement gained enormous publicity, as did the endorsement by Major F. Riddick Jr., former aide to then-Gov. Parris N. Glendening. Steele coupled the Curry endorsement with the endorsement of five Prince George's county council members.[54] Donna Brazile dismissed the Curry endorsement and put more stock in current County Executive Jack Johnson's endorsement of Cardin. Political scientist Ron Walters however called the endorsements "audacious." He proclaimed, "This is going to go through the black community like a rocket.... It's going to be the talk of the county, the state, maybe even the nation."[55] Chair of Maryland's Democratic Party Terry Lierman dismissed black angst and defended the party's relationship with blacks. He stated, "[Those doubting the veracity of the party's commitment] are trying to make an issue out of something that doesn't exist."[56]

Some did not share Lierman's conviction or his optimism about how black party resentment could play out. By October 2006, *The Cook Political Report* labeled Maryland's open seat a "Toss Up," a decisive turn from its prior ranking.[57] For many, the Steele-Cardin campaign represented a problem of navigating legacy and partisan loyalty. Many onlookers made mention of a September 27, 2006 meeting between a frustrated delegation of Maryland's black state senators and party leaders. While Baltimore mayor and 2006 Democratic gubernatorial candidate Martin O'Malley described the meeting between himself, the delegation, Cardin, and Lierman as "cordial," non-elites suspected otherwise.[58] Black elites confirmed these suspicions when Prince George's Senator Nathaniel Exum noted, "They don't take us serious. We're the most loyal constituency, and they don't take us serious. They have never done anything, and they pay us lip service.... We'll have to see how it plays out."[59]

Mfume's numerous gaffes were also changing how the Steele-Cardin contest was playing out, opportunities Steele continued to exploit. These gaffes made it easy for Steele to connect the Democrats' dismissal of the former NAACP president, Steele's changing electoral fortunes, and ambivalent black Democratic allegiance, into a larger story about the Republican Party being "uniquely positioned" to give voice to and act upon black substantive interests. For example, Steele exploited Mfume's decision to wait three days before conceding his primary loss to Cardin. Mfume justified the wait under guise of speculation that absentee and provisional ballots would make the difference. Yet Cardin campaigned as the presumptive victor and challenged Steele to debate. This prompted a statement from Steele's staff: "As much as Congressman Cardin and Democratic Party bosses would like to push Kweisi Mfume out of the race, the Maryland Board of Election still has yet to certify who won Tuesday's primary." Also, "This attempt by Congressman Cardin to anoint himself the nominee is disrespectful to the lieutenant governor's friend, Kweisi Mfume and, more importantly, disrespectful to Maryland voters."[60]

Mfume's concession remarks tried to take the air out of Steele's sails, but his next gaffe, at a pro-unity rally two weeks after the Democratic primary, opened up more space for Steele's appeal to black racial consciousness. This would be the first time that Cardin and Mfume would appear together after the primary election. During the rally headlining Senator Obama, Mfume endorsed Cardin but then added, "We need women in leadership positions in the state. We've got to find a way that African Americans and other minorities are represented statewide in office."[61] That black State House Majority Whip and two-term Delegate Anthony G. Brown was the 2006 Democratic nominee for lieutenant governor seemed unimportant. Steele pounced on Mfume's gaffe by stating: "The challenge of the opportunity is to build a bridge to communities the Democratic Party has taken for granted and has, by its choice of nominee, [decided to tell to wait].... I'm here to say, 'You don't have to wait any longer.'"[62] A *Washington Post* article added legitimacy to Steele's comments when quoting Mfume, who apparently justified his appearance at the event as part "promise keeping" to Senator Mikulski. Mfume remarked, "I am here to fulfill my commitment and my obligation."[63] It was clear that Mfume's endorsement of Cardin came with a "caveat."[64]

Figure 1, which displays the post-primary volatility of public opinion towards Cardin and Steele, makes clear that the lieutenant governor was gaining momentum in his campaign. Notice that a late October poll, conducted by the *Baltimore Sun*, gave the Democrat a six-point lead, with Steele garnering only 43 percent and 5 percent undecided. The *Sun* poll contradicted an earlier *Washington Post* poll that gave Cardin an 11-point lead (with 54 percent) and only 1 percent of respondents identified as undecided. A Mason-Dixon poll conducted at the turn of November reported a Steele disadvantage of three points, and reported that a full 9 percent of respondents remained undecided.

Hoping to build upon Steele's momentum, the Republicans provided another controversial visual depiction of the "Steele Democrats" moniker. It came in the form of a four-page "Democratic Sample Ballot" flier distributed to Prince George's County precincts. It immediately garnered public outcry. The flier was a direct appeal to racial

Figure 1
Post-Primary Volatility in Approval of Steele and Cardin

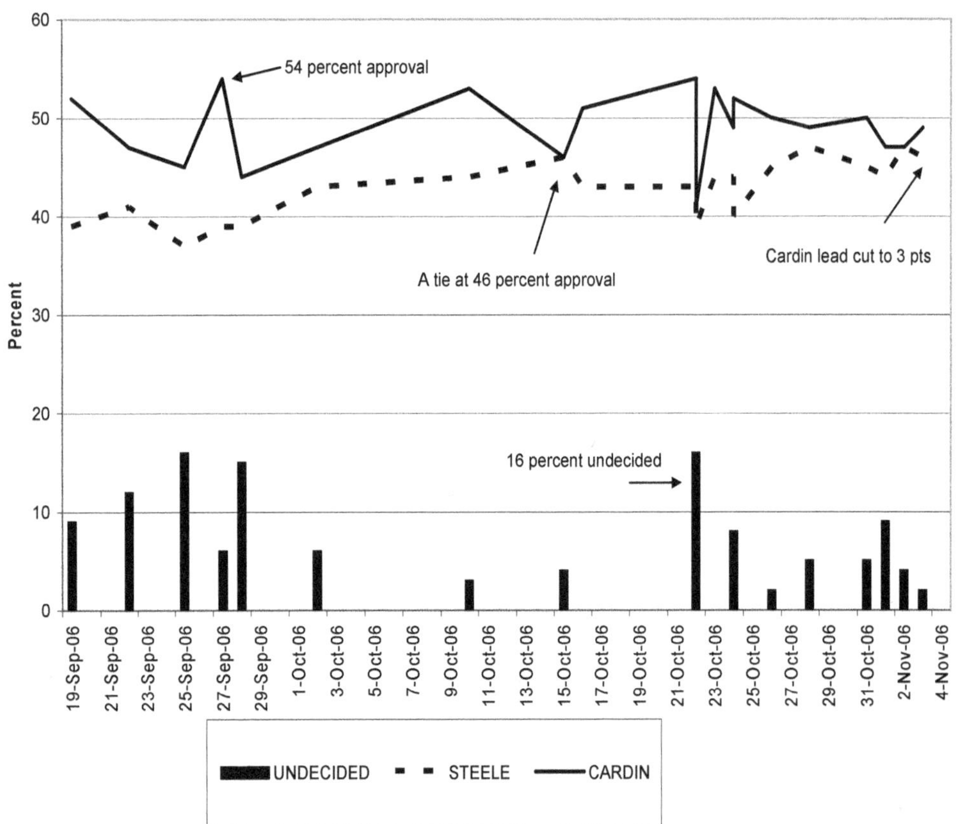

consciousness on multiple levels. First, the cover displayed pictures of Kweisi Mfume, Executive Jack B. Johnson, and former Executive Wayne K. Curry. Second, the inside contained a checked box for Ehrlich and Steele. Candidates for the other offices listed were Democrats. Third, the text, "These are OUR Choices" and "Official Voter Guide" adorned the cover. Fourth, the flier's colors were red, black, and green. Outraged, the Democrats blasted Republicans for fraudulent electioneering and a veiled attempt at either minority vote dilution or voter deception.[65] The Steele campaign claimed that the fliers were suggestive not deceptive.

Election Results

The Democrats successfully nationalized the 2006 midterm elections. The public had grown increasing discontent with Republican scandals, what they perceived as executive and legislative abuses of power, questionable congressional deference to the executive, the war in Iraq, and with President George W. Bush. Making electoral history, a 2006 vote for Democratic candidates was truly a vote against the president.[66] However, Maryland's election environment was contentious for reasons unrelated to national anti-Republican sentiment.[67] Concerns about electronic voting, voter-verifiable technology, and open-source coding caused citizens to cast 1,608,708 votes at the polls along with nearly 156,000 absentee ballots and over 41,000 provisional ballots.

Turnout and Support Data

Turnout reported at 57.53 percent, higher than in 2002 (30.76) and, understandably, lower than in 2004 (78.03). Steele carried 18 of the state's 24 counties but lost to Cardin by ten percentage points (54.2 to 44.2) and 178,296 votes. Table 1 depicts the breadth and depth of the Steele constituency examined against the constituencies built by other Republican candidates. I measure gains and losses by the proportionate share of votes garnered by Steele in 2006 compared to the votes garnered by Ehrlich as a 2002 gubernatorial candidate, by State Senator E.J. Pipkin (R-36) as a 2004 senatorial candidate against incumbent Senator Mikulski, and by President Bush seeking reelection. Looking across the data for Queen Anne's County, the 0.98 figure indicates that Steele retained 98 percent of the 2004 Pipkin constituency, 81 percent of the Bush reelection constituency, and 95 percent of the 2002 Ehrlich constituency. In Prince George's county, Steele bested Pipkin by 24 percent and Ehrlich by 9 percent.

Table 1 confirms Steele's inability to hold onto and build beyond the constituencies supporting previous Republican candidates. This is especially evident in the 18 Bush counties, varying in size, diversity, and geographical proximity to the state's inner corridor. For example, although both carried eastern Maryland, these counties tend to be predominately white, rural, and to *vote* Republican. Moreover, while Steele carried the 18 Bush counties, he was expected to carry those eight (8) giving Republicans a registration advantage: Calvert, Carroll, Frederick, Washington, Allegany, Garrett, Queen's Anne and Talbot. The greatest loss of the Bush constituency occurred in Washington County, a jurisdiction that gave Bush 64.4 percent of the two-party vote in 2004 but gave Steele only 60.8 percent of the vote (and 12,144 less votes). In Baltimore City, Steele outpaced Bush by garnering a greater share of the vote (23 to 17 percent) even while losing by over 75,000 votes.

As Figure 2 shows, reporting votes for Steele by the percentage of a district's black voting-age population, black constituents rejected the candidate despite endorsements by black elected officials and celebrities.[68] In Montgomery County, Steele garnered 31 percent of the vote and lost by over 108,000 votes. In Prince George's County, the lieutenant governor lost by more than 100,000 votes—a ratio of 3.1:1. Within the county's District 24 (an area with a 90 percent BVAP), Steele received 16 percent of vote. Hence, Steele's greatest support came from non-white jurisdictions within the 18 Bush counties (52 percent of the total Steele electorate); e.g., District 36 (with 8.6 BVAP) gave Steele 60 percent of the vote. OLS regression shows for every percentage increase in BVAP, Steele lost 129 votes ($F=26.855$; $p<.000$; adjusted $R^2 = .284$).[69]

Exit Poll Data

Below I analyze the 2006 National Election Poll General weighted national and state sample—with 13,962 and 1,721 respondents, with 1,334 and 394 blacks, respectively.

Table 2 illustrates that Steele exceeded Democratic expectations by garnering 25 percent of the black vote. Comparatively, Republican House and Senate candidates nationwide received 10 and 12 percent, respectively, of the black vote. The lieutenant

Table 1
Steel's Gains and Losses of Republican Constituencies, by County

County	Steele / Pipkin 04	Steele / Bush 04	Steele / Ehrlich 02	Steele Gain / Loss Relative to Bush Vote
Allegany *	1.00	0.68	0.89	+4 B
Anne Arundel *	0.99	0.76	0.89	+3 B
Baltimore City	1.48	0.97	0.91	+6 S
Baltimore	1.06	0.79	0.77	+2 B
Calvert *	0.91	0.73	1.03	+3 B
Caroline *	1.10	0.81	0.95	+1 S
Carroll *	0.95	0.77	0.90	+2 B
Cecil *	0.86	0.72	0.96	+3 B
Charles	0.92	0.69	1.00	+1 B
Dorchester *	1.20	0.81	0.91	+1 S
Frederick *	0.90	0.70	0.97	+2 B
Garrett *	0.95	0.77	1.06	+1 B
Harford *	1.00	0.79	0.89	+2 B
Howard	1.01	0.79	0.88	+1 B
Kent *	1.10	0.87	0.85	+1 S
Montgomery	0.91	0.71	0.85	+2 B
Prince George's	1.24	0.89	1.09	+5 S
Queen Anne's *	0.98	0.81	0.95	+2 B
Saint Mary's *	0.92	0.69	1.02	+5 S
Somerset *	1.13	0.81	0.88	+6 B
Talbot *	1.14	0.86	0.97	+2 S
Washington *	0.85	0.67	0.94	+4 B
Wicomico *	1.04	0.78	1.06	+2 S
Worcester *	1.13	0.80	1.04	0
Average	1.03	0.78	0.94	-

Rounded figures reported.
* Bush County (N=18); Underlined counties reported a 2006 Republican registration advantage.
Note: + 4 B means in that specific county President Bush (B) did 4 percentage points better in 2004 than did Lt. Governor Steele (S) in 2006. For example, in Allegany County, Bush received 64 percent of the vote whereas Steele received 60 percent. In Baltimore City, the vote percentages were 17% (B) and 23% (S) for a +6 S code.
Source: Author calculations of Maryland State Board of Elections data.

Figure 2
Votes for Steele by Percent Black Voting Age Population, by District

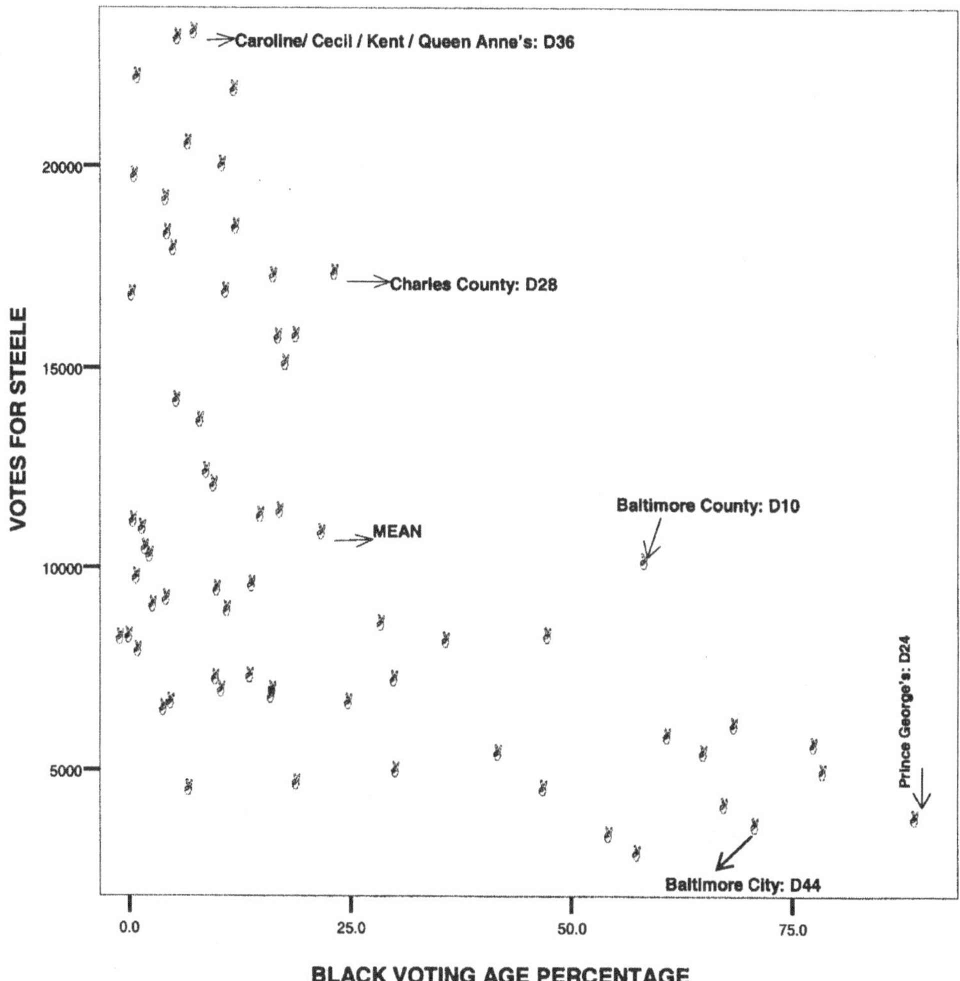

N=65; Votes for Steele = 13650.79 – 129.4 BVAP; p<.000
Source: Author calculations, Maryland State Board of Elections legislative district data.

governor garnered 35 percent of the 18-24 age cohorts, though this segment was the least mobilized. As expected, Steele did well among married blacks (28 percent) and among the more affluent. Other Republican congressional candidates did comparatively worse among married blacks (average 12.5 percent) and among the affluent (average 22.5 percent) making more than $75,000. Steele also bested his Republican counterparts amongst the most educated blacks. Among black college graduates, Steele received 33 percent of the vote while colleagues received an average of 21 percent. Steele failed to capture the majority of Maryland's most affluent and most educated black voters.

Table 2
African American Vote for Steele, by Select Demographic Characteristics

OVERALL (23)	25%
GENDER	
Male (44)	30
Female (56)	20
AGE	
18-24 (6) 35	
25-29 (10)	14
30-39 (17)	25
40-44 (12)	40
45-49 (15)	27
50-59 (24)	22
60-64 (8) 20	
65+ (9) 12	
MARITAL STATUS	
Married (65)	28
Not married (35)	15
INCOME (2005 FAMILY)	
<$15,000 (2)	20
15,000 - 29,999 (7)	12
30,000 – 49,999 (19)	20
50,000 - 74,999 (29)	26
75,000 - 99,999 (19)	31
100,000+ (24)	26
EDUCATION	
Less Than High School (3)	0
High School Graduate (17)	20
Some College (33)	22
College Graduate (31)	33
Post Graduate (17)	24

* Parentheses represent proportion of the Maryland African American exit-poll electorate.

Table 3 confirms similar patterns. Steele earned 17 percent of the black Democratic vote and lost 16 percent of the black Republican vote. He also lost 62 percent of the black conservative vote and 72 percent of the black moderate vote. Among liberal blacks, Steele earned 14 percent of the vote and did better than other Republicans who only earned 5 percent of this segment. Moreover, despite Steele's pro-life stances, he received a small percentage of the Protestant and Catholic vote and of the vote from frequent church attendees. Among those blacks attending church once a week (34 percent of the electorate), Steele received only 25 percent of the vote. This was a 15-point improvement over other 2006 Republican candidates.

The data in Table 4 are most revealing about black perceptions of the Steele campaign. The Democrats effectively portrayed Steele as a *Bush* Republican, and support from Maryland blacks reflected nationwide consternation about the president's agenda. Steele did quite well among blacks who approved of President Bush, voted to express their support for the executive (86 percent), and who believed that Iraq was unimportant to their Senate vote. However, nearly two-thirds of blacks in Maryland and over two-thirds of black nationwide strongly disapproved of Bush's job performance and connected their Senate vote to the Iraq War. Only 5 percent of blacks expressing disapproval of Bush voted for Republican Senate candidates. Steele also fared anemic among blacks who connected the issue of terrorism to their Senate vote (24 percent).

Table 4 shows another dimension of black perception. Thirteen percent of blacks believing that the Democrats only respected their views voted for Steele, and 37 percent of those believing that both parties respected the views of blacks voted for him. Cardin garnered 76 percent of those who believed neither party respected their views. Thirty-seven percent of those blacks who voted for Steele indicated that they had reservations.

Conclusion

The 2006 campaign for Maryland's open U.S. Senate seat reveals the need to modify the deracialization construct for examining the nuances of partisan and racial politics in twenty-first-century America. The deracialization construct is a rational choice explanation of black politics practiced against the backdrop of racial antagonism, socioeconomic stratification, and bloc voting. The construct is therefore akin to the black utility heuristic construct—where individual actions are structured by perceptions of how well blacks are doing and would do under alternative policy regimes.[70] The latter explains black electoral and attitudinal orientations and the former explains black office seeking practices. Both presume future trajectories of black politics will remain amenable to Democratic partisanship. Yet the logic of each construct presents an alternative path, one where black candidates seeking statewide office reject deracialization in order to raise black skepticism about the collective dividend produced by Democratic allegiance.

The campaigns of Kweisi Mfume and Michael Steele were decidedly counter to the proscriptions of the deracialization construct. Each sought, albeit in significantly different ways, to (a) threaten white political power; (b) mobilize black citizens through racial appeals, and (c) to interject issues of race into the contest. Both campaigns reflected consternation over black office seeking under the Democratic banner. Indeed, observers have long pondered about the impact of shifts in black allegiance, with journalists having proclaimed 2006 as the "year of the black Republicans."[71] Of course, the senatorial and

Table 3
African American Vote for Steele, by Party, Ideology, Religion, Church Attendance, and Perceptions of Maryland Economy

PARTY	
Democrat (77)	17
Republican (8)	84
Independent/Something Else (15)	29
IDEOLOGY	
Liberal (29)	14
Moderate (55)	26
Conservative (16)	38
RELIGION	
Protestant / Other Christian (70)	21
Catholic (14)	37
Something Else (10)	21
None (6)	20
CHURCH ATTENDANCE	
More than Once a Week (20)	28
Once a Week (34)	25
A few times a month (20)	27
A few times a year (20)	20
Never (5)	5
PERCEPTION OF MARYLAND ECONOMY	
Excellent (5)	50
Good (50)	27
Not So Good (41)	17
Poor (4)	21

* Parentheses represent proportion of the Maryland African American exit-poll electorate.

Table 4
The Anti-Bush, Anti-Iraq War, Party Legacy, and Candidate Approval Impact on the African American Vote for Steele

PRESIDENT G. W. BUSH'S JOB PERFORMANCE	
Strongly Approve (6)	59
Somewhat Approve (7)	62
Somewhat Disapprove (22)	28
Strongly Disapprove (64)	14
IMPORTANCE OF IRAQ WAR IN SENATE VOTE	
Extremely Important (38)	15
Somewhat Important (27)	24
Somewhat Not Important (23)	33
Not Important at all (12)	37
ISSUE OF TERRORISM IN SENATE VOTE	
Extremely Important (31)	24
Somewhat Important (35)	19
Somewhat Not Important (22)	30
Not Important at all (11)	31
SENATE VOTE TO EXPRESS:	
Support for President G. W. Bush (2)	86
Opposition to President G. W. Bush (53)	5
President G. W. Bush not a factor (42)	42
RESPECTS THE VIEWS OF BLACKS	
Only the Democratic Party (43)	13
Only the Republican Party (1)	67
Both do (28)	37
Neither does (25)	25
REASONS FOR STEELE VOTE:	
Strongly favor candidate	51
Like candidate but with reservations	37
Dislike the other candidate	7

* Parentheses represent proportion of the Maryland African American exit-poll electorate.

gubernatorial defeats of Steele, Lynn Swan (PA), and Kenneth Blackwell (OH) and the black proportion of the Republican vote in 2006 suggest otherwise. On the other hand, harbingers are hard to identify at the time of emergence.

Indeed, voter turnout paved the way for other critiques of rational choice theory. Morris P. Fiorina contended that turnout was "the paradox that ate rational choice theory." [72] The theory was inadequate for explaining the expressive value of participation or for why people voted despite the improbability of their vote being decisive. Similarly, both Mfume and Steele continued to reject deracialization despite the improbability of winning—racial bloc voting within a closed primary system prevented the former from winning and a heavy anti-Republican context prevented the latter. This 2006 Senate contest however could foreshadow bigger problems to come for the Democrats. The Republicans could learn how to organize along *racial* lines as they learned to organize along *organizational* lines to win Congress in 1994; and the Democrats could (as the national party did in 1988 and as Maryland's state party did in 2002) misread black willingness to stay home or to defect. If either occurs, Maryland's 2006 contest could become, in retrospect, the campaign that ate deracialization theory as a prism from which to view trajectories of twenty-first-century black politics. As Prince George's Senator Nathaniel Exum suggested, only time will tell how it "plays out," or, more specifically, how the parties balance black voter aspirations and the need to diversify and solidify their partisan bases.[73]

Notes

1. Jeremy Mayer, *Running on race: Racial politics in presidential campaigns*, 1960-2000 (New York: Random House, 2002); Gary C. Jacobson, "Referendum: The 2006 Midterm Congressional Elections." *Political Science Quarterly* 122 (Spring, 2007), pp. 1-24.
2. Hanes Walton, *African American Power and Politics* (New York: Columbia University Press,1997); Michael C. Dawson, *Behind the mule: Race and class in American politics* (Chicago, IL: University of Chicago Press, 1994); Michael C. Dawson, *Black visions: The roots of* contemporary African-American political ideologies (Chicago, IL: University of Chicago Press, 2001)
3. Joseph McCormick, II and Charles E. Jones, "The Conceptualization of Deracialization: Thinking Through the Dilemma," in *Dilemmas of Black Politics: Issues of Leadership and Strategy*, (ed.) Georgia A. Persons, (New York: HarperCollins College Publishers, 1993), pp. 66-84; Robert B. Albritton, George Amedee, Keenan Grenell and Don-Terry Veal, "Deracialization and the New Black Politics," in *Race, politics, and governance in the United States,* Huey L. Perry (ed.) (Gainesville: University Press of Florida, 1996), pp.96-106; Byron D' Andra Orey and Boris E. Ricks, "A Systematic Analysis of the Deracialization Concept," *National Political Science Review* 11 (2007), pp. 325-334
4. McCormick and Jones (1993:76)
5. Saundra C. Ardrey and William E. Nelson. "The Maturation of Black Political Power: The Case of Cleveland." *PS: Political Science and Politics* 23(June 1990): 148-151.
6. McCormick and Jones (1993:79)
7. Ibid
8. John Wagner and Spencer S. Hsu, "Mfume Jumps In for Sarbanes's Seat," *Washington Post*, March 15, 2005, pg. B05.
9. DeWayne Wickham, "Blacks deserve something in return from Md. Democrats," *USA TODAY*, March 14, 2005, pg. 13A
10. Ibid.
11. Hockstader, "The 'Kweisi Problem'," pg. B07
12. Jon Ward, "Wynn, Cummings back Mfume," *The Washington Times,* August 30, 2006; Matthew Mosk, "Cummings And Wynn To Back Mfume," *The Washington Post,* August 30, 2006; pg. B02
13. Matthew Mosk, "Steele Strives for the Hearts of Black Voters," *The Washington Post*, November 8, 2005, pg. B01
14. Twenty-eight persons filed for the vacant seat, with eighteen in the Democratic primary.
15. Lee Hockstader, "The 'Kweisi Problem'," T*he Washington Post,* June 11, 2006; B07

16. Parris N. Glendening served from 1995-2003.
17. The parallel is Douglas Wilder's successful 1986 bid for Lt. Governor of Virginia that laid the foundation for Wilder's successful and historic 1989 campaign. Until the 2006 election of Deval Patrick, Massachusetts, Wilder was the first popularly elected African American governor since Reconstruction.
18. Marc Fisher, "For Mfume, Race Cuts Both Ways," *The Washington Po*st, July 2, 2006; pg. C01
19. Ibid.
20. Matthew Mosk and Claudia Deane, "Maryland Senate Race May Hinge On Ethnicity," *The Washington Post*, July 2, 2006, pg. A01
21. Gonzales Research & Marketing Strategies, April 4 – 13, 2006; N=819 registered regular voters.
22. Matthew Mosk, "Steele Strives for the Hearts of Black Voters," *The Washington Post*, November 8, 2005, pg. B01
23. Michael Sokolove, "Why Is Michael Steele A *Republican* Candidate?," *New York Times Magazine*, March 26, 2006; Paul Schwartzman and Matthew Mosk, "'Racist' Label by Ehrlich Riles Democrats," *The Washington Post*, September 1, 2004
24. Andrew Green, "Ehrlich bristles at Oreo skeptics," The Baltimore Sun, November 13, 2005, pg. 1B
25. Steele Announcement Speech, Prince George's Community College, October 25, 2005
26. Author interview with Lt. Governor Michael Steele, June 22, 2007.
27. A few weeks before Gilliard depicted Ohio Secretary of State Kenneth Blackwell in blackface.
28. S. A. Miller, "Top Democrats duck on Steele hits," *The Washington Times*, November 3, 2005; Matthew Mosk, "Blog Attack on Steele Decried, Doctored Photo Criticized by Republicans and Democrats," *Washington Post*, October 28, 2005, pg. B04; Jeff Jacoby, "Slurs Fly from the Left," *The Boston Globe*, December 28, 2005, pg. A19
29. Survey based on 489 black Maryland voters. See Matthew Mosk, "Poll Finds Steele May Be Magnet for Black Voters," *Washington Post*, April 6, 2006, pg. B05
30. Richard Miniter, "Democrats Plan Race-Based Campaign Against Black Candidate in Maryland," *The New York Sun*, April 13, 2006,
31. Mosk, *Washington Post*, April 6, 2006
32. Jon Ward, "Plans to knock Steele labeled as 'destructive'," *The Washington Times*, April 7, 2006
33. John Wagner, "Steele Addresses Negative Comments on Bush," *Washington Post*, July 27, 2006, B01
34. Ibid.
35. Dana Milbank, "For One Senate Candidate, the 'R' Is a 'Scarlet Letter'," *Washington Post*, July 25, 2006, pg. A02
36. Ibid.
37. Interview with Steele (June 22, 2007) and Steele supporters (November 7, 2006)
38. Rangers were individuals bundling at least $200,000 for the Bush-Cheney 2004 campaign.
39. Interview with Steele (June 22, 2007)
40. Interview with senior campaign advisor (June 28, 2007).
41. S.A. Miller, "Steele, Cardin wrangle over race in debate," *The Washington Times*, October 4, 2006
42. Interview with senior campaign advisor, June 28, 2007.
43. Transcript for October 29, 2006 edition of Meet The Press, Ben Cardin, Michael Steele. Updated: 10:42 a.m. ET Oct 30, 2006 [Accessed on January 3, 2007; available at ww.msnbc.msn.com/id/15473528/]
44. Robert Barnes and Matthew Mosk, "Poll Puts Maryland Democrats In the Lead," Washington Post, October 29, 2006, A01
45. Matthew Mosk, "Steele Absent From Bush GOP Fundraiser," Washington Post, June 1, 2006, pg. B05
46. S.A. Miller, "Missed fundraiser wasn't a slap at Bush, Steele says," *The Washington Times*, June 4, 2006
47. See Robert Barnes and Matthew Mosk, "Steele Apologies for Holocaust Remarks," *Washington Post*, February 11, 2006, pg. B01
48. Jon Ward, "Steele gaining blacks' support," *The Washington Times*, August 24, 2006
49. Interview with Steele, June 22, 2007.
50. Jon Ward, "Steele gaining blacks' support," *The Washington Times*, August 24, 2006
51. Matthew Mosk, "Angling for Hip-Hop Appeal," *Washington Post*, August 25, 2006, pg. B01
52. Tyson and Turner have two children—a son and a daughter.
53. Matthew Mosk, "Angling for Hip-Hop Appeal," *Washington Post*, August 25, 2006, pg. B01

54. The members were David Harrington (D-Cheverly); Samuel H. Dean (D-Mitchellville); Camille Exum (D-Seat Pleasant); Tony Knotts (D-Temple Hills); and Marilynn Bland (D-Clinton).
55. Ovetta Wiggins, "Black Democrats Cross Party Lines To Back Steele For U.S. Senate," *Washington Post*, October 31, 2006, pg. B01
56. Ibid.
57. *The Cook Political Report*, "2006 Senate Race Ratings," October 20, 2006, pg. 3
58. Doug Donovan, "O'Malley Calls Talk `Cordial'," *The Baltimore Sun*, October 6, 2006, pg. 5.B
59. Jon Ward, "Democrats hit for lack of black candidates," *The Washington Times, October 6, 2006*
60. Jon Ward, "Steele, Cardin: Opening shots," *The Washington Times,* September 14, 2006
61. Ann E. Marimow, "Mfume Endorses Cardin, but Adds Caveat," *Washington Post*, September 28, 2006; pg. A01
62. Ibid.
63. Ibid.
64. Matthew Hay Brow, "Backing Cardin, with a Caveat," *The Baltimore Sun,* September 28, 2006, pg. 1B
65. Ernesto Londono, "Sample Ballots in Pr. George's Misidentify Candidates, " *Washington Post*, November 7, 2006
66. Gary C. Jacobson, "Referendum: The 2006 Midterm Congressional Elections," *Political Science Quarterly* 122(Spring 2007):1-24.
67. A host of problems plagued the September primary—late poll openings, a lawsuit to keep polling precincts open, late or absent election judges, long lines, and concern that electronic voting would disenfranchise the technologically challenged. Governor Ehrlich's comments about ballot security—i.e., that Marylanders vote by absentee ballot, and that those uncertain about their precincts to cast provisional ballots instead of going from site to site—added fuel to the fire.
68. Frequent precinct changes make it impossible to map demographic profile to these small unit lines.
69. A logistic regression running the likelihood of a district giving Steele more than 50 percent of the vote against the percentage of black voting age population produced an Ex(B) for BVAP of .904. This means that a one-unit change in BVAP decreased the odds of a district voting for Steele by 9.6 percent.
70. Michael C. Dawson, *Behind the mule: Race and class in American politics* (Chicago, IL: University of Chicago Press, 1994)
71. Dan Balz and Matthew Mosk, "The Year of the Black Republican?: GOP Targets Democratic Constituency in 3 High-Profile Races," *Washington Post*, May 10, 2006; pg. A01.
72. Morris P. Fiorina, "Information and Rationality in Elections," in *Information and Democratic Processes,* J. A. Ferejohn and J. H. Kuklinski (eds.) (Urbana, IL: University of Illinois Press, 1990), pp.334
73. See the provocative prescription offered to Democrats in Thomas F. Schaller's *Whistling past Dixie: how Democrats can win without the South* (New York: Simon & Schuster, 2006). Black Democrats are, of course, antagonistic towards the sentiment. For an analysis of the dilemma Republicans face in the future, see Michael Fauntroy, *Republicans and the Black Vote* (Boulder, CO: Lynne Rienner, 2007)

Three Wrongs and Too Far Right: The Wrong Candidate, the Wrong Year, and the Wrong State: J. Kenneth Blackwell's Run for Ohio Governor

Wendy G. Smooth
The Ohio State University

In January of 2005, Ohio appeared poised to make history by electing an African American as its next governor. At that early moment, both the Democratic and Republican Parties had strong, viable black candidates. From the Democratic Party, Michael B. Coleman, the mayor of Columbus, Ohio (the state's capital city) emerged as the contending frontrunner, while Secretary of State J. Kenneth Blackwell captured the frontrunner position among Republicans. Both candidates had well established bases capable of mobilizing supporters across the state. Coleman, a pro-growth mayor was credited with leading Ohio's largest city and the only in the state to experience growth in the last ten years. As mayor, he was credited with creating new jobs and overseeing a growing economic base. With deep ties to the state's business community, Coleman had learned to strike the always shaky balance between community interests and big business.

Secretary of State Ken Blackwell was even better positioned to run for governor given his record of winning statewide offices, the first black candidate to do so in the state. Blackwell had also developed a national reputation and was deeply favored among Republicans and equally vilified by Democrats. His national reputation developed in the wake of the 2004 presidential election, in which Ohio's balloting proved as controversial as the voting in the 2000 presidential contest in Florida. In his capacity as secretary of state, Blackwell presided over the elections in Ohio and made national news amidst allegations of widespread voter suppression tactics. Blackwell emerged as a national GOP icon and a party hopeful destined to rise in prominence. Political pundits and national political interests watched with bated breath at the prospects of a Coleman/Blackwell match up. This amazing political first would take place in the nation's foremost political battleground state, which would make Ohio central to deciding the 2008 presidential elections.

Despite such great expectations, by November of 2005 Columbus Mayor Michael Coleman announced that he would not seek the Democratic Party's nomination citing the challenges of running Ohio's largest city and the needs of his family as his reasons for pulling out of the race. Coleman's announcement allowed the Democrats to escape a primary contest between Coleman and Congressman Ted Strickland. Strickland went on to win the nomination. Coleman's exit ended the prospects of a nationally watched battle between two formidable black candidates for governor, a campaign that would have been a first for the nation.

Following Coleman's withdrawal from the race, Democrats quickly coalesced around Congressman Ted Strickland of Lisbon, Ohio, a 12-year congressman representing southeast Ohio, covering a portion of the Appalachian region. Strickland, a Methodist minister and psychologist, established himself as a moderate pro-gun Democrat with humble rural beginnings. Known for sharing his story of living in a chicken coop following the burning of his family's homestead, Strickland connected quickly with rural Ohio voters and steelworkers, the occupation of his father. He campaigned on a platform to clean up Republican corruption and create a stronger economic base for the state. In an overwhelming show of unity among Democrats, Strickland captured over 80 percent of the vote against competitor Bryan Flannery. This set the stage for a strong standing among Democrats in the general election that translated into record setting fundraising and aggressive races up and down the Democratic Party ticket.

Unlike the Democrats, the Republicans engaged in a bitter primary fight, the party's first contested gubernatorial primary since 1988. The primary race between candidates Ken Blackwell and state Attorney General Jim Petro left the party severely fragmented. Blackwell cleverly linked Petro as an insider of the embattled administration of Republican Governor Bob Taft, while situating himself as the lone outsider. He also successfully painted Petro as a liberal who only recently discovered moral values. Petro fought back to no avail. Drawing these differences, Blackwell captured the support of social conservatives across the state. After the entrenched mud slinging fest, Blackwell emerged as the winner capturing 56 percent of the vote with Petro garnering 44 percent. Following the primary, the state GOP faced a difficult task to unite their party, which never fully coalesced in support of the Blackwell candidacy.

Ted Strickland and Ken Blackwell ran the most expensive gubernatorial campaigns in Ohio state history. Voters overwhelmingly supported Democrat Ted Strickland, with Strickland carrying 72 of the 88 counties across the state. Blackwell suffered a brutal loss, garnering only 37 percent of the vote to Strickland's 60 percent, the lowest number of votes of any Ohio Republican candidate since the election of 1912. What factors explain Blackwell's poor showing in the general election? Lavished with promise, Blackwell was considered a rising star in the national Republican Party and a major player in increasing Republican support among blacks not only in Ohio, but across the country. Why did such an esteemed candidate suffer such a bitter defeat?

In this chapter, I argue that Blackwell's loss is attributable to an array of factors. Blackwell was the wrong candidate, in the wrong year and in the wrong state. Despite the national GOP's hopes that this was indeed the year to support a black Republican, the political landscape of Ohio made it nearly impossible for any Republican candidate, much less a black Republican candidate to win in 2006. Even more so, the socially and fiscally conservative Blackwell by all accounts was ideologically too far to the right to hold onto party moderates in such a volatile year for Republicans. Likewise, Blackwell, with his extreme conservative rhetoric, was the wrong black Republican to attract sizeable numbers of crossover black Democrats.

Most studies of black candidates running for high-profile statewide offices have focused on moderate Democrats and Republicans or liberal Democrats. The models evolving from this research implicitly assume that future candidates will also hold such ideological positions. The existing literature on blacks and statewide office speaks little to cases like Blackwell, in which a black conservative is a candidate for statewide office. Ken Blackwell's run for Ohio governor sheds light on our understandings of what non-traditional black candidates running for statewide office might encounter in future elections. As the Republican Party continues to seek out black candidates and voters aggressively, we can expect to see more ideological variances among candidates, including more conservative blacks running for statewide office. Such a strategy might prove successful in a state whose values align with the black conservative candidate. The Blackwell candidacy offers an opportunity to build models that account for the unique challenges such candidates face—challenges that differ from those of their more liberal and moderate counterparts.

Data and Methods

This study is based on analyses of election coverage in major national and local newspapers between the winters of 2005 and 2006. I analyzed coverage of the 2006 Ohio gubernatorial race in national papers, including *The Washington Post*, *The New York Times*, *USA Today*, and *The Chicago Tribune*. I also analyzed the major local Ohio papers, including the *Akron Beacon Journal*, *The Columbus Dispatch*, *The Cleveland Plain Dealer*, *The Cincinnati Enquirer*, *Cincinnati Post*, *Dayton Daily News*, and *Toledo Blade* across the same time period.

In addition to the newspaper coverage, I utilized campaign financing data and the official voter turnout rates from the Ohio Office of the Secretary of State. Finally, I used exit polls conducted by Edison Media Research and Mitofsky International, which consisted of 2, 286 interviews from Ohio. The exit poll data provided the percentages of votes that each candidate received from voters across racial groups, genders, ideological backgrounds, political parties, and religious affiliations. The exit poll also queried voters on their motivations and priorities that may have influenced their votes in the gubernatorial election. Given the limited number of blacks included in the exit poll, I am able to do limited analyses of black voters, but include data where possible.

The Year of the Black Republican in Politics?

Ken Mehlman, then-chairman of the Republican National Committee (RNC), set the party's agenda with a strong emphasis on aggressively attracting black voters. Mehlman went beyond his RNC predecessors in implementing this agenda and began his campaign for black voters by denouncing the Republican Party's historic use of the "southern strategy." Mehlman acknowledged his party's long-employed strategy of using race-based appeals as a means of garnering the support of some white southerners with racist sensibilities.

Mehlman followed his denouncement of the southern strategy with a series of speeches before predominantly black audiences in which he sought to build connections using moral values arguments and pushing the faith-based initiatives. The black church figures prominently into the RNC plans as President Bush's faith-based initiatives are being used to sway black ministers toward support of their party (Muwakkil, 2005).

The centerpiece of the RNC's strategy to attract black voters hinged on the emergence of a star power team of black Republicans running for high-profile statewide offices in key battleground states. *The Washington Post* touted 2006 as the "Year of the Black Republican" pointing to the candidacies of Maryland senatorial candidate Lt. Governor Michael S. Steele, and Pennsylvania gubernatorial candidate Lynn Swann, the former Pittsburgh Steelers football star. The *Post* included Ken Blackwell's success in winning the Ohio primary as the third pillar of the Republican plan. Together, these three black candidates for high-profile offices represented the RNC's key efforts to reshape relations between blacks and the Republican Party (Balz and Mosk, 1995). If the Republicans sought to truly make inroads with black voters by running black candidates for high-profile offices, the party had simply selected the wrong year for Republicans in the states they selected. The RNC also woefully underestimated the extent to which black voters would look to the issues and their political interests in casting their ballots, rather than relying on a crude, more simplistic type of identity politics. Much like Republicans across the nation, Ohio Republicans used the midterm elections and the governor's race to send a message of dissatisfaction to the national party regarding national party scandals, the policies of the Bush administration, and the war in Iraq.

Wrong Year, Wrong State, Wrong Candidate

By the general election in November of 2006, the political landscape indicated that Ohio voters were primed to "throw the rascals out" after 16 years of Republican Party control. Blackwell could not have selected a less favorable year to run as a Republican. He had the misfortune of running as a Republican in a year in which voters were determined to issue a referendum against the Republican Taft administration. The array of scandals faced by the state's GOP, as well as the dismal condition of the state's economy, heavily weighted the governor's race in favor of the Democratic candidate. The low approval rating of the national GOP and the declining support for the war in Iraq did little to bolster the prospects for Ohio Republicans retaining leadership of the state.

To say Ohio Republicans faced a crisis of public trust is an understatement. The Republican governor, Bob Taft, faced ethics violation charges of which he was later found guilty, becoming the first sitting Ohio governor convicted of a crime. His approval ratings sank deeply providing him the honor of holding the lowest approval ratings in the nation. That same year, investigations began regarding a public finance scandal termed by the local media, "Coingate." Coingate involved Thomas Noe, a major Republican fundraiser, who was awarded a generous contract from the state to manage an investment of over $50 million for the Ohio Workers' Compensation Bureau. Noe invested the state's dollars in a rare coin fund, an unusual investment for a public fund. The questionable investments led to conflict of interest charges for the governor's administration and suspicions that money had been funneled to Republican election campaigns to facilitate the deal. Noe and his associates faced federal criminal and civil charges for the secretive rare coin scheme. Coingate further solidified allegations that Ohio had become strictly a "pay to play" state under the Republican administration. Only Republican supporters with a history of sizeable campaign contributions to party candidates would be awarded state contracts.

Blackwell responded to these political conditions by campaigning aggressively against Governor Taft's administration, criticizing the administration more brutally than if he were a Democrat. Blackwell painted the state's Republican leadership as tax and spend Republicans with utter disregard for fiscal responsibility. Needless to say, this strategy won Blackwell few friends among state GOP leaders. It further stressed an already tumultuous relationship between Blackwell and Governor Taft. As Taft faced ethics violations charges, Blackwell regarded the strained relationship as being of little benefit to his election bid.

These deep party divisions, along with the soiled reputations of the Republican administration, left a void in notable Republicans to campaign on Blackwell's behalf. In lieu of local GOP support, Blackwell capitalized on his national party attachments and brought national Republican star power to the state to fundraise and campaign on his behalf, including visits by President Bush, Senator John McCain, and presidential hopeful Mitt Romney. In the final days of the general election, Rudy Giuliani appeared in television ads endorsing Blackwell's fiscal policies, an ad that came too late to truly benefit Blackwell.

Blackwell was indeed saddled with formidable challenges. Moving into the general election, he needed to first, distance himself from the party in government. He needed to strike the artful balance between appealing to his own base of social and fiscal conservatives while also unifying the party, which meant modifying his campaign rhetoric to appeal to the moderates of his party. Rather than build common ground with moderate Republicans, Blackwell instead moved into the general elections maintaining his extreme fiscal and social conservative agenda. As a fiscal conservative, Blackwell advocated for a state flat tax and an extremely legislatively confining constitutional amendment that placed spending caps on the state's budget. Blackwell heavily advertised his 2004 work on an anti-gay marriage bill in the state and his stance against abortion. With these strongly conservative positions, Blackwell gained the endorsement of the Ohio Restoration Project, a group consisting of 2,000 evangelical, Baptist, Pentecostal, and Roman Catholic leaders in a network of so-called "Patriot Pastors." The group set out to build grassroots coalitions in Ohio's 88 counties in hopes of mobilizing conservative voters across the state for Blackwell (Dao, 2005).

Blackwell, as a key player in the RNC's imperative to increase its support among black voters, also set his sights on attracting that coveted prize for the party. As a conservative black Republican, Blackwell faced an uphill battle to dislodge the state's black voters' commitments to the Democratic Party. However, there were strong possibilities that Blackwell could, in fact, attract sizeable numbers of black voters. He had a solid record of doing so. In past elections, Blackwell successfully swayed black voters, garnering between 30 and 40 percent of the black vote in his previous election bids (Will, 2006). Further, studies show that voters are willing to exercise racial loyalty, if provided the opportunity to select a candidate of their own race (Grose, 2007: 326).

Blackwell never completely ignored race in his campaign. To the contrary, he embraced his own perspective of black politics. Blackwell always regards himself as a civil rights activist with a record of working on urban issues, and he often points out his work at the Department of Housing and Urban Development as proof of such commitments. At the same time, he relishes himself as "Jesse Jackson's worst nightmare" (Jones, 2005).

Blackwell's appeals to black voters were on his own socially conservative terms. He counted on the socially conservative beliefs of black voters to trump their more liberal stances on economic and redistributive issues.

Blacks Candidates in High-Profile Statewide Races

Strickland and Whicker (1992) explain that a successful black candidate for statewide office will have crossover appeal with white voters, if the candidate posses certain personal characteristics. A black candidate for statewide office must be a political insider, project a conservative image, and blend with the dominant culture (1992: 208). Based upon this model, Blackwell ran a classic crossover campaign. He was foremost a political insider having served in the state's Republican administration as secretary of state and was also fast becoming recognized as a rising star among party conservatives at the national level. Some even speculated that winning the governor's office in Ohio would place Blackwell in line to secure the 2008 Republican vice presidential nomination (Will, 2006).

Running to the right of the state's GOP, Blackwell positioned himself as a true conservative and keeper of conservative values. Finally he fashioned himself as seamlessly blending with the dominant white culture. Blackwell defied one of Strickland and Whicker most controversial assertions that the ideal black candidate for statewide office must physically "look white" (1992:209). To the contrary, Blackwell physically "looks black" yet maintained an appeal to white voters. Blackwell sought to carefully balance his appeal to white voters with an appeal to black voters. Blackwell understood that securing a sizeable percentage of the black vote was necessary not only to win the race, but also to prove that the Republican Party could appeal to black voters thereby dislodging the Democratic Party's proverbial hold on the black vote. In the midst of his appeals to white social conservatives and white fiscal conservatives, Blackwell used his attachments, albeit limited to the black community, to reach out to blacks, particularly more socially conservative blacks.

Scholars also regard holding prior statewide office, possessing the support of one's party, and having good relationships with the media as fundamental to black candidates winning statewide office (Jeffries, 1995, 1999; McCormick and Jones, 1999; Strickland and Whicker, 1992). Blackwell possessed the appropriate political pedigree to launch a successful bid for the governor's office. He served on the city council of Cincinnati, later served as the city's mayor and by the time of the gubernatorial race had served in two statewide offices as state treasurer and secretary of state. Likewise, Blackwell had carefully steered clear of the pitfalls often afforded to black candidates seeking statewide office. Most importantly, his position as secretary of state meant statewide name recognition beyond his home base of Cincinnati, which would have offered him limited value in a statewide campaign (Sonenshein, 1990; Strickland and Whicker, 1992). In contrast, Blackwell garnered the secretary of state office in a high-profile statewide election immediately before running for governor. He was well supported by the national Republican Party, despite his strained relationships with other state party leaders.

In keeping with the ideal black statewide candidacy, Blackwell staged a largely deracialized campaign with minimal mention of race or race-based issues. Deracialization is a strategy used by candidates to craft a biracial electoral base by de-emphasizing race and avoiding racially divisive issues. The strategy is often used when candidates desire to appeal to voters of other races while maintaining the support of voters of their own race (Wright and Middleton, 2004; McCormick and Jones, 1993). Blackwell strategically used race and pointed out his own blackness in instances when he deemed voters would respond favorably to the idea of making history by electing him the state's first black governor and only the second in the nation's history. This was a successful strategy for Blackwell, one he used in his previous campaigns. He is commonly associated with a series of "first black" honors in Ohio's political history. In lieu of more racialized politics, Blackwell instead focused largely on taxation and moral values as his core campaign issues. Blackwell staged himself as a conservative maverick candidate who stood on his convictions. In contrast to the typical non-threatening image black candidates seeking crossover appeal assume (Wright and Middleton, 2004; McCormick and Jones, 1993), Blackwell presented himself as a passionate conservative unwilling to compromise on his values-driven politics.

Blackwell easily made news and captured the attention of the local and national media. One local journalist captures the sentiment of covering Blackwell writing, "He opens his mouth and news pours out. He has a talent for speaking in quotes and a knack for seeing how they will look in the next day's newspaper, even as he says them." Recognizing Blackwell's charismatic nature, he further writes, "I will miss covering Blackwell. He is fun to be around, blessed with an enveloping personality, and endearing sense of humor and a very big brain" (Hallett, 2006b). Blackwell emerged as a media darling and was often described endearingly as the "six-foot five, broadly built ex-professional football player." Echoing his steadfast, stand on one's convictions persona, Blackwell was drafted by the NFL's Dallas Cowboys after college, but declined his contract during training camp because he refused to play the position he was assigned.

Beyond all of his charismatic personal traits, Blackwell's rags to riches Horatio Alger story enhanced his media appeal. Blackwell's personal story of growing up in the projects of Cincinnati and becoming a millionaire made for the ideal Republican Party narrative. Blackwell earned his millions after selling shares in Blue Chip Broadcasting, a group of 15 urban-formatted Cincinnati radio stations. His rags-to-riches narrative symbolizes what the Republican Party imagines it offers to blacks who are willing to work hard and persevere in the face of hardships. Blackwell's story of racial uplift coincides with black conservative attitudes of self-help through economic empowerment as opposed to blaming whites for the conditions of the black community (Orey, 2004). Together, these factors made Ken Blackwell symbolic of the ideal black Republican and helped to him rise as an iconic figure of the party. He soon became an up and coming, major player for the more conservative factions of the GOP. This positioning on the national forefront made him a media sensation. Quite different from the experiences of many black candidates for high-profile offices (Jeffries, 2002), Blackwell had no problem garnering media attention and coverage.

Blackwell adopted different political strategies from those of most blacks running in statewide races. Opponents wishing to cast black candidates as political outsiders often engage in the "rough politics of values" as a means of defining the black candidate as beyond the mainstream and not in touch with traditional, middle of the road values. This is particularly threatening to black candidates for statewide office who struggle to position themselves as insiders in the eyes of voters (Strickland and Whicker, 1992). Blackwell however used this strategy to his advantage throughout the campaign to attack Strickland as too liberal for Ohio voters. Blackwell portrayed himself as the keeper of morality, often campaigning with a Bible in hand. He took every opportunity to remind voters of his support for the contentious Issue 1, the 2004 ballot issue banning same-sex marriage that rallied Ohio's religious and social conservatives and helped to increase support for President Bush's re-election bid. Blackwell used support of the anti-gay measure as a litmus test of values for Jim Petro during the primary and again with Strickland during the general election.

On two occasions, Blackwell and the state GOP engaged in the lowest form of negative campaigning by using gay-baiting tactics, strategies used to label an opponent as gay or sympathetic to gay issues as a means of distancing the candidate from the mainstream. The first incident involved a state GOP staffer who sent a message to conservative bloggers that Strickland, despite his 18-year marriage to a woman, was in fact gay. The staffer was later fired, but not before the story fully circulated. By mid-October, Blackwell trailed Strickland by 20 percentage point in the polls. At that point, the Blackwell campaign circulated an even more vile story intimating that Strickland was not only himself gay, but also a supporter of child sexual exploitation. Blackwell's campaign built upon a story that one of Strickland's former staffers had been charged with exposing himself to a minor, and suggested that Strickland supported the employee. *The Cincinnati Enquirer* (2006) denounced Blackwell's campaign tactics, labeling them as not befitting of a politician of his stature, yet in the same editorial the paper endorsed his candidacy, the only major Ohio newspaper to do so.

In the end, playing the "rough politics of values" backfired for Blackwell. Since Strickland too had claims to religious convictions and values, Blackwell was ultimately conceived as the extremist. Strickland was able to position himself as a more moderate centrist who also embraced religious values. Strickland, a Methodist minister was often quoted in local papers saying he went into politics "following the example of Jesus Christ." His religious posturing coupled with more moderate politics resonated with Ohio voters as more to the center and Blackwell's values appeared too far out of bounds for Ohio voters.

The Campaign by the Dollars

The 2006 governor's race raised the most money in Ohio's history with the candidates raising a combined $28.3 million. Blackwell raised a total of $12.1 million while Strickland raised $16.2 million. For Blackwell, the primary was an expensive campaign against fellow Republican Jim Petro. The contentious primary race left Blackwell's campaign depleted by more than $5.5 million, over which Blackwell expressed regret (Abraham, 2006). His subsequent fundraising efforts consistently lagged behind those of his Democratic challenger, Ted Strickland. Even after receiving over $1 million dollars from the state Republican Party, Blackwell continued to struggle to match Strickland's fundraising. Strickland raised more money than Blackwell throughout the campaign and ended the campaign with considerable cash on hand. Table 1 shows campaign funds for both candidates across the campaign. Strickland repeatedly attributed his fundraising success to the state's desire for a change in political leadership.

Table 1
2006 Ohio Gubernatorial Race by the Dollars

	Strickland	Blackwell
Post-Primary Election Cash on Hand	$5,129,053	$330,000
Post-General Elections Fundraising	$2.8 million	$304,935
Post- General Election Cash on Hand	$258,486	$11,476
Total Campaign Fundraising	$16.2 million	$12.1 million

Source: Ohio Office of the Secretary of State.

In the last weeks of the campaign, Blackwell's fundraising struggles became more apparent. With limited funds remaining, Blackwell was forced to withdraw his television ads while the Strickland campaign continued a consistent, aggressive television advertising campaign during the final weeks of the campaign (Hallett, 2006).

The General Election: Blackwell and Key Voting Groups

Blackwell successfully motivated his conservative base and they showed up to support him. According to exit poll data, those voters identifying as conservatives supported Blackwell in groves with 71percent of these voters supporting him (See Table 2). The difficulty for Blackwell was that these voters constituted only 32 percent of the electorate. Moderates constituted a much larger share of the electorate. Nearly half of the voters identified as such and Blackwell garnered only 26 percent of their support.

Similar numbers of voters identified as Democrats and Republicans. However, while Strickland secured 92 percent of his party's support. Republican support for Blackwell was far less strong. Of the 37 percent of voters identifying as Republicans, Blackwell garnered 77 percent of their votes. Strickland successfully whittled away one in four Republican voters. Roughly a quarter of independents supported Blackwell (see Table 2).

Blackwell banked heavily on the support of religious conservatives and campaigned aggressively with both black and white congregations across the state. However, positioning his religious values as so far to the right served to alienate some religious voters. Those identifying as Protestants or other Christians constituted 59 percent of the electorate and Strickland fared slightly better with this group than did Blackwell (see Table 3). The second largest group, Catholics, comprised a quarter of the electorate and overwhelmingly supported Strickland.

Beyond religious denominations, the frequency of church attendance is often used to identify religious conservatives across denominational lines. Nearly half of those polled identified themselves as attending church or religious services weekly and these voters were evenly split between the two candidates. Voters attending church or religious services more than once per week comprised 16 percent of those polled and Blackwell fared best among this group garnering 59 percent of these voters' support. Given the small numbers of blacks in the exit poll, I am not able to comment on the number of blacks of various

Table 2
Breakdown of 2006 Ohio Gubernatorial Elections by Ideology and Political Party Affiliation

	Total	Strickland	Blackwell
Ideology			
Liberal	20	92	8
Moderate	48	71	26
Conservative	32	26	71
Political Party			
Democrat	40	92	6
Republican	37	20	77
Independent	23	69	26

Source: Edison/Mitofsky Exit Poll Data based on 2,286 interviews.

Table 3
Breakdown of 2006 Ohio Gubernatorial by Religion and Religious Service Attendance

	Total	Strickland	Blackwell
Religion			
Protestant/Other Christian	59	57	41
Catholic	25	58	38
Jewish	3	93	7
Other	4	79	18
None	9	80	18
Religious Service Attendance			
Weekly	45	49	48
Occasionally	39	68	30
Never	13	81	17

Source: Edison/Mitofsky Exit Poll Data based on 2,286 interviews.

religious denominations supporting Blackwell or those who attend church weekly or more so.

Strickland led Blackwell with every group of traditional swing voters in the state. Women, consisting of 52 percent of the voters polled, supported Strickland in higher numbers with 63 percent of their votes and Blackwell garnering the support of only

34 percent of women voters. Moderate-income families supported Strickland in higher numbers. Three out of five voters with families earning less than $75,000 supported Strickland (see Table 4).

The condition of the state's economy figured heavily in voters' decisions. In general, voters viewed the state's economy in hardship. Sixty three percent of voters interviewed thought the condition of the state's economy was "not so good or poor" and 77 percent of those voters cast ballots for Strickland. In addition, 47 percent of voters considered the job situation in their area as worse off than it was just two years ago while 34 percent viewed the job situation as about the same. Only 17 percent of Ohioans polled viewed the job situation in their area as better than it was two years ago. The pessimistic view of the economy and jobs played to Strickland's strengths and voters supported his position on jobs and the economy. Ohio voters also supported in large numbers an amendment to increase the state minimum wage. Of the 56 percent of voters supporting Issue 2, fully three quarters (75 percent) favored Strickland.

Ohioans views on the war in Iraq bolster the argument that this was indeed a bad year for Republican candidates, as unfavorable feelings about the war informed voters' responses in the gubernatorial election. More than half of those polled (56 percent) disapproved of the war in Iraq and 83 percent of those voters cast their ballots for Strickland. Likewise the declining support for President Bush and his policies were reflected in the gubernatorial race. More than half of Ohioans polled (58 percent) disapproved of the job President Bush was doing and 86 percent of those voters supported Strickland.

Blackwell and The Black Vote

While Blackwell enjoyed name recognition among black Ohioans, he faced the formidable task of persuading blacks to switchover to support a Republican candidate. An

Table 4
Breakdown of 2006 Ohio Gubernatorial Elections by Income

	Total	Strickland	Blackwell
2005 Total Family Income			
Under $15,000	7	72	27
$15,000-$29,000	15	66	32
$30,000-$49,999	23	60	36
$50,000-$74,999	24	63	36
$75,000-$99,000	14	55	41
$100,000-$149,000	9	59	36
$150,000-$199,000	3	56	40
$200,000 or more	5	52	46

Source: Edison/Mitofsky Exit Poll Data based on 2,286 interviews.

equally formidable challenge for Blackwell winning over black voters was overcoming his reputation for engaging in voter suppression tactics during the 2004 elections. Many blacks across the state associated Blackwell with using his power as secretary of state to disenfranchise black voters during the 2004 presidential elections. In going after black voters, Blackwell made several political miscalculations including an over-reliance on black churchgoers, running political ads that were perceived as stereotypical portrayals of blacks, and overstating the connections between black conservatism on social issues and black voting interests.

Concerned that black voters would interpret supporting Blackwell as offering support for Republican candidates more generally, Blackwell launched aggressive black voter education campaigns. The campaigns aimed at convincing blacks to crossover focused on the opportunity to "make black history" by electing Blackwell. Those educating the black community on supporting Blackwell explicitly argued that they were generating support for Blackwell exclusively, and were not asking for general support of the Republican ticket. As one of his black supporters stated, "We don't care what you do further down the ticket, but you need to help this black man get elected" (Hallett, 2006).

As early as the primaries, Blackwell ran ads on urban-format radio stations advising black voters that how they voted in previous election would not prohibit them for casting a ballot for him in the primary. Voters were instructed to request "The Blackwell Ballot" at the polls. In the short span of a radio commercial, these ads cleverly offered voters an education on the open primary system. The ads addressed concerns that blacks who traditionally voted as Democrats would not be able to cast a vote in the Republican primary. The ad offered a short explanation of Ohio's primary system that would allow those traditionally voting as Democrats to vote in the Republican primary. Most importantly, the ads stressed the opportunity to "make black history" by putting the first black candidate in the governor's office in Ohio.

Blackwell relied heavily on black ministers to carry his message and campaigned heavily with black churches seeking to find black voters supportive of the moral values cornerstone of his campaign. Blackwell met with black ministers across the state, including two major black church groups in the Cleveland area—the Black Ministers Conference representing 70 black congregations and the United Pastors in Mission. In addition, Blackwell met with the International Ministerial Alliance in the Dayton area consisting of 35 black congregations.

Beyond the setting of the black church where Blackwell could appeal to blacks on the basis of shared religious values, Blackwell struggled to build connections with other segments of the black community. Blackwell used a series of campaign ads depicting exaggerated caricatures of urban blacks, which many described as offensive. Blackwell's appeals to black voters in urban areas drew criticism across urban newspapers and became a lightening rod among web bloggers. One ad in particular drew widespread attention depicting a black man dressed in an oversized white t-shirt and baggy jeans with bulging eyes suggesting he was frightened beyond extreme. The bulging eyes coupled with the size of his head and hands, which were disproportionately larger than the small body harkened to images of a black Sambo. The ad's commentary encouraged voters to fear Strickland's positions on education, religious freedom, crime, marriage, and economics. Some argued that these ads were reminiscent of previous Blackwell campaigns in which he drew widespread criticism for his portrayal of black men in a barbershop using exaggerated dialect and language that served to mock black cultural spaces (Morris, 2006b). In all, Blackwell's attempts at reaching out to segments of the black community beyond the religious community were strained at best.

Despite these difficulties, at various points in the campaign Blackwell's projection to secure 40-50 percent of the black vote seemed plausible, particularly in light of Strickland's virtual unknown status among black voters across the state. Strickland's congressional district could offer little black support as blacks make up only 2.5 percent of the district. Aware of the critiques that the Democratic Party would simply take the black vote for granted, Strickland aggressively vowed not to do so. Making good on this promise initially proved difficult for Strickland. It appeared that Blackwell would have an opportunity to capitalize on black voters when Strickland struggled to acquire endorsements from key black leaders in the state. A political fault line had developed among Democrats in the state over the selection of the state party chairman and Strickland had supported the candidate that several key black leaders opposed. This cost Strickland initially in the governor's race as several black leaders withheld their endorsements, which were critical to Strickland gaining legitimacy among black voters. After much effort, Strickland narrowly secured endorsements from Congresswoman Stephanie Tubbs-Jones, Columbus mayor and former opponent Michael B. Coleman, and Dayton Mayor Rhine McLin, and only after explicitly addressing concerns for urban areas across the state (Morris, 2006a). Upon gaining these endorsements, Strickland too pursued the black community through visits to black churches across the state, often accompanied by key black community leaders. Further, he ran a series of commercials on gospel and urban formatted radio stations in markets with sizeable black populations.

Blackwell overestimated his appeal to black voters. His staunch social conservative values were not enough to attract the 40-50 percent of the black vote that he projected. Perhaps the largest miscalculation on Blackwell's part was the actual base of black support for a social conservative agenda. Blackwell largely banked on his support for the 2004 amendment banning gay marriage to further solidify his support among black Ohioans. It is commonly understood that the amendment to ban gay marriage in 2004 is responsible for an increase in black voter support for Bush in Ohio and the other 12 states with such amendments on the ballot. However as Smith and Seltzer (2007) illustrate, blacks, while opposing gay marriage, rank this issue as far less important when compared to jobs and the economy or the war in Iraq. Blackwell's experiences with black voters confirm that while blacks in Ohio may hold socially conservative views on issues like same-sex marriage, their voting interests are focused on more traditionally liberal issues such as the availability of jobs, the condition of the economy, and the war.

Black voters are estimated to comprise 8 percent of the overall vote in statewide elections (Hallet, 2006a); however, exit poll data suggest the numbers were higher in this gubernatorial election. Figure 1 illustrates the distribution of the black population across the state and shows the distribution of Blackwell and Strickland's support by county. Ohio's black voting population is clustered in Cuyahoga, Franklin, and Hamilton counties, the three counties make up the urban centers of the state—Cleveland, Columbus, and Cincinnati.

Table 5 indicates that in the precincts accounting for 90 percent or more of the state's black residents—Cuyahoga (Cleveland), Franklin (Columbus), and Hamilton (Cincin-

Figure 1

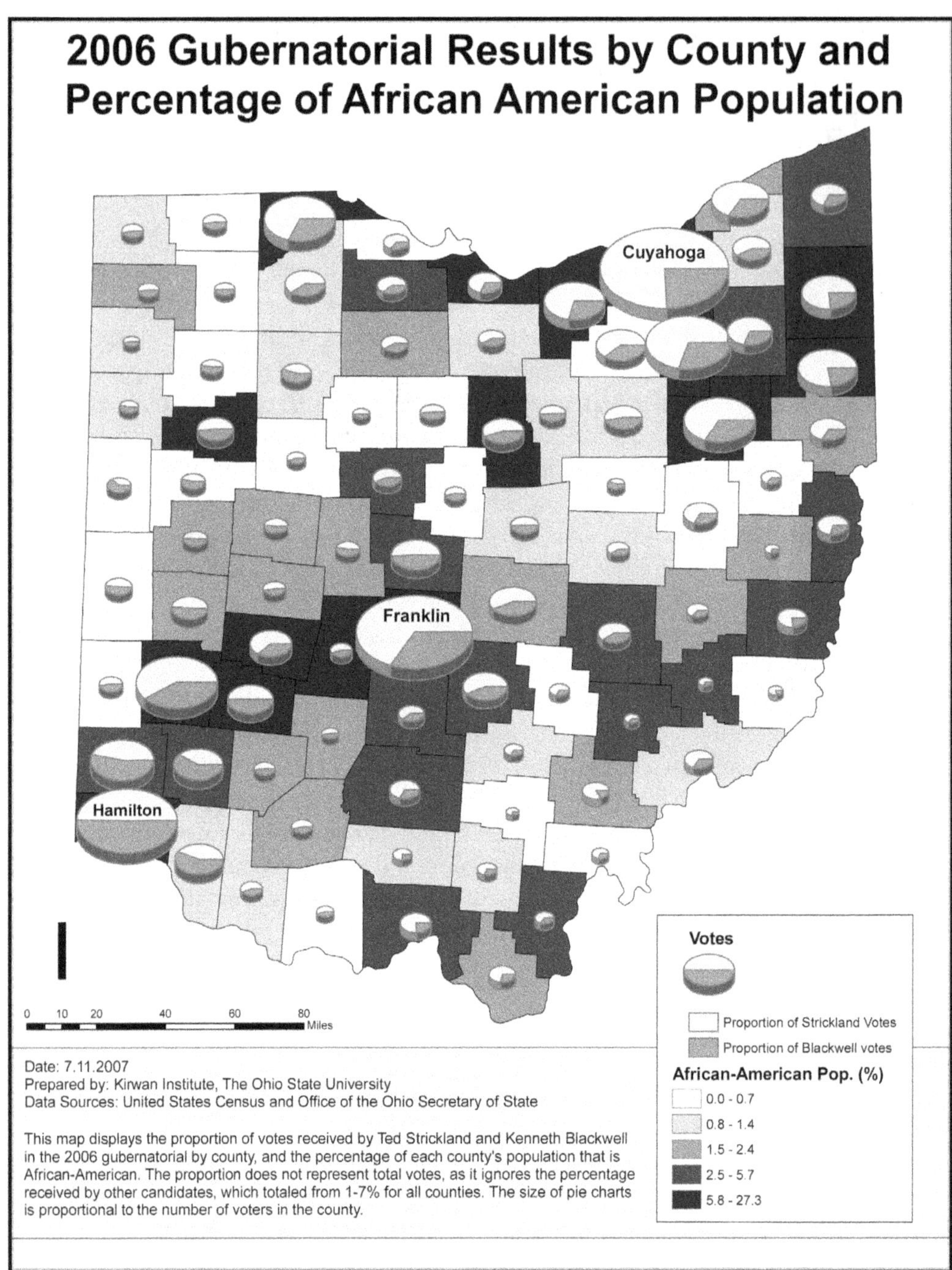
2006 Gubernatorial Results by County and Percentage of African American Population
Cuyahoga
Franklin
Hamilton
0 10 20 40 60 80 Miles
Votes
Proportion of Strickland Votes
Proportion of Blackwell votes
African-American Pop. (%)
0.0 - 0.7
0.8 - 1.4
1.5 - 2.4
2.5 - 5.7
5.8 - 27.3
Date: 7.11.2007
Prepared by: Kirwan Institute, The Ohio State University
Data Sources: United States Census and Office of the Ohio Secretary of State
This map displays the proportion of votes received by Ted Strickland and Kenneth Blackwell in the 2006 gubernatorial by county, and the percentage of each county's population that is African-American. The proportion does not represent total votes, as it ignores the percentage received by other candidates, which totaled from 1-7% for all counties. The size of pie charts is proportional to the number of voters in the county.

nati) counties, it is clear that Blackwell did not capture the 40 to 50 percent of the vote he expected. Instead, his best showing occurred in his home county of Hamilton. Surprisingly, Blackwell did not win Hamilton County, but evenly split the votes with Strickland. Blackwell was able to carry the neighboring counties of Butler and Clermont. Outside of his home county and neighboring counties, as Figure 1 shows, Blackwell's stronghold was located along the western edge of the state. He carried several counties along the western border of the state with largely white populations.

According to exit poll data in Table 6, blacks constituted 12 percent of exit poll participants. Overall, Strickland garnered 77 percent of the black vote in comparison to 20 percent for Blackwell. A slight gender gap emerges among black men and women, with black men (26 percent) supporting Blackwell more than black women (19 percent). This data is in keeping with studies showing that women, regardless of race are more likely to support more liberal democratic candidates than are their male counterparts (Smooth, 2006). For Blackwell, miscalculations regarding the appeal of socially conservative values to black voters and a series of advertising missteps proved how out of step he was with black voters and their voting interests.

Conclusion

Blackwell's emphasis on moral values, a rarity among Republican candidates in 2006 races made him too far to the right for the majority of Ohio voters, including the state's Republicans who tend to run more moderate campaigns. Blackwell never took into account the need to pull support from moderate Republicans particularly moving into the general elections. Some imagined that he would successfully meld together the most unlikely of coalitions between blacks who tend to be socially conservative and white social and fiscal conservatives. However, Blackwell could not attract a sizeable number of black supporters. These political miscalculations cost him heavily.

While Blackwell's role as secretary of state during the 2004 presidential election earned him star power among the conservative arm of the national Republican Party, we must surmise that his reputation for voter suppression in the minds of black voters made

Table 5
Registered Voters and Voter Turnout in Ohio Counties with Large African American Populations

Ohio Counties	Total # of Registered Voters	Total # of Votes Cast	% of Total Votes Cast	Votes for Strickland	Votes for Blackwell
Cuyahoga	1,054,670	468,056	44.38	335,306 (72%)	107,234 (23%)
Hamilton	566,930	296,420	52.29	139,451 (47%)	141,374 (48%)
Franklin	766,652	385,863	50.33	241,536 (62%)	122,601 (32%)

Source: Office of the Ohio Secretary of State.

Table 6
Breakdown of 2006 Ohio Gubernatorial Elections by Race, Gender, and Ideology

	Total	Strickland	Blackwell
Race			
Whites	84	58	40
Blacks	12	77	20
Hispanic/Latino	2	-	-
Gender			
Men	48	58	40
Women	52	63	34
Race/Gender			
White Men	41	55	42
White Women	43	60	37
Non-White Men	7	70	26
Non-White Women	9	78	19

Source: Edison/Mitofsky Exit Poll Data based on 2,286 interviews.

him unacceptable to become the state's first black governor. Black voters in Ohio, as in other states sent the message that in order to appeal to them as voters candidates will have to speak to issues of concern to the black community. Black politics is far more sophisticated than simple appeals based on identity politics, as the Republicans nationally misunderstood. Black voters again showed that they are issue-based voters and will support candidates that appeal to them as such.

Blackwell's gubernatorial bid offers lessons to future black republicans seeking high profile statewide offices and the Republican National Committee which will likely take the lessons learned to heart as they continue to strategize for increasing black support for their party. The question raised by this race is that if Kenneth Blackwell was the wrong candidate, what type of candidate will persuade black voters to crossover? This is likely a question that RNC strategists are pursuing. For students of black politics, we must begin to develop models that account for these possibilities as well.

References

Abraham, Lisa. 2006. "Key Race Days Ahead-Blackwell Not Giving Up. Strickland Not Taking Win for Granted." *Akron Beacon Journal* (October 22).

Austin, Sharon D. Wright and Richard T. Middleton, IV. 2004. "The Limitations of the Deracialization Concept in the 2001 Los Angeles Mayoral Election. *Political Research Quarterly*, 57 (June): 283-93.

Balz, Dan and Matthew Mosk. 2006. "The Year of the Black Republican? GOP Targets Democratic Constituency in 3 High Profile Races." *The Washington Post* (May 10).

The Cincinnati Enquirer. 2006. "Blackwell for Governor." *The Cincinnati Enquirer* (October 22).

Dao, James. 2005. "Movement in the Pews Tries to Jolt Ohio" *The New York Times* (March 27).

Grose, Christian R., 2007. "Cues, Endorsements, and Heresthetic in a High-profile Election: Racial Polarization in Durham, North Carolina? *PS: Political Science* (April): 325-332.

Hallett, Joe. 2006a. "Role of Skin Color is Uncertain in Ohio's Gubernatorial Race." *The Columbus Dispatch* (August 13).

———. 2006b. " Blackwell Never Put His Best Foot Forward, and Paid the Price." *The Columbus Dispatch* (November 19).

Jeffries, Judson L. 2002. "Press Coverage of Black Statewide Candidates: The Case of L. Douglas Wilder of Virginia." *Journal of Black Studies* 32 (July): 673-97.

———. 1999. " U.S. Senator Edward W. Brooke and Governor L. Douglas Wilder Tell Political Scientists How Blacks Can Win High-Profile Statewide Office." *Political Science Quarterly* 32 (September): 583-87.

———. 1995. "Douglas Wilder and the Continuing Significance of Race" An Analysis of the 1989 Gubernatorial Election." *Journal of Political Science* 23: 87-111.

Jones, Tim. 2005. "The anti-Obama-Ohio's Bible-quoting Secretary of State Tests the GOP with His Ultra-conservative, Unpredictable Style." *The Chicago Tribune* (February 11).

McCormick, Joseph and Charles E. Jones. 1993. "The Conceptualization of Deracialization: Thinking Through the Dilemma." in *Dilemmas of Black Politics*, ed. Georgia Persons. New York: Harper-Collins.

Morris, Phillip. 2006a. "Blackwell Taking Aim at Ohio's Black Voters." *Plain Dealer* (Cleveland) (May 2).

———. 2006b. "Blackwell's Stereotypical Appeal to Blacks Isn't Very Appealing." *Plain Dealer* (Cleveland) (July 25).

Muwakkil, Salim. 2005. "GOP's Faith-Based Quest for a Touch of Color." *The Chicago Tribune* (April 10).

Orey, Byron D. 2004. "Explaining Black Conservatives: Racial Uplift or Racial Resentment?" *Black Scholar* 34 (Spring): 18-22.

Smith, Robert C. and Richard Seltzer. 2007. "The Deck and the Sea: The African American Vote in the Presidential Elections of 2000 and 2004" in *The National Political Science Review* 11: 253-270.

Smooth, Wendy G. 2006. "Journeying from the Shadows to the Spotlight: African American Women and Electoral Politics From Shirley Chisholm to Carol Moseley Braun" in *Gender and Elections in America: Change and Continuity through 2004*. eds Susan J. Carroll and Richard L. Fox. New York: Cambridge University Press.

Sonenshein, Raphael J. 1990. "Can Black Candidates Win Statewide Elections?" *Political Science Quarterly* 105 (Summer): 219-41.

Strickland, Ruth Ann. and Marcia Lynn Whicker. 1992. "Comparing the Wilder and Gantt Campaigns: A Model for Black Candidate Success in Statewide Elections." *PS: Political Science and Politics* 25(June): 204-12.

Will, George F. 2006. "Governor's race in Ohio could be pivotal." *Desert News* (Salt Lake City) (Feb 19).

Williams, Sherri, Joe Hallett and Mark Niquette. 2006. "Lack of Support; Blackwell Won Few of the White Conservative or Black Votes He Thought He Could Expect." *The Columbus Dispatch* (November 19).

Southern Racial Etiquette and the 2006 Tennessee Senate Race: The Racialization of Harold Ford's Deracialized Campaign

Richard T. Middleton, IV
University of Missouri-St. Louis
Sekou M. Franklin
Middle Tennessee State University

In November 2006, Harold Ford, Jr., an African American congressman from Memphis, Tennessee, ran as the Democratic Party's senatorial nominee against Chattanooga mayor and multi-millionaire, Bob Corker, the Republican Party nominee. The Senate race was among the most closely watched contests of the 2006 mid-term elections, because a Ford victory would increase the Democratic Party's chances of regaining control of the Senate for the first time in a decade. Ford would have also become the South's first black senator who was elected by a *popular* vote and the region's first black senator since Blanche K. Bruce's selection by the Mississippi legislature (1875-1881).

Ford's Senate campaign marked a significant departure from black electoral politics in Tennessee. Although blacks have won many political victories in Tennessee, rarely has an African American candidate campaigned and won in a statewide election. In the nineteenth century, Y.F. Yardley, a Knoxville city councilman, ran for governor in 1872, and Samuel McElwee campaigned for the speaker of the House a decade later. Yet both lost these bids, and between 1887 and 1964, blacks were not even elected to the state legislature.[1] Two blacks ran for governor in the years following the civil rights movement. William Butler of east Tennessee ran for governor in 1974 and Rev. Ed Sanders of Nashville ran as an independent 2002, however, both were soundly defeated.

Similar to most states, especially in the South, Tennessee's racially conservative culture marginalized black electoral politics. Its patrimonial political culture, which privileges politically powerful families and wealthy candidates, and archaic legislative districts,[2] which for decades, disenfranchised black and urban voters, also made it difficult for blacks to win statewide political campaigns.[3] Moreover, Tennessee's black population is relative small compared to other southern states—blacks comprise only 17 percent of the population—and most blacks reside in the western region of the state in and adjacent to Memphis-Shelby County. The state's geographic complexity has allowed blacks to garner victories in the western black belt, and to a lesser extent, in the midstate's Nashville-Davidson County, but little success in the mostly white, homogenous and conservative counties of eastern Tennessee.

Nevertheless, Ford's campaign was enhanced by relatively favorable coverage by the national and state media, not only during the 2006 Senate race, but throughout his ten years in the House of Representatives.[4] Many political commentators were impressed by Ford's willingness to work with Republicans and his active membership in the Blue Dog Coalition and the Democratic Leadership Council, two moderate/conservative Democratic Party organizations.[5] In fact, they viewed Ford as a race-neutral/non-racial, young black leader and his centrist brand of leadership as a viable alternative to civil rights leaders and black progressives inside of the Democratic Party.[6]

Despite Ford's race-neutral centrism, racial politics still had an important impact on the Senate race. On October 20, as Ford and Corker were in a virtual tie, the Republican National Committee (RNC) aired a political advertisement, which purported that Ford had associational ties with a blonde-haired, Caucasian-looking woman who said she met him at a Playboy party during the 2005 Super Bowl weekend celebrations. The commercial, generally referred to as the "Bimbo" ad,[7] was clearly designed to prime embedded racial stereotypes, and convince white voters that a Ford victory would violate the South's traditional customs regulating relations between black men and white women.

This chapter analyzes the 2006 Senate race in Tennessee and gives close attention to Ford's electoral strategy and crossover appeal to moderate and conservative voters. The first part of this chapter explains how racial cues or symbolic appeals that prime racial stereotypes can limit the potential effectiveness of crossover or deracialized campaigns. This is followed by a discussion of recent trends in the deracialization literature.[8] We then turn our attention to Ford's efforts to exert a *normalizing effect* over critical policy issues.[9] The normalizing effect describes what happens when black candidates in statewide elections or biracial jurisdictions attempt to neutralize racially or ideologically divisive issues. They will often embrace an electoral strategy that normalizes their image, or situate their politics as mainstream or centrist, in order to attract moderates, centrists, and even conservative whites.[10]

We further discuss how the Republican National Committee (along with Corker's implicit consent) racialized what had essentially been a deracialized campaign by Ford. The ad was intended to convince a critical segment of the (white) electorate that Ford did not abide by the traditional norms and etiquette regulating black-white relations. The advertisement implied that black men (i.e., Ford) must exercise restraint and not encroach upon the sanctity of white women. In addition to the ad, some political observers believed that a Republican Party-sponsored circular in eastern Tennessee counties, which urged residents to vote in order "preserve your way of life," was also racially coded.[11] Other forms of racial priming included a radio commercial criticizing Ford with African drums beating in the background, a campaign flyer that darkened Ford's skin color, and another radio commercial sponsored by a political organization, Tennesseans for Truth, criticizing Ford's connection to the Congressional Black Caucus.[12]

This set of tactics was similar to one that was promoted by white candidate, James Hahn, against Antonio Villaraigosa, a Mexican American, in the 2001 Los Angeles mayoral election primary run-off. Hahn ran an advertisement that depicted images of a crackpipe and graffiti-covered buildings along with Villaraigosa's image. Hahn also promoted print as well as television advertisements that implied Villaraigosa lacked the moral fortitude to thwart gang violence, pedophilia, and drug trafficking.[13] As evidenced by both the 2001 Los Angeles mayoral race, as well as the 2006 Tennessee Senate race, candidates of color have increasingly become the targets of racially coded messages that in effect racialized what otherwise have been deracialized campaigns.

As part of this discussion, we present data from Mason-Dixon Polling Research firm, as well as pre-election data from a November 1-4, 2006 *USA Today*/Gallup poll and a National Election Poll exit poll. These data allow us to gauge the impact of the "Bimbo" ad and assess whether Ford's normalizing tactics (his infusion of religion (Christianity) in the campaign, and harsh criticisms of gay marriage and illegal immigration) effectively mobilized white and moderate/conservative voters. Additional discussion, using ecological regression, is offered to examine Ford's crossover appeal in select counties.

The Southern Custom of Racial Etiquette as a Framing Device

Research on U.S. southern culture has found that an elaborate etiquette of race evolved during the Civil War era to govern race relations in the South.[14] This etiquette, "created a system of behavior that served to reinforce the supremacy of the white race and the inferiority of the black."[15] One particularly rigid aspect of this etiquette was the belief that "white women were too 'pure' for liaisons with black men."[16] The evolution of this dogma in the U.S. South dates back to the American colonial period when race mixing between blacks and whites was admonished by white governing elites.[17] During this period in American history, the law generally provided for more harsh treatment for interracial relations between *white females* and *black males*. One such example was a 1664 Maryland statute that decreed children born to such relationships carried the status of the father and were to be enslaved for a period of 30 years while the mother was to be banished from the colony.[18]

Anti-miscegenation laws were enacted, beginning as early as 1662 in Maryland, in an effort to stem the mixing of blacks with whites. According to legal historian Christine Hickman, the presence of a relatively large mixed black-white population (mulatto) in the colonies was one of the catalysts for the passage of this race-based type of legislation.[19] White colonial leaders saw the mulatto as evidence that the purity of the white woman and white race was being encroached upon.[20] The rule of hypodescent was legislatively and/or judicially adopted in many states in order to socially stigmatize the participating parties who engaged in interracial fornication as well as their progeny. Pursuant to the rule of hypodescent, any individual of some varying degree of mixed black-white blood was assigned the status of their socially (and, according to some, biologically) inferior bloodline—the Negro. The state of Tennessee espoused a particularly strict form of the rule of hypodescent—the infamous "one-drop" rule, which provided that "anyone having any African blood in their veins was a person of color."[21]

During the post-Civil War period and into the Jim Crow era, punishment for breaching southern racial etiquette came in the form of extralegal repercussions, such as lynchings.[22] As F. James Davis notes, "the racial etiquette was complex, and the penalties for not learning and following it well could be severe. There were countless lessons to be learned...."[23] The murder of Emmett Till, a young black boy, in Money, Mississippi, for having allegedly whistled at a white woman serves as one of the most grim, yet classic examples of the severity of an allegation that a black male breached the most stringent of the rules of southern racial etiquette.

Given the deeply embedded nature of a racial etiquette in the South, one can understand how even in modern-day Tennessee, the Republican National Committee's allegation of Harold Ford having connections to a sexually energized and provocatively dressed, blonde-haired, white woman could foment racial sentiments among conservative and rural white voters and cause Ford's race to become a critical framing device for mobilization against him.

Recent Trends in the Deracialization Literature

At the time of this writing, thirty years has passed since Charles V. Hamilton first posited the idea of African American candidates strategically reaching out to white voters by emphasizing policy issues that would tend to appeal to a broader spectrum of constituents versus focusing on issues salient primarily to black voters.[24] Twenty years after the publication of Hamilton's seminal work, Huey Perry edited a volume in which a number of scholars examined the campaign strategies utilized by various African American candidates in light of Hamilton's thesis.[25] Perry's aim was to test Hamilton's deracialization theory to discern if African American candidates who had ascended to high profile elected offices had actually utilized a deracialized strategy, and if so, what implications did such an approach have on the socio-economic prospects for African Americans.

Recent trends in the deracialization literature present a number of findings that are positioned to shape how political scientists think about electoral politics into the next decade and beyond. Much of this recent literature looks at how candidates of color are portrayed, the amount of exposure they receive by media outlets, and how this affects their ability to attract important crossover votes from whites and moderate conservatives. For example, in a study of the 2001 Los Angeles mayoral election, Timothy Krebs and David Holian analyze how a candidate's race affects the occurrence of negative campaigning.[26] Krebs and Holian argue that one of the major challenges of minority candidates (that is, candidates of color) in a white dominated electoral climate is "how to craft a political style to appeal to, or at least not energize, voters least likely to support a minority candidate, voters for whom a candidate's race matters."[27] Their findings suggest that candidates of color who choose to run deracialized campaigns face an interesting dilemma. On the one hand, such candidates must attack their opponents significantly less than white candidates, in an overall effort to deracialize their appeal. On the other hand, according to Krebs and Holian, when candidates of color are not front-runners, but rather, strong contenders, they have more of a strategic need to attack or at least respond to attacks. In doing so, however, such candidates are more likely to lose the support of voters who are already least likely to support a candidate of color. For example, Krebs and Holian find that Villaraigosa likely did not aggressively attack James Hahn or vociferously respond to Hahn's attack ads because doing so would have reinforced stereotypes of Villaraigosa as an "angry kid from the streets [of a Latino neighborhood]."[28] They go on to note that Villaraigosa could not afford to attack because his low favorability among swing voters was a function, in part, of his race.

Other recent studies have also probed into the role media exposure and portrayals of candidates of color in deracialized electoral contexts. For example, Baodong Liu investigates the interaction between media exposure as an agent of deracialization and its associated effect on white voting behavior.[29] In particular, Liu finds that positive media exposure by white-controlled media outlets can serve as a legitimizing source for an African Americans who desire to present themselves in a racially non-threatening manner. In an analysis of electoral politics in New Orleans, Louisiana, Liu finds that endorsements that emanated from a white-controlled newspaper (*Times-Picayune*) provided legitimacy to African American candidates who ran deracialized campaigns which, in turn, increased their level of white crossover support.[30] Implicitly, then, such media endorsements serve as a racial cue—one that signifies that a candidate of color is a friend of the white community. On the other hand, negative media exposure has been found to limit the effectiveness of deracialized campaigns run by candidates of color.

As mentioned previously, Austin and Middleton investigate negative campaigns advertisements that were employed by James Hahn in the 2001 Los Angeles mayoral election to attack his competitor, Villaraigosa's, character and play upon negative stereotypes of Mexicans as drug dealers and criminals. In particular, Austin and Middleton find that Villaraigosa's, "attempts to widen his appeal beyond white liberals and Latinos failed primarily because the Hahn campaign's print and televisions ads made it impossible for him to maintain a non-threatening image on the issue of crime."[31] In the case of the 2001 Los Angeles mayoral election, Hahn's favorability rating increased dynamically after the negative advertisements made the airwaves and landed on the streets.

The Normalizing Effect

The preceding discussion sets the tone for our following analysis of Harold Ford's deracialized campaign strategy. In our discussion, we focus on how Ford attempted to exert a *normalizing effect* over critical policy issues to enhance his ability to attract crossover votes from whites and moderate conservatives. The normalizing effect describes what happens when a candidate attempts to remove race from a campaign, as well as convince whites that she or he has more in common with them on a host of non-black issues (i.e., gay rights, immigration rights, etc.), which presumably, have been receptive to civil rights and liberal groups. The expectation is that the normalizing effect can neutralize the race variable and liberal issues, and convince white moderates and conservatives that a black candidate subscribes to their preferred belief systems.

Ford tried to normalize his image in the white community by embracing positions that are opposed by many of his liberal supporters. For example, he voted for the congressional bill to ban gay marriage,[32] and he supported Tennessee's constitutional amendment to ban gay marriage that was on the November ballot. His stance on immigration was also in concert with many conservatives in the state and he attacked his opponent, Corker, for being soft on illegal immigrants. In addition, he repeatedly invoked religious symbolism during the campaign, which appealed to state's Bible belt culture and white evangelical voters.[33] This was a surprise since there was no prior evidence that Ford held orthodox Christian beliefs. In addition, Ford was at best moderate on economic issues, and at worse, rejected progressive economic policies.[34]

The RNC-sponsored attack ads raised additional concerns about the effectiveness of deracialization and the normalizing strategies, and whether they can prevail over sophisticated efforts to racially prime, race-neutral campaigns. Despite the contention by some researchers that negative attacks backfire and demobilize voter turnout,[35] some political observers give credence to their effectiveness.[36] When campaign ads are delivered late in an electoral contest, such as the "Bimbo" commercial, they may be more effective in shaping voter attitudes, because it allows voters to use the most recent information they have about a candidate to evaluate their performance.[37] Furthermore, the effectiveness of racial priming tactics is enhanced if the targeted candidates fail to condemn or offer authoritative responses to the attack ads.[38]

Interestingly, a version of the "Bimbo" ad was aired by the National Republican Senatorial Committee during the first week of October. Yet, the national media expressed little outrage about the ad, in part, because unlike the RNC-sponsored ad several weeks later, it didn't make a direct connection between Ford and a Caucasian woman. The ad, designed as a counterattack to Ford's appeal among social conservatives, stated that Ford partied with "Playboy playmates in lingerie."[39] Ford denounced the ad by insisting that Republicans were the ones lacking in moral character, as exemplified in their efforts to hide the scandal involving Congressman Mark Foley, the Florida Republican who made sexual advances to underage, male congressional pages.

Ford also said that Republicans injected his racial background into the campaign after Tennesseans for Truth sponsored a radio ad that said: "[Ford's] daddy handed him his seat in Congress and his seat in the Congressional Black Caucus, an all-black group of congressmen who represent the interest of black people above all others."[40] Yet despite these earlier political advertisements, and despite his strong response to them, he failed to authoritatively condemn Republicans of racial priming after the "Bimbo" ad was first aired on October 20. When asked to respond to the ad, he called it "smutty," and days later explained his reason for attending the Playboy party as, "I like football, and I like girls."[41] Furthermore, he refused to call the ad racist and said about Republicans, "You have to ask them about race. I don't focus on those things."[42] Ford's response underscores the challenge with deracialization. If, as Mendelberg suggests, candidates are better suited to diminish racially charged attack ads by publicly condemning them,[43] this becomes difficult if a candidate is stubbornly committed to race-neutralism. After all, if Ford had publicly condemned the "Bimbo" ad as racist, it would have racialized the campaign, and given legitimacy to the fact that black and white Tennesseans were racially polarized. Ford's response and his bachelor status may have further harmed his image among family values moderates and conservatives.

In the remainder of the chapter, we offer a detailed analysis of Ford's normalizing strategy, while controlling for a host of socio-demographic and political variables. Yet before engaging this discussion, we discuss the data and methodology, and then examine the impact of the RNC-sponsored playboy bunny advertisement on the campaign. Afterward, we discuss Ford's overall support in the week before the election and on the day of the election.

Data and Methods

This chapter draws upon data from a *USA Today*/Gallup poll conducted from November 1-4, 2006 and a National Election Pool (ABC News/Associated Press/CBS News/CNN/Fox News/NBC News) exit poll administered on November 7. The pre-election poll allows us to measure for two outcomes. We look at approval ratings of the "Bimbo" advertisement (1=approve, 0=disapproval), while controlling for socio-demographic variables (race, gender, age, social class (low-income and college-educated respondents), and jurisdiction/locality (rural and east Tennessee voters). Since we are interested in the influence of swing voters, measured as self-identified moderates and independents, we included these variables in the analysis. Finally, we looked at whether general opinions about political advertisements influenced approval/disapproval ratings of the advertisement. Another logistic regression model was constructed with the same variables in order to measure Ford's support among prospective voters a week before the election. Approval of the playboy ad, election interest, and whether the respondents voted in the 2002 election were also added as independent variables.

We conducted a third logistic regression for the exit poll with Senate vote (1=Ford, 0=Corker) serving as the dependent variable. We controlled for socio-demographic variables: race, gender, age (30-59=reference category), jurisdiction (rural/town=reference category), region (East Tennessee voters=reference category),[44] and social class (measured by education). Due to Ford's bachelor status, we included three measures (married voters, single women, parents) to determine his appeal to voters from varying family types. An additional variable was included to determine if concerns about the economy impacted the Senate race.

The exit poll did not ask specific questions about the "Bimbo" ad, but it did ask if "either of the candidates for U.S. senator attacked the other unfairly." We included this as an independent variable, as well as three proxy measures of partisanship (independent voters, approval of George Bush, and approval of Tennessee's incumbent Democratic governor, Phil Bredesen). We expect Bredesen supporters to vote for Ford and Bush supporters to reject him. Three measures are included to test the *normalizing effect*: support for the state's anti-gay marriage amendment; if the respondents believed immigration was an important issue; and support from white evangelicals/born-again voters.[45]

In addition, we performed a secondary analysis of black voter turnout and black-white racial polarization on the day of the election. Ecological inference, refined by political scientist Gary King,[46] is a useful tool for assessing racial polarity between blacks and whites.[47] This approach is commonly used by scholars to study voter intensity and transitions, as well as racially polarized voting.

Findings and Discussion

The RNC-sponsored, "Bimbo" advertisement was designed to convince a critical segment of the electorate that Ford had violated the southern traditionalism and etiquette which forbid black men from associating with white women. Similar to many racially charged campaign tactics, the ad operated as a framing device that appealed to the state's conservative population.[48] As Table 1 points out, voter attitudes shifted after the first airing of the "Bimbo" advertisement. Six weeks before the election, Ford had a six-point lead over Corker, although a sizeable number of voters had neither favorable nor unfavorable views of the two candidates. By mid-October, the race was a virtual dead heat, yet after the ad was aired, Corker's favorability rating over Ford increased by eight percentage points.

It is debatable whether these shifting attitudes were attributed to the advertisement or other factors. The "Bimbo" ad was one of many negative ads levied by both cam-

Table 1
Favorability/Approval Ratings of Harold Ford, Jr. and Bob Corker Before and After the "Playboy Bunny" Political Advertisement

	FAVORABLE	UNFAVORABLE	NEUTRAL
Conducted Before Ad First Aired - September 25 – September 27, 2006			
Harold Ford, Jr.	44%	30%	22%
Bob Corker	38%	35%	24%
Conducted Between October 18 – October 20, 2006			
	FAVORABLE	UNFAVORABLE	NEUTRAL
Harold Ford, Jr.	45%	36%	18%
Bob Corker	46%	27%	26%
Conducted After Ad First Aired - November 1 – November 3, 2006			
	FAVORABLE	UNFAVORABLE	NEUTRAL
Harold Ford, Jr.	39%	44%	15%
Bob Corker	47%	33%	17%

Source: The Mason-Dixon Tennessee Polling & Research, Inc. administered the surveys for the Memphis Commercial Appeal and Chattanooga Times Free Press. A total of 625 registered Tennessee voters were interviewed statewide by telephone.

paigns. Further, Bob Corker reorganized his campaign staff in late September. Though some political observers viewed this as a setback for Corker, it may have worked to his advantage because he brought in Tom Ingram to run his campaign. Ingram, the chief of staff for Senator Lamar Alexander, the Republican senator from Tennessee, refocused Corker's message, and used his in-state networks to boost Corker's image. In addition, Corker survived a brutal primary season, in which his opponents, former congressmen Ed Bryant and Van Hilleary, harshly criticized him for running negative attacks. Some conservatives also believed Corker was too moderate to adequately represent the Republican Party. This created tension and acrimony among the three camps (Corker, Bryant, Hilleary). In fact, Bryant and Hilleary did not actively campaign for Corker until late in the campaign season. These factors may have harmed Corker's support, and boosted Ford's standing, in September.

To gain more insight into the effectiveness of the Playboy bunny ad, we conducted logistic regression of a pre-election poll conducted a week before the election. Table 2 displays the regression estimates. As expected, disapproval of the ad was found among moderates and respondents who had negative views about the election-oriented, television commercials. However, independent voters and social class did not significantly distinguish sentiments about the ad.

Table 2
Logistic Regression Measuring Approval of the "Bimbo" Advertisement

(Pre-Election Poll, November 1-4, 2006)

Independent Variables	B	
Independents	-.05	(.51)
Negative Political Ads	-1.1*	(.31)
East TN	-.41**	(.24)
College Ed.	-.33	(.26)
Whites	1.81*	(.75)
Rural TN	.23	(.25)
Men	.64*	(.23)
Moderates	-.73*	(.73)
Young Adults	.94*	(.37)
Low-Income	-.42	(.31)
Constant	-2.24*	(.80)

-2 Log Likelihood 499.745
Chi-Square 53.195*

*p<.05, **p<.10

Source: The survey is a USA Today/Gallup Poll, November 1-4, 2006. The survey was obtained from the Roper Center. The N=1,001, but because of missing data, only 616 respondents were included in the logistic regression.

Racial background, as expected, significantly influenced how voters interpreted the ad. Whites were much more likely to approve of the ad and did not find it offensive. Approval of the ad was also found among men. Given Ford's youth, we incorrectly expected young adults/youth to be more critical of the ad. This was surprising since Democratic Party insiders insisted that the party made significant inroads in capturing the youth vote during the mid-term elections.[49] Young people—both Democrats and Republicans—found few problems with the advertisement, perhaps because they have less knowledge about the sophisticated use of racial cues.[50] Young people also have less memory of southern traditionalism. In contrast to their parents and grandparents, the state's young voters are more cosmopolitan (urban and suburban) and may not have entrenched predispositions against interracial relationships. If racial priming activates pre-existing racial schemas,[51] then this may have less of an effect on young voters than older ones. Further, Ford's refusal to admonish the ad as racist—he condemned the ad, but for other reasons—may have misled younger voters about the intention of the "Bimbo" advertisement, especially since young adults (18-29) have historical distance from southern etiquette and Jim Crow politics.

We further expected rural voters and eastern Tennesseans to approve of the ad, because it may have allied hidden stereotypes they had about Ford. Yet there was no statistical significance between rural and urban/suburban voters, and surprisingly, voters from eastern Tennessee, the state's conservative stronghold, disapproved of the ad compared to those from other parts of the state. Sentiments among rural voters may be explained by Ford's aggressive campaigning in rural Tennessee. Furthermore, even though the state's rural voters tend to be more conservative than urban voters, there is some variation that may have offset the impact of the ad. There is a sizeable (over 100,000) and politically active, black population that makes up 30 percent of the population in rural/small town, western Tennessee counties outside of Memphis.[52] Moreover, Ford is a close ally of Congressman John Tanner, a conservative Democrat from western Tennessee's eighth congressional district, who actively campaigned for Ford. Tanner's congressional district includes 19 counties (18 out of 19 counties are rural) in western and middle Tennessee. This may have offset Corker's influence in rural eastern Tennessee.

We conducted another logistic regression, displayed in Table 3, to assess Ford's support among prospective voters the week before the election. Those who approved of the "Bimbo" ad and whites were most likely to support Bob Corker. Our only surprise was that we mistakenly believed Ford's centrism would attract independent voters who expressed greater approval of Bob Corker.

The Ford campaign, however, neutralized Corker's support among men, and he won approval from moderate voters in the week leading to the election. If this were to remain true on November 7, it would suggest that Ford's crossover appeal cut into some voters who were expected to support Republicans. On the other hand, working to Ford's disadvantage was his poor showing in the pre-election survey among those who voted in the 2002 mid-term elections. This indicates that active voters—voters who routinely participate in elections—were more receptive to Corker than Ford.

Additional insight on Ford's electability and crossover appeal was found in the exit poll survey. Unlike the pre-election survey, immigration, religiosity, and gay marriage questions were included in the exit poll. As indicated in Table 3, whites and college-educated voters were likely to vote for Corker, although there were no distinguishing results between men and women. Ford also performed poorly among married couples and single women. This may be due to attacks, such as the "Bimbo" ad, which in addition to racial priming, also attacked his bachelor status.

The larger concern is whether Ford was able to soften white resistance to his candidacy by embracing issues that were appealing to the state's conservative base. In terms of the normalizing variables (immigration, gay marriage, religiosity), he was successful at neutralizing the vote among white evangelicals. Corker won the vote among the respondents who ranked illegal immigration as an important issue in the campaign and those who voted for the constitutional ban on gay marriage. Although it is beyond the scope of this study, further research should consider whether Ford damaged his own campaign by accentuating these two issues. One may discover that Ford inadvertently helped to mobilize anti-gay marriage voters and opponents of illegal immigration, who otherwise may have stayed home, and this enthusiasm spilled over and benefited the Republican Party. At least in regards to gay marriage, the Republican Party has been fairly effective at linking anti-gay/civil union, state policies with its voter mobilization efforts during high profile elections.

It is also worth mentioning that Ford's vocal opposition to gay marriage and harsh criticisms of illegal immigration were, for the most part, supported by blacks. Although national political/civil rights groups such as Rev. Jesse Jackson's Rainbow/Push Coalition, the Leadership Conference on Civil Rights, and the Congressional Black Caucus, have supported anti-discrimination legislation pertaining to the LGBT (Lesbian, Gay, Bisexual, Transgender) and immigration rights' communities, rank-and-file blacks have expressed uneven support for these issues. In fact, blacks overwhelmingly voted for Tennessee's constitutional ban on gay marriage (over 80 percent) and as much as two-thirds indicated that illegal immigration is an important issue.[53] This suggests that black candidates such as Ford can use normalizing strategies on wedge issues—even those issues that are condemned by civil rights groups—and still avoid harsh criticisms from rank-and-file blacks. This is particularly the case in the South where socially conservative, faith-based leaders and institutions play a dominant role in the daily lives of blacks.

Though Ford did not win the white evangelical vote, his religious appeals may have neutralized this group. This was a surprise considering that Tennessee is the epicenter of the Bible-Belt politics and home to the religiously conservative, Southern Baptist Convention (SBC). Ford's counterbalance of the white evangelical vote may shed light on a shifting pattern among evangelicals. Since the 2004 presidential election, evangelical organizations such as the SBC have engaged in an intra-denominational struggle over the trajectory of their organization. Some evangelical leaders have urged their organizations and networks to abandon their blind support of the Republican Party.[54] Progressive groups have also initiated conversations throughout the state to counteract the Christian Right's influence. For example, the Tennessee Alliance for Progress, a statewide social justice organization, sponsored the "Doing Justly" project. Launched in October 2006, the project entailed a series of ecumenical dialogues with religious leaders about social justice issues.

We expected economic concerns to be a driving factor behind Ford's support, considering that many Democrats campaigned on economic populist issues (i.e., trade policy, wages, job displacement, etc.) during the 2006 mid-term elections. The lack of concern among voters about the economy may reveal that Ford didn't spend enough time emphasizing this issue. Some political observers believed Ford chose to focus less attention on the economy, and the Tennessee economy in particular, because this may have inadvertently sparked criticisms of Governor Phil Bredesen, a conservative Democrat and close ally of Ford.[55] Yet Ford's campaign and the voters deserved an in-depth discussion of the economy. Tennessee experienced approximately 90 plant closings from 2001-2004 and the governor led a successful effort to downsize and cut health care benefits to over 600,000 Medicaid recipients (over 200,000 of these recipients were disenrolled from TennCare, the state's Medicaid program).[56] Unfortunately, none of these issues took center stage in the campaign and Ford gave more attention to gay marriage, religiosity, and immigration.

Age was partially significant in predicting the Senate vote. Senior citizens (above 60 years old) were most likely to vote for Ford than voters between 30-59 years of age. This paralleled a national trend in which senior citizens, mainly because of concerns about health care, the costs of prescription drugs, and social security, were more inclined to support Democrats.[57] Partisanship was an influential indicator of the Senate vote. President Bush supporters and supporters of Phil Bredesen, the state's Democratic governor, were more inclined to vote for Corker and Ford, respectively. It also appears that as the election neared, Ford won over some self-identified independent voters. Although independents supported Corker in the pre-election poll, on the day of the election, there was no statistical significance between their vote for Corker and Ford.

The only jurisdictional (region or locality) indicator that significantly influenced the election was region. Middle and western Tennessee voters, compared to those from eastern

Table 3
Logistic Regression Assessing Approval and Vote for Harold Ford, Jr.

Independent Variables	**Model 1 (Pre-Election Poll)**	**Model 2 (Exit Poll)** **B**	
Whites	-3.93* (1.0)	-3.5* (.65)	
Men	-.07 (.20)	-.15 (.21)	
Married	____	-.87* (.32)	
Single Women	____	-.84* (.42)	
Parents	____	-.16 (.21)	
College Educated	-.15 (.23)	-.78* (.20)	
Low-Income (under $30,000)	.12 (.26)	___	
18-29 yrs. old	-.58 (.45)		
			Age*
		.28 (.31)	18-29 yrs.
		.67 (.26)*	60 yrs. and over
Negative Ads	.43 (.36)	____	
Attack Ads	____	3.3* (.41)	
Both Attacked	____	-2.9* (.35)	
Ban Gay Marriage	____	-1.2* (.25)	
Immigration (Important)	____	-.69* (.22)	
Economy (Important)		.43 (.27)	
White Evangelicals	____	-.07 (.21)	

Table 3 (cont.)

East Tennessee	-.21 (.20)		
		Region*	
		.50 (.20)	Middle/West*
		-.13 (.28)	Southwest
Rural Voters	.06 (.22)		
		Locality	
		-.48 (.57)	Urban
		-.67 (.23)	Suburban
Playboy Ad	-1.45* (.32)	____	
Election Interest	.13 (.26)	____	
Vote 2002	-.75* (.31)	____	
Moderates	1.2* (.21)	____	
Gov. Phil Bredesen	____	2.3* (.22)	
Independents	-.99** (.57)	-.24 (.20)	
Pres. GW Bush	____	-3.0* (.19)	
Economy (Important)	____	.43 (.27)	
Constant	3.89* (1.1)	5.5* (.88)	
-2 Log Likelihood 603.188 Chi-Square 142.609*		-2 Log Likelihood 864.292 Chi-Square 1660.658*	

*p <.05, ** p < .10 *p <.05, ** p < .10

Source: Model 1 uses the same pre-election poll that was used in Table 2. The model excludes variables with missing data, so the original sample size (1,001) was reduced to 538. Weights were included in the exit poll. Also, variables with missing data were excluded from the sample (2,651), but the final results are measured on 1,822 cases.

Tennessee, were more likely to vote for Corker. This was predicted by every political observer of Tennessee politics because eastern Tennessee is a conservative stronghold. Ford anticipated making inroads in eastern Tennessee counties. Indeed, his electoral outreach in eastern Tennessee counties was similar to Governor Bredesen, who won a narrow victory over Congressman Van Hilleary in the 2002 gubernatorial contest. Bredesen's victory was partially attributed to cutting into Republican strongholds in eastern Tennessee. In the same election season, Bredesen won or tied in 22 of the counties that were won by Republican senatorial candidate, Lamar Alexander, nine of which were in eastern Tennessee. In eastern Tennessee's largest county, Knox County (Knoxville), Alexander won 62 percent of the vote, but many voters split their tickets and cast their votes for Bredesen, who tied his Republican challenger. Ford, on the other hand, won only 30 of the 59 counties that threw their support behind Bredesen and only three of the counties that voted for Alexander. He won only two counties in eastern Tennessee compared to 14 counties for Bredesen, and he was soundly defeated in Knox County. Thus, it is likely that Ford did not do well enough in eastern Tennessee, and Bredesen's coattails were influential in counties that traditionally vote for or leaned to the Democrats.

We fully expected Ford to lose among rural and small town residents, yet this was not the case. But as we stated earlier, Ford made an aggressive attempt to win over rural voters, especially in western and middle Tennessee. Corker, on the other hand, did fairly well in all of the metropolitan areas (Chattanooga-Hamilton County, Knoxville-Knox County, Wilson County, Williamson County, and Rutherford County) outside of Memphis-Shelby County and Nashville-Davidson County.

It is also worth revisiting the impact of political advertisements. The exit poll asked the respondents: "Did either of these candidates for U.S. senator attack the other unfairly?" Those who believed Ford was unfairly attacked held strong feelings about the race and were much more likely to vote for Ford. Yet, Corker received an unanticipated bounce from the advertisements among those who believed that both candidates unfairly attacked each other. This last point is worth considering. If there was a backlash against the "Bimbo" ad—and it appeared that there was as exhibited with the criticisms of many national media personalities—Republicans may have offset these criticism by convincing voters that Democrats (and Ford) had also initiated negative political advertisements.

In all of the regression analyses, race is a constant theme. Despite Ford's attempts to deracialize his campaign, race served as lens through which voters made their decisions. Though Ford made explicit appeals to white voters, and perhaps convinced some of them to vote for him, he was not able to neutralize race. This indicates that even when candidates use race-neutral appeals or de-emphasize salient issues that appeal to blacks, they still find it difficult to convince voters that race doesn't matter.[58] This is because the candidates' opponents may be already pre-positioned for racial priming and more receptive to sophisticated uses of racial coding.[59]

Further evidence of racial polarity—and Ford's biracial appeal—can be examined by looking at black and white voter trends in the Senate race. We conducted ecological regressions of 1,069 precincts or voter tabulation districts (VTDs).[60] Although our analysis only covers 21 of 95 counties in the state, it includes six of the seven largest metro areas/counties (Memphis-Shelby County, Nashville-Davidson County, Knoxville-Knox County, Chattanooga-Hamilton County, Williamson County, and Clarksville-Montgomery County). The remaining counties have smaller populations and encompass small towns/rural communities.[61] The VTDs chosen for this study are disproportionately in Democratic leaning counties, since we included the two largest counties, Memphis-Shelby and Nashville-Davidson Counties. As Table 4 points out, almost 56 percent of the voters in our sample are from Democratic Party precincts and the average black population in each precinct was 24 percent. To address the selective bias, we disaggregated the large counties and conducted a second ecological regression analysis.[62]

In both regression models, one sees a tremendous amount of consolidation among blacks in support of Ford. Although racial polarization exists, Ford was able to garner 40-42 percent of the white vote in both models, which is the same number identified in the exit poll. Yet what may have worked to Ford's disadvantage, notwithstanding his abil-

Table 4
Racial Polarity in the 2006 Tennessee Senate Race

Model I

	(Percentages)			
(Per Precinct)		Ford		
Total Voter Turnout	41 %			
Black Population	24 %	Blacks	94 %	(S.E. .01)
Democratic Voters	56 %	Whites	42 %	(S.E. .01)

Model II (Excludes Memphis-Shelby County and Nashville-Davidson County)

	(Percentages)			
(Per Precinct)		Ford		
Total Voter Turnout	40 %			
Black Population	13 %	Blacks	91 %	(S.E., .002)
Democratic Voters	48 %	Whites	40%	(S.E., .01)

Note: Gary King's EiZ package is used for these two models.

ity to garner 40 percent of the white vote, was that as one moves away from Memphis and Nashville, the black population shrinks in size and the proportion of Ford's white supporters also decreases. This indicates that Ford's base of support was in traditional Democratic Party strongholds, that he probably did not garner enough support in homogenous (white) counties outside of the two central cities/counties.

Also, working to Ford's disadvantage was that voter turnout in black precincts was lower than what his campaign predicted. The campaign hoped for presidential-election turnouts (about 300,000 blacks voted for John Kerry) among blacks.[63] The campaign also targeted 65,000 blacks in Memphis who voted in presidential elections, but not in mid-term elections.[64] Yet, in a separate study of the 2006 Senate race, Franklin found that only 35 percent of the black voting age population in Memphis-Shelby and Nashville-Davidson Counties turned out to vote.[65] This percentage, if it holds across the state, would account for only 228,000 out of the approximately 650,000 voting age blacks, thus falling short of Ford's expectations. Accordingly, if Ford's loss was partially attributed to a lower than expected black voter turnout, he may have himself to blame. His focus on the normalizing variables mentioned earlier in this study, and inattention to economic security issues, may have convinced some blacks to stay home rather than vote.

Conclusion

This study uses a two-tiered analysis (logistic and ecological regression) to assess Harold Ford's deracialization strategy. One of our objectives was to explain how racial cues or symbolic appeals that prime racial stereotypes can limit the potential effectiveness of crossover or deracialized campaigns. In particular, we looked at how a Republican National Committee advertisement ("Bimbo" ad) racialized what had essentially been a deracialized campaign by Ford. The ad was intended to convince a critical segment of the (white) electorate that Ford did not abide by the traditional norms and etiquette regulating black-white relations. The advertisement implied that black men (i.e., Ford) must exercise restraint and not encroach upon the sanctity of white women. This discussion set the tone for our examination of Ford's biracial appeal and whether the South's traditional mores regarding black-white relations, religion, immigration, and gay marriage impeded his ability to win over whites, moderates, and even some conservatives. We argued that Ford focused on a host of traditional, non-racial issues such as religiosity and gay marriage, as well as accentuated illegal immigration as an important campaign issue, in order to distance himself from liberal policy positions that are perceived to be supportive by black candidates. We referred to this as the normalizing effect. We believe that in a hotly contested campaign, conservatives will make a concentrated effort to link black candidates with a broad range of liberal policy issues, such as immigration and gay marriage. The reason for this has a lot to do with the nature of southern politics. For better or worse, black candidates and elected officials, even moderate ones, are often looked at by different constituent groups of the liberal-progressive axis to advance various causes.

The normalizing effect was only partially effective. Ford neutralized the white evangelical vote, but those who felt strongly about illegal immigration as well as opponents of gay marriage, were more likely to vote for Ford's opponent, Bob Corker. Ford also neutralized support in some rural communities, although much of this can be attributed to his aggressive campaigning in these areas, and the influence of Congressman John Tanner, Ford's ally, in some western and middle Tennessee counties. Ford, however, was less successful in convincing voters from eastern Tennessee to support his campaign. His campaign also failed to capture single women, married voters, and college-educated voters.

As stated earlier, despite Ford's better than predicted performance among white voters, race was still a deciding factor in the election. Whites were more supportive of the "Bimbo" advertisement, and in the pre-election and exit polls, race was a significant factor. Ford, however, fell short of a presidential-election-year turnout in the black community.

Notes

1. Mingo Scott, *The Negro in Tennessee Politics and Governmental Affairs, 1865-1965: "The Hundred Years Story"* (Nashville, Tennessee: Rich Print. Company, 1964, c1965); James B. Jones, *Knoxville's African American Community, 1860-1920* (Nashville, Tennessee: Tennessee Historical Commission, 1989), 38-44.
2. Terry Tomziac and Mario Perez-Riley, "Effects of *Baker v. Carr* on the Distribution of Influence in the Tennessee General Assembly: An Application of Linkage Policy," in *The Volunteer State: Readings in Tennessee Politics*, eds. Dorothy F. Olshfski and T. Simpson, III, (Knoxville: Tennessee Political Science Association, 1985), 95-113.
3. Sekou Franklin, "Black Political Agency in Tennessee from Reconstruction to the Twenty-First Century," in Wornie Reed, eds. *African Americans in Tennessee* (forthcoming).
4. This included a front-cover expose in *Newsweek*, sympathetic commentaries from the conservative *Washington Times* and Fox's Brit Hume, and even a pre-election interview on HBO's *Real Time with Bill Maher*. See Jonathan Darman, "The Path to Power," *Newsweek*, October 30, 2006, available at http://www.msnbc.msn.com/id/15366095/site/newsweek/. Also, Harold Ford, Jr.'s campaign website listed all of his favorable media coverage, available at http://www.haroldfordjr.com/index.php?option=com_content&task=view&id=157.
5. Sekou Franklin, "Style, Substance, and Situational Deracialization: Racial Polarization and the Tennessee Senate Race," Paper presentation for the National Conference of Black Political Scientists' Annual Conference, March 21-25, 2007.
6. Jackson Baker, "Is Harold Ford Really a New Generation of Democrat—or Is He Just Another Ford?" (Political Notes) *Nashville Scene*, October 21, 2006, available at http://www.nashvillescene.com/Stories/News/Political_Notes/2006/10/12/Family_Matters/index.shtml; and Roger Abramson, "Prince

Harold: The Sky Could Be the Limit for Harold Ford, Jr. Conventional Wisdom Be Damned," *The Nashville Scene*, March 18, 2004, available at http://www.nashvillescene.com/Stories/News/2004/03/18/Prince_Harold/index.shtml.

7. It is unclear whether this was the official name of the ad. However, most political commentators referred to it as the "Bimbo" ad. Some referred to it as the "Playboy" ad or the "Call me" ad.
8. For more discussion of how the use of racial cues can limit deracialized campaigns, see Sharon Wright Austin and Richard T. Middleton, IV, "The Limitations of the Deracialization Concept in the 2001 Los Angeles Mayoral Election," *Political Research Quarterly* 2004; 57 (2) (June 2004): 283-293, and Timothy B. Krebs and David B. Holian, "Competitive Positioning, Deracialization, and Attack Speech: A Study of Negative Campaigning in the 2001 Los Angeles Mayoral," *American Politics Research* 2007; 35; 123.
9. Franklin, "Style, Substance, and Situational Deracialization."
10. Ibid.
11. No Author, "Put Party Affiliation in Check; Vote Early," *Chattanooga Times Free Press* (November 1, 2006): B8.
12. Andy Sher, "Corker Calls for RNC to Pull Ad," *Chattanooga Times Free Press* (October 21, 2006): B1.
13. Austin and Middleton, "The Limitations of the Deracialization Concept in the 2001 Los Angeles Mayoral Election."
14. See for example, David R. Goldfield, *Black, White, and Southern: Race Relations and Southern Culture, 1940 to the Present* (Baton Rouge: Louisiana State University Press, 1990); Brattain, Michelle, "Miscegenation and Competing Definitions of Race in Twentieth-Century Louisiana," *Journal of Southern History* vol. 71 (August 2005): 62-658; William J. Harris, "Etiquette, Lynching, and Racial Boundaries in Southern History: A Mississippi Example," *The American Historical Review* vol. 100, no. 2 (April 1995): 387-410; James F. Davis, *Who is Black: One Nation's Definition* (University Park, PA: Pennsylvania State University Press, 1991).
15. David R. Goldfield, *Black, White, and Southern: Race Relations and Southern Culture, 1940 to the Present* (Baton Rouge: Louisiana State University, 1990), 2.
16. Gail Bederman, *Manliness and Civilization: A Cultural History of Gender and Race in the United States, 1880—1917* (Chicago, IL: Univ. of Chicago Press, 1995), 3.
17. Martha Hodes, *White Women, Black Men: Illicit Sex in the Nineteenth-Century South.* (New Haven, CT: Yale University Press, 1997).
18. Christine B. Hickman, "The Devil and the One Drop Rule: Racial Categories, African Americans, and the U.S. Census," *Michigan Law Review* vol. 95, no. 5. (Mar., 1997), 1161, 1173.
19. Ibid., 1178.
20. Trina Jones, "Shades of Brown: The Law of Skin Color," *Duke Law Journal* vol. 49, no. 6 (April 2000): 1487, 1501, note 41.
21. Paul Finkelman, "The Crime of Color," 67 *Tul. L. Rev*. (June 1993): 2063, 2110.
22. See William J. Harris, "Etiquette, Lynching, and Racial Boundaries in Southern History: A Mississippi Example," *The American Historical Review* vol. 100, no. 2 (Apr., 1995): 387-410.
23. Davis, *Who is Black*, 64.
24. Charles V. Hamilton, "Deracialization: Examination of a Political Strategy." *First World* 1977 (March/April): 3-5.
25. Huey Perry, ed., *Race, Politics, and Governance in the United States* (Gainesville, Florida: University Press of Florida, 1997).
26. Timothy B. Krebs and David B. Holian, "Competitive Positioning, Deracialization, and Attack Speech: A Study of Negative Campaigning in the 2001 Los Angeles Mayoral Election," *American Politics Research* 2007; 35; 123.
27. Ibid., 142.
28. Ibid.
29. Baodong Liu, "Deracialization and Urban Racial Contexts," *Urban Affairs Review* vol. 38, no. 4 (2003): 572.
30. Ibid.
31. Austin and Middleton, "The Limitations of the Deracialization Concept in the 2001 Los Angeles Mayoral Election," 283, 291.
32. Karen Tumulty and Perry Bacon, Jr., "Why Harold Ford Has a Shot," *Time Magazine*, August 6, 2006, available at http://www.time.com/time/magazine/article/0,9171,1223381,00.html.
33. Erik Schelzig, "Faith Continues to be Prominent Issue in Tennessee Senate Race," *Political News* (AP Wire) (November 4, 2006).

34. See "Black Point Man for the Right," *The Black Commentator* no. 120, January 6, 2005, available at http://www.blackcommentator.com/120/120_cover_harold_ford_pf.html; Jackson Baker, "Is Harold Ford Really a New Generation of Democrat—or Is He Just Another Ford?" (Political Notes) *Nashville Scene*, October 21, 2006, available at http://www.nashvillescene.com/Stories/News/Political_Notes/2006/10/12/Family_Matters/index.shtml; and Roger Abramson, "Prince Harold: The Sky Could Be the Limit for Harold Ford, Jr. Conventional Wisdom Be Damned," *The Nashville Scene*, March 18, 2004, available at http://www.nashvillescene.com/Stories/News/2004/03/18/Prince_Harold/index.shtml.
35. Stephen Ansolabehere and Shanto Iyengar, *Going Negative: How Political Ads Shrink and Polarize the Electorate* (New York: Free Press, 1995); Stephen Ansolabehere, et al., "Does Attack Advertising Demobilize the Electorate?" *American Political Science Review* 1994: 88: 829-838; Richard R. Lau, et al., "The Effects of Negative Political Advertisements: A Meta-Analytical Assessment," *The American Political Science Review* vol. 93, no. 4. (December 1999): 851-875.
36. Steven E. Finkel and John Geer, "A Spot Check: Doubt on the Demobilizing Effect of Attack Advertising," *American Journal of Political Science* vol. 42, no. 2 (1998): 573-595; Kim F. Kahn and Patrick J. Kenney, "Do Negative Campaigns Mobilize or Suppress Turnout? Clarifying the Relationship between Negativity and Participation," *The American Political Science Review* vol. 93, No. 4. (Dec., 1999): 878; Paul Freedman and Ken Goldstein, "Measuring Media Exposure and the Effects of Negative Campaign Ads," *American Journal of Political Science* vol. 43, no. 4 (October 1999): 1189-1208; Ken Goldestein and Paul Freedman, "Campaign Advertising and Voter Turnout: New Evidence for a Stimulation Effect," *The Journal of Politics* vol. 64, no. 3. (August 2002): 721-740; John Geer, *In Defense of Negativity: Attack Advertising in Presidential Campaigns*. (Chicago, Illinois: University of Chicago Press, 2006).
37. Craig Leonard Brians and Martin P. Wattenberg, "Campaign Issue Knowledge and Salience: Comparing Reception from TV Commercials, TV News and Newspapers," *American Journal of Political Science* vol. 40, no. 1 (Feb., 1996): 172-193.
38. Tali Mendelberg, *The Race Card: Campaign Strategy, Implicit Messages, and the Norms of Equality* (Princeton, NJ: Princeton University Press, 2001); Nicholas A. Valentino, Vincent L. Hutchings, and Ismail K. White, "Cues That Matter: How Political Ads Prime Racial Attitudes during Campaigns," *The American Political Science Review*, Vol. 96, No. 1. (Mar., 2002), pp. 75-90.
39. Andy Sher, "Attack Ads Dominate Corker-Ford Contest," *Chattanooga Times Free Press* (October 5, 2006): A1.
40. Sher, "Corker Calls for RNC to Pull Ad."
41. Steve Inskeep, "In the News and on the Air: Call Me!" (Morning E-Dition), National Public Radio, October 26, 2006, available at http://www.npr.org/templates/story/story.php?storyId=6386670&sc=emaf.
42. David Espo, "GOP Consultant Cuts Ties with Wal-Mart, (*The Associated Press*) *The Washington Post*, October 27, 2006, available at http://www.washingtonpost.com/wp-dyn/content/article/2006/10/27/AR2006102701340.html.
43. Mendelberg, *The Race Card*, 2001.
44. All reference categories rely upon "simple" contrasts in the SPSS statistical program.
45. With the exception of the simple contrasts, the independent variables in the three logistic regressions are all coded as dummy variables.
46. Gary King, *A Solution to the Ecological Inference Problem* (Princeton, NJ: Princeton University Press, 1997).
47. Kent Redding and David R. James, "Estimating Levels and Modeling Determinants of Black and White Voter Turnout in the South, 1880 to 1912," *Historical Methods* 34, 4 (Fall 2001): 141-159.
48. MSNBC's Patrick Buchanan said "the RNC ad isn't 'racist' because Ford "likes Playboy bunnies. Almost all of them are white," October 27, 2006, available at http://mediamatters.org/items/200610270015.
49. Panel Presentation by Seanna Brandmeir (President of the Tennessee Young Democrats), "Election 2008," Tennessee Alliance for Progress' Compass IV Conference, Nashville, Tennessee, April 14, 2007.
50. For example, Daniel Stevens found that individuals with less sophistication about campaigns, and politics in general, may inaccurately process the intent behind negative attack ads. See Stevens, "Separate and Unequal Effects: Information, Political Sophistication and Negative Advertising in American Elections," *Political Research Quarterly* vol. 58, No. 3. (Sep., 2005): 423.
51. Mendelberg, *The Race Card*; Valentino, Hutchings, and White, "Cues That Matter."
52. Nate Hobbs, "Activist Lifts Voice for Rural Blacks in W. Tenn.," *The Commercial Appeal* (January 17 1994): 1A.

53. The National Election Pool exit poll of the 2006 Senate race in Tennessee.
54. E.J. Dionne, "A Shift Among the Evangelicals," *The Washington Post* June 16, 2006, http://www.washingtonpost.com/wp-dyn/content/article/2006/06/15/AR2006061501790_pf.html; Michael Erard, "Don't Stop Believing: Renegade Bloggers Besiege the Southern Baptist Convention," *The Texas Observer*, July 13, 2007, http://www.texasobserver.org/article.php?aid=2547.
55. Sekou Franklin (co-author) thanks his student, Ben Neal, for special insight on this subject. Mr. Neal is a student activist with the Democratic Party and works in Congressman Bart Gordon's office Murfreesboro, Tennessee.
56. Data for plant closures were obtained by Sekou Franklin (co-author) from the Tennessee AFL-CIO, which has identified plant closures for the state's worker investment areas. For information on Medicaid cuts, see "TennCare Once Was Model for Public Health Care, But Now Is Cautionary Tale. Over 1,000 HIV Patients Left With No Coverage," *AIDS Alert* vol. 21, no. 1 (January 2005): 4-5.
57. See the Pew Research Center for People and the Press survey conducted from November 1-4, 2006, p. 8.
58. Charles L. Prysby, "The 1990 U.S. Senate Election in North Carolina," in Perry, ed. *Race, Governance, and Politics in the United States* (Gainesville, FL: University of Florida Press, 1996), 30-43.
59. Valentino, Hutchings, and White, "Cues That Matter."
60. Tennessee's voter tabulation districts are officially called "pseudo" districts. These districts do not provide exact counts of the voting age population. Moreover, Tennessee has experienced a population boom in recent years, and some central city neighborhoods in Nashville-Davidson County, Memphis, and Chattanooga have experienced gentrification since data for the VTDs were collected.
61. Anderson, Meigs, and Sullivan Counties represent eastern Tennessee. Although Sullivan County is majority white and is considered a racially homogenous district, it has a black representative (Nathan Vaughn) in the state legislature. Representing the western portion of the state are Hardeman, Haywood, Tipton, and Madison. These areas, excluding Dyer, have the largest concentration of rural blacks and fairly active voter mobilization coalition called the Rural West Tennessee African American Affairs Council. Bedford, Giles, Maury, and Robertson represent middle Tennessee.
62. David Waters, "Ford Country?; These Rural West Tennessee Near Always Lead to the Winner," *The Commercial Appeal* (October 31, 2006): A1.
63. See the comments by Michael Powell, Ford's campaign consultant. Andy Sher, "Ford Looks to High Black Turnout in U.S. Senate Race," *Chattanooga Times Free Press* (November 4, 2006): B2.
64. Erik Schelzig, "Ford Tries to Energize Black Vote in West Tennessee," *The Associated Press State & Local Wire* (October 30, 2006).
65. Franklin also uses Gary King's ecological regression analysis to measure black voter turnout. See Sekou Franklin, "Style, Substance, and Situational Deracialization: Harold Ford, Jr.'s Governance and Electoral Strategy," Working Paper, 2007.

Racial Threat, Republicanism, and the Rebel Flag: Trent Lott and the 2006 Mississippi Senate Race

Byron D'Andra Orey
University of Nebraska, Lincoln

I want to say this about my state: When Strom Thurmond ran for president we voted for him [Lott said, with a chuckle]. We're proud of it. And if the rest of the country had followed our lead we wouldn't have had all these problems over all these years. — Trent Lott, 2002 (Kiker, 2002).

Over 50 years ago, in his seminal book *Southern Politics in State and Nation*, V.O. Key wrote, "in its grand outlines the politics of the South revolves around the position of the Negro" (1949: 5). According to Key (1949), "those whites who live in counties with populations 40, 50, 60, and even 80 percent Negro share a common attitude toward the Negro" (5). The phenomenon described by Key has since been labeled as racial threat or more specifically, "black threat" (Giles and Hertz, 1994). Arguably, whites who live in high-black-density areas perceive blacks to be a threat to their social, political and economic hegemony.

More recently, a revisionist group of scholars has found empirical support that runs counter to the black threat hypothesis. Contrary to the racial polarization that is caused by the racial threat phenomenon, these scholars find a positive relationship between black population-density and the phenomenon of whites forging alliances with blacks. In other words, whites are found to be more likely to join alliances with blacks in defeating racially conservative candidates or supporting African-American candidates (see for example Voss, 1996; Carsey, 1995; Sadow, 1996). When applying this line of thinking to the southern context, one might draw the conclusion that there has been a "declining significance of race" in explaining political behavior in the South. The current research seeks to address this issue by examining competing explanations for white political behavior in the South. Indeed, the failure of this research to consider additional racial-explanations has left the literature incomplete. In an effort to achieve this feat, the 2006, United States Senate race in Mississippi, featuring a white racially conservative incumbent, Trent Lott, is employed as the case for analysis. To be sure, recent research has failed to find support for the racial threat hypothesis. The research here, however, contends that other variables associated with race, and by extension racism, persist in explaining white political behavior in the South.

This article is expected to be more theoretical in its composition when compared to the other articles in this symposium. Why? First, the lack of survey data has forced me to employ aggregate-level data such as election returns and United States Census indicators. As a result, consistent with my prior research (see e.g., Orey, 1998; Orey, 2001), I have decided to take advantage of these aggregate-level data by testing the racial threat hypothesis. This is more than appropriate, given the comments made by Lott, captured in the opening epigraph. Moreover, the election's close proximity to the 2001 Mississippi state-flag-referendum, to maintain the Confederate flag as a part of the Mississippi state flag, grants me the opportunity to examine the Lott vote as a function of the white vote for the Confederate flag. Finally, there simply is not much of a qualitative story to tell, regarding the 2006 Senate race, because of Lott's incumbency advantage and his opponent's near invisible campaign.

This article proceeds with a brief overview of the 2006 Senate race. Secondly, the article traces the evolution of the link between the white vote in Mississippi and the Republican Party. Thirdly, a review of the extant literature on racial threat is offered. After introducing the hypotheses, and the data and methods sections, a systematic analysis of the white vote for Trent Lott is presented. Lastly, the article closes with a discussion and summary of the findings.

The 2006 Mississippi Senate Race

The above epigraph provides the backdrop for the current analysis. Those words were spoken by U.S. Senator Trent Lott during the 100th birthday celebration for longtime Senator Strom Thurmond. Given Thurmond's stance on segregation in 1948, many perceived Lott's statement to be racially insensitive. Despite the senator's efforts to apologize for his comments, reports by the media eventually forced the leadership of the Republican Party to pressure the senator into resigning his position as Senate majority leader.

Lott's comments were expressed at a time when Mississippi was recovering from an embarrassing flag-referendum, whereby its citizens voted overwhelmingly to keep the Confederate flag as a part of the state's official flag.[1] On average, whites have responded that the flag represents Mississippi's rich heritage, while many African Americans see the flag as offensive, serving as a symbol of racial hatred and a reminder of slavery. According to a statewide, pre-referendum poll conducted by *The Clarion Ledger* newspaper, approximately 76 percent of whites indicated that, "The Confederate battle symbol is a part of the state's proud history and traditions, and therefore should not be removed from the flag" (*The Clarion Ledger*, 2001: 3).[2] Approximately 69 percent of African Americans responded that "the Confederate battle symbol is offensive and divisive to some groups and should be removed" (*The Clarion Ledger*, 2001: 3).

In assessing both the flag referendum and the Lott vote, some glaring similarities are detected. First, almost identical to the flag outcome, Lott received roughly two-thirds of the vote. Secondly, the vote was clearly polarized along racial lines, with whites overwhelmingly supporting the Confederate flag and Trent Lott and blacks voting overwhelmingly against the Confederate flag and against Lott.

Lott's major contender in the general election was an African American Democratic candidate, Erik Fleming. Fleming, a state legislator, was first elected to office in 1999. During his bid for the U.S. Senate, he soundly defeated his opponent, Bill Bowlin, in the runoff of the Democratic primary. In addition to Fleming, Harold Taylor ran on the Libertarian ticket and received very little support in the race (approximately

1.5 percent). Lott won decisively, receiving over 60 percent of the vote to Flemings 35 percent.

As an incumbent, Lott easily filled his coffer with campaign contributions. According to records posted by the Federal Election Commission, he possessed roughly $1.4 million cash on hand at the end of September, 2006. His campaign had a beginning cash balance of $773,404. Over time, Lott was able to raise an estimated $2.3 million, while spending approximately $1.7 million. Fleming, on the other hand, struggled to mount a serious campaign because of the dearth of campaign funds. While he did manage to film a 30-second campaign ad, he was unable to gather enough funds to run the ad on television. During the same reporting period, records reveal that Fleming, who was making his first run for a statewide office, had $2,474 cash on hand. He started the campaign season with a zero balance. At the end of September 2006, he had raised $26,961 and spent $24,507. Fleming's inability to raise funds was very similar to Lott's 2000 opponent, Troy Brown. Brown, also an African American, raised approximately $40,000 in campaign funds. Lott defeated Brown by a 66-32 percent-margin. Additionally, in 1994, despite having raised approximately $345,000, Ken Harper (a white candidate) was soundly defeated by Lott, receiving only 31 percent of the vote, compared to 69 percent for Lott. So, despite having raised more money than both Fleming and Brown, Harper actually performed the worst, suggesting that Lott's victories were attributed almost entirely to his incumbent status and his Republican affiliation.

This article seeks to investigate whether additional explanations exist in explaining Lott's landslide victory, following his verbal faux pas in 2002. Given Lott's racially insensitive comments at the Strom Thurmond birthday bash, the current author is inclined to believe that race played a role in the outcome of the 2006 election. One plausible theoretical-explanation is that V.O. Key's racial threat thesis still reigns true, even in the *new South.* That is, the Lott vote can be traced to those whites who live in close proximity to blacks.

Black Population Density and the White vote: Cooperation or Conflict?

Whites who find themselves in high black density areas can either join alliances with blacks to form voting coalitions, or they can engage in "turf wars," and vote as a bloc. Along the threat lines, Kinder and Sears (1981) argue that African Americans may pose a threat to white's perceived "good life." In other words, whites perceive the physical presence of blacks as a zero-sum game, whereby blacks might infringe upon their social, political and/or economic dominance.

Overall, the findings in the black-density literature have been mixed. Indeed, Forbes (1997) states that empirically, "roughly equal numbers of studies show positive, zero, and negative effects of contact" (112). Wright (1977) provides support for Key's thesis in an analysis examining the white vote for Wallace in the 1968 presidential election. Using both individual-level data and an aggregate measurement of black density, Wright concludes that black density has an indirect effect on the white vote for Wallace. Giles and Buckner (1993, 1995) also provide confirmation for the racial threat hypothesis in their examination of the white vote for David Duke across parishes in Louisiana in the 1990 United States Senate race.

Contrary to the racial threat hypothesis is the social contact hypothesis. This hypothesis holds that as majority group-members interact with members of the minority, they become more racially tolerant. Carsey (1995) provides empirical support for the social contact hypothesis. The author reports that, the higher the black density in precincts in New York City and Chicago and boroughs in New York City, the higher the probability that a white person voted for the black candidate. Voss (1996), in challenging the evidence reported by Giles and Buckner (1993), finds support for the social contact hypothesis by reporting a negative estimated effect of racial density on vote choice for parishes (the name for counties in Louisiana) in Louisiana that are at least 75 percent urban. Voss (1996) reports that those whites in Louisiana who reside in urban areas, and areas with high black densities, were least likely to have voted for David Duke in the 1990 U.S. Senate race, the 1991 gubernatorial open primary, and the 1991 gubernatorial runoff. Based on his findings, Voss points to the whites living in the suburbs as being the most likely supporters of Duke. Voss (1996) continues by stating that whites should be most threatened in majority-black cities where they have lost their political edge and in areas where poverty and crime have the potential to "exacerbate racial strife" (1163).

The current research builds on the black density model by linking the support for Lott with support for the Confederate flag. In doing so, this research provides an empirical link to the "Southern Strategy" often used by candidates to mobilize white support in the South. That is, by including a variable to tap white voters' support for a racially charged symbol such as the Confederate flag, the current research is able to examine whether the rhetoric voiced by Lott was successful in attracting racially conservative supporters. The next section traces the evolution of the Southern Strategy in Mississippi.

Strange Bedfellows: The Party of Lincoln and Southern Whites

To be sure, Mississippi once was the epitome of a one-party state and the anchor of the "Solid South." In recent years, however, the state has undergone a dramatic transformation towards a two-party state. Arguably, some of this change can be linked to issues pertaining to race. Key writes, "on the surface at least, the beginning and the end of Mississippi politics is the Negro" (229). Giles and Hertz (1994) point to Key's racial threat hypothesis in explaining the observed positive-relationship between the number of whites who identify as Republicans and the percentage of blacks in a parish. Additionally, Knuckey (2005) concludes that beginning in 1994, Republican identification among whites in the South was a direct function of resentful attitudes toward blacks. In an effort to better understand the relationship between race and the Republican Party in the South and beyond, a digression is necessary for the purpose of outlining the history of this phenomenon.

Arguably, one can trace the marriage between white Mississippians and the Republican Party back to 1964. During that year, Barry Goldwater of Arizona, was one of eight non-southern senators to vote against the Civil Rights Act. This played a major role in his ability to mobilize southern supporters, such as Senator Strom Thurmond of South Carolina. As a result, Goldwater was able to win the support of five southern states. Among those five states, four had voted the Democratic ticket for 84 years (Califano, 1991: 55). Among the Southerners supporting Goldwater, Mississippians led with approximately 87.1 percent of their state's vote (Edsall and Edsall, 1992). The Deep South was sold on Goldwater's strategy. Columnist Robert Novak summarizes Goldwater's strategy as follows:

> Soft pedal civil rights. While stopping short of actually endorsing racial segregation, forget all the sentimental tradition of the party of Lincoln. Because the Negro and Jewish votes are irrevocably tied to the

> Democrats anyway, this agnostic racial policy won't lose votes among the groups most sensitive to Negro rights. But it might work wonders in attracting White southerners into the Republican party (Edsall and Edsall, 1992: 39-40).

The South's attraction to Goldwater was clearly linked to the senator's opposition to the Civil Rights Act. Indeed, some southerners saw the civil rights movement as a potential threat to their economic and political hegemony. As a result, they pledged, at least at the presidential level, their votes to the Republican Party. In 1964, for example, Wirt A. Yerger, Jr., chairman of the Mississippi Republican Party, warned party officials that civil right leaders and liberals were registering black voters in Mississippi at higher rates than whites (Edsall and Edsall, 1992). In an effort to counter this threat, Yerger announced that the "Mississippi Republican party is planning a White conservative voter registration campaign.... If we want responsible conservative government in Mississippi, unregistered White conservatives must register and vote" (Edsall and Edsall, 1992: 44).

Goldwater's stance on civil rights, along with his newly captured southern base, reversed the Republican Party's long-term association with racial liberalism and served as the impetus behind Richard Nixon's Southern Strategy. Goldwater transformed the way in which presidential candidates campaigned for the white vote in the South. Richard Rovere, who was by Goldwater's side for much of his tour in the South, states that Goldwater

> did not, to be sure, make any direct racist appeals. He covered the South and never, in any public gatherings, mentioned "race" or "Negroes" or "Whites" or "segregation" or "civil rights." ... He talked about them all the time in an underground, or Aesopian language—a kind of code that few in his audiences had any trouble deciphering. In the code, ... "Criminal defendants" means "Negroes," "States' rights" means "Opposition to civil rights" (Kinder and Sanders, 1996: 225).

In 1968, Nixon followed the lead of Goldwater and gave his campaign a face-lift compared to his 1960 presidential race. Nixon started by selecting Spiro T. Agnew, a border-state governor from Maryland, who was primarily known for "law and order," which became a major theme in Nixon's campaign. Also, Nixon surrounded himself with Senator Strom Thurmond, the Dixiecrat presidential candidate of 1948.

Following the strategy invoked by Nixon, Ronald Reagan learned to perfect the use of racial codewords. According to Walton (1997, 20), "Reagan and the Republican party developed their crucial political technique, the re-introduction of racial cleavages for partisan political advantage." Edsall and Edsall (1992) write "Reagan paralleled Nixon's success in constructing a politics and a strategy of governing that attacked policies targeted toward Blacks and other minorities without reference to race..." (138). Following the 1980 Republican National Convention, Reagan, with the encouragement of then U.S. Representative Trent Lott, began his campaign trail for the presidency at the Neshoba State Fair in Philadelphia, Mississippi (Black and Black, 2002: 216). Philadelphia was the home of the 1964 slayings of civil rights workers James Chaney, Andrew Goodman, and Michael Schwerner during Freedom Summer. During the sixteenth anniversary marking the deaths of these civil rights workers, Reagan spoke openly about his support for "states rights and other issues dear to the old south" (Walton, 1997: 20). An unnamed official in the Reagan administration summarizes Reagan's use of the Southern Strategy as follows:

> You start out in 1954 by saying "Nigger, nigger, nigger." By 1968 you can't say "nigger"; that hurts you. Backfires. So you say stuff like forced busing, states' rights, and all that stuff. You're getting so abstract now [that] you're talking about cutting taxes, and all these things you're talking about are totally economic

> things and a by-product of them is [that] Blacks get hurt worse than Whites. And subconsciously may be that is part of it. I'm not saying that. But I'm saying if it is getting that abstract, and that coded, that we are doing away with the racial problem one way or the other. You follow me, because obviously sitting around saying "We want to cut this," is much more abstract than even the busing thing and a hell of a lot more abstract than "Nigger, nigger" (Lamis, 1990: 26).

Dating back to the 1964 presidential campaign, many white Mississippians have coalesced with conservative whites from other states to create a cohesive "southern bloc" during presidential elections. In recent years, this group of voters has been labeled as "Reagan Democrats." Black and Black (1992) sum the Republicans' Southern Strategy up by stating,

> From Goldwater's vote against the Civil Rights Act of 1964 and Nixon's vocal opposition to "forced busing" in 1968 to Ronald Reagan's coolness toward civil rights laws in the 1980s and George Bush's veto of the Civil Rights Act of 1990, Republican presidential nominees and Republican presidents have consistently taken significant positions in opposition to the wishes of most Blacks (296).

As discussed above, codewords such as "state rights" have often been used as a strategy by Republicans to mobilize conservative southern whites. For example, during his bid for the 2000 Republican nomination for president, then Texas Governor George W. Bush, stated that the Confederate flag controversy ongoing in South Carolina was a "State's" issue. Within the same context, former U.S. Attorney General John Ashcroft, once a Republican senator, expressed strong support for the Old Confederacy. In an interview with *Southern Partisan*, Ashcroft praised the magazine by stating,

> Your magazine also helps set the record straight. You've got a heritage of doing that, of defending Southern patriots like Lee, Jackson and Davis. Traditionalists must do more. I've got to do more" (*Southern Partisan*, 1998: 2).

Based on the above discussion, Trent Lott's comments appear to be consistent with the Republican Party's Southern Strategy. In fact, the Thurmond incident was not an isolated case for Lott. As a U.S. Congressman, Lott voted against all civil rights legislation; opposed the Martin Luther King, Jr. holiday bill and the funding for the commission to commemorate the holiday; and he lobbied the Reagan administration in an effort to grant tax-exempt status to private segregated schools (Beachler, 2001: 592). In 1999, Lott was linked to the neo-segregationist Council of Conservative Citizens, an organization dedicated to preserving white supremacy (Merida, 1999).

Given the southern strategy adopted by the Republican Party, the current research posits that Lott received overwhelming support from whites and very little support from blacks. Formally it is stated:

H_1: White voters provided more support for Lott, than did blacks.

It also is expected that the use of the southern strategy by Lott increased his support from those whites who supported the Confederate flag during the 2001 Mississippi flag referendum.

H_2: An increase in white support for the Confederate flag will lead to an increase in support for Trent Lott.

Based on Key's racial threat thesis, it is expected that whites who live in close proximity to blacks are expected to support Lott.

H_3: An increase in the black population will lead to an increase in white support for Lott.

Data and Methods

The data compiled for this research are derived from two sources: the Secretary of State's Office and the U.S. Census. Consistent with the work of Key (1949), the unit of analysis for this project is the county. In addition to Key, a number of contemporary studies have relied heavily on the county as the unit of analysis (see Giles and Buckner, 1993). One potential reason for the reliance on the county as the unit of analysis is data limitations, as is the case here. In the absence of survey data, aggregate-level analyses have been employed to examine voting behavior. As a result, researchers have had to depend heavily on census data. The county is used as the unit of analysis because, while voting-age population data is available at the precinct level, many of the control variables used to examine voting behavior are not available at this level.

Dependent Variable

The dependent variable in this analysis is the estimated white support for Trent Lott. The data used to construct this variable include election returns, collected from the Mississippi Secretary of State's office, and voting age population data collected from the United States Census.[3] All of these data are aggregate-level data and are collected at the precinct-level. Unfortunately, reliable individual-level data are not available for this analysis. The general problem of moving from data on aggregated tabulation units to data on individuals is known as the problem of ecological inference. Given the use of aggregate-level data, we must acknowledge that we are confronting the "ecological fallacy"—the possibility of making false inferences about individuals from aggregate data. Gary King (1997), however, has proposed a method designed to specifically "correct for aggregation bias"[4] and by extension reduce the potential of succumbing to the ecological fallacy. King's method expands upon the Duncan-Davis method of bounds and incorporates the deterministic method of bounds with maximum likelihood estimates.

Table 1 is included for the purpose of assisting us better understand the model and technique used to derive our estimates. According to Table 1, we can take advantage of the only observable data that we have, those data in the marginal cells, and work our way back to those unobservable quantities within the body of the table. Based on Table 1, X_i represents the fraction of the voting age population who are black and T_i represents the proportion of the voting age population who voted for candidate A. The unobservable quantities of interest are B_i^b the proportion of blacks who vote for candidate A and B_i^w, the proportion of whites who vote for candidate A. Both B_i^b and B_i^w (and the standard errors) are calculated for each county using the estimation procedure, EI, developed in King (1997).[5]

Independent Variables

One of the primary purposes of this project is to test the racial threat hypothesis. This hypothesis is tested by employing an interaction between the Black Population variable and the Urban variable (Voss 1996). The Black Population variable is measured based on the percentage of blacks in a county, as reported by the U.S. Census. Unlike Giles and Buckner (1993), however, I chose to use the total black population rather than the number of black registered voters. This is because whites perception of the threat that blacks pose is based on whites perception of the size of the black population as a whole, not just the number of black registered voters. In other words, the author here rejects the notion that white voters think rationally by calculating the number of blacks who are eligible to vote. Rather, my position is that their perception is based on the number of blacks that they see. In addition, urban population is operationalized as the percent of a county that is classified as urban, as defined by the 2000 Census. The interaction term is simply a multiplicative term consisting of the Percent Black × Percent Urban. Additionally, this analysis seeks to examine the impact of the white vote for the Confederate flag on support for Trent Lott. Similar to the Dependent variable, the white vote for the flag is estimated using EI.[6]

In addition to the aforementioned variables, other variables have been employed as controls to ensure that the model is fully specified. Consistent with Giles and Buckner (1993), we posit that those whites socialized outside of Mississippi will be less likely to support Lott. Here, based on data derived from the U.S. Census, the percentage of the white population that migrated into the state from other states is employed. Bonacich (1976) contends that working-class whites, who are argued to be in direct competition with African Americans, are likely to be racially conservative. These whites view job competition as a zero-sum game, whereby African Americans are given an edge through such programs as affirmative action, and as a result, whites lose out. As a result, we expect that poor whites will be more likely to support Lott, when compared to higher-income whites. The income variable is based on the per-capita white income level as defined by the 2000 United States Census. Additionally, unemployment is measured as the percentage of whites that are unemployed.

Oliver and Mendelberg (2000) find that white hostility toward blacks is shaped more by their low educational level than by their residential proximity to blacks (see also Giles and Evans, 1985). In this analysis we control for the percentage of whites that possess a high-school diploma as capturing education. We classify whites with less than a high-school degree as being among the lower educated, whereas someone with a high-school degree and higher is considered highly educated. That distinction made, the research here expects a positive relationship to occur between the vote for Lott and those counties with a high

Table 1
The Ecological Inference Problem

Race	Vote Choice: Referendum A	Referendum B	Voting Age Population
Black	B_i^b	$1 - B_i^b$	$\mathbf{X_i}$
White	B_i^w	$1 - B_i^w$	$\mathbf{1 - X_i}$
	$\mathbf{T_i}$		$\mathbf{1 - T_i}$

Note: In each precinct, noted as i, both X_i (fraction of the voting age population who are black) and T_i (fraction of the voting age population who voted in the referendum) along with N_i not shown here, (the number of voting age people, not included in the Table) are observed. (fraction of voting age blacks who vote) and (fraction of voting age whites who voted) are unobserved and are inferred from the aforementioned aggregate variables.

percentage of whites with lowly educated whites. Beck (1977) suggests that the different age cohorts experienced different socialization in the South. Thus, we expect those individuals who were socialized in the Old South to preserve their heritage by supporting the rebel flag. Here, a variable is constructed to capture the percentage of a county's white population that is 65 and older.

For ease of interpretation, I have mapped all of the variables, with the exception of income, onto a [0, 1] interval. The current analysis employs weighted least squares regression, whereby the standard errors of the point estimates for the white vote are assigned as weights (see Table 2, cf. King, 1997: 90).

Findings

The first step in this analysis is to determine whether racially polarized voting existed in the 2006 Senate race. An analysis of the descriptive statistics reveals that the average white support for Lott was approximately 86 percent, compared to roughly 21 percent from blacks. At first glance, the 21 percent support by blacks may be somewhat alarming, given Lott's comments. In explaining the black vote, an outside observer might point to Lott's contrite apologies on Black Entertainment Television, in a last-minute effort to save his Senate majority leader position. A closer investigation, however, reveals that a high percentage of Lott's support came from Lott's home region, the Mississippi Gulf Coast. Indeed, Lott received roughly 37 percent of the black vote from the counties on the coast. In Hancock County he received an amazing 65 percent of the black vote. Arguably, blacks supported Lott on the coast, not because the region served as Lott's home away from Washington, but, because it is the home of Keesler Air force Base. In addition to providing a number of civilian jobs for blacks, the base strongly enhances the coast's economy. Another plausible explanation is that blacks may also have felt that Lott would be more influential in helping to rebuild the coast in the aftermath of Katrina, given his senior status.

Moving beyond the descriptive statistics presented here, the results from the regression analysis are presented in Table 2. Overall, the model performs extremely well, achieving statistical significance, as is indicated by the probability of the F-statistic. In addition, the adjusted R^2 is impressive, suggesting that 73 percent of the variance of Lott support is explained by the current model.

In testing the racial threat hypothesis, it was expected that white urbanites who lived amidst large populations of blacks, would be more likely to support Lott. Based on this line of reasoning, the results reported in Table 2 would force us to reject the racial-threat hypothesis. Here, the coefficient for the Urban x Black variable is highly significant, but in the opposite direction of what would be expected under the contemporary racial threat hypothesis. According to the results, whites who live in urban areas, with high populations of blacks, are less likely to support Lott. Figure 1 provides a plot of the effect of Percent Black on white vote for Lott, as a function of the urban population. That is, as the urban population increases from county to county, the impact of the Percent Black (racial threat) variable decreases. Despite the negative slope presented in Figure 1, however, the impact of the Percent Black variable on vote for Lott remains positive (albeit marginal), even when the Percent Urban variable is set at its maximum level. That is, when the urban population is .85 (maximum), a 40-point increase in the black population

Table 2
White Support for Trent Lott
(2006 U.S. Senate Race)

	b		s.e.	
Black	0.15	**	0.07	
Urban	0.04		0.05	
Black x Urban	-0.10	**	0.04	
Flag Vote	0.63	***	0.05	
Less than High School Education	-0.50	***	0.18	
Income	5.00E-06		5.00E-06	
Unemployment	-2.79		1.86	
65 and older	-0.46		0.34	
In-Migration	-2.82	***	0.75	
Constant	0.47	***	0.14	
N			82	
F			26.06	***
R2			0.77	
Adj. R2			0.74	

***p<.01; **p<.05; *p<.10

Figure 1
Effect of Urbanization on the Racial Threat Coefficient

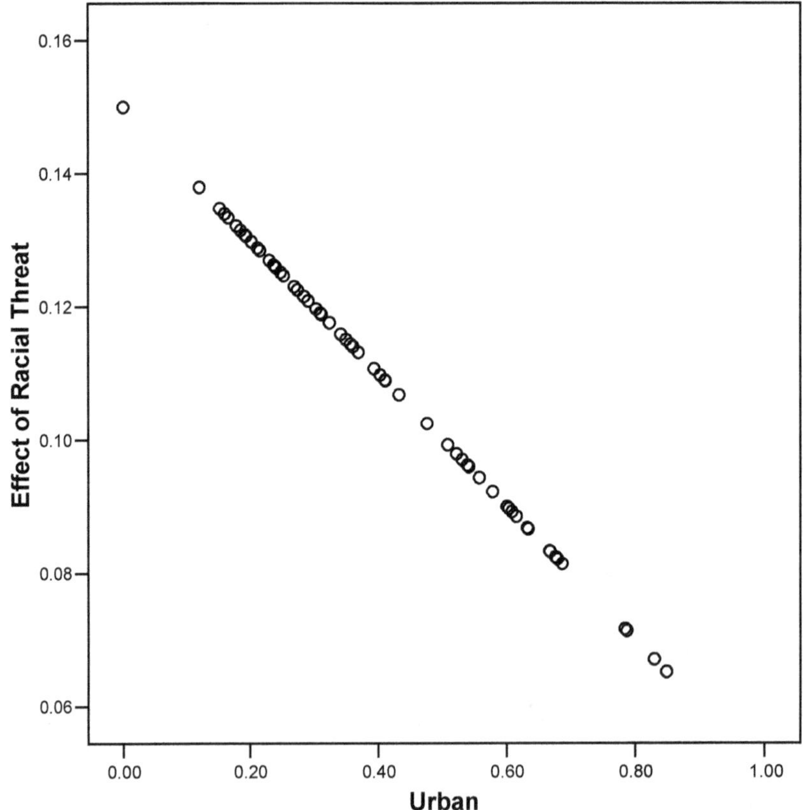

(i.e., a two standard deviation in the Percent Black) results in a 2.4 percent increase in white support for Lott.

Here, it is necessary to re-frame the contemporary discussion of the racial threat phenomenon in order to fit our current case. Much of the debate in the extant literature has focused on states with substantial urban and suburban populations. Key's original work, however, focused on the rural South. Indeed, Key writes, "cities seem to be less dominated in their political behavior than rural areas by consideration of the race question" (1949: 673). Thus, the current research returns to the work of Key by assessing the case of Mississippi. According to Figure 2, the bulk of the majority-black counties in Mississippi are rural. In returning to the illustration presented in Figure 1 then, the findings here are said to provide support, albeit marginal, for the racial threat hypothesis. According to these results, a 40-point increase in the black population leads to an estimated six percent increase in the white support for Lott.

In addition to the racial threat hypothesis, it was posited that those whites who supported the Confederate flag referendum would be more likely to support Lott, when compared to those whites who supported a change in the state flag. Table 2 provides strong evidence supporting this hypothesis. The coefficient is highly significant and the magnitude is

Figure 2
Urban and Black Populations in Mississippi

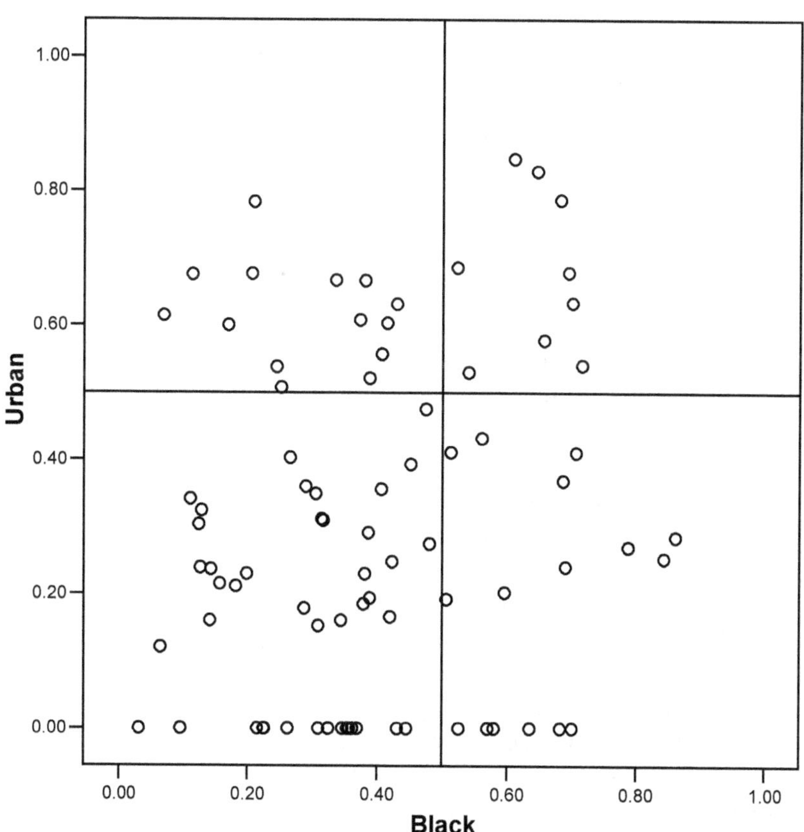

high. Based on the results of the regression, the model produces a coefficient score of approximately .62. This can be interpreted to indicate that a 22-point increase (i.e., a two standard deviation increase) in the flag vote increases white support for Lott by roughly 14 points, *ceteris paribus*.

In addition to the main hypotheses tested here, whites who possess less than a high school degree were found to be less likely to support Lott. Based on Table 2, a 12-point increase (i.e., a two standard deviation) in whites with less than a high school degree, leads to a six-point decrease in support for Lott. These findings might be tapping class. In other words, those whites with less than a high-school degree might be economic liberals, given their low levels of education. Similarly, counties with high proportions of individuals who migrated from outside the South, had a negative influence on white support for Lott. Here, a two-point increase in the percentage of individuals who migrated from outside the South, decreases the white vote for Lott by three points.

Conclusion

The research here set out to examine the impact of race on political behavior in the South. Previous work examining the racial threat hypothesis seemed to imply that there was a declining significance of race in the South. Indeed, a recent group of revisionists have found that blacks and whites are more likely to coalesce as opposed to engage in conflict when choosing political candidates. The current research sought to build on the extant literature, by offering a competing explanation for racially conservative political behavior, beyond the simple notion of racial threat. Specifically, this article employed white support for the Confederate flag as a competing variable for white support for Trent Lott.

The findings reveal that the size of the black population does impact the white vote for a racially conservative candidate. The current demographics in the state of Mississippi are very comparable to the demographics during Key's assessment of the South. Hence, given Key's original focus on the rural South, the current research finds support for the racial threat hypothesis. Specifically, the research at hand finds that whites were more likely to support Trent Lott in rural areas that possessed high populations of blacks. In addition, the research here also introduced a competing explanation for the support of a racially conservative candidate. White support for the Confederate flag in Mississippi was found to be positively associated with the white vote for Trent Lott. These findings are consistent with Lott's racially insensitive comments made during a birthday bash for Senator Strom Thurmond.

Lott won his reelection bid by a landslide, in lieu of his comments. As expected, the vote for the senator was polarized along racial lines, with whites supporting Lott and blacks supporting the African-American candidate, Erik Fleming. Contrary to conventional wisdom, however, Lott's support was not entirely made up of white voters. There were some blacks who supported Lott's candidacy. Given Lott's comments and previous behavior, one might ask, "why would blacks support him?" A number of plausible explanations exist in explaining Lott's higher than expected black votes. First, name recognition associated with incumbency is sure to have been a factor. Secondly, blacks on the Mississippi Gulf Coast were found to provide the bulk of support for Lott. These blacks may have supported Lott because of his strong support for Keesler Air Force Base, which helps to boost the economy on the coast. Lastly, many blacks may have believed that Lott would be more sensitive to helping rebuild the region, in the aftermath of Katrina, given that he resides there himself. Among those whites not supporting Lott included whites who lived among individuals who migrated from outside of the South and whites with less than a high-school degree. This meant that much of Lott's support came from whites with at least some college experience. These findings are counterintuitive, as theories related to racial attitudes suggest that education would lead to more tolerant racial attitudes. The Southern Strategy, however, may have made it less difficult for highly educated whites to support Lott. In other words, Lott's comments were not explicit, and he did not invoke any race-specific epithets. Hence, similar to the white vote for the Confederate flag, where whites couched their support as being based on "heritage" and not "hate," whites could have justified their support for Lott, by focusing on his seniority status in the Senate.

The implications of this study point to a continuing significance of race in Mississippi. Indeed, Mississippi has not elected a statewide black officeholder since the state legislature elected Blanche K. Bruce to the U.S. Senate in 1874. Despite his comments, Lott was not penalized by Mississippi's white voters. The implications here, however, are by no means relegated to Mississippi. To be sure, leaders in the Republican Party forced Lott to resign his post as Senate majority leader. Following the senator's reelection, however, he was elected to the party's number two position of minority whip. Lott's election to a leadership position following his remarks accentuates the continuing significance of race in American politics and not simply the South.

Notes

1. In my previous research, I found that white support for the Confederate flag was explained by old-fashioned racism (see, Orey 2004). Specifically, old-fashioned racism, the belief that blacks are inferior to whites, trumped the new racism, the belief that blacks violate traditional values such as the work ethic, self-reliance and individualism, in explaining white support for the flag.
2. The *Clarion Ledger* is printed in Jackson, Mississippi.
3. The website for the election returns is: http://www.sos.state.ms.us/elections/2006/primary/general-countyrecaps.asp.
4. King's method makes three assumptions: 1) that each precinct's Black and White percentages together are one drawn from bi-variate normal distribution, truncated so that both fall within the 0% and 100% range; 2) in each precinct, the estimated black vote (βb_i) and the estimated white vote (βw_i) are mean independent of racial density; and 3) that the values of the proportion voting (T_i) "in different precincts are independent after conditioning on X_i" (King 1997, 94).
5. The current analysis employed EI, version 1.9 it is available at http://gking.harvard.edu.
6. The website for the flag referendum returns is: http://www.sos.state.ms.us/elections/FlagVote/FlagResults.asp. All results that were not in a scanable format were collected from Ms. Tony Terry of the Secretary of State's Election office. The demographic data were collected from the U.S. Census website, http://www.census.gov using the 2000 Redistricting data (P.L. 94-171).

References

Beachler, Donald W. 2001. "All about Race? Electoral Politics in Mississippi." *Politics and Policy.* 29: 585-599.

Beck, Paul. 1977. "Partisan Dealignment in the Postwar South." *American Political Science Review* 71: 477-96.

Black, Earl and Merle Black. 2002. The Rise of Southern Republicans. Cambridge, MA: Harvard University Press.

———. 1992. *The Vital South.* Cambridge, MA: Harvard University Press.

Bonaich, Edna. 1976. "Advanced Capitalism and Black-White Relations in the United States." *American Sociological Review* 41: 34-51.

Carsey, Thomas. 1995. "The Contextual Effects of Race on White Voter Behavior." *The Journal of Politics* 57: 221-228.

Califano, Joseph, Jr. 1991. *The Triumph and Tragedy of Lyndon Johnson*. New York: Simon & Schuster.

Edsall, Thomas Byrne and Mary D. Edsall. 1991. *Chain Reaction.* New York: W. W. Norton

Forbes, H.D. 1997. *Ethnic Conflict: Commerce, Culture, and the Contact Hypothesis*. New Haven, CT: Yale University Press.

Giles, Michael and Melanie Buckner. 1993. "David Duke and Black Threat: An Old Hypothesis Revisited." *Journal of Politics* 55: 702-13.

————. 1995. "David Duke and the Electoral Politics of Racial Threat," in John C. Kuzenski, Charles Bullock III, and Ronald Keith Gaddie, eds., *David Duke and the Politics of Race in the South*. Nashville, TN: Vanderbilt University Press.

Giles, Michael and Arthur Evans. 1985. "External Threat, Perceived Threat and Group Identity." *Social Science Quarterly* 66: 50-66.

Giles, Michael and Kaenan Hertz. 1994. "Racial Threat and Partisan Identification." *American Political Science Review* 88: 317-326.

Key, V.O. 1949. *Southern Politics in State and Nation*. New York: Alfred A. Knopf.

Kiker, Douglas. 2002. "A Whole Lot of Trouble." December 11, 2002. http://www.cbsnews.com/stories/2002/12/11/politics/main532739.shtml

Kinder, Donald and David O. Sears. 1981. "Prejudice and politics: symbolic racism versus racial threats to the good life." *Journal of Personality and Social Psychology* 40: 414-31.

Kinder, Donald R. and Lynn Sanders. 1996. *Divided By Color: Racial Politics and Democratic Ideals*. Chicago: University of Chicago Press.

King, Gary. 1997. *A Solution to the Ecological Inference Problem: Reconstructing Individual Behavior from Aggregate Data*." Princeton: University of Princeton Press.

Knuckey, Jonathan. 2005. "Racial Resentment and the changing Partisanship of Southern Whites." *Party Politics* 11: 5-28

Lamis, Alexander P. 1990. *The Two-Party South*. Expanded rev. ed. New York: Oxford University Press.

Merida, Kevin. 1999. "3 Consonants and a Disavowal." Http://www.ferris.edu/htmls/othersrv/isar/Institut/CCC/disavow.htm.

Oliver, J. Eric and Tali Mendelberg. 2000. "Reconsidering the Environmental Determinants of Racial Attitudes." *American Journal of Political Science* 44: 574-589.

Orey, Byron D'Andra. 2004. "White Racial Attitudes and Support for the Mississippi State Flag." *American Politics Research* 32: 102-116.

————. 2001. "A New Racial Threat in the New South: A (Conditional) Yes." *American Review of Politics* 22: 233-255.

————. 1998. "The Race Race in Black and White: The 1995 Louisiana Gubernatorial Election." *Southeastern Political Science Review* 26: 909-920.

Sadow, Jeffrey D. 1996. "David Duke and Black Threat: Laying to Rest an Old Hypothesis, Revisited," *American Review of Politics* 17: 59-68.

Southern Partisan. 1998. http://www.southern-partisan.com/johnashcroft.html.

The Clarion Ledger. 2001. http://www.clarionledger.com/news/0102/08/q1html. "Statewide Survey of Mississippi Voters on flag issue." February 8, 2001 pp 1-3.

Voss, Stephen. 1996. "Beyond Racial Threat: Failure of an Old Hypothesis in the New South." *Journal of Politics* 58: 1156-70.

Walton, Hanes. 1997. *African American Power and Politics: The Political Context Variable*. New York: Columbia University Press.

Wright, Gerald C., Jr. 1977. "Contextual Models of Electoral Behavior: The Southern Wallace Vote." *American Political Science Review* 71: 497-508.

Part II

The Evolving Developmental Context of Black Politics and Praxis

Statewide Races in Maryland: Unusual Beginnings of a New Era in Electoral Politics?

Walter W. Hill
St. Mary's College of Maryland

Introduction

Despite the pessimism in some of the literature examining the plateau in the number of offices with black elected officials, Maryland voters elected two African Americans to statewide office in recent elections. In 2002 and 2006 an African American was elected to the position of lieutenant governor. In Maryland, both the governor and lieutenant governor run on the same ticket. A somewhat anomalous feature of the 2002 Maryland's governor's race is that the Republicans won, with an African American on the ticket, in a highly Democratic state. Why did this happen? The Democrats regained this seat in the following election. The conventional wisdom is that the Democrats ran a weak candidate in the 2002 governor's race, resulting in a rare defeat for the party. However, the Republican win resulted in one of the few cases of an African American being elected to a statewide office since the end of Reconstruction, and the first African American elected to that position since the office was created in the state.

Contrary to the conventional wisdom, I hypothesize that the African American candidate had the surprising effect of not increasing the black vote. Rather, ironically, the candidate had the effect of increasing the support of swing white voters. Different dynamics resulted in another African American winning a statewide election in the next cycle. The country may be entering an era where African Americans can win statewide or national offices.

The Situation in Maryland

Maryland is divided into 23 counties and the city of Baltimore. It is one of the states that require voters to select a party affiliation when they register to vote. It is typically said that there are twice as many Democrats as Republicans in Maryland. The *Congressional Quarterly* (2002) reports that 57 percent of voters are registered as Democrats, 30 percent as Republicans, and 13 percent in other categories. In recent presidential elections, the state has consistently voted for the Democratic candidate. The last exceptions were Reagan's landslide in 1984 and Bush in 1988. The state has voted for the Democratic nominee in all subsequent elections for president. The conventional wisdom is that Democrats can win statewide elections by carrying the jurisdictions along the Baltimore to Washington,

D.C. corridor. Washington, D.C., of course, is not in Maryland, but its suburbs in Maryland and Virginia are heavily populated and the Maryland suburbs represent a large fraction of the state's total vote. The immediate Maryland suburbs of Washington are Montgomery County and Prince George's County. Over half of John Kerry's votes in the 2004 presidential election came from three counties, Montgomery, Prince George's, and Baltimore. Another 13 percent came from Baltimore City. African Americans are a clear majority of the population in Baltimore City and Prince George's County. In the 2004 race for the U.S. Senate, the Democratic candidate, Barbara Mikulski, received 65 percent of the vote. She came close to receiving enough votes from simply the 3 largest jurisdictions to defeat her opponent. In other words, she would have nearly won the election had all Democrats in the rest of the state stayed home!

The 2002 Election

In 1998 Parris Glendening, the Democratic incumbent, ran for governor and easily won the election. Kathleen Kennedy Townsend was on the ticket as lieutenant governor. They had faced the same Republican candidate, Ellen Sauerbrey, in a close election in 1994. Townsend was the Democratic nominee for governor in the 2002 election. She was highly favored to win given the Kennedy name and her experience at the top levels of Maryland politics.

In the 2002 race, the Republicans nominated Robert Ehrlich. He had represented a U.S. congressional district outside of Baltimore City. He chose Michael Steele to run as lieutenant governor. Steele had extensive experience in the GOP. It was joked that Ehrlich had picked the only black Republican in the state as a running mate (Martin, 2002: 11).

Townsend shocked Democrats by choosing Charles Larson, the former head of the US Naval Academy, as her running mate. Democrats were upset, because, among other reasons, her choice was a lifelong Republican. This pick for the number two spot on the ticket was taken as an indication of poor judgment on Townsend's part. One possible alternative was Isiah Leggett. Leggett is from Montgomery County and he may have helped the Democrats win more of the suburban Washington vote. He has since become the first African American elected to the position of county executive, the top post, in the most populous county in the state.

The *a posteriori* interpretation of the results of the 2002 election was that the Democrats fielded a weak candidate. Her choice for lieutenant governor simply highlighted her inability to make informed political decisions. But, we might well ask, how could one recognize in, say, the spring before the election, that the candidate was weak? The candidate had the proper previous experience, and had good name recognition. How much could she lose in a poor campaign? The problem is that observers cannot define candidates as weak because they lose elections, and then say that those who lose elections are therefore weak candidates. Researchers looking at electoral behavior need a better definition. I need not find a definition for the state pundits here, as I believe another viewpoint better explains the data, but I need to note the conventional wisdom about Townsend and how it gives little insight to the election.

I collected election data for Maryland's 23 counties and Baltimore City.[1] An initial analysis appears in table 1. We might suspect a good procedure would be to use a multiple regression with the proportion vote for the Democrat in 2002 regressed on the vote in the presidential election in 2000 and the governor's election in 1998 and perhaps other

Table 1
Vote for Democrat in 2002 Given Previous Election Results

			Dependent Variable Proportion vote for the Democrat 2002		
B		st. error	t	Sig	
Constant		-0.163	0.028	-5.823	0.000
Pdem1998		0.755	0.175	4.306	0.000
Pdem2000		0.403	0.156	2.582	0.017
	F=201.68	p=0.000	r=0.975	df=2,21	
			Dependent Variable Proportion vote for the Democrat 2002		
B		st. error	t	Sig	
Constant		-0.166	0.031	-5.278	0.000
Pdem1998		1.180	0.066	17.768	0.000
	F=315.42	p=0.000	r=0.967	df=1,22	

The independent variables are the Democratic proportion of the two party vote for governor in 1998 and president in 2000.

previous elections. However, because of multi-collinearity between elections, it is difficult disentangle the independent effect of the two earlier elections. Hence, we treat this more or less as a stepwise procedure and see the better equation is the bivariate regression with the vote in the 2002 governor's campaign regressed on the previous governor's election in 1998.

Taking the percentage vote for the Democrat is a typical procedure when looking at sequential election data (Fair, 2004; Lewis-Beck, 1998). It is well known from critical election theory that voting behavior at the national level tends to be consistent in subsequent elections. Exceptions tend to occur with realignments and anomalous elections. We expect the same to be true in state elections, perhaps even to a greater extent as some states are known to consistently favor one parry or the other. This model shows a very strong statistical relationship between the two sequential governor's races, which is consistent with the theory. There is a strong correlation in the party vote in elections. It is interesting that a closer inspection of this model shows that the Democrats lost votes across the state in 2002. We may interpret the constant as an offset. The constant can be seen as saying the Democrats would be predicted to lose as much as 16.5 percent of their 1998 vote in a hypothetical heavily Republican county. The slope of 1.178 says the Democrats will increase their vote as counties become more Democratic, but they will just barely make this up in the hypothetical heavily Democratic county. In short, by this measure, the Democrats lost votes across the board. A county with 50 percent of the electorate supporting Glendening-Kennedy in 1998 would expect to win 42.4 percent of the two-party vote when Kennedy-Larson ran for the Democrats in 2002. The results in table 1 are consistent with the view that Townsend was a weak candidate, but leave open the question of what substantively happened below the state level. Let me suggest an alternative model that might better explain the recent election.

Table 2
Change in the Vote for the Democrat in 2002

	Dependent Variable, Vote Gain for the Democrat in 2002			
	B	st. error	t	sig
Constant	-1575.68	1003.15	-1.571	0.131
DemGov98	1.01	0.016	61.305	0.000
F=3758.3	r=0.997	p=0.000	df=1,22	

Table 3
The Proportional Gain in Vote for Parties in 2002

	mean	st. dev.	N	t	sig
Gain-Democrat	0.90	0.097	24	-4.92	0.00
Gain-Republican	1.30	0.132	24	11.24	0.00

The null hypothesis for the t test is the mean equals 1.00.

Consider a simple description of voting behavior that says that there are three categories of voters. There are partisan voters who will consistently vote either for the Democrat or Republican (we ignore minor parties). We also know that the turnout in presidential election years is greater than in off-year elections, so there is also some chance that a registered voter with either party preference will not go to the polls. The final category of voters is independent or swing voters. So we see three categories of voters: partisan Democrats, partisan Republicans, and swing voters. Partisan voters will vote for their party or not vote. Swing voters will vote for either party, or chose not to vote. This model suggests one should look at voting behavior within each of the 3 categories. We examine turnout in each category.

First, look to see if the Democrats consistently lost votes. Again county level data are used when regressing the number of votes for the Democrat in 2002 (not a percent) on number of votes for the Democrat in 1998. Table 2 summarizes the results.

In the typical county, Democrats had 1,576 fewer votes in the 2002 governor's election than they received in the 1998 governor's race. This loss is statistically significant, but it suggests, in a state of 5 million people, in an election that was not seen as close, a poor campaign was not the only explanation.

Consider the proportional change in votes for the Democrats and Republicans in 2002. Here it will be defined as the number of votes the party received in 2002 divided by their vote in 1998.

What does this mean? In the average county, the Democrats only obtained 90 percent of the vote they had in the previous off-year election. The simplest explanation is that a substantial portion of their voters did not bother to show up. Note, counties are of varying sizes so the actual loss is a weighted mean of the values of the variable. Exceptions to the general pattern occurred in two counties. The Democrats actually increased their vote by 5 percent in the large jurisdictions of Montgomery and Prince George's.

One possible explanation was that there was ticket splitting to prevent the same party controlling the executive and legislative branches, so called Madisonian voting (Lewis-Beck, Michael S. and Richard Nadeau, 2004). The name is taken from Madison's idea of checks and balances. Analysts give no evidence of this in Maryland. Other literature on ticket splitting, for example, Burden and Kimball (2002: 145) or Fiorina (1996) focuses on grand systemic demographic features of the electorate and realignment. Given the Democratic win in 2006, realignment does not seem to be the case in Maryland. It seems much more likely that the election was unusual in some way. The outcome was equivalent to an anomalous election at the national level.

What happened to the Republicans in 2002? On average the GOP increased their vote by 30 percent. From where did these votes come? We can look at the counties where the greatest gain took place. These are in the northeastern part of the state and are typically classified as Baltimore suburbs. They are neither the western mountainous regions, nor the southern or eastern region whose economies were traditionally characterized by agricultural production.

Interestingly, the black population in these areas is low. The conventional wisdom was that Steele would bring black votes into the Republican Party. In fact, what happened is that the Ehrlich and Steele ticket won by increasing turnout in essentially white counties. Analysts have described voters in these counties as "Reagan Democrats" in the past. Perhaps now they are simply swing voters. The regional characterization does not seem entirely satisfactory as the Republican gains were in many parts of the state. The GOP was of course helped by the decreased turnout of the Democrats. The lower Democratic turnout is consistent with the conventional wisdom that Townsend ran a poor campaign, however we see that the accepted explanation cannot be the entire story.

Our result is consistent with the model that there are several types of voters. Consider the loyalist, the person who consistently votes for their party. A substantial number of Democratic Party loyalists did not bother to vote in 2002. Republican loyalists voted. The decision to vote will depend on the campaign or candidate, but also other things such as national events or even the weather. The other main category of voter is the swing voters. I suspect these voters, in Maryland, tend to be nominally registered as Democrats. They may switch parties for someone they perceive as a good candidate. In the 2002 governor's race a substantial number of swing voters in fact voted Republican.

We have the observed, a decrease in the Democratic vote by about 30,000 and an increase in the Republican vote by about 190,000. The Democrats would have lost had their 2002 vote total been identical to their vote in 2002. Note that the total two-party vote in 2002 was around 1.7 million. I hypothesize that having an African American on the ticket, even one that would be characterized as conservative, made the Republican Party seem more acceptable to moderate white voters. Some swing voters who might vote Republican, but were unhappy about some of the extreme conservative positions of the GOP, might have felt more comfortable voting Republican with an African American on the ticket. The choice of the lieutenant governor could have been seen as a signal that an Ehrlich administration would be sensitive to moderate views and it would not be in the pocket of extreme conservatives.

Swing Voters

One way to obtain a rough measure of the size of the swing voter is to look at the election data for 2004. Throughout the presidential campaign, Maryland was considered a safe Democratic state. Kerry was never seriously challenged by Bush in the Old Line State. We can use the U.S. Senate race of that year to gain information about the strength of voter partisanship. The popular Democratic Senator Mikulski was running for reelection. She had represented the state for several terms, having first won the seat in 1986.

Mikulski received more votes than Kerry in all 24 jurisdictions of the state. Clearly, some voters in every county voted for President Bush on the Republican side at the top of the ticket and then voted for the incumbent Democratic senator. We can take as a measure of the swing vote the difference between the percent vote for Kerry and the percent vote for Mikulski in each county. Clearly, other voter behavior was possible. For example, a voter might have decided not vote for president, and then voted for Mikulski. I can use this operationalization as a rough indication of the swing vote. This type of undervote is known to be unusual.

We then want to see if this swing vote is correlated with the Republican gain in 2002 for the governors race. If there is a positive correlation, it is evidence that the Ehrlich-Steele ticket was able to attract some of this vote. The results of testing this idea are shown in Table 4.

The swing vote is correlated with the Republican gain, suggesting that a sufficiently large proportion of this group voted Republican in 2002 for the GOP to win the governor's seat. I conclude that Ehrlich and Steele were able to win with this swing vote. A contributing factor was a number of Democrats staying home in 2002. The swing vote was much more important than the poor showing of Democrats.

The 2006 Election

By the time of the 2006 election, the national view of the war in Iraq had completely changed. President Bush's popularity had dropped from a peak of over 90 percent in October 2001 to around 30 percent. The national dynamics clearly had a decisive effect on some congressional elections. However, all congressional incumbents who ran in Maryland won reelection. Maryland had an open U.S. Senate seat. Senator Paul Sarbanes, a popular incumbent who had held the chair since the 1976 election, decided not to run for reelection. Steele decided to run for that seat on the Republican side. He faced no serious opposition within the GOP. There were two main contenders on the Democratic side, Kweisi Mfume and Benjamin Cardin. Mfume had represented a U.S. congressional district in Baltimore and previously led the NAACP. Cardin was in the U.S. House and represented a suburban Baltimore district. It is generally acknowledged that the Democrat leadership decided not to support Mfume. Arguably, the most prominent person making the charge was Wayne Curry, the former head of the Prince George's County delegation (Thomas-Lester, 2006; Williams, 2006).

Mfume had lost the invisible primary, the race for funds and endorsements, by the summer of 2006. He campaigned with little overhead at the grassroots level. He lost in the September primary. His supporters said that Mfume lost while being abandoned by party leadership in the state. The way that he lost prompted some black Democrats, such as Curry, to support Steele openly in the general election. After the primaries, the

Table 4
Prevalence of Swing Vote

	Dependent Variable Republican Gain 2002			
	B	st error	t	sig
Constant	0.087	0.084	1.04	0.312
Swing Vote	1.801	0.073	2.68	0.014

F=7.17 r=0.496 p=0.014 df=1,22

The swing vote is defined as the proportion of the two party vote for Mikulski in 2004 minus the proportion of the two party vote for Kerry in the same year. The Republican gain is the proportion change in the Republican vote for governor in 2002 relative to the Republican vote for governor in 1998.

lieutenant governor was the remaining African American candidate seeking the Senate seat. Curry took the position that the state Democratic leadership had not given a viable African American a fair opportunity to win a Senate seat, it made sense to support an African American Republican attempting to win the same seat.

The other statewide race was for the governor's office. Ehrlich ran for reelection picking Kristen Cox as a running mate. Cox was the state secretary of the Department of Disabilities. Many candidates announced on the Democratic side, but there were two main contenders for the September primary. The two Democratic candidates were Douglas Duncan, head of the Montgomery County Council, and Martin O'Malley the mayor of Baltimore. Duncan campaigned on a number of issues including criticism of the school system in Baltimore City, and tax issues.

Democrats feared that a prolonged and divisive campaign between Duncan and O'Malley would drain funds going to the party, and provide ammunition for Republicans in the general election. Also, given that the primary would occur relatively late in the election cycle, it would prevent the party from presenting a unified message until late in the year. With respect to the last point, some Democrats in state government unsuccessfully attempted to move the primary from September to June.

Hints that there were problems with Duncan's campaign surfaced in January 2006. After Baltimore Mayor O'Malley named "House Majority Whip Anthony G. Brown (D-Dist 25 [Mitchellville]) his running mate on Dec. 12, 2005, aides to Duncan said he would select his running mate before the start of the General Assembly." Duncan did not make an announcement before the beginning of the General Assembly in January. Democrats wondered why he would miss this self-imposed deadline (Dennison, 2006). It turned out that Duncan dropped out of the race well before the primary citing a personal reason, depression (Jamison, 2006). His departure in fact worked to the advantage of the Democrats as O'Malley found himself in a position were he need not defend himself in the pre-election period from attacks from the left. He was able to move towards the center and concentrate on defeating the Republican in the general election. Significantly, unlike Kathleen Kennedy Townsend, O'Malley chose an African American to be his running mate.

On the Republican side, there were hints that Steele might have problems on the campaign trail. Matthew Mosk (2006a) pointed out that Steele offended Jewish leaders at the

Baltimore Jewish Council by referring to stem cell research as the same thing as Nazi experiments. He confused the issue more by saying he supported embryonic research on a conservative talk show interview. At about the same time, his communications director, Leonardo Alcivar resigned.

After the September primary, campaign advertisements were evident. Arguably, the most discussed television commercial was aired by Steele shortly after the primary. Steele appeared saying that, "politicians in Washington say one thing, but do another." They "play the angles." If you "wanted real change," claimed the commercial, Steele was "your man." He portrayed himself as an outsider. A follow-up commercial showed Steele with a dog and portrayed the lieutenant governor as a friendly fellow who loves animals and who anticipated that Democrats would say nasty things about him. The commercials were generally recognized as well crafted.

Democrats took a while to respond. Steele was shown as a party insider. Most striking were commercials showing pictures of him with President Bush. An amusing follow-up said that the dog shown in Steele's commercial "wasn't even his dog." The levity of the late September commercials deteriorated into a number of dark advertisements by both sides as the election approached.

At the election, Democrats gained votes relative to their 2002 showing and the Republicans lost votes. Both the Democratic gains, and the Republican losses were consistent across the state. Democratic gains are consistent with the hypothesis that Townsend ran a poor race in 2002. We also find it consistent with the hypothesis that there was a core of Democratic voters who decided not to go to the polls in 2002. However, this is not the entire story.

On the Republican side, we see two possible hypotheses. One is that the combination of Ehrlich and Steele attracted one type of swing voter in 2002. Having them run separate races weakened this link. An alternative possibility is that there were national trends that gave Democrats in Maryland an advantage.

With respect to the hypothesis that national trends doomed Republican candidates in Maryland, there were no other statewide elections that might be used as control cases. Ideally a researcher would like to find Democrats and Republicans who ran statewide in several elections get an estimate of the effects of national trends on the GOP in Maryland. The next best option is to look at state's elections for the U.S. House of Representatives. Of the 8 U.S. congressional districts in Maryland, two were won by Republicans in 2002. Both incumbent Republicans retained their seats in 2006. One congressional district is concentrated on the rural eastern shore and reaches to the Atlantic Ocean. This district does have voters in the Baltimore suburbs. The other district stretches from the Baltimore region to the Appalachian Mountains. Although the incumbent Republican won both races, their percent of the two-party vote in the most recent election was about 8 percent less than in 2002. I have a similar estimate from the more competitive districts won by Democrats.[2] I take an 8 percent Republican loss as a rough estimate of the effect of national trends on candidates in Maryland.

In a post-mortem, Mosk and Marimow (2006b) said the governor's attacks on Baltimore hurt his team's chances of getting black support. I think it should be pointed out that there is not evidence that a Republican could make serious gains in Baltimore City. The demographics of a low-income, African American, urban area along with the Republicans not having an African American on the governor's team did not bode well for the GOP in a large city.

The *Post* article further says Steele won 25 percent of the black vote, while Ehrlich, the Republican governor, obtained 15 percent. These numbers seem to have become conventional wisdom. This was not better than the 23 percent they got in Prince George's County in the last election. Our data are more sanguine and suggest that neither Republican received more than 15 percent of the black vote. This topic is a current research project. Steele, for example, received 24 percent of the two-party vote in Prince George's county and in Baltimore. It seems unlikely that no whites voted for him. However, the overall point of Mosk and Marimow is well taken. Despite urging by some prominent black officer holders, the black vote did not switch to the Republican Party in 2006.

Let me add a personal note. In interacting with Steele campaign workers in my district as a curious citizen at one outdoor local festival shortly before the September primary, my impression was that the staff was at best indifferent to the black vote. This was in dramatic contrast to speaking with those working at the Cardin table and those at the Mfume table.

Majority-Minority Seats

The most blatant barriers to black participation were lifted with the passing of the Civil Rights Act and Voting Rights Act (Philpot and Walton, 2005). A result was the number of black elected officials increased dramatically (Bositis, 2001; Dawson, 1990; Gomes and Williams, 1992; Joint Center for Political Research, 1994; Williams, 1990). The vast majority of congressional seats held by African Americans are from districts with majority-black populations. A strategy for winning seats in jurisdictions with a substantial minority of African Americans was to win the black vote, Latinos, plus the white liberal vote and some of the Asian vote. The exemplar here was Harold Washington who won the election for mayor of Chicago in 1983 (Kleppner, 1995: 153). At that point, a strategy for black political candidates was to win a solid majority of the black vote, plus a fraction of the white liberal vote. The number of blacks in office seems to have reached a peak in the middle 1990s using these strategies. Racial bloc voting remains (Kraus and Swanstrom, 2005) and it will limit expansion of black elective officeholders. Supreme Court decisions, in particular the *Shaw v. Reno* case in 1994, dampened redistricting efforts to increase the number of majority-black districts. The Democrat defeat at the polls in 1994 further soured enthusiasm for the drawing of highly irregular lines for additional majority-minority districts.

Integrated Districts

African Americans are not a majority in any state in the Union. To win statewide offices it is necessary for any candidate to win a substantial number of white votes. Although there is some evidence from that intolerance has not waned (Mondak and Sanders, 2003), public opinion polls in the last decade tend to say candidates from almost any major demographic group can win votes across the board. A standard public opinion poll question asks respondents whether they would vote against a candidate solely on demographic considerations. *The New York Times* (13 August 2000) reports the results of public opinion polls conducted since the 1950s asking adults, "If your party nominated a generally well-qualified person for president who happened to be _______ would you vote for that person?" The interviewer fills in the blank with female, Catholic, African American, Jewish, etc. Within the last half century the ratings for all categories rose, some dramatically. The percent of Americans saying they would vote for a black candidate rose from 37 percent in the 1950s to 95 percent. The story appeared in the context of Al Gore, picking Connecticut U.S. Senator Joseph Lieberman to be the Democratic candidate for vice president. Lieberman was considered squeaky clean, unlike the then-current President Bill Clinton. The Connecticut Senator was seen as a moderate Democrat, but hawkish on foreign policy. The *Times* article was surely inspired by the fact that the senator is Jewish and had a good chance of becoming vice president.

The results from the last two elections for statewide office in Maryland indicate that African Americans can win statewide or even national offices. Both elections have unique features making it difficult to know the extent to which the situations generalize beyond Maryland. It may be time for minority candidates to pursue seriously these statewide positions.

Discussion and Conclusion

The Civil Rights Act and Voting Rights Act of 1964 and 1965 resulted in increasing black participation in the political process. Increasing numbers of blacks were able to vote given these laws. Following the increase in voting rates, there followed an increase in African American officeholders. The number of black elected officials approached a plateau in the middle 1990s using the prevalent electoral strategy. By concentrating on a strategy that focused on local elections, many blacks won these elections, but few blacks reached statewide office. This pattern was broken in Maryland as two different African Americans have won the position of lieutenant governor in the last two statewide elections. How, and why they won was different in the two cases.

The state is heavily Democratic. I have shown that Republicans won the top two offices in 2002 by, among other reasons, having a candidate running for executive office who had the ability to attract swing votes by having an African American on the ticket. Ironically, the increase in support did not come from counties with mainly minority constituents. I suspect by having an African American on the ballot, albeit a conservative one, Ehrlich appeared more moderate than Republicans running for the office in very recent memory. He was thereby able to attract swing voters in the election.

In the case of the 2006 election, the Democrats won by mobilizing their core constituents. The party ran a candidate who had been mayor of the largest city in the state. His selection of an African American running mate responded to an error by the previous Democratic candidate for governor. Blacks who may have felt shunned by the Democratic Party leadership when the party opposed Mfume over Cardin in the Senate race may have been mollified by seeing Brown in the lieutenant governor's position as a reasonable compromise.

These two elections may herald a new era of African Americans winning elections at the state level. The reasons for African Americans appearing on the ballot varied for both parties, and the reason for victory, when it occurred, was different for both parties.

Acknowledgments

* Research on this manuscript was conducted while the author was a visiting scholar at the University of Michigan in Ann Arbor. He wishes to thank University personnel for assistance. Comments on an earlier version of this manuscript by Thomas Botzman, Joseph McCormick, Hanes Walton, and anonymous referees improved the quality of the paper. Remaining errors are, of course, the responsibility of the author.

Notes

1. In April 2007, election data were available at: http://elections.state.md.us/elections.
2. The research design using congressional districts won by Democrats has less validity than that using Republicans. The Democrats won six congressional districts. In two districts the Democrat was not the incumbent in 2002. Another two districts are majority-minority districts in which Republicans did not seriously compete. For example, Cummings won with 98 percent of the vote. One of the remaining two seats is held by Hoyer, one of the highest ranking Democrats in the House. Hoyer ran without a Republican opponent in 2006. Hoyer's strongest opponent, Warner from the Green Party, received 16 percent of the vote.

References

Bositis, David A. 2001. *Black Elected Officials*. Washington, D.C.: Joint Center for Political and Economic Research.

Burden, Barry C. and David C. Kimball. 2002. *Why Americans Split Their Ticket*. Ann Arbor, MI: University of Michigan Press.

Dawson, Michael C., Ronald E. Brown and Richard C. Allen. 1990. "Racial Belief Systems, Religious Guidance and African-American Political Participation." *National Political Science Review*, 2: 22-44.

Dennison, Thomas. 2006. "Duncan's running mate selection delayed." *Montgomery County Gazette (Maryland)*, January 11: page 20.

Fair, Ray. 2004. *Prediction of Presidential Election*. Washington, D.C.: Congressional Quarterly Press.

Fiorina, Morris. 1996. *Divided Government* 2nd Edition. Needham Heights, MA: Allyn & Bacon.

Gomes, Ralph C and Linda Faye Williams. 1992. *From Exclusion to Inclusion*. Westport, CT: Greenwood Press.

Jamison, Kay Redfield. 2006. "Acknowledging Depression: Public Figures Perform A Service In Revealing Mental Illness." *Washington Post*. June 25: b07.

Joint Center for Political Research. 1994. *Black Elected Officials*. Washington, D.C.: Joint Center for Political Research.

Kleppner, Paul. 1995. "Mayoral Politics Chicago Style: The Rise and Fall of a Multiethnic Coalition, 1983-1989." *National Political Science Review*, 5: 152-180.

Kraus, Neil and Todd Swanstrom. 2005. "The Continuing Significance of Race: African American and Hispanic Mayors, 1968-2003." *The National Political Science Review*, 10:54-70.

Lewis-Beck, Michael. 1998. *Forecasting Elections*. Washington, D.C.: Congressional Quarterly Press.

Lewis-Beck, Michael S. and Richard Nadeau. 2004. "Split-Ticket Voting: The Effects of Cognitive Madisonianism. "*The Journal of Politics*," 66:97-112.

Martin, Jurek. 2002. "Political Dynasty May Join Endangered Species List." *Financial Times*, September 28/29.

McCormick, Joseph, 2nd. 2007. "An Anatomy of a 'Sacrificial Lamb': The Lynn Swann's 2006 Campaign for Governor." Unpublished. A version was presented at the NCOBPS meeting in March 2008 in Chicago.

Mondak, Jeffery, Jr. and Mitchell S. Sanders. 2003. "Tolerance and Intolerance, 1976-1998." *American Journal of Political Science*, 47: 492-502.

Mosk, Matthew. 2006a. Steele Disappoints on Stem Cells. *Washington Post*, February 18: b1.

Mosk, Matthew and Ann E. Marimow. 2006b. Election Review. *Washington Post*, Nov. 9: a1.

New York Times. 2000. "He's just Red, White and Blue." *New York Times,* August 13: 1.

Philpot, Tashi S. and Hanes Walton, Jr. 2005. "An Historical Election in Context: The 2001 Atlanta Mayoral Election." *The National Political Science Review*, 10: 43-53.

Thomas-Lester, Avis. 2006. "Leaders Say They Endorsed Republican to Wake Democrats." W*ashington Post*, November 6: b4.

Vandeltel, Jim and Juliet Eilperin. 2002. "Congress Gives Bush Authority for War in Iraq." *Washington Post*, October 11: a1, a6.

Williams, Linda F. 1990. "White/Black Perceptions of the Electability of Black Political Candidates." *National Political Science Review*, 2: 45-64.
Williams, Ovetta. 2006. "Black Democrats Cross Party Lines to Back Steele for US Senate: Prince George's Politicians Lash Out at State Party." *Washington Post*, October 31: b1, b4.

Electoral Cycles in Racial Polarization and the 2006 Senate Elections

Richard Forgette
University of Mississippi

Marvin King
University of Mississippi

Introduction

Is there a growing electoral divide in American politics? This question evokes substantial discussion and disagreement. Popular pundits and pollsters are more likely to answer that there is a widening electoral divide along partisan, cultural, and racial lines. In *The Two Americas*, Greenberg (2005) argues that electoral trends reflect a deepening division between Republicans and Democrats. He argues that this electoral pattern manifests itself into a "politics of parity" in which issues among elites become deadlocked. Given the close electoral parity, elite partisans are more inclined to promote issue agendas that harden and mobilize support among their electoral base rather than risking a loss of this base. Strong academic evidence also supports the claim of growing partisan polarization (DiMaggio, Evans, Bryson, 1996; Evans, 2003). Brewer and Stonecash (2007) present evidence of growing cultural and economic class-based electoral cleavages, and Streb (2002) reports evidence of persisting race-based party polarization.

Other academic research, however, provide a more muted and complex picture of trends in electoral polarization. Fiorina et al. (2005) argues this culture war rhetoric is largely a myth. He concludes the electorate is closely but not deeply divided, dispelling the case of geographically based, "Red" state versus "Blue" state, partisan polarization. Bernhardt et al. (2006) suggest that media bias might be responsible for political party polarization. Ansolabehere et al. (2005) also provides reasons to doubt the veracity of "culture war" claims. First, the authors assert that party polarization has actually shrunk over the last 100 years, thus the current crisis of polarization found in the mass media takes a myopic view of American political history. Second, the typical American voter is an ideological moderate on economic issues. Consequently, the term "culture war" implies a division in American society that really does not exist. Last, for most Americans, economic concerns still outweigh moral issues in elections.

In this work, we assess one aspect of electoral polarization: whether voter assessments of incumbents vary by election proximity. We focus particularly on party-based racial polarization—whether white and black voters *assess elites differently* as an election nears.

We refer to this election season pattern as a "political-racial cycle" in which incumbent approval polarizes between white and black respondents as an election approaches. We are also interested in a second campaign hypothesis, whether campaign intensity promotes racial polarization. We test these campaign hypotheses that campaign proximity or intensity promotes racial polarization while controlling for alternative hypotheses, notably whether racial polarization is a rational response to ideological extreme incumbents.

Our research examines a new data source, monthly tracking poll data of U.S. senators. We analyze voters' assessments of Senate incumbents using monthly SurveyUSA, tracking poll data aggregated by state for every Senate incumbent. The unit of analysis is statewide senator approval rates by race, gender, ideological cohort, party, and other categorical variables for 15 months leading up to the 2006 midterm election. This cross-sectional time-series data provides unique analytical leverage for evaluating campaign effects. Since we have data on all 100 U.S. senators and only 33 stood for reelection in 2006, the data provides a natural experiment for isolating the effects of election proximity, campaign intensity, and voter attributes on electoral polarization.

The essay proceeds as follows. In the next section, we review relevant literature and report evidence of trends in electoral polarization between elections. The following section presents our hypotheses and analysis of party-based racial polarization. We conclude with a discussion of our results and their implications.

Explanations of Electoral Racial Polarization

What might explain variation in the electoral racial divide? If racial discrimination and tensions have lessened in American politics, why might there not be a corresponding decline of party-based, racial polarization? Earlier studies provide different responses to these questions. Abramson, Aldrich and Rohde (1994) suggest that racial polarization is a persisting norm, and Carmines and Stimson (1980 and 1989) argue that in the post-civil rights era parties polarized on racial issues and the politics of civil rights.

There are sectional consequences to race-based party polarization. Valentino and Sears (2005) find the linkage between racial conservatism and partisanship in presidential voting stronger in the South than the non-South, and regional differences in nonracial ideology or nonracial policy preferences cannot explain this relationship. In other words, only racial issues explain the stronger link between racial conservatism and partisanship in the South.

An examination of party polarization and race reveals that blacks have overwhelmingly voted Democratic for at least two generations with no trends in actual voting behavior suggesting a shift (Shaw, 1997). Blacks perceive larger differences in the parties than do whites (Glaser, 1995). This is noteworthy because blacks see these differences while they are comparatively less politically sophisticated than whites. Glaser (1995) hypothesizes that blacks see large partisan differences because historically Democrats have treated African Americans better and this appears to matter in identifying important differences.

Culture, Class and Issues as Polarizing Agents

In addition to race, Adams (1997) writes that all culture war issues have the potential to polarize the parties. Layman (1999) concurs that cultural issues exhibit a tendency to divide along partisan lines and since 1980, the Republican Party has sought separation from the Democrats by emphasizing morality and family value-type issues (Layman and Carsey, 2002).

However, Lindaman and Haiden-Markel (2002) claim that not every culture war issue has the capacity to polarize the parties. Party elite opinion is sometimes unrelated to mass opinion. Some issues only divide elite partisans and do not divide the party in the electorate. The polarizing issues tend to be election-specific phenomena.

Brewer and Stonecash (2001) assert that income matters more than race as a polarizing agent, especially as it relates to issues of individualism, government regulation, and taxes. Likewise, Nadeau and Stanley (1993), in a study limited to native southern whites, find evidence for substantial class-based party polarization. Finally, Stonecash (2006) reports that from 1970-2004 as class divisions increased—as judged by the Gini Index—so did class-based voting.

Besides class-based polarization, Abramowitz and Saunders (1998) support the argument that increased ideological polarization of the parties explains the shift in party loyalties in the electorate in the 1990s because "clearer differences between the parties' ideological positions make it easer to choose a party identification based on their policy preferences."

Figure 1

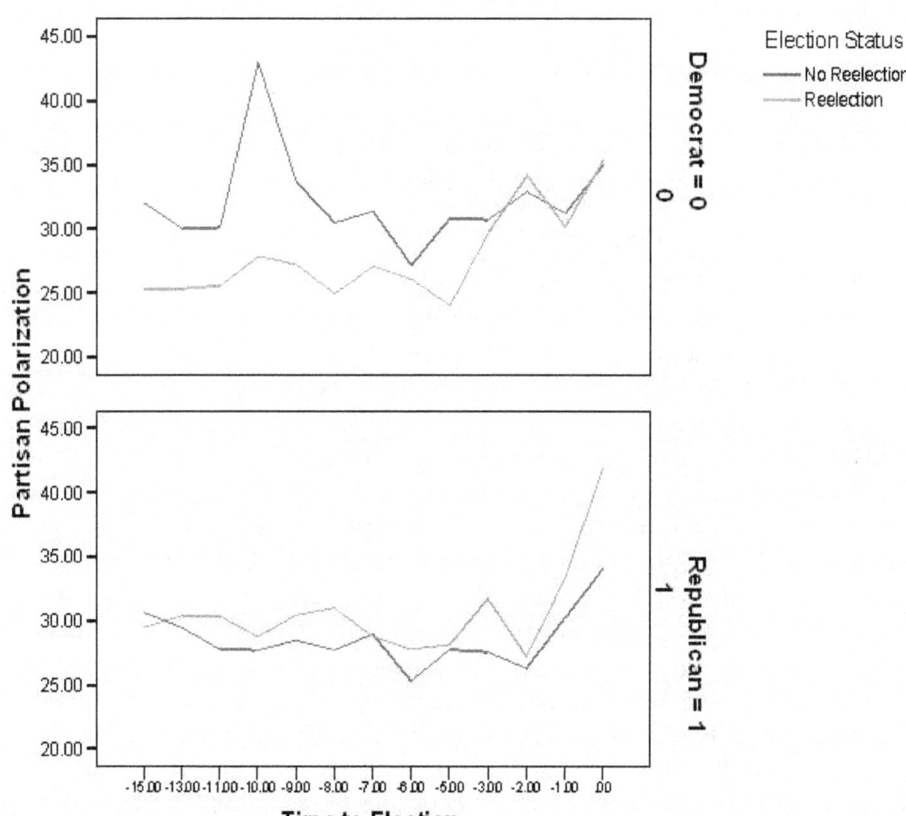

Sinclair (2002) notes that congressional parties emphasize particular issues in order to frame the policy agenda during election campaign cycles. Parties behave in this manner because an issue must be salient to polarize the electorate (Adams, 1997). An even more nuanced view of the role of issues in campaigns is that voters polarize along specific issues only when a candidate and voters agree on which issues are important and that party "owns" the issue (Abbe et al., 2003). For instance, Abramowitz (1995) identifies abortion as the most important non-economic issue of the 1992 presidential race. Following Adams, we should expect to see polarization only on issues deliberately put on the campaign agenda by the political parties.

There are, of course, election specific variables affecting ideological party polarization. These election specific variables include national political conditions, which Abramowitz (2006) reminds us matter in Senate elections. President Bush is a polarizing political figure (Jacobson, 2006), so much that he exacerbated ideological polarization and increased turnout (Abramowitz and Stone, 2006).

Finally, campaigns produce their own set of dynamics as it relates to party polarization. It is reasonable to imagine that the themes and intensity of a particular campaign might exacerbate cleavages in the electorate. While most research focuses on the presidency in this regard, Miller (1981) notes that citizens evaluate Senate and House candidates differently. There is more focus in senatorial campaigns on issues as well as candidate competency and integrity. House campaigns tend to focus more on the personal appeal of candidates and their responsiveness to constituents. Given Miller's findings, it is reasonable to expect polarization along the issues in a Senate campaign.

Abramowitz and Segal (1992) note that incumbents in small states might have an advantage in Senate races because it is easier for incumbents in smaller states to develop home-style relationships with their constituents. Lee and Oppenheimer (1999) explain this is because large state senators must devote more time to fundraising their governing suffers, making them more vulnerable to challengers.

Polarization and SurveyUSA Data

The 2006 SurveyUSA tracking poll data present some descriptive evidence of campaign effects on electoral polarization. We measure electoral polarization by taking the absolute value of marginal differences between group cohorts. For instance, racial polarization is measured as the absolute value of ($\text{Black Approval}_{it}$ - $\text{White Approval}_{it}$) for Senator i in month t leading up to the November 2006 election. Partisan and ideological polarization is similarly measured using differences between Republican / Democrat and liberal / conservative identifiers.

There is strong reason to expect electoral polarization in the 2006 election. The 2006 election results clearly indicated a pro-Democratic national tide with Democrats gaining six Senate seats, all taken from Republican incumbents, and 30 House seats. In fact, this Democratic tide in the 2006 election was unique as the first election in U.S. history in which a party retained all of its current House and Senate seats. The electorate's disapproval of the Iraq War and the corresponding low approval rating of President Bush largely generated the strong Democratic tide. According to Pew Survey data, a higher proportion of voters (compared to previous midterm elections) cast their 2006 ballot as a negative evaluation of presidential performance (Pew Research Center, 2006). Polls also indicated that voters' attributions of Iraq War to Bush policies, though, sharply divided along partisan lines. Democratic voters in 2006 strongly aligned with Democratic candidates.

The 2006 tracking data reflect these campaign trends. Voters' assessments of their home-state senator's job approval changed significantly over the election cycle. Figures 1-3 present partisan, ideological, and racial polarization trends over 15 months leading up to the November election. The horizontal axis displays the months to election with "0" indicating November 2006. Polarization, again, is the absolute difference between partisan, ideological, or racial groups. The figures indicate that polarization increases over the electoral cycle for both senators up for reelection (in-cycle) and those not up for reelection (out-cycle). However, partisan polarization is slightly greater for the in-cycle Republican senators and racial polarization is greater for Senate Democrats. Overall, the rate of ideological polarization grew 60 percent between August 2005 and November 2006. Partisan polarization grew 40 percent over the same period. Other sources of electoral polarization—gender, age, education, religiosity—show no clear increase over the election cycle.

Racial polarization rates also increased, though the trend was evidently more erratic reaching a low point in January 2006. The difference between in-cycle and out-cycle senators also grew over the election cycle. Figure 3 reports racial polarization trends separated by Republican and Democratic incumbents. Nearly all of this increase in racial polarization over the election cycle occurred among Senate Democrats.

Figure 2

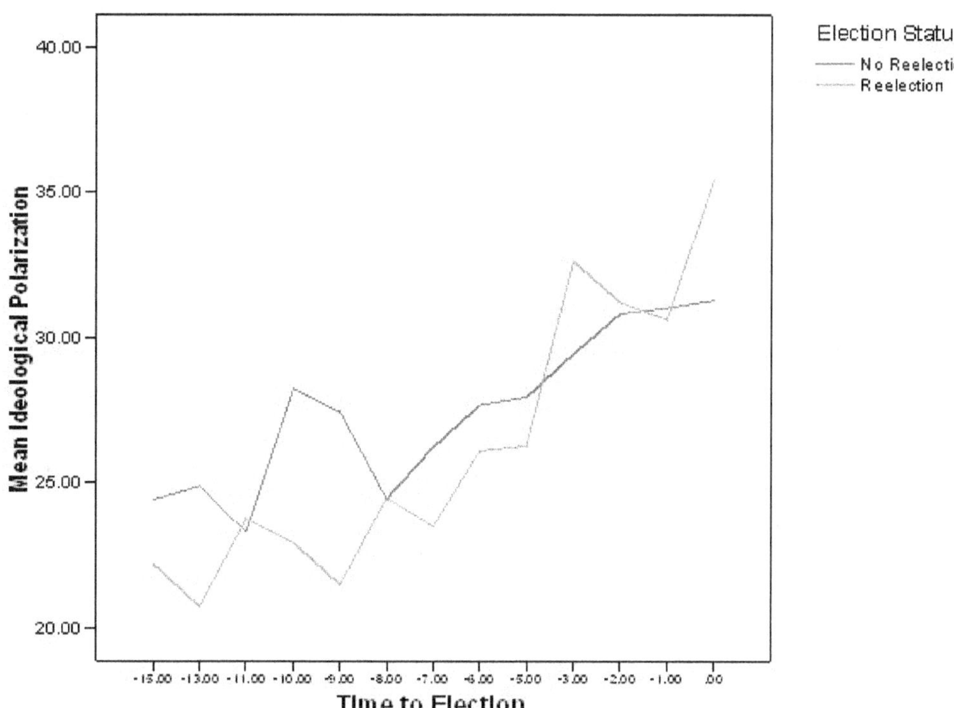

Collectively, these graphs indicate that electoral polarization varies over time, and appears to grow with election proximity. In the next section, we propose and test hypotheses explaining a political racial cycle.

Hypotheses and Analysis

Despite voters' relatively stable partisan and ideological predispositions, voter approval of individual incumbents' performance varies dramatically over time. With nine of ten African American voters casting votes for Democrats in national elections, one might expect Republican incumbent approval among African Americans to be low. The SurveyUSA tracking poll data, however, indicates that over 40 percent of African Americans approved of their Senate Republican incumbents' performance over the election cycle. As the earlier figures show, though, black and white voters' approval ratings polarize along ideological and partisan lines as Election Day gets closer. Contested campaigns necessarily require voters to make judgments that are more discerning.

How do we explain this apparent political racial cycle? We discuss several explanations for racial polarization in this section and present empirical results evaluating these

Figure 3

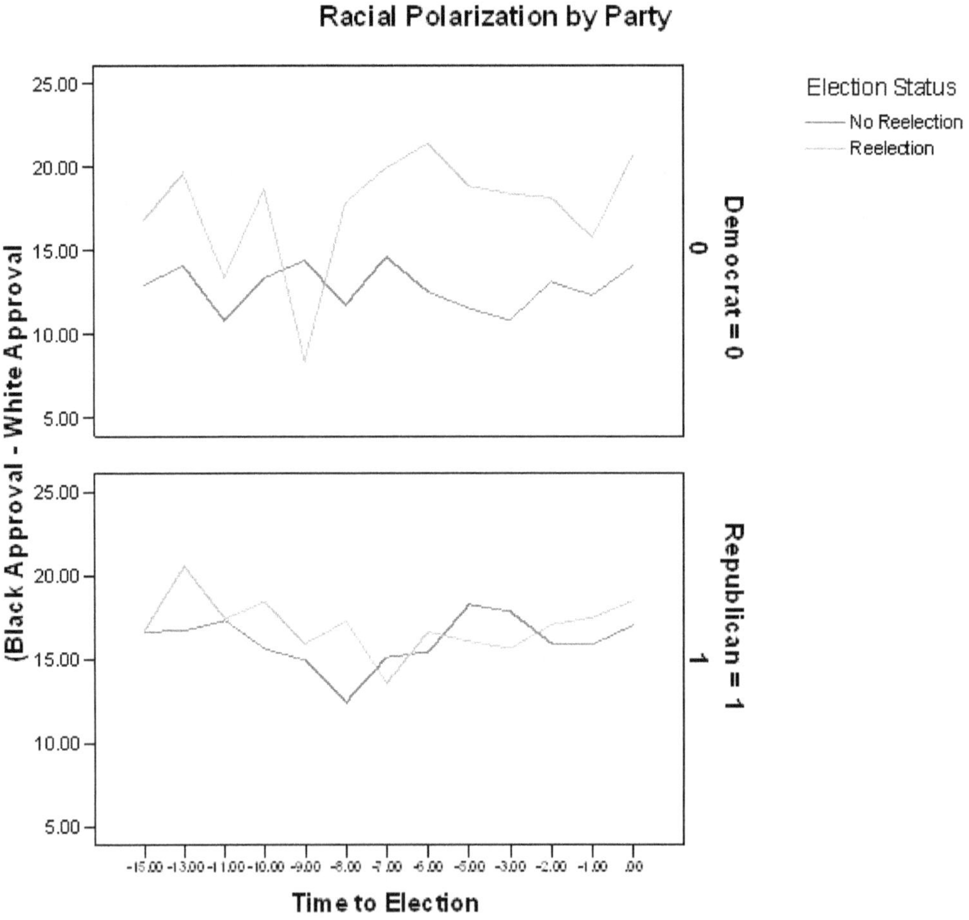

Racial Polarization by Party

hypotheses. Particularly, we contrast the campaign-based explanation from a rational explanation. A campaign-based explanation suggests that racial polarization grows as a direct result of campaigns. The campaign issues, themes, and intensity tend to polarize voters as the election draws close. Following this campaign explanation, a political racial cycle is evidence of a persisting cultural divide that limits prospects for biracial electoral coalitions. Kinder and Sears (1981) claim that a soft or symbolic racism exists which does not allow for overt expressions of racism, yet still has the effect of leading whites to oppose racial policy. A symbolic or soft racism in electoral campaigning may promote racial polarization as elections near and campaign intensity increases.

We argue that two variables would indicate evidence for this campaign-driven hypothesis. First, we hypothesize that campaign proximity promotes racial polarization. Voters are more likely to polarize along racial lines as Election Day gets closer. The *campaign proximity* variable takes the value of "1" for in-cycle senators (up for reelection) for the three months preceding the election and "0" otherwise.

A campaign-based explanation also would imply that campaign intensity positively relates to racial polarization. Candidates in very competitive races may choose campaign themes that intentionally mobilize black voters or white voters along party lines. Southern politics particularly provides anecdotal evidence of candidates supposedly promoting issues or campaign tag lines late in a campaign season intentionally to mobilize white or black voters. Following this campaign explanation, greater campaign intensity promotes racial polarization.

Senate challenger spending is our measure of this *campaign intensity* variable. One manifestation of challenger quality is spending. Westlye (1991) acknowledges challenger spending has merit because there is a strong assumption that campaign intensity is present when a challenger raises considerable money, especially when it is at least half that of the incumbent. Krasno (1994) concludes that challenger "quality" is a factor that most determines Senate election competitiveness. For this reason, our essay uses challenger spending as a proxy for *campaign intensity*.

Campaigns alone, though, may have little effect on increasing racially polarized electorates. A political racial cycle may be wholly a rational response by voters to cast votes according to incumbent actions. A rational explanation for the political-racial cycle implies that racial polarization is more pronounced when Senate incumbents have more ideologically extreme voting records. More partisan and ideological senators, along with a rational African-American electorate, may promote a political racial cycle. Surveys demonstrate a persisting racial divide along attitudes toward economic and racial conservatism, though less so on social issues (Pew Research Center, 2005). Blacks, regardless of income-level, are more likely than whites are to think that government has an active role in promoting economic security and racial justice.

Following a rational explanation, an ideologically divided black and white electorate becomes more polarized as reelection of an ideologically polarizing incumbent nears. An incumbent ideology variable, *DW-Folded*, is measured by taking the absolute value of a senator's first dimension DW-Nominate score. In successive models assessing black and white voters' approval, we include the Senate Republican and Democratic DW-Nominate scores separately to test senator ideology effects.

We include a second test of this rational explanation for racial polarization. As discussed earlier, the Bush administration's Iraq policy greatly affected 2006 campaigns. A variable is included for a senator's position on current Iraq policy. We construct an index measure ranging from -3 to 3 using three final Senate roll-call votes cast in the 109th Congress relating to the Bush administration's Iraq policy. Higher values denote opposition to current policy.

Senators may be more responsive to larger voting blocs within their reelection constituency. A *Black Vote Share* variable is measured by the percent of African Americans as a share of a state's voting age population. In the so-called "Black Belt" states—a roughly crescent-shaped region that sweeps from Virginia through Louisiana—African Americans currently represent between one-sixth and nearly one-third of the electorate. For Democrats, the black vote in southern states ranges from one-third to over half of the Democratic vote in competitive races. These southern states have higher rates of racial polarization given their histories, and in contemporary elections, racial polarization may play an important tactical value in mobilizing a winning electoral coalition.

We test these campaign, rational, and voting bloc size hypotheses using the SurveyUSA monthly tracking data of U.S. senator approval ratings leading up to the 2006 election. The dependent variable for the initial set of regressions is the absolute value of the margin between black and white approval for any senator in any state. We include a lag of the dependent variable as an independent variable to address autocorrelated errors in each time-series. The fixed effects model includes month and state dummy variables correcting for time and cross-sectional autocorrelation effects.

The first column of Table 1 reports the racial polarization regression results. These results indicate no support for campaign-based hypotheses of racial polarization. Neither campaign intensity nor the campaign proximity variable has a significant effect on racial polarization. The results do support the rational hypotheses of racial polarization, though. A senator's ideology (DW-Folded) and Iraq policy position both appear to relate significantly to rates of racial polarization.

We also evaluate whether these variables affect changes in black and white incumbent approval differently over the election cycle. The second and third columns in Table 1 show results with black approval and white approval ratings as the dependent variable, respectively. These results offer some insights into why overall racial polarization rates change. The black approval model indicates support for a rational explanation of political racial cycles. African American voters respond to incumbents' voting ideology. They are more likely to approve of liberal Democrats and disapprove of conservative Republicans in states with incumbent reelections. Interestingly, these results also indicate that challenger spending suppresses black and white incumbent approval.

Overall, while our results do not question the enduring racial divide in American national elections, they do provide some perspective. Notably, racial polarization appears not to be an intentional countering between black and white voters. As elections approach, African Americans largely respond to rational voting cues from incumbent senators. Black voters approve of incumbents in greater rates when the incumbent has a liberal voting record. Once controlling for incumbent ideology, we find that campaign proximity alone generally does not promote racial polarization. Furthermore, campaign intensity (as measured by challenger spending) reduced both black and white polarization during the 2006 election.

Table 1
Fixed Effects Model of Racial Polarization, Black and White Approval Among 2006 Senate Incumbents

	DV = Racial Polarization	DV = Black Approval	DV = White Approval
(Constant)	9.072**	29.333**	7.173**
	(1.511)	(2.266)	(1.035)
Campaign Proximity	1.167	1.758	.982*
	(1.513)	(1.971)	(.548)
All -- Black	-.044	.084**	.014
	(.031)	(.04)	(.011)
Opposition to Iraq Policy	-.382**	-1.448**	-.042
	(.145)	(.479)	(.132)
Challenger Intensity	.000	.005**	.007**
	(.000)	(.000)	(.000)
DW- Folded	-4.091**	---	---
	(1.897)	---	---
DW - Republican	---	-12.728**	-1.393**
	---	(2.551)	(.707)
DW - Democrat	---	-18.847**	.763
	---	(3.763)	(1.027)
Lag (Racial Polarization)	.435**	---	---
	(.027)	---	---
Lag (Black Approval)	---	.356**	---
	---	(.027)	---
Lag (White Approval)	---	---	.878**
	---	---	(.015)
F	18.837	26.735	236.413
Sig.	.000	.000	.000

Entries represent unstandardized coefficients. Standard errors in parentheses.
* $p < .1$; ** $p < .05$

Discussion

This essay seeks to understand better the puzzle of contemporary racial polarization. In the 2006 U.S. Senate elections, we found evidence of a political racial cycle even when there was no demonstrable evidence that race played a major role as a campaign issue. In actuality, the war in Iraq and an unpopular president dominated the election. We proposed several potential explanations to understand this puzzle of political racial cycles.

Our empirical evidence indicates that black voters rationally respond to ideological polarization among Senate incumbents as elections approach. We find that black approval drops significantly for more conservative Republican senators and more moderate Senate Democrats. Like Shaw (1997), we find no trend for black voters away from the Democratic Party. Our findings also support Glaser's (1995) conclusions that black voters are relatively politically sophisticated. There is a distinction between black approval of Republican incumbent job performance and actually voting for that Republican. Still, black voters' job approval rationally declines as incumbents cast more conservative votes.

Dawson (1994) provides perhaps the most relevant long-term explanations. First, perceptions of a political party's responsiveness to the black community drive black partisanship. Blacks do not believe the Republican Party works hard on their issues while believing the opposite about the Democratic Party. The implications are such that even if "black" issues are not paramount in any given campaign, the assumption made by black voters is that Democrats, not Republicans will support their issues. Second, group solidarity characterizes African American voting behavior and group interests are the chief concern for black voters. Our analysis shows that as elections approach, partisan cues draw in black voters.

Fauntroy (2006) notes the wide divide between partisanship and ideology. What keeps blacks from forming a lasting identification with the GOP is that Republican ideology is too far to the right for the vast majority of American blacks. Only a relative few can countenance Republican policy to the point that they will actually vote Republican, which is what these results show. Our results show that blacks will abide Republican incumbents, but not routinely vote for them. Utilizing a Downsian perspective, Dawson (1994) suggests that the two-party system does not provide blacks with meaningful choices and the Democratic Party becomes the de facto black political party. This line of reasoning is consistent with a rational approach to partisanship. As elections become more proximate, black partisanship takes over the collective black voting calculus.

Finally, the GOP finds itself in a dilemma with itself (Fauntroy, 2006). If it actually seeks black votes by moderating its social policies, it risks losing certain conservative voters. Yet, seeking black votes with rhetoric only and no substantive policy overtures to black voters equates to little black support at the ballot box. These results counter Fiorina's (2005) finding that polarization is largely limited to political elites. We find that sharp distinctions between partisan, ideological, and racial groups grow as elections approach. The implications are that electoral polarization is hardening partisanship for core Democrats and core Republicans. As blacks are core Democratic partisans, we should expect racial polarization.

References

Abbe, Owen, Jay Goodliffe, Paul Herrnson, and Kelly Patterson. 2003. "Agenda Setting in Congressional Elections: The Impact of Issues and Campaigns on Voting Behavior." *Political Research Quarterly* 56: 419-430.

Abrajano, Marisa A., Jonathan Nagler and R. Michael Alvarez. 2005. "A Natural Experiment of Race-Based and Issue Voting: The 2001 City of Los Angeles Elections." *Political Research Quarterly* 58: 203-218.

Abramowitz, Alan. 1994. "Issue Evolution Reconsidered: Racial Attitudes and Partisanship in the U.S. Electorate." *American Journal of Political Science* 38: 1-24.

Abramowitz, Alan. 1995. "It's Abortion, Stupid: Policy Voting in the 1992 Presidential Election." *Journal of Politics* 176-186.

Abramowitz, Alan and Kyle Saunders. 1998. "Ideological Realignment in the U.S. Electorate." *Journal of Politics* 60: 634-652.

Abramowitz, Alan and Kyle Saunders. 2005. *Why Can't We All Just Get Along? The Reality of a Polarized America.* Manuscript.

Abramowitz, Alan and Walter Stone. 2006. "The Bush Effect: Polarization, Turnout, and Activism in the 2004 Presidential Election." *Presidential Studies Quarterly* 36: 141-154.

Abramson, Paul, John Aldrich, and David Rohde. 1994. *Change and Continuity in the 1992 Elections.* Washington, DC: CQ Press.

Adams, Greg. 1997. "Abortion: Evidence of an Issue Evolution." *American Journal of Political Science* 41: 718-737.

Ansolabehere, Stephen, James Snyder, Aaron Strauss, and Michel Ting. 2005. "Voting Weights and Formateur Advantages in the Formation of Coalition Governments." *American Journal of Political Science* 49: 550-563.

Bartels, Larry. 2000. "Partisanship and Voting Behavior, 1952-1996." *American Journal of Political Science* 44: 35-50.

Bernhardt, Dan, Stefan Krasa and Mattias Polborn. 2006. *Political Polarization and the Electoral Effects of Media Bias.* Manuscript.

Bowler, Shaun, Stephen Nicholson, and Gary Segura. 2006. "Earthquakes and Aftershocks: Race, Direct Democracy, and Partisan Change." *American Journal of Political Science* 50: 146-159.

Brewer, Mark and Jeffrey Stonecash. 2001. "Class, Race Issues, and Declining White Support for the Democratic Party in the South." *Political Behavior* 131-155.

Brewer, Mark and Jeffrey Stonecash. 2007. *Split: Class and Cultural Divides in American Politics.* Washington, DC: CQ Press.

Campbell, Angus, Philip Converse, Warren Miller and Donald Stokes. 1964. *The American Voter.* New York: Wiley.

Carmines, Edward G. and James A. Stimson. 1980. "The Two Faces of Issue Voting." *American Political Science Review* 74: 78-91.

Carmines, Edward G. and James A. Stimson. 1989. *Issue Evolution: Race and the Transformation of American Politics.* Princeton, NJ: Princeton University Press.

Dalager, John. 1996. "Voters, Issues, and Elections: Are the Candidates' Messages Getting Through? *Journal of Politics* 58: 486-515.

Dawson, Michael. 1994. *Behind the Mule: Race and Class in African-American Politics.* Princeton, NJ: Princeton University Press.

DiMaggio, Paul, John Evans, and Bethany Bryson. 1996. "Have America's Social Attitudes Become More Polarized?" *American Journal of Sociology* 102: 690-755.

Evans, John. 2003. "Have Americans' Attitudes Become More Polarized?—An Update." *Social Science Quarterly* 84: 71-90.

Fauntroy, Michael. 2007. *Republicans and the Black Vote.* Boulder, CO: Lynne Reinner.

Fiorina, Morris P, with Samuel J. Abrams and Jeremy C. Pope. 2005. *Culture War? The Myth of a Polarized America.* New York: Pearson Longman.

Franklin, Charles H. 1993. "Senate Incumbent Visibility over the Election Cycle." *Legislative Studies Quarterly* 18: 271-290.

Glaser, James M. 1995. "Black and White Perceptions of Party Differences." *Political Behavior* 17: 155-177.

Greenberg, Stanley. 2004. *The Two Americas: Our Current Political Deadlock and How to Break It.* New York: St. Martin's Press.

Hetherington, Marc. 2001. "Resurgent Mass Partisanship: The Role of Elite Polarization." *American Political Science Review* 95: 619-631.

Jacobson, Gary. 2006. *A Divider, Not a Uniter: George W. Bush and the American People.* New York: Pearson.

Joslyn, Mark. and Donald Haiden-Markel. 2000. "Guns in the Ballot Box: Information, Groups, and Opinion in Ballot Initiative Campaigns." *American Politics Quarterly* 28: 355-378.

Kaufmann, Karen. 2002. "Culture Wars, Secular Realignment, and the Gender Gap in Party Identification." *Political Behavior* 24: 283-307.

Kinder, Donald and David Sears. 1981. "Symbolic Racism Versus Racial Threats to 'The Good Life.'" *Journal of Personality and Social Psychology.*

Kohut, Andrew. 2006. "The Real Message of the Midterms." Pew Research Center.

Layman, Geoffrey C. 1999. "Culture Wars' in the American Party System: Religious and Cultural Change Among Partisan Activists Since 1972."*American Politics Quarterly* 27: 89-121.

Layman, Geoffrey C. and Thomas M. Carsey 2000. "Ideological Realignment in Contemporary American Politics: The Case of Party Activists." Presented at the Annual Meeting of the Midwest Political Science Association, Chicago.

Layman, Geoffrey C. and Thomas M. Carsey. 2002. "Party Polarization and Party Structuring of Policy Attitudes: A Comparison of Three NES Panel Studies." *Political Behavior* 24: 199-236.

Lindaman, Kara and Donald P. Haiden-Markel. 2002. "Issue Evolution, Political Parties, and the Culture Wars." *Political Research Quarterly* 55: 91-110.

Miller, Warren. 1981. Policy directions and presidential leadership: alternative interpretations of the 1980 presidential election. Paper presented at the Annual Meeting of the American Political Science Association.

Nadeau, Richard and Harold Stanley. 1993. "Class Polarization in Partisanship among Native Southern Whites, 1952-90." *American Journal of Political Science* 37: 900-919.

Shaw, Daron R. 1997. "Estimating Racially Polarized Voting: A View from the States." *Political Research Quarterly* 50: 49-74.

Sinclair, Barbara. 2002. "The Dream Fulfilled? Party Development in Congress, 1950-2000." In John C. Green and Paul S. Herrnson, eds., *Responsible Partisanship? The Evolution of American Parties Since 1950*, 121-140. Lawrence, KS: University Press of Kansas.

Sniderman, Paul, James Glaser and Robert Griffin. 1991. "Information and Electoral Choice." In *Reasoning and Choice: Explorations in Political Psychology*, eds., Paul Sniderman, Richard Brody, and Philip Tetlock. Cambridge, UK: Cambridge University Press.

Stokes, Donald. 1966. "Some Dynamic Elements of Contests for the Presidency." *American Political Science Review* 60: 19-28.

Stonecash, Jeffrey. 2006. "The Income Gap." *PS: Political Science and Politics* 39: 461-465.

Streb, Matthew J. 2002. *The New Electoral Politics of Race.* Tuscaloosa, AL: University of Alabama Press.

Valentino, Nicholas and David O. Sears. 2005. "Old Times There Are Not Forgotten: Race and Partisan Realignment in the Contemporary South." *American Journal of Political Science* 49: 672-688.

Zaller, John R. 1992. *The Nature and Origins of Mass Opinion.* New York: Cambridge University Press.

The Early Electoral Contests of Senator Barack Obama: A Longitudinal Analysis

Hanes Walton, Jr.
University of Michigan

Robert C. Starks
Northeastern Illinois University

On November 2, 2004, the state of Illinois once again made political history by sending the second of two most recent African Americans to the United States Senate. When Senator Barack Obama arrived, Illinois matched Mississippi as the only two states in the Union to have sent two African Americans to the Senate. Mississippi sent two African Americans in the Reconstruction Era, 1868-1880, while Illinois has sent two during the twentieth and twenty-first centuries. Louisiana and Massachusetts are the only other states to have sent an African American to the Senate (one each).

However, what is unique and different about Illinois is that it has sent one African American female and one African American male and both came in the period, 1992-2004. Until 1913, U.S. senators were elected by state legislatures. With the ratification of the 17th Amendment to the Constitution on April 8, 1913, candidates for the Senate had to run statewide and be elected by the popular vote of the people in each state.[1]

Besides, Illinois, only Massachusetts has popularly elected an African American to this body, Senator Edward Brooke in 1966 and 1972.[2] Again, the difference here is that both of Illinois' African American senators have been Democrats, while all of the others, including Senator Brooke, have been Republicans.[3] In fact, four of the six that have been sent to the Senate were Republicans. Hence, Illinois and only Illinois have sent the two African American Democrats.[4]

The uniqueness here is not simply the state of Illinois. The candidate is also unique. He is an African American with a Kenyan father and a white mother from Kansas.[5] He is unique not only because of his racial background, but also in terms of his electoral career. Unlike all of the other previously elected African American senators, Senator Obama comes out of the Illinois State Senate, whereas his predecessors, Senator Moseley-Braun, came out of the Illinois State House and Cook County Recorder of Deeds Offices and Senator Brooke who was a two-term elected attorney general from Massachusetts, Senator Obama had been elected for his third term to the State Senate representing the 13th Senate District from the city of Chicago. Thus, it is his electoral contests in this district and others that is the subject and focus of this chapter.

Data and Methodology

Just prior graduating from college in 1983, Senator Obama writes in his autobiography that he "decided to become a community organizer."[6] So, "I wrote to every civil rights organization I could think of, to any black elected official in the country with a progressive agenda, to neighborhood councils and tenant rights groups. When only one wrote back... I decided to find more conventional work for a year."[7] And after the passage of some time, "a consulting house to multinational corporations agreed to hire me as research assistant."[8] However, within a few months he turned in his resignation at the consulting firm and began looking in earnest for an organizing job. Once again offers were slow to come in but the college graduate got a job offer from a prominent civil rights organization in New York City.[9] During the job interview, the director of the organization offered him a job, "which involved organizing conferences on drugs, unemployment, housing" and working with the Republican Cabinet secretary at the Department of Housing and Urban Development in Washington, DC. The young college graduate declined the job because he "needed a job closer to the streets."[10]

While waiting on other organizing job offers to surface, Obama "spent three months working for a Ralph Nader offshoot up in Harlem. Then a week passing out flyers for an assemblyman's race in Brooklyn (the candidate lost and Barack never got paid).[11] Eventually, a call came from the head of the Calumet Community Religious Conference (CCRC), an organization of more than twenty suburban churches in Chicago, that Marty Kaufman would be in New York the following week to interview Obama.[12] Wanting to hire a trainee for their new city organizing drive, the job was offered on the spot, and Obama within a week moved to Chicago.

Arriving in Chicago during the historic election of African American mayor Harold Washington in 1983, he would leave his community organizing position a year after Washington's reelection and death, in 1988 to attend Harvard law School. Obama's father had attended the graduate school there in 1963 upon his graduation from the University of Hawaii.[13]

When Obama graduated in 1991, he went back to Chicago and by 1992 he "directed Illinois Project Vote, which registered 150,090 new voters." Thus, here were the beginnings, initially a community organizer in the South Side of Chicago and then a statewide voter registration organizer and activist.

Then it happened. "When a seat in the state legislature opened up in 1996, some friends persuaded me to run for office, and I won," wrote Obama. Table 1 offers a comprehensive and systematic portrait of the different electoral contests that Senator Obama was involved in prior to his winning his senate seat. Overall, Senator Obama has run in five primary elections, four general elections, for a total of nine elections. Of these nine elections, he won eight of them and lost one.

As to the offices, he has run in six elections for the Illinois State Senate winning all of them, one election for a congressional seat in the House of Representatives, which he lost, and two elections for the United States Senate, both of which he won. As to his congressional race, he ran for it while he was in the Illinois State Senate due to the fact that election laws in Illinois do not prohibit one from holding one elected position and simultaneously running for another. In that race he took on an eight-year incumbent.

Table 1
The Categories and Types of Elections Contested by Barack Obama: 1996–2004

Year	Primary Elections	Number Elections	Total	Results
State Senate Races				
1996	X	X	2	Won
1998	X	X	1	Won
2002	X	X	0	Won
U.S. Congressional Race				
2000	X	-	3	Lost
U.S. Senate Races				
2004	X	X	20	Won
Grand Total	5	4	26	8 Wins/1 Lost

Source: Adapted from the State Board of Elections, Official Vote, Primary Election General Primary March 17, 1992–2004 and Official Vote General Election, November 3, 1992–2004.

Table 2 indicates the number of opponents that Senator Obama faced in his primary and general elections during his entire electoral career. There were no opponents in his state senate primaries, three opponents in his congressional House of Representative race and seven opponents in his United States Senate race. All total, he has had some ten opponents in his primary races.

In his general election contests, Senator Obama faced opponents in two of his three state senate races. Only in his last general election contest, 2002, did he not have any opponents. As for his congressional general election, he lost in the primary election and therefore did not proceed to that general election. His three opponents in this race appeared in the primary. However, in the Senate races, both at the primary and general election ones he had more opposition than in all of his other contests combined. Seven opponents in the primary and a whopping thirteen in the general election. In fact, in these two races, he had twenty opponents compared to only six in all of his other contests.

Therefore, the data for this study will be the election return data for all nine of his elections and similar data for all of his opponents in these elections. This official data will permit the study to develop a comprehensive portrait of the electoral trends, patterns and tendencies in his support. In addition, it will be able to follow the nature and scope of his electoral coalitions through these nine elections.

At this point, a word has to be said about the methodology, which is used to assess and evaluate the electoral trends, patterns, and tendencies as well as the coalitions over time. Both descriptive and probability statistics will be employed to produce empirical analyses of these nine elections, so that both a description of these electoral contests can be had as well as an explanation about how the victories and loses were attained. And from our findings, this case study hopes to generate several testable propositions to be

Table 2
The Number of Opponents Faced by Barack Obama in Primary and General Elections: 1996–2004

Year	Number of Primary Election Opponents	Number of General Election Opponents	Total
State Senate Races			
1996	0	2	2
1998	0	1	1
2002	0	0	0
U.S. Congressional Race			
2000	3	NA	3
U.S. Senate Races			
2004	7	13	20
Grand Total	10	16	26

Source: Adapted from the State Board of Elections, Official Vote, Primary Election General Primary March 17, 1992–2004 and Official Vote General Election, November 3, 1992–2004.

used in other studies that hopefully will emerge in the future. Such empirical insights will go a long ways in helping students and scholars to understand African American Senate elections given the current dearth of academic and scholarly information on this aspect of African American politics.[14]

The Political Context: Voter Turnout in Illinois

Chicago has always been a successful city for the rise and growth of African American politicos. Political Scientists Harold Gosnell writes: "as far back as 1876, when the colored people comprised only 1 percent of the total population of the city, one of them, John W. E. Thomas, was sent as their representative to the capitol at Springfield by the Republican voters of the Second Senatorial District of Chicago."[15] After making this remark, Gosnell continues with the observation that "Representative Thomas was not reelected until 1882, but after that date there has never been a session of the Illinois General Assembly, which has lacked a colored representative."[16]

After the arrival of these state legislators came the first African American congressman from the state, in 1928. This was not only a major political breakthrough, but it also shocked the nation, and particularly the South, simply because the last African American in Congress (who just happened to be from the South) was eliminated by the region-wide disenfranchisement in 1901.[17] This African American congressman, Oscar DePriest, was a Republican. Two years into the New Deal, in 1934, African American voters in the South Side of Chicago replaced him with a Democrat, Arthur W. Mitchell, and this election greatly disturbed the southern white party elites.[18] But the rise of African American politicos did not stop there.

In 1983, African Americans and their electoral coalition allies elected an African American mayor, Harold Washington.[19] Four years later they reelected him, but he died shortly thereafter. The next major political breakthrough was the election of an African American female to the United States Senate in 1992, followed by Senator Obama's election in 2004. Thus, it can simply be said that up to this point no other state or city has matched the political achievements of this state and in the city of Chicago.

Besides having a politically active African American population and strategic acting politicians, the political landscape in Illinois is unique in that electoral power in the state is highly concentrated and located predominately in a single county. Political scientists in studying this unusual electoral phenomenon have written: "With the decline of the rural population, it is no surprise that the voter-rich areas in Illinois are clustered mainly in the state's northeast corner. Both parties must begin any serious political campaign by focusing on this small geographic area where the vast majority of people live."[20] They continue by noting, "Democrats have the same kind of advantage in Illinois that they have in New York. Fifty percent of the statewide Democratic vote for president typically originated from Cook County (especially Chicago)."[21]

Having made these insights about the geographic concentration of Illinois's population and voting electorate, they focus upon Chicago and add: "Chicago remains the Democratic stronghold that it has been for decades. Its population has become more diverse as upwardly mobile whites have fled and blacks and Hispanics have moved in... African Americans and Latinos are now core Democratic constituencies.... White ethnics control fewer of the city's wards, and white politicians are dependent upon the nonwhite vote to an extent never before seen in history." Thus, Chicago and the African American electorate are central to a political party's victory in both statewide and national elections.

Beyond Cook County but including it, Table 3 lists the counties that form the electoral bases for each of the major parties in the state, as well as the total percentage of the party

Table 3
Illinois's Top Ten Strongest Counties for Republicans and Democrats in the 1988–2000 Presidential Contests

Rank	Democratic	Republican
1	Cook (Chicago)	Cook (Chicago)
2	DuPage (Wheaton)	DuPage (Wheaton)
3	Lake (Waukegan)	Lake (Waukegan)
4	St. Clair (East St. Louis)	Will (Joliet)
5	Madison (Granite Cite-Alton)	Kane (Elgin)
6	Will (Joliet)	McHenry (Crystal Lake)
7	Winnebago (Rockford)	Sangamon (Springfield)
8	Rock Island (Rock Island)	Winnebago (Rockford)
9	Peoria (Peoria)	Madison (Granite City-Alton)
10	Kane (Elgin)	McLean (Bloomington)
Percentage of Total Vote	73.5	66.1

Source: James Gimpel and Jason Schuknecht Patchwork Nation: Sectionalism and Political Change in America Politics (Ann Arbor: University of Michigan Press, 2003), p. 355.

vote that is derived from these ten counties. Thus, while Illinois is essential a competitive two-party state, voter turnout can help to ensure victory for either of the parties in statewide and national elections. From the table it is clear that the Democratic Party has an electoral edge over the Republicans in the densely populated areas of the state.

Figure 1 furnishes us with the degree of voter turnout for the entire state over time. Not only is turnout greater in general elections that in primary elections, other extant data reveals that Democrats in the time period in Figure 1 had turned out in larger numbers than Republicans, giving the party the advantage that it now has in Illinois politics. This type of turnout clearly laid the electoral foundation for the state senate and U.S. Senate victories that Senator Obama achieved in his elections. He never had to worry about turnout in his state senate primary elections because he never had any primary opposition. He did face opposition in his House of Representatives race and U.S. Senate races, but even then he chose to run in presidential years, 2000 and 2004, when turnout was always higher than in mid-term election years.

The State Senate Electoral Contests of Barack Obama: 1996, 1998, and 2002

In 1996, the long-term incumbent in the 13th State Senate District, Alice Palmer, asked attorney and voter registration activist Barack Obama to run for her seat. Not only did he agree, he entered the Democratic state primary on March 17, 1996. No one qualified to run against him. With no opponents in the state senate primaries, he won each time the Democratic Party's nomination.

Figure 1
Voter Turnout in the Primary and General Elections in Illinois: 1982-2004

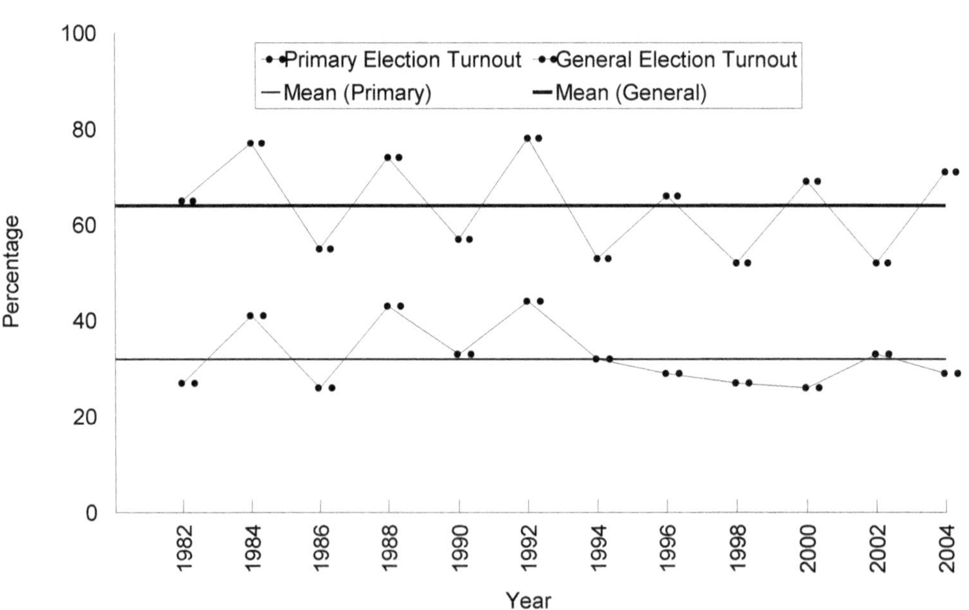

Source: Adapted from the State Board of Elections, *Official Vote, Primary Election, General Primary March 17, 1992-2004 and Official Vote, General Election, November 3, 1992-2004.*

Primary opposition might not have surfaced, but he did face general election opponents in two of his three general election contests. Yet, in each of those elections, he captured a mean percentage of 85.7 percent. In his last state senate general election in 2002 he had no opponents.

Table 4 provides both the votes and the percentages, which Obama received in each of his primary and general election contests in the 13th State Senate District in Illinois. Although he received 100 percent of the primary vote each time, his total primary votes did not change much. For the first two elections they remained about the same C the mean vote was 16,536 C but in 2002 his vote total nearly double reaching a high of 30,938 votes.

However, there is a degree of similarity in the total vote count for Obama between the primary and general election. Although his general election vote total is three times as high as his primary vote total, the difference here is that the general election vote total is quite stable over all three elections. The range of his vote total runs from a high of 48,717 in this third election in 2002 to a low of 45,486 in his second election in 1998. Surprisingly, his middle level vote total of 48,592 votes came in his initial general election in 1996. But that year, he faced two opponents a Republican and a third-party candidate. By the time of his second state senate election, he only faced a Republican candidate. Thus, Obama means general election vote was 47,498.3 votes, while the mean vote for his Republican opposition was 6,494 votes.

Overall, with no primary opposition and the opposition in the general election garnering only a mean vote of 9.5 percent, Obama state senate contests were essentially a Democratic affair. The African American vote for African American Republican candidates in the South Side of Chicago has been a minuscule vote because this electorate has been aligned with the Democratic Party since 1934. Hence, winning the vote of African American Democrats nearly ensures victory at least at the ward, precinct, state, legislative and senatorial and some congressional districts levels.[22] All that Obama needed in these state senate electoral contests was a good turnout to win.

The Congressional Electoral Contest of Barack Obama: 2000

In 1998 when Obama was reelected to the Illinois Senate, he was elected to a four-year term. But two years into the four-year term, Obama decided to run for the 1st Congressional District seat held by long-time incumbent Bobby Rush of the Black Panther Party notoriety. This seat had been held by numerous political notables in the Windy City such as William Dawson, Ralph Metcalfe, Bennett Stewart, Harold Washington, and Charles Hayes.[23] Congressman Rush had initially won the seat in 1992 and had won reelection three times before the 2000 elections. Literally Rush had been in Congress some eight years. Thus, unlike his state senate elections where he faced no opposition in the Democratic primaries, this time Obama would face a seasoned incumbent as well as two other major challengers.

Shown in Table 5 are the results for the four candidates in the 2000 Illinois First Congressional District race. Under Illinois's election laws, a candidate may hold an elected office and run for another one at the same time. However, even with two successful electoral contests behind him, State Senator Obama suffered his first election defeat. The four-term incumbent Congressman Rush soundly defeated this newcomer by capturing almost two-thirds (62.5 percent) of the total vote cast. State Senator Obama came in second

Table 4
The Votes and Percentages in the 13th Illinois State Senate District for Candidate Barack Obama: 1996–2002

Year	Candidate	Primary Election Vote	Primary Election Percentage	Candidate	General Election Vote	General Election Percentage
1996	B. Obama	16,279	100	B. Obama	48,592	82.2
				D. Whitehead	7,461	12.6
				R. Peyton	3,091	5.2
					59,144	100.1
1998	B. Obama	16,792	100	B. Obama	45,486	89.2
				Y.B. YattuDah	5,526	10.8
					51,012	100.0
2002	B. Obama	30,938	100	B. Obama	48,717	100.0

Source: Adapted from State Board of Elections, *Official Vote Primary Elections General Primary, March 17, 1996–2002 and Official Vote General Elections, November, 1996–2002.*

with less than one-third (29.2 percent) of the vote cast. The rest of the opposition in the 2000 race captured less than a tenth (8.4 percent) of the vote. In fact, even if the Obama vote is combined with that of the other two challengers, it would still be significantly less than the vote that the incumbent received.

Although this was a presidential election year when turnout is highest, and that Obama's mean primary vote up to this point was 16,536 and that he increased it by 10,885 it was still less than half of the incumbent Congressman Rush's vote. The incumbent beat Obama by 31,351 votes. In fact, had Illinois been a state with a runoff primary and it is not, Obama would have still lost the primary simply because the incumbent won a clear-cut majority. Thus, the very best that can be said of State Senator Obama performance is that he significantly increased his electoral base in the city of Chicago and his political exposure. He increased his name recognition among the Cook County Democratic electorate. And this increase base of support shows up two years later when he runs for reelection to his state senate seat when he captures some 30,938 votes. This was 14,402 votes beyond his primary mean and 3,517 votes beyond his congressional primary totals. In sum, State Senator Obama foray into a congressional election contest and his subsequent State Senate reelection proved that he was able to attract a larger electoral group of supporters in a relative short period of time.

The U.S. Senatorial Contests of Barack Obama: 2004

Four years after his first attempt to represent the people of Illinois in Congress and two years after his reelection to the State Senate, Obama announced for the open U.S. Senate seat in the state. Prior to his announcement, an African American female Carol Moseley-Braun had won a U.S. Senate seat in 1992 but lost it in her reelection bid in 1998,[24] the same year that Obama won his first reelection to the State Senate. Thus, six years after an African American U.S. senator had lost her seat, another African American was making a bid for it.

Former Senator Moseley-Braun was now an announced candidate for the Democratic Party's nomination for president. She made the announcement shortly after New York civil rights activist Al Sharpton had announced that he was running for the Democratic Party's nomination for president.[25] Despite these unique contextual features surrounding this senatorial primary, there was the matter of the open seat election itself, which would attract numerous candidates. This is usually the case when no incumbent is involved.

Therefore what one sees in Table 6 in the Democratic primary is a total of some eight different candidates that attracts about 1.2 million voters to the polls. Besides State Senator Obama, this open-seat race also attracted another African American candidate, Joyce Washington that had just come off in 2002 a race for the lieutenant governorship. Said race had proven to this candidate that she could build a statewide electoral coalition even if she had never held elective office before.

Yet in spite of this unique electoral context, State Senator Obama won the Democratic primary going away. He captured a majority of the vote, 52.8 percent and this was double his second-place opponent, Hayes who won only 23.7 percent of the total vote cast. The other African American in the race, Washington, won only one percent of the total vote cast.

In terms of votes, State Senator Obama captured more than 600,000 votes of the 1,242,996 total votes cast. To this date, this was Obama's best primary showing in his

Table 5
The Vote and Percentage in the 1st Congressional District Democratic Primary: 2000

Year	Candidate	Primary Election Vote	Primary Election Percentage
2000	Bobby Rush	58,772	62.5
	Barack Obama	27,421	29.2
	Donne E. Trother	6,590	7.0
	George C. Roby	1,296	1.4
	Total	94,079	100.1

Source: Adapted from State Board of Elections, *Official Vote, Primary Election General Primary, March 27, 2000.*

entire electoral career.[26] Having won his election, Obama would go on to represent the Democratic Party in the November 2, general election.

But before the general election occurred, the Republican party nominee, Jack Ryan, became involved in a sex scandal with his movie star wife, Jeri Ryan, and withdrew from the Senate race. In order not to let this seat go unchallenged, the Republican party at this late date asked a number of other well known personalities in the state to accept the party's nomination, but all refused. Then, the party went out of state and asked two-time African American Senate candidate from Maryland and two-time Republican presidential candidate Alan Keyes to come to Illinois and run against Democratic party nominee Obama.[27] He accepted while vigorously denying that he was a carpetbagger.

Once again Table 6 shows that in this general election contest, Obama captured nearly three-fourths (70 percent) of the total vote cast, while Keyes won less than one-third (27.15 percent) of the total vote. The other five candidates won less than three percent (2.9 percent) of the total vote. Clearly, Obama seriously defeated the carpetbagger from Maryland, who had only a token electoral base in the state from his previous participation in the Republican presidential primaries in the state. While this performance was greater than both of his previous runs as demonstrated in Table 7 it surely was not enough to be competitive and/or defeat the hometown boy. It was an embarrassing defeat for Keyes and an immediately step up for Senator-elect Obama who was now being touted as a national candidate as a possible future vice-presidential nominee.[28] The best that the data in Table 7 indicates about Keyes is that the voters in Illinois were much more willing to vote for him for senator than for president. In fact, they were a lot more willing.

Conclusions: Testable Propositions from a Case-Study

Figure 2 provides a longitudinal look at the level of voter support for Obama in both his primary and general elections in Illinois over his electoral career. This figure starts off with the primary vote for African American incumbent State Senator Alice Palmer in 1992 before she gave up her seat to Obama and shows his percentage where he had no opposition in the primaries with the years of 2000 and 2004 where he did have opposition in the primaries. The mean primary vote for Obama stands at 77.5 percent.

Again the starting percentage is that for incumbent Palmer but drops as soon as Obama began his general election contest. Of the four general election contests, Obama has had

Table 6
The Vote and Percentage in the 2004 Illinois U.S. Senate Race for Candidate Barack Obama: Primary and General Elections

Year	Candidate	Votes	%
	Primary Election		
2004	B. Obama	655,923	52.8
	D. Haynes	294,717	23.7
	M.B. Hull	134,453	10.8
	M. Pappas	74,987	6.0
	G. Chico	53,433	4.3
	N. Skinna	16,098	1.3
	J. Washington	13,375	1.1
	E.J. Hunt	10	0.0
	Total	1,242,996	100.0
	General Election		
	B. Obama	3,597,456	70.0
	A. Keyes	1,390,690	27.1
	A. Franzer	81,164	1.6
	J. Kohn	69,253	1.4
	M. Kuhnke	2,268	0.04
	S. Doody	339	0.0
	Others	350	0.0
	Total	5,141,520	100.1

Source: Adapted from the State Board of Elections, Official Vote Primary Election General Primary, March 11, 2004, p. 8 and Official Vote General Election November 3, 2004, p. 17.

opposition in three of them and his mean general election vote is 88.2 percent. This indicates that of the two categories across time, Obama has performed better in the general elections than in the primaries and this is due essentially to his loss in the 2000 congressional primary. His vote percentage in this election was by far and away significantly below his primary mean.

When comparing his performance in the 2004 election to that of the African American presidential candidates, Moseley-Braun and Al Sharpton, and senatorial candidate Joyce Washington as seen in Table 8, it appears that the state's electorate liked Obama far better than they liked all of the other African American candidates combined. In fact, these candidates barely garnered any support from the electorate, including the African American electorate. They failed to increase the turnout in the state, much less any serious electoral coalition. Simply put, they made quite a poor showing. In the case of former Senator Moseley-Braun, this could be credited to the fact that she withdrew from the race even

Table 7
The Vote and Percentage for Alan Keyes's Presidential and Senatorial Races in Illinois: 1996–2004

Year	Vote	Percentage	Office
1996	30,052	3.7	President
2000	66,066	9.0	President
2004	1,390,690	27.1	Senate

Source: Adapted from Richard Scammon, Alice McGillivray and Rhodes Cook (eds.) *America Votes 22*, (Washington, D.C.: Congressional Quarterly, 1996) p. 58; Richard Scammon, Alice McGillivray and Rhodes Cook (eds.) *America Votes 24* (Washington, D.C.: Congressional Quarterly, 2000), p. 37 and 42; and Illinois State Board of Elections, *Official Vote, Primary Election, General Primary* (March 16, 2004), pp. 1 and 8.

Table 8
The Vote and Percentage for African American Presidential and Senatorial Candidates in Illinois's Primary Election: 2004

Office	Candidate	Vote	Percentage
Senate	B. Obama	655,923	5.8
President	C. Moseley-Braun	53,249	4.4
President	A. Sharpton	36,123	3.0
Senate	J. Washington	13,375	1.1

Source: Illinois State Board of Education, *Official Vote Primary Election, General Primary, March 16, 2004*, p. 8 and Illinois State Board of Election, *Official Vote, General Election, November 2, 2004*, p. 17.

Table 9
Comparison of the Democratic and Republican Vote and Percentage for the Presidential and Senatorial Candidates in Illinois: 2004

Office	Candidate	Vote	Percentage
	Democratic Party		
Senator	B. Obama	3,597,456	69.97
President	J. Kerry	2,891,550	58.82
	Differences	+705,906	+15.15
	Republican Party		
President	G. Bush	2,345,946	44.48
Senator	A. Keyes	1,390,690	27.05
	Differences	-995,256	-17.43

Source: Adapted from Illinois State Board of Elections: Official Vote, General Election November 2, 2004, pp. 1–28.

Figure 2
The Percentage of the Vote Cast in the Illinois's 13th State Senate District for Candidate Barack Obama in the Primary and General Elections: 1992-2004

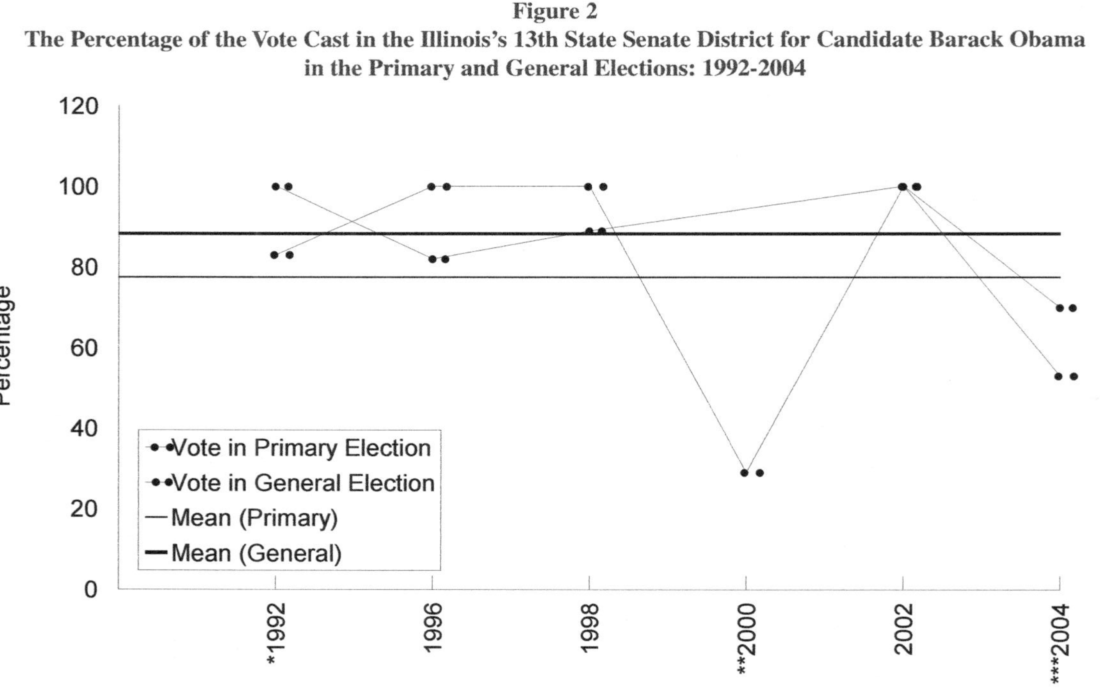

Source: Adapted from the State Board of Elections, Official Vote, Primary Election, General Primary March 17, 1992-2004 and Official Vote, General Election, November 3, 1992-2004.
* = Candidate is the incumbent African American Alice J. Palmer.
** = Year that State Senator Obama ran for the House of Representative Seat, in Congressional District.
*** = Year that State Senator Obama just ran for the United States Senate Seat.

before the Iowa Caucus and the New Hampshire presidential primary took place. Thus, those individuals who voted for her were voters who simply wanted to remain loyal to her in spite of the fact that she was no longer running. And even though she had withdrawn, she still got more votes than the Reverend Al Sharpton.

Therefore, in the final analysis, it was not so much the uniqueness of the political context as much as it was the political accident that emerged before the general election in which the main Republican nominee had to quit the race and a carpetbagger without roots in the state became the major party challenger. This last-minute replacement had no time to build a successful electoral coalition in the state that could rival that of Obama. Hence, he went down to a great defeat.

Moreover, when one compares Obama's senate victory with the presidential outcome in the state the sheer size and magnitude of his victory can be put into perspective. Table 9 permits us to see the relationship between Obama electoral support and that for the Democratic and Republican presidential candidates in the 2004 election. Obama ran significantly ahead of his own party's presidential ticket of John Kerry and John Edwards. He captured some 705,906 more votes than the ticket, which was some 15.2 percentage points greater and at the county level Obama beat Kerry in every county of the state as he did with all of his senatorial opponents. In addition, although the incumbent President Bush ran ahead of his senatorial candidate Alan Keyes, Obama outpolled the incumbent Republican president by nearly 1.3 million votes. This almost equaled the total number of votes that Keyes received in the election. Thus, both Obama and Kerry outpolled both Bush and Keyes.

Table 10
The Testable Propositions Empirically Deduced from the Barack Obama Senate Elections

Number	Hypotheses
1	White crossover voting is essential for victory in African–American Senate elections
2	High African–American voter registration is essential in victorious African–American Senate elections
3	High voter turnout is essential in victorious African–American Senate elections
4	African–American Senate candidates need to run to help attain victory in African–American Senate elections
5	Scandals that eliminate the main Republican candidate helps to secure victory in African–American Senate elections
6	The political experiences of the African–American Senate candidate is germane
7	Concentration of state electorates in a few counties around Chicago provide the African–American Senate candidate with a balance-of-power position in African–American Senate election

Overall, the Obama 2004 electoral performance was exceptional in mobilizing the state's electorate behind him and as such it generates a series of testable hypotheses for the further study of African American senate elections. In Table 10 was derived from Obama's successful senate elections certain hypothesis about the: (1) Illinois's population and its concentration, (2) the state electorate, especially the dominance of the African American electorate in the state's largest county, Cook County, (3) the qualifications and biracial campaign of the African American candidate, (4) a weak and/or scandal-laden opposition candidate, and finally (5) substantial crossover voting in the election in behalf of the African American candidate. All of these independent variables can be tested for their influence and impact in shaping the final outcome of the election. Findings from these categories of testable hypotheses will go a long way in generating an empirical theory about the nature and scope of African American senate elections.

Although these testable propositions were generated from aggregate election return data, thereby giving us an empirical portrait at the group level, these findings can surely be tested in the future with other aggregate data and can also be used in an exploratory manner with individual level data. In fact, given the cross-level nature of the proposed future research, it is essential that these future researchers understand and keep in mind that these group-level findings might not hold up at the individual level.[29] With this caveat taken in consideration, the empirical study and rending of African American senate elections can begin in earnest. Here is one of the first steps.

Notes

1. Karen O. Connor and Larry J. Sabato, *American Government: Continuity and Change* 2006 Edition, (New York: Longman, 2006), pp. 88-89. Alan Abramowitz and Jeffrey Segal, *Senate Elections* (Ann Arbor: University of Michigan Press, 1992), pp. 12-26.
2. John Becker and Eugene Heaton, Jr., "The Election of Senator Edward W. Brooke," *Public Opinion Quarterly* Vol. 31 (Fall, 2967), pp. 346-358.
3. Katherine Tate, "African American Female Senatorial Candidates: Twin Assets of Double Liabilities?" in Hanes Walton, Jr., *African American Power and Politics: The Political Contextual Variable* (New York: Columbia University Press, 1997), pp. 264-281.
4. Roger K. Oden, "The Election of Carol Moseley Braun in the U.S. Senate Race in Illinois," in Huey L. Perry, (ed.) *Race, Politics, and Governance in the United States* (Gainesville: University of Florida Press, 1996), pp. 47-64.
5. Barack Obama, *Dreams from My Father: A Story of Race and Inheritance* (New York: Three Rivers Press; Barack Obama, *The Audacity of Hope* (New York: Crown Publishers, 2006); and see also Mary Mitchell, "Memoir of a 21st Century History Maker," *Black Issues Book Review* Vol. 7 (January-February, 2005), ;o. 18-21.
6. *Ibid.*, p. 133.
7. *Ibid.*, p. 135.
8. *Ibid.*
9. *Ibid.*
10. *Ibid.*, p. 139.
11. *Ibid.*
12. *Ibid.*, p. 140 and 150.
13. *Ibid.*, pp. 287-289. See also, Michael Preston, "The Election of Harold Washington: An Examination of the SES Model in the 1983 Chicago Mayoral Election," in Michael Preston, Lenneal Henderson, Jr., and Paul Puryear (eds.), *The New Black Politics: The Search for Political Power* 2nd Edition (New York: Longman, 1987), pp. 139-171.
14. At this writing thee are no comprehensive and systematic studies of African American Senators. For them most recent work on a single Senator and his family, Lawrence Otis Graham, *The Senator and the Socialite* (New York: HarperCollins, 2006). At best one can only find such studies of African Americans in the House of Representatives. See Katherine Tate, *Faces in the Mirror: African Americans and Their Representatives in the U.S. Congress* (Princeton: Princeton University Press, 2003)

and her article, "African American Female Senatorial Candidates: Twin Assets or Double Liabilities," in Walton, op. Cit. William Clay, *Just Permanent Interest: Black Americans in Congress, 1870-1991* (New York: Amistad Press, 1992); LaVerene Gill, *African American Women in Congress: Forming and Transforming History* (New Jersey: Rutgers University Press, 1997). And Sheila F. Harmon-Martin, "Black Women in Politics: A Research Note," in Hanes Walton, Jr., (ed.), *Black Politics and Black Political Behavior* (Westport, Connecticut: Praeger, 1994), pp. 209-218.

15. Harold Gosnell, *Negro Politicians: The Rise of Negro Politics in Chicago* (Chicago: University of Chicago Press, 1966), pp. 65-66.
16. *Ibid.*, p. 66. See Also Lee McGriggs, *Black Legislative Politics in Illinois: A Theoretical and Structural Analysis* (Washington, DC: University Press of America, 1977).
17. Gosnell, op. cit., pp. 163-195.
18. Dennis S. Nordin, *The New Deal's Black Congressman: A Life of Arthur Wergs Mitchell* (Columbia: University of Missouri Press, 1997).
19. Dianne Pinderhughes, *Race and Ethnicity in Chicago Politics: A Reexamination of Pluralist Theory* (Urbana: University of Illinois Press, 1987). See also Paul Kleppner, *Chicago Divided: The Making of a Black Mayor* (DeKalb, Illinois: Northern Illinois University Press, 1985); William Grimshaw, *Bitter Fruit: Black Politics and the Chicago Machine 1931-1991* (Chicago: University of Chicago Press, 1992), and Henry Young, *The Black Church and the Harold Washington Story* (Bristol, Indiana: Wyndham Hall Press, 1988).
20. James Gimpel and Jason Schuknecht, *Patchwork Nation: Sectionalism and Political Change in American Politics* (Ann Arbor: University of Michigan Press, 2003), p. 353.
21. *Ibid.*
22. See Hanes Walton, Jr., "Black Presidential Participation and the Critical Election Theory," in Lorenzo Morris (ed.), *The Social and Political Implications of the 1984 Jesse Jackson Presidential Campaign* (New York: Praeger, 1990), pp. 49-64. And his "Remaking African American Public Opinion: The Role and Function of the African American Conservatives," in Gayle T. Tate & Lewis Randolph (ed.), *Dimensions of Black Conservatism in the United States: Made in America* (New York: Palgrave, 2002), p. 147, Figure 8.1 which compares the Republican vote in Chicago's African American congressional district with those of New York. It went from a high of nearly 50 percent to about 15 percent.
23. Tate, *Black Faces in the Mirror*, pp. 183-195. See Robert Singh, *The Congressional Black Caucus: Racial Politics in the U.S. Congress* (Thousand Oaks, California: Sage Publications, 1998), Table 2.2, pp. 31-32. See also Robert C. Smith, "The Black Congressional Delegation," *Western Political Quarterly* Vol. 34 (1981), pp. 203-221; and Shirley Washington, *Outstanding African Americans of Congress* (Washington, DC: United States Capitol Historical Society, 1998), pp. 73-78.
24. Barbara Mikulski, et al., *Nine and Counting: The Women of the Senate* (New York: Perennial Books, 2001), p. 236.
25. Hanes Walton, Jr. and Robert C. Smith, *American Politics and the African American Quest for Universal Freedom* 3rd Edition (New York: Longman, 2006), pp. 133-139.
26. Kenneth Weeks, "Favorite Son," *Black Enterprise* Vol. 35 (October, 2004), pp. 88-97.
27. Hanes Walton, Jr. and Lester Spence, "African-American Presidential Convention and Nomination Politics: Alan Keyes in the 1996 Republican Presidential Primaries and Convention," *National Political Science Review* Vol. 7 (1999), pp. 188-209.
28. Christopher Benson, "Barack & Michelle Obama: Begin Their Storied Journey," *Savoy Magazine* Vol. 1 (February, 2005), pp. 61-69, 103106.
29. Christopher Achen and W. Phillips Shively, *Cross-Level Inference* (Chicago: University of Chicago Press, 1995).

The Third Wave: Assessing the Post-Civil Rights Cohort of Black Elected Leadership

Andra Gillespie
Emory University

Introduction

By all accounts, African Americans[1] are being introduced to a third generation of black elected leadership. Ironically, this new phase, like the phases that preceded it, is called "new black politics." What distinguishes this new batch of leaders from their predecessors is their generation (i.e., they were born or came of age after the civil rights movement), their education (i.e., they were educated in Ivy League and other white institutions), and their potential (i.e., they have realistic chances to hold higher executive and legislative positions more frequently than any other generation of black leaders) (Reed and Alleyne, 2002).

This latest wave of black politicians is not immune from criticism. Not least among critics' concerns is whether these new black politicians will advance the substantive and strategic policy goals of the African American community. Yes, some of these women and men can realistically become senators and even president, as Barack Obama has so aptly demonstrated, but at what price? Will they have to abandon a civil rights agenda to gain the electoral advantage needed to attain high office (Martin, 2003)?

Implicit in this discussion of new black politicians is their relative chance for success and the means by which these politicians emerge onto the political spectrum. Is the emergence of this cohort of leadership an organic development emanating from black communities, or are these politicians overly ambitious instrumentalists who are exploiting their racial background for political traction? What is more, does this cohort of elected leadership have a chance at developing a loyal base of black voters, or are they being propped up by white elites seeking to divide and conquer black communities?

The answers to these questions are important because the stakes are so high. The new cohort of black elected officials receive such notoriety because their probability of attaining high office is perhaps greater than it has been for any generation of blacks in the United States. If this cohort of elected leadership meets expectations, ascending in critical numbers to governor's mansions, the U.S. Senate and even the White House, what are the implications for black communities? Clearly, these leaders will be in an unprecedented position to shape public policy. Thus, it seems that the big question is not just what pundits think about new black politicians, but what constituents think about these candidates and whether the material conditions of African Americans will improve under their leadership.

In the pages that follow, I trace the emergence of this new cohort of black leadership. I draw on the Black Leadership literature to see how scholars in the past defined and assessed black leadership. Indeed, they created multiple, yet similar typologies to evaluate leadership. I then use the basic demographic record of the current crop of young black elected leadership to introduce a new model of black leadership, which I in turn apply in describing the post-civil rights cohort.

New Black Politics throughout History

There have been three iterations of new black politics in the post-civil rights era: the widespread election of the first black elected officials in the 1970s; the successes of black candidates in major elections in majority-white jurisdictions in the 1980s; finally, the current rise of young, black moderates, many of whom challenge members of the first wave of black elected officials in majority-black cities and congressional districts. Each wave of black politicians is significant for the barriers that its members traversed. They are also important to study because the rise of each class of black elected officials is concurrent with innovations in campaign strategy. However, despite the campaign innovations, scholars studying these waves of black elected officials have been careful to question whether the programmatic agenda of these black elected officials aligns with the interests of black constituents.

New Black Politics: Phase I

Charles Hamilton notes that after the passage of Voting Rights Act, the focus of black politics, in a literal and academic sense, shifted from the judicial to the legislative/electoral arena. Now that blacks largely had the franchise, the goal became to channel that electoral power into legislative policies that would benefit blacks (Hamilton, 1982). Putting black officials in office was a key first step in achieving that agenda. Indeed, from 1965 to 1988, there was a more than thirteen fold increase in the number of black elected officials (Tate, 1994: 1; see also Williams, 1987: 112).

The elected officials of the first wave of new black politics faced tremendous obstacles. As trailblazers coming on the heels of the civil rights movement, they had to run in still racially tense environments. Furthermore, they had to reconcile with the white portions of their constituency that may have been skeptical of them as leaders (Smith, 1990).

Furthermore, these new black elected officials had difficulty implementing their agenda. As Linda Williams notes, "urban blacks today have reached city hall precisely at the moment when the real power to deliver jobs, money, education and basic services is migrating to higher levels of government and the private sector" (Williams, 1987: 129). She observes that first-wave black politicians came to power during a period of national economic decline and decreased federal aid to cities. As a result, first-wave black mayors were hampered in their efforts to provide redistributive relief to their constituents. What little aid they were able to provide tended to focus on ameliorative policies such as affirmative action and set-asides, which disproportionately benefited middle-class black residents. What is more, blacks ascended to the mayoralty in cities, which severely proscribed their power, limiting some from having control over important functions such as taxation (Williams, 1987: 128-129).

William Nelson further notes that the notion of new black politics being the collective agent for improvement of the whole black community is easier said than done. Using

Cleveland as an example, he notes that uniting blacks around a permanent agenda is difficult. Carl Stokes was able to unite blacks under one political banner. However, that union dissolved when Stokes stepped down as leader of Cleveland's black political organization. Diversity of opinion and ambition, then, undermined some attempts for political unity (Nelson, 1982). Moreover, Robert Smith observes that the legislative record of these officials, with respect to their progressive, black politics agenda, has been limited. They only have been able to develop downtown space, implement municipal affirmative action programs, and respond to police brutality (Smith, 1990).

New Black Politics: Phase II

One of the distinguishing features of each wave of new black politics has been the new black candidates' campaign style. While candidates in each wave of new black politics have had some measure of crossover appeal, observers have attributed more crossover appeal to each subsequent generation of new black political candidates. For example, Ardrey and Nelson (1990) note that black elected officials elected in new black politics' first wave, who were largely civil rights leaders, transferred the confrontational style from the movement to the electoral and legislative arena.

Many scholars viewed 1989 as a watershed year for black politics. In November 1989, blacks ascended to the mayoralty for the first time in Seattle (Norm Rice), New Haven (John Daniels), Durham (Chester Jenkins), and New York City (David Dinkins). Most notably, Douglas Wilder was elected governor of Virginia, making him the country's first black governor since Reconstruction. This cluster of elections is particularly important given that these men were elected in majority-white jurisdictions with at least 40 percent of the white vote (McCormick and Jones, 1993: 66, 68).

With their elections, Wilder and his peers ushered in the second wave of new black politics. The second wave is characterized by the prevalent use of a deracialized campaign strategy. McCormick and Jones define a deracialized campaign as one being "in a stylistic fashion that diffuses the polarizing effects of race by avoiding explicit reference to race-specific issues, while at the same time emphasizing those issues that are perceived as racially transcendent, thus mobilizing a broad segment of the electorate" (McCormick and Jones, 1993: 76). McCormick and Jones (1993) go further to articulate this strategy by noting that candidates employing such a strategy convey "*a nonthreatening image*," (76) "avoid employing direct racial appeals in organizing the black community" (76), and "*should avoid emphasis of a racially specific issue agenda* (77).

Douglas Wilder clearly exemplifies the deracialized strategy. Strickland and Wheeler note that Wilder, "adopted mainstream and even fiscally conservative positions. He was also able to avoid discussing overtly racial issues" (Strickland and Wheeler, 1992: 210). For example, Wilder's campaign theme was "the 'New Virginia Mainstream,'" and he made law and order, drug enforcement, and his support for the death penalty a key part of his platform (Jones and Clemons, 1993: 140).

While this strategy may be electorally effective, some find it morally troubling and wonder what the implications are for the pursuit of a pro-black political agenda. Earl Sheridan (1996), in his article, "The New Accommodationists," implicitly likens such a strategy to Booker T. Washington's Atlanta Compromise when he writes that instead of lauding black elected officials who deemphasize race to get elected, "America needs Black leaders who will continue the legacy of the 1960s, not the 1890s—men and women who will call for meaningful change in our society" (Sheridan, 1996: 169). He fears that in an attempt to gain office by any means necessary, these officials would abandon the issues of concern to the black community to get votes and would shortchange black interests to stay in power (Sheridan, 1996: 165-166).

McCormick and Jones are a little less fearful of the implications of using a deracialized electoral strategy, but they, too, brace for less progressive politics as a result of the strategy. They write that "In the absence of such demands from a politically organized African American community, there is little reason to expect African American elected officials who capture office in predominantly white political jurisdictions to be in the vanguard of articulating racially-specific policy issues" (McCormick and Jones, 1993: 78). That being said, they proffer that even these politicians will occasionally have to make some explicitly racial overtures to their black constituents, lest these officials lose an important base of support in their communities (McCormick and Jones, 1993: 78).

However, much of the handwringing over the implications of deracialization as a strategy of second-wave black politicians was short-lived. Second-wave politicians experienced a number of setbacks that prevented that cohort from making a long-term impact on the communities they represented. Some setbacks were structural. Doug Wilder, for instance, was constitutionally barred from seeking a second consecutive term as governor of Virginia. Others, such as David Dinkins, had very short tenures in office due to poor public perceptions. (See Kim 2000 for an example of Dinkins alienating black constituents.) However, for a number of politicians in the second wave, they suffered electoral defeats that marked the end of their electoral pursuits. For instance, Harvey Gantt twice lost his bid to represent North Carolina in the U.S. Senate to Jesse Helms in what were racially vitriolic campaigns. Andrew Young lost a bid to be Georgia's governor by wasting time campaigning for white votes in southern Georgia at the expense of campaigning in his base in and around Atlanta. Thus, according to the various authors studying the rise of second-wave politicians in the late 1980s and early 1990s, deracialized candidates overestimated racial goodwill outside of the black community and paid a high electoral price for ignoring black voters (Wilson, 1993; Davis and Willingham, 1993).

Moreover, from an academic perspective, many authors challenged the notion that pure deracialization was even going on in the first place. Mary Summers and Phillip Klinkner, for instance, argue that John Daniels did not run a deracialized campaign in his successful bid to become New Haven's first black mayor. They point to his progressive campaign platform, his integral role in introducing community policing to New Haven and his creation of a needle exchange program, in addition to his willingness to discuss his race on the campaign trail, as evidence that Daniels was not a deracialized candidate (Summers and Klinkner, 1996). Additionally, Lenneal Henderson studied Kurt Schmoke's ascendance to the mayoralty of Baltimore and reached similar conclusions. He contends that Schmoke's efforts at economic redevelopment were racially transcendent, but that Schmoke was not trying to distance himself from black communities. Thus, Schmoke was a "transracial[ized]" black politician and not a deracialized black politician (Henderson, 1996: 172-173).

New Black Politics: Phase III

The current wave of new black politics very much resembles the second wave in that this wave is characterized by ambitious politicians with more moderate politics. What distinguishes this group from its predecessors is its youth and connection to civil rights history. The figures associated with the third wave of new black politics were born after 1960, immediately before or after the passage of all the major civil rights legislation (see Traub, 2002). For example, Barack Obama was born in 1961; Cory Booker was born in 1969; Harold Ford, Jr. and Kwame Kilpatrick were born in 1970. As a result, these figures benefited from the fruits of the struggle and were able to grow up in integrated neighborhoods and attend predominantly white schools from kindergarten to graduate school. However, their youth also means that some perceive this generation as being less likely to relate to the civil rights struggle (see Bositis, 2001: 3-11). While second-wave new black politicians were charged with deliberately not having been active in the civil rights movement, they at least had the benefit of having been eyewitness to the monumental changes that took place in the 1950s and 1960 (see Sheridan 1996: 166).[2] In addition, others view this generation as being untested and unable to point to any record upon which to base their claims of being better legislators or government executives or to a clear agenda around which to organize their candidacies (Martin, 2003).

This perceived lack of identification with the struggle is what raises so much skepticism among older black elites when evaluating this emerging generation of leadership. In an interview with *Savoy* magazine, Ronald Walters voiced the suspicion that this new generation was merely a tool of white elites who wanted to replace more acerbic, older black leaders with less threatening, younger black leaders:

> [The white power structure] would rather supplant [the old guard] with a far more accommodating leadership. They are going to pit them against the so-called old leadership because they have been threatened by the interests and power of the black leadership who really have the influence and control of black people (Walters, quoted in Martin, 2003: 56).

In addition to having had their race consciousness questioned, this generation has also been accused of hubris. David Bositis acknowledged in an interview that young black leaders "imagine themselves as governors, United States Senators, and even President" (Bositis, quoted in Martin, 2003: 56). When Harold Ford, Jr. ran to unseat Nancy Pelosi as House minority leader in 2003, his efforts were rebuffed even by members of the Congressional Black Caucus. Walters notes that Ford's attempted power grab failed because he had not spent years currying favor and garnering support from his colleagues in the House Democratic Caucus. "To step out there because you've got a pretty face and no agenda," Walters said, "you're going to lose every time" (Walters, quoted in Martin, 2003: 56).

If there is anything that does distinguish the third wave of new black politics from the first two waves, it may be that it is the synthesis of the first and second waves. Where we witnessed civil rights activists turned legislators challenge the white power structure in the first wave, and where we witnessed second-wave politicians attempt to join the white power structure, we now see third wave politicians who behave like second-wave politicians and challenge first-wave incumbents for power,[3] often in majority-black jurisdictions, and often with extensive mainstream media support. For instance, Alexandra Starr predicts that moderate politics would probably propel more black candidates to national office (2002). James Traub goes so far as to say that the success of people like Cory Booker and Artur Davis against the Sharpe Jameses and Earl Hilliards of the world would be a "balm to white liberals, whose politics have been so heavily determined by an agonized sense of 'what black people want,' as defined by the black leadership class.

And it will be a boon to the Democrats, for it will help heal the ideological rifts within the party" (Traub, 2002: 1).

Analytical Concerns with Phases II and III of New Black Politics

The academy has not been immune from being infatuated with second- and third-wave new black politics because of the non-threatening dimension of their electoral strategy. Strickland and Whicker acquiesce to racism in American society and propose a crossover model for black electoral success. This model calls for espousing conservative positions on issues, deemphasizing race, and having worked outside the civil rights movement. While they do all this, these candidates are supposed to excite and maintain a black voting base (Strickland and Whicker, 1992: 208-209).

Strickland and Whicker acknowledge that catering to whites while not alienating blacks is easier said than done. However, their key mistake is assuming that black voters will be loyal to any black candidate. While that is a gross overgeneralization of black voting preferences in and of itself, Strickland and Whicker fail to account for the situation when two blacks would run against each other. Who should black voters choose, then? In their study of congressional elections, Canon, Schousen, and Sellers (1996) studied the electoral success of black candidates pitted against other black candidates in majority-minority districts. They argue that when first-wave new black politicians run against second- or third-wave new black politicians, the second- or third-wave new black politician will win if whites, who should be a sizable minority of the constituency, vote as a bloc. They assume that whites are more likely to support moderate blacks. However, they do concede that if blacks vote as a bloc, the first-wave new black politician has a better chance of winning.

This focus on which black candidates appeal to white voters (as opposed to which black candidates can best represent the interests of black voters) is what is so troubling to students of black politics. Ronald Walter's aforementioned quote captures this concern (Martin, 2003, 56). Indeed, it is this fixation with keeping whites happy that seems to be an anathema to black self-determination, if only because the focus on this type of black politics shifts the focus away from blacks.

Critics must respond to the question, though, of whether these candidates are out of touch, though. Reed and Alleyne note that the hallmark of third-wave new black politics is their "philosophic mix of political pragmatism, pro-business sensibility, and social progressivism" (Reed and Alleyne, 2002: 84). Martin notes that, "today's black elected official may be more concerned with closing the digital divide, increasing economic opportunities for people of color, and school vouchers…" (Martin, 2003: 54). Are these positions really out of touch with the policy preferences of black constituents? David Bositis would have to concede that these candidates may not be out of touch with their constituents. Reporting the results of the Joint Center's 2002 National Opinion Poll, he notes that a majority of blacks were in favor of vouchers, that younger blacks identified less with the Democratic Party, and that blacks are far more concerned about the economy, foreign affairs, and education than they are about racism (Bositis, 2002: 6, 7, 10). What is more, when the Joint Center compared the political attitudes of black elected officials to the black electorate, they found that generational differences in attitudes among blacks generally paralleled generational differences among black elected officials (Bositis, 2001: 21).

Skeptics need also to consider the substantive critiques levied against older generations of black leadership. While Walters chided the younger generation of black elected officials for being overly ambitious but substantively unfocused and proclaimed that the older generation of black leaders "really have the influence and control of black people" (Walters, quoted in Martin, 2003), he has also acknowledged elsewhere that the earlier vanguard of leadership encountered institutional barriers that limited their effectiveness in providing benefits for blacks (Smith and Walters 1999, 135). His colleague, Robert Smith, argued that post-civil rights elected officials assumed power, but were co-opted by the establishment and thus accomplished very little of their intended programmatic agenda to improve the lives of African Americans. The reality that even the first wave of black politicians failed to deliver policy redress to their black constituents led Smith to boldly proclaim in the title of his book that "We Have No Leaders" (Smith, 1996). This reality begs the questions of whether younger, post-racial candidates really can do more harm than good, relative to the previous generation of leadership, for the advancement of basic African American policy interests, such as ending systemic inequality.

Examining the Typologies of Black Leadership

The exercise of classifying a new, post-racial cohort of leadership is deeply rooted in previous studies of black leadership. In those studies, scholars went to great efforts to classify leaders. The classification scheme they chose varied on the margins, but all focus on identifying distinct leadership styles within the black community based on the leaders' style in dealing with the white power structure.

The extant typologies of black leadership go back to the late 1930s. In 1937, Guy Johnson defined black leaders as either "gradualists" or "revolutionaries" (Ladd, 1966: 148). As their names suggest, gradualists acquiesced to the realities of second-class citizenship in the United States, and revolutionaries challenged the racial caste system. In the classic tome *An American Dilemma*, Gunnar Myrdal created the accommodationist/protest paradigm to classify black leaders. Accommodationists are akin to Johnson's gradualists; and protesters are analogous to Johnson's revolutionaries (Ladd, 1966: 148; see Myrdal, 1944: 720).

Walters and Smith (1999) outline other major typologies created in the early 1960s to define black leadership. James Q. Wilson, for instance, defined black leadership styles on two dimensions. In his view, black leaders were either militants or moderates, basing his typology on the methods these leaders used to achieve specific classes of civil rights goals. Militant leaders used direct action or protest techniques to achieve racial integration, which Wilson termed a "status" goal; moderate leaders, in contrast, tended to try to negotiate with whites to achieve concrete, "welfare" goals for black communities (Wilson, 1960: 218, 235). Thus, a militant leader would lead a protest to achieve a measure of social accommodation for blacks equal to whites while moderate leaders might appeal to white power structures behind the scenes to achieve goals such as more goods and services targeted to black communities (Wilson, 1960: chapter 9).

Drawing on Wilson's scholarship, Everett Ladd uses the notion of welfare and status goals, along with rhetorical style and tactics to create his own typology of leadership. Like Wilson, he notes that at the extremes are conservatives and militants. However, he also notes that there is an intermediate class of leaders known as moderates. Militant leaders seek status goals using confrontational tactics and rhetoric. Conservative leaders seek welfare goals using acquiescent, non-confrontational strategies and rhetoric (usually behind the scenes). Moderate leaders are a hybrid: they seek welfare and status goals depending on the situation using non-confrontational rhetoric. However, they often take advantage of the presence of militants to achieve their goals. They are able to position themselves as the reasonable alternative to the militants and attempt to get access to dominant power structures along these lines (Ladd, 1966: chapter 4).

In her study of black politics in Durham, North Carolina, Elaine Burgess also extends the definition of black leadership beyond the protest-accommodation binary to include other, intermediary types of leadership. In her typology, there were four types of black leaders. On one end of the spectrum were conservative leaders, the old, established black leadership which acquiesced to racial domination and with which the white power structure was more comfortable. Moderates tended to be upper-class blacks who did not devote their full-time and energy to addressing racial issues. They tended to emerge to prominence working on non-racial issues, and they were committed to being part of biracial groups working to address city challenges. Liberals were those black leaders, often from professional backgrounds, who were uncompromising in their commitment to achieving civil rights for blacks. However, their tone was non-confrontational, and they were perceived to be non-threatening, especially in relation to radicals. Radicals were the leaders most prone to be outspoken and to engage in direct action to achieve civil rights. In Burgess' view, they were clearly inspired by Martin Luther King (Burgess, 1962: 181-185; Walters and Smith, 1999: 18).

While there are some clear differences in the typologies mentioned above, their similarities are striking. All of them use a linear continuum to judge a leader based on how radical he or she is. They judge the extent to which a person is radical based on the extent to which these leaders wish to work with powerful whites and whether or not a leader tries to achieve his/her goals through protest or negotiation.

All of the aforementioned studies took place in the midst of the civil rights movement and reflect the diversity of opinion about the efficacy of certain tactics. It would seem logical that in the wake of the legislative victories of the civil rights movement that there would perhaps be some changes in how leadership was defined and categorized. For instance, at the time Burgess was writing, she noted that conservative leaders were losing their prominence in the black community and even white leaders realized that this cohort of leadership's influence in the black community was waning. It seemed to be that racial moderates would fill the role of racial conservatives (Burgess, 1962: 181). Moreover, Robert Smith (1980) contends that in the wake of the Black Nationalist movement, many black elites were radicalized. Thus, even some of the more conservative elements of the black community would likely have been socialized into affirming some measure of race pride, whether it be through membership in a racially specific professional association or some other avenue of racial particularism.

Despite these radical social changes, our understanding of the basic types of black leadership has not changed that much, though there has been some innovation. Walters and Smith acquiesce to the protest-accommodation paradigm in their book. They concede that protesters are far less prevalent, and they contend that most leaders are now accommodationists. They do provide some innovation when they identify different ways black leaders gain legitimacy. One can argue that Walters and Smith define leadership legitimacy on a two-dimensional scale, with white and black acceptance being the x and y axes respectively. Leaders accepted by both black and white communities are "consensus" leaders. Those embraced by the white community and not the black community are called "external" leaders. Those embraced by the black community and not the white community are called "community" leaders. Those who lack credibility in both black and white communities are considered "auto-selected" leaders (Walters and Smith, 1999: 217).

While Walters and Smith's two dimensional rendering of racial acceptability is helpful, in reality, they are only judging legitimacy on racial acceptance. Still, others have continued to use the simple binary to define black candidates and politicians. David Canon, Matthew Schousen and Patrick Sellers (1996), for instance, used the terms "old style" and "new style" to describe black candidates running against each other in majority-minority congressional districts. Old-style candidates ran in the protest, confrontational spirit of the civil rights movement and were thus the racialized candidates; new-style candidates ran racially transcendent campaigns that were more palatable to some of the blacks and the remaining whites in these districts.

Lenneal Henderson (1996), in contrast, creates perhaps the most complex version of race leadership to date. While keeping with the one-dimensional model of racial radicalism (He defines black leaders on a continuum from non-racial to hyper-racial, with deracialized, racialized and transracialized candidates as the intermediate points), he argues that both electoral and policy considerations should factor into how one categorizes black politicians. Black candidates run differently when running against whites and when running against other blacks, and that should be taken into account. Moreover, race politics plays out differently in different parts of the policy process. An elected official could set the agenda for a policy in a racially transcendent tone, for instance, but once the policy was implemented, it could be judged to be highly beneficial for blacks. Likewise, a policy could be introduced as explicitly helping blacks, but by the time it was passed and implemented, might not achieve its intended purpose. Thus, Henderson suggests the importance of looking at the ends elected officials achieve in office rather than the means by which they get to office before judging them (Henderson, 1996: 172-171). Unfortunately, Henderson's typology is very preliminary and in the end, still very unidimensional.

A Multi-Dimensional Assessment of Black Elected Leadership

Is there a better, perhaps more complex way to judge and examine black leadership? For this new cohort of elected officials, I would like to proffer a new model of leadership that creates more complex typologies and presents a more nuanced, and hopefully, more accurate picture of what we know about the post-civil rights cohort of black leadership to date. While this model incorporates the traditional militant to moderate axis (under the rubric of crossover appeal), it also adds two more important dimensions: expected career trajectory (ambition) and preexisting connections to the black establishment. These axes are far from simple, and in the next paragraphs, I will explain the criteria that go into determining a politician's position on these axes.

Crossover Appeal

As shown before, the militant-moderate continuum has figured prominently in studies of black leadership for nearly seventy years (Walters and Smith, 1999; Ladd, 1966; Burgess, 1962; Wilson, 1960; Canon, Schousen and Sellers, 1996). While it is extremely antiquated to judge black politicians on whether they believe in acquiescing to second-class citizenship for blacks anymore (Indeed, it would be hard to find a credible black leader arguing for a rollback on the gains of the civil rights movement), the dimension still has analytic merit. Politicians who run deracialized campaigns, for instance, would naturally be far less militant and more likely to have greater levels of crossover appeal than those who do run racialized campaigns.

Additionally, perceptions of moderation and militancy also spill over into policy issues. An elected official's degree of crossover appeal can affect his policy agendas and/or how she frames issues in the pursuit of achieving certain racial policy goals. For instance, a militant official, or one with less crossover appeal, may pursue the ending of police brutality and frame it as a racial issue. A moderate counterpart may either not address the issue entirely or frame it as being disadvantageous to the pursuit of law and order in order to maintain his/her crossover appeal. A more militant leader may champion affirmative action, while a moderate leader seeking crossover appeal may focus on more racially neutral issues such as traditional economic development.

Perceived Career Trajectory

If one reads the mainstream press, he or she can often find examples of black politicians in the new cohort being touted as presidential material (see Dionne, 2004: Benson, 2006). Clearly, there are members of this cohort besides Barack Obama who clearly aspire to be president one day and appear to be better positioned to achieve their goals than any other generation of black politicians. However, there are members of this cohort who seem content to remain in the positions they currently hold for the foreseeable future.

The career trajectory dimension seeks to make distinctions between politicians who appear to be upwardly mobile (i.e., they aspire to statewide or national office) and those who do not. Often, the personal backgrounds of politicians influence their ambitions. Pauline Stone studied the ambitions of black elected officials in Michigan in the late 1970s. Using a typology developed by Joseph Schlesinger (1966: 10), she identified politicians with "progressive" ambitions (those who wanted to seek higher office), "static" ambitions (those who wanted to maintain their current positions), and "discrete" ambitions (those who wanted to step down from their current offices) (Stone, 1980: 96). She found that politicians with discrete ambitions were more likely to have been drafted from the grassroots. In contrast, politicians with progressive ambitions were more likely to be young, well educated, and less committed to pure partisan politics (Stone, 1980). For the purposes of this analysis, politicians with long trajectories will have progressive ambitions, while politicians with short trajectories will have static or discrete ambitions.

There are three factors that influence a politician's being categorized as having a long or short career trajectory. First, a politician has to want (or appear to want) to pursue higher office. This is important for a number of reasons. Because these officials have not served in prominent office for a short period of time, their future ambitions figure prominently into popular evaluations of them because for now, we really cannot judge their record of achievement. Moreover, the perceived ambitions of these officials have been a point of criticism. Recall that Ronald Walters criticized this cohort of politicians for being too ambitious, for seeking higher office before they had paid their dues (Martin, 2003: 56).

Second, the media also plays a role in generating buzz about a black candidate's future prospects. Adolph Reed, Jr. noted in his analysis of Jesse Jackson, Sr.'s 1984 presidential campaign that the mainstream media hyped Jackson's candidacy. Jackson had no chance of winning the Democratic nomination for president, yet because of the inordinate amount of media attention afforded to Jackson, he emerged from that campaign as the perceived spokesman for black America, with no consideration of his actual legitimacy as a leader in the black community (Reed, 1986: chapter 8). It may very well be that some of these officials are media constructions; or conversely, the perception that some of these candidates are mere media constructions could have a very negative impact on their legitimacy in black communities (Walters and Smith, 1999: 217).

Finally, there are structural and political considerations that do impact the future career trajectories of some of these officials. Black elected officials representing majority-minority enclaves in overwhelmingly white states may have difficulty winning statewide elections. Similarly, ambitious black elected officials living in the District of Columbia, such as Mayor Adrian Fenty, would have to move to a state to pursue higher political office. Finally, elected officials who fail to achieve policy goals in office or get mired in scandal jeopardize their chances to make credible runs for higher political office.

Connections to the Black Establishment

The final dimension of the model assesses the strength of young black politicians' connections to the black establishment. Part of this analysis looks at political socialization. Some young black politicians have clear connections to traditional centers of black political power. They are either the scions of political or activist families (i.e., Harold Ford, Jr. and Jesse Jackson, Jr.) or have been politically socialized in traditional black institutions, whether it be serving on the staff of an established black politician or working with prominent civil rights organizations such as the NAACP. Others are clearly new players to the body politic and lack the traditional political connections to the black establishment. Having connections to traditional black centers of power can be invaluable. Those with access to the establishment could gain a fundraising or endorsement advantage, while those without those establishment ties have to raise money or win endorsements from scratch.

Being part of the establishment or being a newcomer to the political scene could have significant implications for the types of agendas young black politicians advance and the tone they use to advance those agendas. Someone who is a newcomer to the political scene may be more likely to ruffle feathers or to challenge the elders. Those with establishment connections may be less likely to challenge their elders, who literally could have raised them or their childhood friends. This decreased likelihood to challenge the system could have significant consequences for the advancement of black politics and the improvement of the material lives of black people. Those less likely to challenge the status quo may in fact be less likely to provide the needed innovations to advance African American interests.

Assessing linked fate also figures prominently into evaluations of a young black politician's connections to the black establishment. Michael Dawson (1994) noted that middle-class blacks, who may physically remove themselves from core black communities when they gain affluence and move to the suburbs, often maintain physical and psychic connections to black communities through a number of means. They can return to these communities for things as mundane as church and hair appointments. They may still leave relatives behind in these core communities, which solidifies their connections to these communities. Finally, the fact that middle-class blacks still experience racial discrimination still plays a radicalizing force. These factors combine to give middle-class blacks a sense that their fate is tied to the fate of other blacks, which in turn leads them to support policy positions (such as welfare spending) that non-blacks of the same class status are far less likely to support. Thus, some young black politicians with no roots in traditional black communities at all may be far less likely to advance a political and policy agenda that would advance the civil rights interests of black communities.

Typologies of the Third Wave

Having articulated the factors that contribute to the political identities of young black elected officials and aspirants of the post-civil rights generation, it is important to see how those factors interact and how this affects the classification of young black politicians.

If we look at the three definitional axes (crossover appeal, perceived career trajectory, and connections to the black establishment), and scale them dichotomously (ranking people as low or high relative to each other on the scales), this yields eight possible archetypal permutations, as shown in Table One. For the rest of this section, I will provide a thumbnail sketch of these typologies, devoting most of the attention to the observed archetypes.

New Black Politicians with Strong Credentials

Ivy League Upstarts

The Ivy League Upstarts, which include Senator Barack Obama and Newark, New Jersey Mayor Cory Booker, are among the most visible of the post-civil rights cohort of black elected leadership. This subset is defined by high crossover appeal, high levels of ambition, and weak ties to the black political establishment. This sub-cohort tends to be highly educated, graduating with advanced degrees from prestigious, majority-white institutions. For example, Obama graduated from Columbia University and Harvard Law School; Booker graduated from Stanford, Oxford University (as a Rhodes Scholar), and Yale Law School. They are also receive a lot of buzz in the mainstream media and appear to be anointed as members of the next wave of black leaders because of their credentials. For instance, a month before Barack Obama delivered his now-famous keynote address to the 2004 Democratic National Convention, columnist E.J. Dionne dubbed Obama, "a media darling in this year's election.... Already there's speculation that he may be the first African American president of the United States—and he's only a state senator" (Dionne, 2004: A29). The week after Cory Booker won his election to lead New Jersey's largest city, *New York Times* columnist Josh Benson noted that people were already discussing Booker's next political office (Benson, 2006, 14:1). Indeed, these gentlemen receive a lot of attention for their poise and for projecting a non-threatening image, similar to the deracialized candidates of Phase II.

However, these candidates are also embattled, at least at first, in black communities. Both Booker and Obama suffered defeats early in their careers, when they challenged established black leaders in Newark and Chicago for political power. Those campaigns were marked by noticeably high levels of racial vitriol, where they were condemned for not being black enough and for being interlopers who at best did not know enough about they communities they aspired to represent to lead them and at worst were insincere instrumentalists who planned to exploit and gentrify their communities for political gain

Table 1
Typologies of Third Phase Black Politicians

	Typology	Crossover Appeal	Ties to the Black Establishment	Perceived Trajectory	Example	Political Opportunity Structure	Challenges Facing This Sub-Cohort
Dominant Characteristic: Strong Credentials	*Ivy League Upstarts*	High	Weak	Long	Obama, Booker	Systemic Failure in Their Jurisdiction	They have to answer the charge that they are racially inauthentic and only seek to exploit black communities for their personal political gain.
	Local Kids Made Good	High	Weak	Short	Fenty, Davis, Ellison, McTeer-Hudson	Systemic Failure in their Jurisdiction	The political environment in which they run makes it more difficult (but not necessarily impossible) for candidates to achieve higher office, either because of structural constraints or unresolved racial tension.
Dominant Characteristic: Strong Connections To Black Establishment	*Rebrands of Their Parents*	High	Strong	Long	Ford	Generational Succession + Long Term Dynastic Planning	Their ties to the black establishment, and their parents' racialized political records could undermine their crossover appeal.
	Deracialized Sequels	High	Strong	Short	Mitchell	Generational Succession + Demographic Shift Privileging Non-Blacks	This group largely limits themselves deliberately from attaining higher office.
	Chips Off the Old Block	Low	Strong	Short	Kilpatrick, Clarke, Meek, Jackson	Their Parents Pave the Way	This group may face the most pressure to maintain the political status quo, even if that hurts black advancement.
	New "Old Standard Bearers"	Low	Strong	Long	Jackson?	Demographic Shift Favoring Blacks	In order to have viable long term career trajectories, they have to cultivate crossover support.
Dominant Characteristic: High Levels of "Street Credibility"	*New Activists*	Low	Weak	Long	Powell	Rising Internal Class Warfare; Increased Lower Class Participation	It is extremely difficult to maintain a long career trajectory without cultivating crossover appeal and establishment ties.
	Rebels Without a Chance	Low	Weak	Short	Hutchins	Most Likely To Emerge as the Result of a One-Time Disturbance	The emergence of viable candidates from this cohort is unlikely without other resources.

Source: Author's compilation. 2008.

(see Curry, 2005; Lawrence, 2000). While Ivy League Upstarts typically rebound from these initial defeats, their emergence onto the political scene raises important normative questions about class, racial authenticity, and linked fate.

In addition to the normative debate surrounding these candidates about linked fate and their ability to hold the best interests of black communities at heart is the inherent pressure to perform that is placed on these officials. These candidates often run on good government platforms, in response to what they perceive to be failures of previous administrations to deliver goods and services effectively to their communities. When they get elected to office, they are expected to produce results immediately, and if they do not produce, then their constituents may be less forgiving at the next election.

Local Kids Made Good

The Local Kids Made Good, which include Washington, D.C. Mayor Adrian Fenty, Greenville, Mississippi Mayor Heather McTeer Hudson, Minnesota Congressman Keith Ellison and Alabama Congressman Artur Davis, are very similar to the Ivy League Upstarts, but they receive far less attention. They, like the Ivy League Upstarts, are extremely well educated, have crossover appeal, are committed to good government and are generally political newcomers, but they are perceived to have shorter career trajectories. As a resident of Washington, D.C., Fenty does not have the option of running for governor or being able to run to be a voting member of Congress. Thus, barring Washington, D.C. obtaining statehood, the D.C. delegate earning full voting privileges in Congress, or Fenty moving to an actual state, his elected political career is probably limited. Ellison, the first Muslim elected to Congress, has expressed no interest yet in running for statewide office at either the state or federal level, so we have to code his progressive ambitions as low for now.

Artur Davis and Heather McTeer Hudson, on the other hand, are potentially constrained by the political and racial conditions in their respective states. While Davis has actively contemplated seeking higher office, he has already had to rule out a 2008 U.S. Senate bid. Alabama voters are predicted to support the Republican candidate for president, and Davis figured that voters would be unlikely to split their ballots to vote for him as the U.S. Senate candidate. While Davis is actively considering a gubernatorial bid in 2010, he will have to overcome the hurdle that race may pose in his election. Alabama has never elected a black to any statewide office (Evans, 2007). Thus, while he harbors similar political aspirations to Obama and Booker, it is unclear at this point as to whether race relations in the Deep South will hamper his efforts to achieve his long-term goals.

Hudson is notable because unlike Fenty and Davis, she was the first black person to be elected to her post. In fact, Hudson is the first black mayor in the Mississippi Delta, which is 70 percent black (Byrd, 2004). As such, her obstacles relate to larger issues of political incorporation. With blacks in her region being largely unable to translate their numerical dominance into political power, it is difficult to project that Hudson would be able to easily win higher political office.

New Black Politicians with Strong Ties to the Black Establishment

Chips off the Old Block

The Chips off the Old Block are the children of prominent black politicians or civil rights leaders who used their lineage as a steppingstone to a political career. This sub-cohort includes people such as Florida Congressman Kendrick Meek, New York Congresswoman Yvette Clarke and Detroit Mayor Kwame Kilpatrick, all children of prominent politicians (former Congresswoman Carrie Meek, former New York City Councilwoman Una Clarke, and Congresswoman Carolyn Cheeks-Kilpatrick respectively). This sub-cohort is probably most diverse in terms of its orientation. While most of them espouse more moderate politics than their parents, they are perceived to have less crossover appeal than their counterparts who are largely defined by their credentials and who lack political lineages. These politicians clearly have connections to the black establishment and are thus less likely to have their commitment to black communities called into question. However, they are less likely to be perceived as having a long career trajectory. For those serving in the House of Representatives, if they continue their congressional careers, they are likely to gain seniority and committee chairmanships, but as of yet, they do not appear likely to take the risk of running for statewide or national office. As illustrated by the case of Mayor Kilpatrick, they may become implicated in political scandals that circumscribe future political opportunities (see Star News Services, 2005).

Rebrands of Their Parents

Rebrands of Their Parents are a different breed of black dynastic heirs. They have high crossover appeal, strong ties to the black establishment and long perceived career trajectories. Rebrands are very similar to Ivy League Upstarts, but they differ on the establishment dimension. Because these politicians have ties to the black establishment—indeed, they are often children of Phase I and II politicians—they tend to be less susceptible to charges of racial inauthenticity levied at Ivy League Upstarts.

Former Tennessee Congressman Harold Ford, Jr. typifies this category. Ford assumed the Memphis congressional seat held by his father in 1996, but he clearly had higher political ambitions and cultivated a national political presence. Al Gore chose him to deliver one of the keynote addresses at the 2000 Democratic National Convention because "He's a rising star. He has a bright future. And he's from Tennessee" (Gore, quoted in Brosnan, 2000). After the 2002 midterm elections, Ford made an unsuccessful bid to be minority leader of the House of Representatives. In 2006, Ford came within three percentage points of becoming Tennessee's first black United States senator. Therefore, unlike the Chips off the Old Block, who currently do not publicly evince an interest in seeking office beyond the posts they currently hold, Rebrands of Their Parents use their parents' old seats as springboards to seek high offices that their parents could only dream of attaining.[4]

However, because Rebrands got their political starts at their parents' knees, they could be constrained by their families no matter how hard they try to escape the proverbial apple tree. If a family's reputation is mixed, it can cause problems for the Rebrand candidate. When Ford ran for the Senate in 2006, his family's ethical issues became a campaign obstacle. For instance, his opponent, Bob Corker, ran an ad ("Family Ties") noting that Harold Ford, Jr. was a puppet for his father, (Strategic Perception, 2006). This ad clearly was meant to prime antipathy for members of the Ford family, who has had more than its share of ethics charges levied against them (see Davis and Sher, 2006).

New "Old Standard Bearers"

There is the potential for an ambitious black politician to emerge with strong black establishment ties and low crossover appeal. The New "Old Standard Bearer" embodies these characteristics. They would likely be the scion of an established black activist or political family whose political base is rooted in the black community. If the conditions were ripe, A New "Old Standard Bearer" would then try to use his/her family's good name to reap win elective office. Certain conditions must be in place first, though, in order to make this a viable possibility. For instance, these candidates would have to generate just enough crossover appeal to effectively split the white vote, thus making black voters the crucial swing vote in their particular contest. In any case, the demographics of a particular jurisdiction would have to change such that blacks made up a decisive portion of the electorate. Currently, no one really fits the description of a New "Old Standard Bearer." However, there is a chance that Jesse Jackson, Jr. (who otherwise is a Chip off the Old Block) could fit this category. In fall 2006, Jackson began to publicly explore the possibility of challenging Richard Daley for the Chicago mayoralty. While he ruled out a run in November 2006, the possibility remains for him to consider a mayoral, gubernatorial or senatorial bid in the future—though one cannot speculate about his chances at this time (see Mihalopoulos, 2006; Mihalopoulos and Washburn, 2006; "Rep. Jesse Jackson, Jr. Won't Run...", 2006). That Jackson even publicly considered running for another office suggests that he might have higher political ambitions.

The Other Types—Deracialized Sequels; New Activists; and Rebels without a Chance

The final three typologies represent different permutations of the three relevant dimensions by which to judge the black politicians of this generation. However, as of yet, no one has been elected at the national or large city executive level who embodies these combinations of characteristics. The paragraphs that follow describe the characteristics of lesser known politicians who could emerge and fit this type and will explain why it may be difficult (though not impossible) for some types of black politicians to emerge.

It is most likely that a Phase III new black politician will emerge onto the national stage who fits the characteristics of a *Deracialized Sequel*. Like Rebrands of Their Parents, these politicians have high crossover appeal and strong ties to the black establishment. However, unlike Rebrands of Their Parents, they choose to have short career trajectories. A Deracialized Sequel politician is most likely to emerge in an area accustomed to black leadership, but has a large enough non-black population that requires that black candidates reach out to non-black constituents in order to be politically viable.

While one cannot point to a prominent mayor or member of Congress who fits this type, former Baltimore City Councilman and mayoral candidate Keiffer Mitchell does provide an example of this type of politician. Mitchell, the grand-nephew of the late Maryland Congressman Parren Mitchell and scion of a legendary black activist family in Maryland, served on Baltimore's City Council for 11 years before running for the Democratic nomination for mayor of Baltimore in 2007. Mitchell represented a diverse city council ward and was comfortable reaching across racial and class lines. Mitchell clearly attempted to capitalize on his family's reputation to be elected mayor of Baltimore. However, at an August 14, 2007 debate (which the author attended), Mitchell announced that he had no intention of running for higher office after serving as mayor.

Despite Mitchell's pledge to devote his career to Baltimore politics, his campaign efforts were hampered in part because of family drama. Mitchell's father, who initially served as treasurer of his campaign, was forced to resign after it was alleged that he had used campaign funds for non-campaign expenses. Mitchell's father then evicted his son's campaign out of office space he rented to them. By the time that this scandal emerged, Mitchell already trailed the eventual nominee and winner, Sheila Dixon, in polling by double-digit margins. The scandal, though, presented a new distraction at best and further hampered his efforts. In a *Baltimore Sun* poll taken weeks before the September 11 primary, 16 percent of voters said that the scandal did make it less likely for them to vote for Keiffer Mitchell (Brewington, 2007).

New Activists are characterized by low crossover appeal, weak ties to the black establishment and long perceived trajectories. Because of the low crossover appeal and weak ties to the black establishment, it is hard to conceive that any successful, young, black politician would emerge who fits this type. However, there are certain conditions which make the emergence of a New Activist more plausible. If class divisions between upper- and lower-class blacks exacerbate and the black lower class organizes politically around a new and different set of leaders than middle- and upper-class blacks (see Dawson, 1994: 208-209), those leaders would likely fit the description of New Activists. The New Activists would be able to maintain their political power so long as lower-class blacks remain a politically cohesive voting bloc; and they might even be able to expand their political base beyond a city or even a congressional district if they were able to effectively use a populist appeal to reach out to poor non-blacks. However, given the fact that all of these conditions have to emerge simultaneously in order for this to be a viable type, it is less likely that New Activists will make up a sizable subset of Phase III black politicians.

That being said, potential candidates are emerging who fit the mold of New Activists. Kevin Powell, a reality TV star turned author/activist, challenged Brooklyn Congressman Edolphus Towns for the Democratic nomination in New York's 10th Congressional District in 2008. Towns, a thirteen-term congressman, won his 2006 primary against New York City Councilman Charles Barron with only a plurality of the vote in a three-person field. This showing, on the heels of narrow primary wins in 1998 and 2000, suggested that he was politically vulnerable. Towns also made a big strategic misstep when he endorsed Hillary Clinton in the 2008 Democratic presidential primary. Fifty-eight percent of Towns' district voted for Barack Obama. Powell hoped to use all of these vulnerabilities, plus his own assertion that Towns was unresponsive to the needs of his constituents, to gain a foothold in the congressional primary. Despite his notoriety as an original cast member of MTV's *The Real World* and his potential appeal to young people, though, Powell was not successful. Towns eventually beat Powell by a two-to-one margin in 2008 (Hicks, 2008a; Hicks, 2008b; Gross, 2008).

Rebels without a Chance are characterized by low crossover appeal, weak ties to the black establishment and a short career trajectory. Because Rebels without a Chance lack conventional resources that are needed to win elections (i.e., support from black elites and non-black voters), they only succeed in cases where they have massive grassroots support among largely disaffected black voters, who would certainly have to comprise a majority of the electorate. Given the structural obstacles impeding Rebels without a Chance (i.e., they may not have majority support in their constituency depending on the demographic makeup of their jurisdiction; they may not have access to the resources needed to run campaigns such as money or professional staff; and they have to mobilize potentially discouraged and inefficacious voters), it is difficult for a successful Phase III black politician to emerge in this mode.

Despite the long odds of success, though, Rebel without a Chance candidates have emerged recently. Markel Hutchins, an Atlanta minister, rose to prominence as the spokesperson for the family of Kathryn Johnston, a 92-year-old Atlanta woman who was shot to death by police during a bungled no-knock warrant arrest in 2006. In February 2008, Hutchins challenged Congressman John Lewis for the Democratic nomination for Georgia's 5th Congressional District. Clearly, Hutchins was attempting to translate his stature as a young activist into political power. He also hoped to tap into voter disappointment with Lewis' original endorsement of Hillary Clinton over Barack Obama in the 2008 presidential primaries. However, he was unable to unseat Lewis, who won nearly 70 percent of the vote in a three-person field. Hutchins only garnered 16 percent of the vote (see Galloway, 2008; Smith, 2008).

It is still too early to predict the political futures of both Kevin Powell and Markel Hutchins. They will first have to win elective office before we can predict their career trajectories and properly categorize them. However, it is clear that they tried to capitalize on their opponents' strategic errors (i.e., supporting a losing presidential candidate) and public dissatisfaction with that political error to win political office. They are clearly presenting themselves as "men of the people" and not overly qualified technocrats or scions of political families in their political campaigns.

It is important to note the differences between candidates like Powell and Hutchins. Powell has fashioned himself as a telegenic political organizer (Hicks, 2008a), while Hutchins, in his causes and cadence, assumes the role of a classic civil rights leader. This framing may put Hutchins at a disadvantage (even in Atlanta) if voters prefer more moderate black candidates (see Canon et al., 1996). Powell still lacks complete crossover appeal, as he is perceived to be an "activist of the hip hop generation" (Hicks, 2008b). However, given Powell's small celebrity, he may be able to cultivate a political base of voters under 45, which could serve him well in future elections (He has already vowed to run again in 2010) (Hicks, 2008c). For this reason, I tentatively classify Powell as a New Activist, and Hutchins as a Rebel without a Chance.

Analysis and Further Questions

The typologies listed above serve a two-fold purpose. First, they are designed to show the diversity among this class of individuals—a diversity that is often obscured in the popular press with their preoccupation with a few of these elected leaders. Moreover, the typologies help to organize our assessment of these leaders and give us some uniform metrics by which to judge them.

They typologies are not meant to be a monolith, though. There are other important considerations that the typologies do not take into consideration. I would like to briefly touch on these points.

Where Are the Women?

One of the interesting and troubling aspects of this research into the third wave of black elected officials is the relative absence of women on the national scene. Not until Yvette Clarke's election in November 2006 had any black woman born after 1960 achieved any measure of prominence in a federal office (She has since been joined by Congresswoman

Laura Richardson, who replaced the late Juanita Millender-McDonald). While Heather McTeer Hudson is an example of a young, black, female mayor, she leads a city with a population of less than 50,000 residents (United States Census Bureau, 2007).

There could be a reason to explain this apparent dearth of young, female black politicians. Jennifer Lawless and Richard Fox (2005) have found that women who are well situated professionally to run for political office (i.e., they come from the pipeline professions of law, education, politics, or business) are less likely to consider running for office and less likely to actually run for office once they have considered the possibility. Moreover, when they do consider running for office, women are more likely to consider running for a lower-level office (i.e., local government as opposed to state government) than men. On a small scale, Lawless and Fox's findings mirror what we observe in the cohort of young black politicians. The women who are running for office are concentrating their efforts at the state and local level. Yvette Clarke started out as a city councilwoman; Heather McTeer Hudson is mayor of a small city. Similarly, Alicia Thomas Morgan of Georgia, Jennifer McClellan of Virginia, Jill Carter of Maryland, and Grace Spencer of New Jersey are examples of Phase III female elected officials who serve as state legislators. These women stand in contrast to Harold Ford, Jr. and Jesse Jackson, Jr., whose first elections were for their congressional seats. However, only time will tell if these observations are temporary and these women use these first seats as steppingstones to higher political office.

Phase 2.5

In addition, there are also some elected officials who by virtue of their age, were not considered in this analysis, but who deserve mention because their politics closely resemble the politics of the younger cohort. Massachusetts Governor Deval Patrick is especially notable. (Congresswoman Donna Edwards also fits into this category.) Born in 1956, Patrick is too old to be considered part of the post-civil rights cohort, but he has the profile and politics of an Ivy League Upstart—he is Harvard-educated and worked in the Clinton administration. In many ways, Patrick's personal narrative draws on the themes of being on the racial vanguard characteristic of previous phases of black leadership and melds it with the post-racial pragmatism of some of the Phase III leadership. He is from the South Side of Chicago and was one of the first blacks to be afforded a prep school education through a program targeted to poor students of color. As a young lawyer, he worked in Darfur and for the NAACP Legal Defense Fund. He followed that with a stint in the Clinton Justice Department (Civil Rights Division) and work in the private sector (Anderson, 2006). Thus, because of his age and the breadth of his experience, Patrick and those like him are able to appeal to both blacks and whites apparently without the same need to prove their racial authenticity that the ways that their Ivy League Upstart counterparts have had to prove.

Conclusion

To be sure, the younger generation of leadership has not amassed enough power or seniority as a whole to affect widespread change in the black community. Thus, it remains to be seen whether their strategies and agenda produce favorable or unfavorable outcomes for blacks. However, we can apply what we now know about this emerging generation of black leadership to developing important questions to guide future research. I conclude with three of these questions, which will hopefully lead to more questions and further lines of inquiry on this topic.

First, we know that the new crop of young, black elected officials is more diverse than it would appear to be in the mainstream media, who focuses mostly on those with Ivy League credentials and crossover appeal. Indeed, most young black politicians inherited their seats from their parents. Will the exodus of Phase I and II black politicians from the scene free this sub-cohort to innovate black politics? Or will this group of dynastic heirs assume the oppositional mantle of their parents and vie for influence with their popular peers who have fewer ties to the black establishment?

Second, the age, class status and upbringing of these politicians raises larger questions for the study of black public opinion. Does this new generation of leadership reflect the larger generation that they came from, or are their preferences artifacts of calculated political ambition? If the values, perspectives and policy preferences of these politicians reflect the values of their cohort of blacks generally (as Bositis [2002] suggests), then this means that we have to reevaluate conventional wisdoms about how blacks develop linked fate and about how they choose parties, candidates and policy preferences. Further study of this cohort may provide further credence to Adolph Reed's argument that class differences within the black community betray multiple black agendas (see Reed, 2000: chapter 1).

Finally, we will eventually have to ask whether the campaign, legislative, and governing approach of this new generation of politicians will actually be more successful in delivering goods and services to African American communities. This question becomes especially important as more minority groups make legitimate claims for recognition, representation, and scarce resources. Moreover, the question reflects the nearly 20-year skepticism over deracialization generally. Robert Smith gloomily predicted that deracialization "is not likely to be able to arrest and reverse the decline of the black community, and ... it suggests that even black leadership itself may be turning away from the problem" (Smith, 1993: 220). If the new generation of black leaders turns away from problems that face the black community or is unable to deliver on their promises, then this could have a negative impact on already deep divisions within black communities. Moreover, it could lead to a deeper secondary marginalization of blacks deemed less socially desirable even within the black community (see Cohen, 1999). By reflecting on these issues sooner rather than later, hopefully this line of research can use lessons from the past 40 years of black elected leadership to chart a course for greater policy advancement in the future.

Notes

1. The terms "black" and "African American" will be used interchangeably in this chapter to describe people of African descent living in the United States.
2. Sheridan uses Douglas Wilder as a example of a second-wave politician who refused to identify with the civil rights struggle, saying that he opted to make money than advocate for change in the 1960s. Whatever one can say about Wilder's personal politics, given his age, no one can argue that he missed being personally affected by Jim Crow growing up in Richmond, Virginia (Sheridan, 1996: 166).
3. To be sure, there are earlier examples of young, moderate blacks challenging leaders from the older, civil rights generation as early as the 1980s. Ardrey and Nelson note that Michael White challenged the combative, divisive tactics of George Forbes and beat him for the mayoralty of Cleveland. There are other examples of black politics going against other black politicians in the 1980s and early 1990s. The notable victors include Dennis Archer (Ardrey and Nelson, 1990; Nordlinger, 2002).
4. Please refer to footnote 3 for a definition of high office. If I define a Rebrand broadly as someone who wins his/her parent's seat and then seeks higher office, then Congresswoman Yvette Clarke qualifies

as a Rebrand. She took over her mother's New York City Council seat. Winning a congressional seat could qualify as a step up. However, because this analysis defines high offices as offices higher than congressional seats, Congresswoman Clarke is classified as a Chip off the Old Block until she pursues a U.S. Senate seat, the New York governorship, or the presidency of the United States.

Bibliography

Anderson, Lisa. 2006. "Chicago-born, Leading in Mass: Deval Patrick Rose from Poverty, Bids to Be State's 1st Black Governor." *The Chicago Tribune*. 29 October 2006.

Ardrey, Saundra C. and William E. Nelson. "The Maturation of Black Political Power: The Case of Cleveland." *PS: Political Science and Politics*. 23(2): 148-151.

Benson, Josh. 2006. "Next for Booker? (Get Used to the Question)." *The New York Times*. 14 May 2006, 14:1.

Bositis, David A. 2002. *2002 National Opinion Poll: Politics*. Washington: Joint Center for Political and Economic Studies. Retrieved from www.jointcenter.org.

Bositis, David A. 2001. *Changing the Guard: Generational Difference among Black Elected Officials*. Washington, DC: Joint Center for Political and Economic Studies.

Brewington, Kelly. 2007. "Mitchell, Father Renew Their Feud." *Baltimore Sun*. Retrieved from baltimoresun.com. 24 September 2007.

Brosnan, James W. 2000. "Youngest Congressman to Speak To Democrats." *Cleveland Plain Dealer*. 6 August 2000.

Burgess, M. Elaine. 1962. *Negro Leadership in a Southern City*. Chapel Hill: University of North Carolina Press.

Byrd, Veronica. 2004. "'My Generation Can't Just Complain. We Have To Get Involved." *Essence*. October 2004. Retrieved from findarticles.com, 14 June 2007.

Canon, David T., Matthew Schousen, and Patrick Sellers. 1996. "The Supply Side of Congressional Redistricting: Race and Strategic Politicians, 1972-1992. *The Journal of Politics*. 58(3): 846-862.

Cohen, Cathy. 1999. *The Boundaries of Blackness: AIDS and the Breakdown of Black Politics*. Chicago: University of Chicago Press.

Curry, Marshall (Director). 2005. *Street Fight* [DVD]. United States: Marshall Curry Productions.

Davis, Marilyn and Alex Willingham. 1993. "Andrew Young and the Georgia State Elections of 1990." In *Dilemmas of Black Politics*. Georgia Persons (ed.). New York: Harper Collins. 147-175.

Davis, Michael and Andy Sher. 2006. "State GOP Mailing Focuses on Ford Family." *Chattanooga Times Free Press*. 2 November 2006. B2.

Dawson, Michael C. 1994. *Behind the Mule*. Princeton: Princeton University Press.

Dionne, E.J. 2004. "In Illinois, a Star Prepares." *The Washington Post*. 25 June 2004. A29.

Dovi, Suzanne. 2002. "Preferable Descriptive Representatives: Will Just Any Woman, Black or Latino Do?" *American Political Science Review*. 96(4): 745-754.

Evans, Ben. 2007. "Davis Won't Challenge Sessions for Senate Seat In 2008." *Associated Press State and Local Wire*. 8 January 2007.

Galloway, Jim. 2008. "Hutchins to Seek Lewis' Seat." *Atlanta Journal-Constitution*. 23 February 2008. Retrieved from ajc.com. 20 September 2008.

Gross, Courtney. 2008. "Democratic Primary Results by Congressional District." Posted on *The Wonkster* blog (http://www.gothamgazette.com/blogs/wonkster/2008/02/06/primary-results-by-congressional-district/). 6 February 2008. Retrieved 20 September 2008.

Hamilton, Charles V. 1982. "Foreword." In *The New Black Politics: The Search for Political Power.* Edited by Michael B. Preston, Lenneal J. Henderson Jr. and Paul Puryear. New York and London: Longman Publishers. xvii-xx.

Henderson, Lenneal J., Jr. 1996. "The Governance of Kurt Schmoke as Mayor of Baltimore." In *Race, Governance, and Politics in the United States*. Huey L. Perry (Ed.). Gainesville: University of Florida Press. 165-178.

Hicks, Jonathan. 2008a. "Brooklyn Congressman and Veteran of Tough Primaries Faces New Fight." *New York Times*. 28 April 2008. Retrieved from nytimes.com. 20 September 2008.

Hicks, Jonathan. 2008b. "Accused of Being Out of Touch, a 25-Year Congressman Campaigns for Dear Life." *New York Times*. 4 September 2008. Retrieved from nytimes.com. 20 September 2008.

Hicks, Jonathan. 2008c. "Towns's Challenger Vows to Run Again." Posted on *City Room Blog* of nytimes.com. *New York Times*. 28 April 2008. Retrieved from http://cityroom.blogs.nytimes.com/2008/09/16/townss-challenger-vows-to-run-again/#more-3963. 20 September 2008.

Jones, Charles E. and Michael Clemons. 1993. "A Model of Racial Crossover Voting: An Assessment of the Wilder Victory." In *Dilemmas of Black Politics*. Georgia Persons (Ed.). New York: Harper Collins. 128-146.

Kim, Claire. 2000. *Bitter Fruit: The Politics of Black-Korean Conflict in New York City*. New Haven: Yale University Press.

Ladd, Everett C. 1966. *Negro Political Leadership in the South*. Ithaca: Cornell University Press.

Lawless, Jennifer and Richard Fox. 2005. *It Takes a Candidate: Why Women Don't Run for Office*. Cambridge and New York: Cambridge University Press.

Lawrence, Cynthia. 2000. "Rush Wins in 1st: Did Obama Deliver a Wake-Up Call to Rush?" *Chicago Sun-Times*. 22 March 2000. Retrieved from www.jessejacksonjr.org. 14 June 2007.

Martin, Roland. 2003. "Ready or Not…" *Savoy*. March 2003. 52-56.

McCormick, Joseph II and Charles E. Jones. 1993. "The Conceptualization of Deracialization: Thinking Through The Dilemma." In *Dilemmas of Black Politics*. Georgia Persons (Ed.). New York: Harper Collins. 66-84.

Mihalopoulos, Dan. 2006. "Jesse Jackson Jr. Will Probably Run for Mayor of Chicago." *The Chicago Tribune*. 6 September 2006.

Mihalopoulos, Dan and Gary Washburn. 2006. "Jesse Jackson Jr. Said to Decide Against Running for Chicago Mayor." *The Chicago Tribune*. 8 November 2006.

Myrdal, Gunnar. 1944. *An American Dilemma*. New York: Harper and Brothers.

Nelson, William E.. 1982. "Cleveland: The Rise and Fall of the New Black Politics." In *The New Black Politics: The Search for Political Power.* Edited by Michael B. Preston, Lenneal J. Henderson Jr. and Paul Puryear. New York and London: Longman Publishers. 187-208.

Nordlinger, Jay. 2002. "Some 'Dissident.' Doin' the Skin-Color Nasty. A Bit of Righteous Kvetching. Etc." *National Review Online*. 28 May 2002. Retrieved from LexisNexis Academic Universe (web.lexis-nexis.com/universe). 20 January 2003.

Reed, Adolph. 1986. *The Jesse Jackson Phenomenon*. New Haven: Yale University Press.

Reed, Adolph. 2000. *Class Notes: Posing as Politics and Other Thought on the American Scene*. New York: The New Press.

Reed, K. Terrell and Sonia Alleyne. 2002. "What It Takes to Win." *Black Enterprise*. November 2002: 82-95.

_______. "Rep. Jesse Jackson Jr. Won't Run for Chicago Mayor." *Jet*. 27 November 2006.

Russakoff, Dale. 2002. "In Newark Race, Black Political Visions Collide." *TheWashington Post*. 14 May 2002. Retrieved from LexisNexis Academic Universe (web.lexis-nexis.com/universe) January 2003.

Schexnider, Alvin J. 1996. "Analyzing the Wilder Administration Through the Construct of Deracialization Politics." In *Race, Governance, and Politics in the United States*. Huey L. Perry (Ed.). Gainesville: University of Florida Press. 15-28.

Schlesinger, Joseph. 1966. *Ambition and Politics: Political Careers in the United States*. Chicago: Rand McNally and Company.

Sheridan, Earl. 1996. "The New Accommodationists." *Journal of Black Studies*. 27(2): 152-171.

Smith, Ben. 2008. "US HOUSE: Incumbents win all primary races. Lewis Avoids RunoffDespite Two Opponents." *Atlanta Journal-Constitution*. 16 July 2008. Retrieved from ajc.com. 20 September 2008.

Smith, Robert C. 1990. "Recent Elections and Black Politics: The Maturation or Death of Black Politics? *PS: Political Science and Politics*. 23(2): 160-162.

Smith, Robert C. 1993. "Ideology as the Enduring Dilemma of Black Politics." In *Dilemmas of Black Politics*. Georgia Persons (Ed.). New York: Harper Collins. 211-225.

Smith, Robert C. 1996. *We Have No Leaders*. Albany: State University of New York Press.

Smith, Robert C. and Ronald Walters. 1999. *African American Leadership*. Albany: State University of New York Press.

Star News Services. 2005. "Kwame's Woes: Conflict Follows Detroit Mayor In His Battle for a Second Term." *Windsor Star* (Ontario, Canada). 16 July 2005.

Starr, Alexandra. 2002. "We Shall Overcome, Too." *Business Week*. 15 July 2002. Retrieved from LexisNexis Academic Universe (web.lexis-nexis.com/universe). 20 January 2003.

Strategic Perceptions (Producer). 2006. "Family Ties" [Political Advertisement]. Hollywood: Strategic Perceptions, LLC. Retrieved from http://nationaljournal.com/members/adspotlight/2006/11/1106tnsen2.htm, 14 June 2007.

Strickland, Ruth Ann and Marcia Lynn Whicker. 1992. "Comparing the Wilder and Gantt Campaigns: A Model for Black Candidate Success in Statewide Elections." *PS: Political Science and Politics*. 25(2): 204-212.

Summers, Mary and Phillip Klinkner. 1996. "The Election and Governance of John Daniels as Mayor of New Haven." In *Race, Governance, and Politics in the United States*. Huey L. Perry (Ed.). Gainesville: University of Florida Press. 127-150.

Tate, Katherine. 1994. *From Protest to Politics: The New Black Voters in American Elections*. New York and Cambridge: Russell Sage Foundation/Harvard University Press.

Traub, James. 2002. "The Way We Live Now: 9-8-02; The Last Color Line." *The New York Times Magazine*. 8 September 2002. Retrieved from LexisNexis Academic Universe (web.lexis-nexis.com/universe) 20 January 2003.

United States Census Bureau. 2007. "American Factfinder: Greenville, Mississippi." Retrieved from http://factfinder.census.gov 14 June 2007.

Williams, Linda. 1987. "Black Political Progress in the 1980's: The Electoral Arena." In *The New Black Politics: The Search for Political Power.* Second Edition. Edited by Michael B. Preston, Lenneal J. Henderson Jr. and Paul Puryear. New York and London: Longman Publishers. 97-136.

Wilson, James Q. 1960. *Negro Politics: The Search for Leadership*. Glencoe, Illinois: The Free Press.

Wilson, Zaphon. 1993. "Gantt Versus Helms: Deracialization Confronts SouthernTraditionalism." In D*ilemmas of Black Politics*. Georgia Persons (Ed.). New York: Harper Collins. 176-193.

Black Identity: What Does It Mean for Black Leaders?

Jas M. Sullivan
Louisiana State University

Black identity (in its various conceptions) has been used in political science to study black attitudes toward policy preferences and voter participation (Dawson, 1994; Tate, 1993). For example, with respect to policy preferences, Tate (1993) found a relationship between racial group identification and blacks' opinions on affirmative action; Kinder and Winter (2001) found a correlation between racial group closeness and blacks' support of social welfare programs; and White (2007) found explicit and implicit racial verbal cues activate racial thinking about policy issues—specifically, "explicit references to race most reliably elicited racial thinking by activating racial in-group identification" (1). Additionally, Dawson (1994) concluded that racial identity continues to be stronger than identities based on class, gender, religion, or any other social characteristics as appreciation of attitude toward a range of policy issues.

Research has also shown a relationship between black identity and political interest and voter participation. Specifically, Tate (2003) found that "black identification was significantly related to black political interest and to voter participation in congressional elections; however, it was unrelated to political knowledge and to political efficacy" (142). Olsen (1970: 688-92) and Verba and Nie (1972: 161) found blacks with a strong sense of racial identity or group consciousness participated at higher rate in politics. Dawson's (2001) findings in *Black Visions* reveal the impact black identity (as measured by linked-fate) has on various ideological support. For example, he finds that believing one's fate is linked to that of the race is a strong predictor for economic nationalism (130), supportive of black feminist orientations and ideology (157, 164), allowing more women to become members of the clergy (349), and warmth for lesbians (348).

However, the link between black identity and preferences toward black leaders has not been fully examined. The objective of this article is to ascertain whether feelings toward black leaders are shaped by one's black identity (i.e., linked fate and racial salience). Using the 1996 National Black Election Studies data, the results suggest black identity is a significant predictor of feelings toward Louis Farrakhan, Jesse Jackson, Carol Moseley-Braun, and Kweisi Mfume. A strong sense of black identity, however, is not a significant predictor of feelings toward Clarence Thomas and Colin Powell. As a result, these findings certainly suggest that differences in how blacks feel about a black leader will depend on their perceptions of the leader's attitude and beliefs about being black, their own attitudes and beliefs about being black, and where they fall on various demographic measures. In the next section, I begin with discussing, briefly, the theories of racial identity, and then explain, specifically, theories of black identity. Then, using the data, I show that racial identity affects feelings toward certain types of black leaders.

Theories of Racial Identity

Racial identity is an ambiguous and socially constructed concept. It implies a "consciousness of self within a particular group" (Spencer and Markstrom-Adams, 1990: 292). It's the "meanings a person attributes to the self as an object in a social situation or social role" (Burke, 1980: 18), and it relates to a "sense of people-hood, which provides a sense of belonging" (Smith, 1989: 156). The "level of uncertainty about the nature of racial identity" (Herring et al., 1999: 364) and the "indicative confusion about the topic" (Phinney, 1990: 500) is illustrated by the lack of a standard definition. Nevertheless, according to symbolic interactionism, "racial identity is treated as one of the many identities contained within self" (White and Burke, 1987: 311), and it is given fundamental and overriding importance in the United States. For example, Winant (1995) explains "racial identity outweighs all other identities. We are compelled to think racially, to use the racial categories and the meaning systems into which we have been socialized.... It is not possible to be 'color blind,' for race is a basic element of our identity.... For better or worse, without a clear racial identity, an American is in danger of having no identity" (31-32).

Racial identity formation is produced by the everyday "interactions and challenges" (Davis and Gandy, 1999: 367) that an individual encounters. It is affected by socioeconomic status and situational context (Cornell and Hartman, 1998). It is "dynamic and changing over time, as people explore and make decisions about the role of race in their lives" (Phinney, 1990: 502). In other words, racial identity is "achieved through an active process of decision making and self-evaluation" (Phinney, 1990: 502). Thomas (1970), Cross (1971), and Banks (1981) have proposed the idea that racial identity development is a "progressional process which occurs in a hierarchical sequence from racial unconsciousness to racial pride and commitment" (Gay, 1985: 49). For example, Cross' (1978) five stages to identity development include: pre-encounter, encounter, immersion-emersion, internalization, and internalization and commitment. In essence, these stages represent a process by which people come to a "deeper understanding and appreciation of their race" (Phinney, 1990: 500); even so, a deeper understanding may not translate into a greater acceptance of their racial identity; nevertheless, it has an affect on behavior.

The importance of this is that "positive racial identification for most racial minorities does not happen automatically; nor does it for all individuals. When it does happen, it is learned" (Gay, 1985: 49). This suggests that racial identity sentiments and attitudes are heterogeneous even among people of the same race, because individual's experiences and encounters differ. Let's now turn our attention to theories of black identity.

Theories of Black Identity

Black identity is "emerging, changing, and complex" (Hecht and Ribeau, 1991: 503). Banks (1981) has suggested that "there is no one identity among blacks that we can delineate, as social scientists have sometimes suggested, but many complex and changing identities among them" (129-139). Due to its multifaceted nature, scholars have conceptualized black identity in a variety of different ways: "racial categorization" (Jaret and Reitzes 1999), "common fate or linked fate" (Gurin et al., 1989; Dawson 1996), "racial salience" (Herring et al., 1999), "closeness" (Allen et al., 1989; Broman et al., 1988; Conover 1984), "black separatism or racial solidarity" (Allen and Hatchett 1986; Allen et al., 1989), "racial self-esteem" (Porter and Washington 1979), "Africentrism" (Grills and Longshore 1996), and "racial awareness and consciousness" (Jackson 1987). Others suggest black identity has "multiple dimensions" (Seller et al., 1998) and formation occurs over time through various "stages" (Cross 1978). Consequently, several different psychometric scales have been used to tap the different dimensions of black identity.

The psychometric scales most often employed range from one question to sometimes over sixty questions, depending on how black identity is operationalized. Furthermore, scholars use different measures to tap the same aspect of black identity. For example, when black identity is operationalized as closeness, *American National Election Studies* asked respondents to rate their closeness to blacks as whole (Campbell et al 1960; Lau 1989); *National Survey of Black Americans* assessed closeness with sub-groups of blacks such as poor, middle class, or the aged (Ellison 1991; Harris 1995); and National Black Election Studies asked respondents their closeness to blacks in Africa and America (Gurin et al., 1989). These are three vary different psychometric questions measuring the same aspect of black identity. Recognizing the various dimensions and measures of black identity, scholars have forged ahead with the understanding that no one conceptualization of racial identity or psychometric scale is better than the other.

Regardless of complex nature of black identity, scholars have focused their attention on exploring the factors shaping black identity and the effect black identity has on human behavior. Let's begin with the factors shaping black identity. Black identity is affected by socioeconomic status and situational context. Studies have suggested that social and demographic factors (Broman et al., 1988; Allen et al., 1989), childhood socialization (Gecas 1981; Gecas and Schwalbe 1986), interracial interaction (Rosenberg 1975; McGuire et al., 1978), social class (Gecas 1999), age (Broman et al., 1988; Porter and Washington 1979), family and friends (Gecas and Mortimer 1987; Hughes and Demo 1989), and socioeconomic status (Allen et al., 1989; Broman et al., 1988) are important factors influencing black identity. Additionally, Broman et al., (1988) found people who were older, Southern, and less educated scored higher on an index measuring closeness to other blacks.

Demo and Hughes (1990) examined the social structural process and arrangements related to racial group identification. They found that group identity is shaped by the content of parental socialization. In particular, "feelings of closeness and black group evaluation are enhanced by positive interpersonal relations with family and friends" (372). Interracial contact has also been found to shape black identity. Harris (1995) explored the impact of childhood interracial contact on adult black identity. The findings suggest that "interracial contact in childhood weakens adult feelings of closeness to other blacks" (243). Similar findings were also found in the Demo and Hughes (1990) study, in which they discovered that the impact of interracial interaction depends on timing; specifically, "contact during childhood and adolescence has a negative impact on the black group identity; however, interracial relationships during adulthood promote positive black group evaluations" (372). Social movements have also been shown to affect racial identity. Condi and Christiansen (1977) found that there has been "significant shift in identity structure of blacks and that the Black Power movement was an important causal factor in effecting change" (53).

Residential racial composition, competition, and conflict have been shown to affect black identity. Conflict theorists argue group identity and cohesiveness increase as a result of conflict with an adversary (Coser 1965), and competition theorists argue competition among racial-ethnic groups in work and community settings will also increase the likelihood people will attach more importance to their racial-ethnic identity (Olzak and Nagel 1986). Jaret and Reitzes (1999) explored black identity changes in different social settings. Their findings indicate black identity changes across various settings; specifically, black identity is more important for blacks at work and least important at home. In addition, changes in black identity are affected by racial composition of the local area. They find that blacks "living in areas that are 'intermediate' in percentage black say that their racial-ethnic identity is more important to them than do blacks living in areas with 'low' amounts of black residents or with 'high' amounts of black residents" (725). These findings have, however, been challenged by the data collected in similar studies.

Contrary to the findings of Jaret and Reitzes (1999), Bledsoe et al. (1995) found those who live in neighborhoods with more blacks score significantly higher on the racial solidarity scale; mixed-neighborhoods show less solidarity than those who live in more heavily black neighborhoods (449). The major reason is because "those who live in mixed-race neighborhoods have more frequent and intimate contact with whites; surrounded by white friends, acquaintances, neighbors, merchants, and service providers, these blacks may simply perceive less reason to engage in collective action on behalf of blacks" (450).

The link between black identity and preferences toward black leaders, however, has not been fully examined, and purpose of this research is to do exactly that. I ask the following question: Are blacks' feelings toward black leaders influenced by black identity? Specifically, I examine the impact of linked fate and racial salience on blacks' feelings toward Louis Farrakhan, Jesse Jackson, Carol Moseley-Braun, Kwesi Mfume, Clarence Thomas, and Colin Powell. Just as black identity has affected policy preferences and support for various ideologies, I expect that feelings toward these black leaders will be influenced by black identity.

Data and Methodology

The data used in the study is from the 1996 National Black Election Study (NBES). This data provides information on the attitudes and political preferences of the black electorate during the 1996 presidential election, and contains both pre- and post-election components. Questions regarding demographic information were also asked of survey respondents. The data used in this study is from the group of respondents from the pre-election component.

Dependent Variable

The dependent variable in this study is the feeling thermometer score. Scores were recorded for the following black leaders: Louis Farrakhan, Jesse Jackson, Carol Moseley-Braun, Kwesi Mfume, Clarence Thomas, and Colin Powell. In the 1996 NBES study, respondents were asked to rate their feelings toward various black leaders on a scale of 0 (least favorable) to 100 (most favorable). If the respondent rated the person at the 50 degree mark, it meant they felt neither warm nor cold toward them. If respondents didn't recognize the person's name, they didn't rate that person. The specific question asked of respondents was: using the thermometer, how would you rate Louis Farrakhan? Respondents were then given the following choice of options: (a) select a number between 0 and 100; (b) doesn't recognize name; (c) don't know where to rate/can't judge; or (d) refused/no answer.

Independent Variables

The independent variables in this study include: black identity measures (linked-fate and racial salience), educational level, family income, sex of respondent, age, and political ideology. Previous discussion on black identity has illustrated that scholars have conceptualized black identity in a variety of different ways, and have utilized several different psychometric scales to tap the different dimensions of black identity. The two most prevalent ways black identity has been conceptualized in political science research is through the notions of linked-fate and racial salience.

Both linked-fate and racial salience taps cognitive orientations toward in-groups, and assesses the essential nature of group identity. Several measures have been utilized to capture the idea of linked-fate and racial salience, and the most frequent ways have been by asking the following questions: "Do you think what happens generally to black people in this country will have something to do with what happens in your life?"; and "People differ in whether they think about being black—what they have common with blacks. What about you—do you think about this a lot, fairly often, once in a while, or hardly ever?" The first question taps linked-fate; while the second taps racial salience. Both of these questions were asked of respondents in the 1996 NBES, and I rely on these as measures of black identity for this research.

Analyses

The data was analyzed using ordinary least squares (OLS) to identify whether black identity influences feelings toward the following black leaders: Louis Farrakhan, Jesse Jackson, Carol Moseley-Braun, Kwesi Mfume, Clarence Thomas, and Colin Powell. Separately, each of the five black leaders was subjected to the same model. Descriptive statistics for each of the variables are reported in Table 1. The number of participants differed for each black leader, because only raw thermometer scores were included into the analysis. For example, doesn't recognize name, don't know where to rate, and refused/no answer responses were not included.

Table 2 gives results for the multiple regression results. The findings show that linked-fate was a strong predictor for feelings toward Farrakhan, Jackson, Mfume, and Moseley-Braun. Those who believe what happens to blacks in this country will have something to do with what happens in their life felt more favorable toward these black leaders, as seen in Figure 1. Racial salience, on the other hand, was significant only for Farrakhan; specifically, favorability toward Farrakhan increased, among those who thought a lot about being black.

While racial identity measures were not strong predictors of favorability for Powell and Thomas, Figure 1 shows that among those who don't believe their fate is linked to other blacks were more favorable toward Powell and Thomas.

Political ideology was not significant on feelings toward black leaders; however, the significance of socioeconomic variables differed for different black leaders. For Farrakhan

Table 1
Descriptive Statistics for Dependent & Independent Measures for Each Black Leader

	Farrakhan (n=901)		Jackson (n=964)		Mfume (n=364)		Moseley-Braun (n=469)		Thomas (n=906)		Powell (n=868)	
	M	*SD*	*M*	*SD*	*M*	*SD*	*M*	*SD*	*M*	*SD*	*M*	*SD*
Thermometer Score	51.2	30.93	70.38	24.74	69.05	26.78	63.49	25.62	41.81	27.36	66.33	25.96
Linked-fate	.81	.39	.81	.39	.84	.37	.82	.39	.81	.39	.82	.39
Racial Salience	1.10	1.12	1.08	1.13	1.21	1.13	1.18	1.13	1.10	1.12	1.10	1.13
Political ideology	2.63	2.02	2.65	2.02	2.47	1.86	2.49	1.84	2.62	1.98	2.59	1.94
Educational level	4.10	1.62	4.04	1.63	4.76	1.82	4.48	1.76	4.15	1.63	4.11	1.63
Family income	10.64	22.52	10.26	22.04	9.99	19.78	10.57	21.91	10.49	22.12	10.51	22.28
Sex of respondent	1.63	.48	1.64	.48	1.59	.492	1.62	.49	1.63	2.74	1.63	.48
Age	2.70	1.53	2.76	1.53	2.68	1.42	2.79	1.52	1.10	1.12	2.79	1.56

Table 2
OLS Results of Independent Variables on Feelings toward Black Leaders

	Farrakhan		Jackson		Braun		Mfume		Thomas		Powell	
Variable	**b**	**Beta**	**b**	**Beta**	**b**	**Beta**	**b**	**Beta**	**b**	**Beta**	**b**	**Beta**
Linked-fate	8.15**	.10	7.47**	.12	6.77*	.10	15.07*	.21	-2.35	-.03	2.53	.04
	(2.72)		(2.13)		(3.16)		(3.84)		(2.49)		(2.34)	
Racial-salience	2.11*	.08	1.28	.06	1.34	.06	1.28	.05	.68	.03	.90	.04
	(.95)		(.74)		(1.06)		(1.28)		(.87)		(.81)	
Political ideology	-.32	-.02	-.63	-.04	-.61	-.04	.09	.01	.42	.03	.03	.00
	(.54)		(.43)		(.67)		(.77)		(.50)		(.48)	
Educational level	.25	.01	-.33	-.02	3.05**	.21	3.72**	.25	-2.43**	-.14	2.43**	.15
	(.65)		(.51)		(.67)		(.78)		(.59)		(.55)	
Family Income	-.00	-.00	.05	.04	-.04	-.03	-.00	-.00	.05	.04	.04	.03
	(.04)		(.04)		(.05)		(.07)		(.04)		(.04)	
Sex of Respondent	-2.19	-.03	4.72**	.09	3.15	.06	2.02	.04	-1.80	-.03	-3.79*	-.07
	(2.15)		(1.68)		(2.41)		(2.83)		(1.96)		(1.83)	
Age	-2.24**	-.11	-1.34*	-.06	.54	.03	.47	.03	.14	.01	.48	.03
	(.68)		(.53)		(.78)		(.98)		(.63)		(.58)	
R^2=	.19		.18		.28		.36		.16		.18	

NOTE: b = unstandardized regression coefficient with standard error in parenthesis; Beta = standardized regression coefficient.
$^*p < 0.05$; $^{**}p < 0.01$

Figure 1
Effects of Linked-Fate on Feelings toward Farrakhan, Jackson, Mfume, Moseley-Braun, Powell, and Thomas

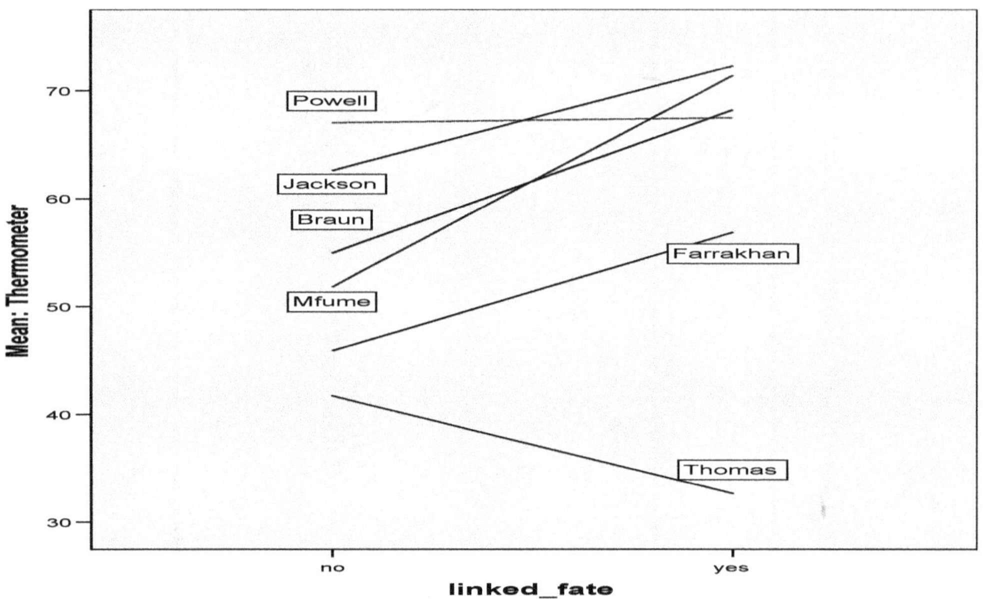

Figure 2
Effects of Education on Feelings toward Mfume, Moseley-Braun, Powell, and Thomas

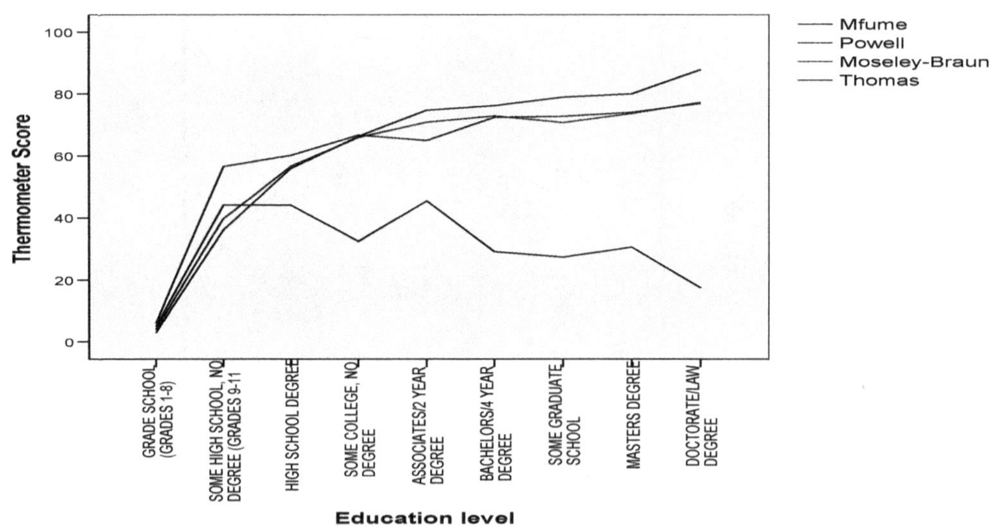

and Jackson, age of the respondent's influenced favorability. For example, the younger the respondents, the more favorable toward these black leaders. Sex of the respondent was significant on feelings toward Jackson and Colin Powell. Females were more likely to feel favorable toward Jackson; while males were more likely to feel favorable toward Powell. Education level was a strong predictor of feelings toward Moseley-Braun, Mfume, Thomas, and Powell. Specifically, favorability increased with higher the education for Moseley-Braun, Mfume, and Powell. See Figure 2 for the effects of education on feelings toward Moseley-Braun; however, for Thomas, the higher the education level, the lower blacks felt favorable.

In short, the findings indicate that black identity does have an impact on feelings toward some black leaders. In particular, while both racial salience and linked-fate are important in shaping feelings toward Farrakhan and Jackson, only linked-fate was significant for Mfume and Moseley-Braun. However, neither racial salience nor linked-fate was a strong predictor of feelings toward Powell and Thomas. Finally, the significance of demographic characteristics varied, depending on the black leader.

Conclusion

The general findings reveal black identity (along with several demographic factors) does affect black voters' feelings toward black leaders. This is an important finding, because we now have an insight into the factors shaping black voter's feelings toward black leaders. Specifically, simply being a black leader will not generate favorable feelings among the black electorate—differences in how blacks feel about a black leader will depend on their perceptions of the leader's attitude and beliefs about being black, their own attitudes and beliefs about being black, and where they fall on various demographic measures.

In regards to the findings, several important questions arise. Why was it that favorability toward Farrakhan, Jackson, Mfume, and Moseley-Braun increased amongst those who believed that their fate was linked to other blacks, while, favorability toward Thomas and Powell increased amongst those who did not believe that their fate was linked to other blacks? Do the signals these black leaders send (regarding their own black identity), through their words and deeds, have an impact on the black electorate? In other words, the findings suggest, among black leaders who portray the idea that their race is a central part of who they are found increased favorability among those blacks who themselves felt their fate was linked to other blacks; while black leaders who portray the notion that their race is not a central part of who they are found increased favorability among those blacks who themselves felt their fate was not linked to other blacks.

While these black leaders don't come out and directly say that their fate is either linked or not linked to other blacks, their actions and words do bring some clarity to their positions. For example, I argue that speaking out against racial inequalities, voicing support for race-centred policies such as affirmative action, and forming organizations like the Nation of Islam and the Rainbow/PUSH Coalition sends a message to the black electorate that race is an important characteristic linking them together. However, black leaders like Powell and Thomas often shy away from race issues, and do not support racial preference policies and affirmative action programs. Rarely do they see things in racial terms. For example, Thomas, in a recent Supreme Court case disagreed that Dallas prosecutors systematically excluded black jurors in the trial of Texas death row inmate Thomas Miller-El; however, the irony was that he was the lone dissenter in that case. Furthermore, they often de-racialize themselves to the point that the black community considers them an outsider and questions their "blackness." These leaders, through their deeds and words, portray the idea that race is not a central part of their lives, and ultimately, represent an image that race is not an important aspect linking them together with the rest of the black community. Thus, this research, in part, suggests attraction to a black leader will depend on shared racial identity positions.

Let's explore the case of Barack Obama. It was not too long ago (i.e., early on during the Democratic primaries) that some suggested Obama was not "black" or "black enough" for reasons stemming from his cultural heritage (his mixed ancestry) and his lack of expressed positions on race issues. Even Obama expressed the following: "There are elements within the black community who might suggest 'Well, he's from Hyde Park' or 'He went to Harvard' or 'He was born in Hawaii, so he might not be black enough" (Fletcher, 2007: 2). To this type of thinking, he explained in his book, *The Audacity of Hope*, "I've never had the option of restricting my loyalties on the basis of race, or measuring my worth on the basis of tribe." Nevertheless, Debra J. Dickerson, a black author and essayist, declared that "Obama isn't black" (Swarns, 2007: 1) in the American racial context, "because he does not embody the experiences of most blacks whose ancestors endured slavery, segregation, and the bitter struggle for civil rights" (Swarns, 2007: 1). Debra Dickerson further explained:

> I've got nothing but love for the brother, but we don't have anything in common. His father is African. His mother was a white woman. He grew up with white grandparents. Now, I'm willing to adopt him. He married black. He acts black. But there's a lot of distance between black Africans and African-Americans" (Swarns, 2007: 3).

With regards to policy, early in the primary campaign, Obama rarely interjected policies that were directly related to race. His policy stances spoke generally to the welfare of the whole community—instead of singling out one group over another. For example, in his address at the 2004 Democratic National Convention, Obama stated:

> For alongside our famous individualism, there's another ingredient in the American saga. A belief that we're all connected as one people. If there is a child on the South Side of Chicago who can't read, that matters to me, even if it's not my child. If there's a senior citizen somewhere who can't pay for their prescription drugs, and has to choose between medicine and the rent, that makes my life poorer, even if it's not my grandparent. If there's an Arab American family being rounded up without benefit of an attorney or due process, that threatens my civil liberties. It is that fundamental belief, it is that fundamental belief, I am my brother's keeper, I am my sister's keeper that makes this country work. It's what allows us to pursue our individual dreams and yet still come together as one American family. E pluribus unum. Out of many, one. There is not a Black America and a White America and Latino America and Asian America—there's the United States of America.

Even during Jena Six controversy, Obama's voice was silent on the issue. This prompted Jesse Jackson to publicly criticize Obama for not getting personally involved. Jackson stated: "If I were a candidate, I'd be all over Jena. Jena is a defining moment, just like Selma was a defining moment" (Associated Press, 2007: 1). Jackson further went on to say that Obama was "acting like he's white" (Associated Press, 2007: 1).

For these reasons, there had been some ambivalence early on in the primary season among blacks toward his candidacy. According to the *Washington Post*-ACB poll taken December 2006 and January 2007, Hillary Clinton was "preferred" 3 to 1 over Obama by black Democrats and 4 out of 5 black Democrats viewed her "more favorably" than Obama (Fletcher, 2007: 2). Some black legislators had endorsed Clinton, instead of Obama, and the chairwoman of the Congressional Black Caucus, Carolyn Cheeks-Kilpatrick, said she was "99% sure her group would not support Obama en masse the way the powerful women's political organization Emily's List was backing Hillary Clinton" (Bacon, 2007: 1). Oddly enough, Obama found himself a stranger among the black electorate.

What has changed since the early primary season to warrant such overwhelming support for Barack Obama among the black electorate? Did Obama successfully send signals, regarding his own racial identity, to the black electorate? Before answering this question, two points must be reiterated: this research shows that black voters overwhelmingly feel their fate is linked; and the regression analysis reveals an increased favorability for Farrakhan, Jackson, Mfume, and Moseley-Braun—suggesting that those leaders who portray the idea that their race is a central part of who they are found increased favorability among those blacks who themselves felt their fate is linked to other blacks. I argue that Obama sent clear signals that solidified the link between him and the black electorate, by voicing support for policies that are important to the black community, gaining prominent black endorsements, and winning the first primary contest. More importantly, certain experiences confronted by Obama during the primary election (which were not of his doing) further solidified this bond.

Let's begin with those actions that Obama undertook in signaling to the black electorate that race is a central and an integral part of his identity. First, during the Rev. Jeremiah Wright controversy, he delivered a prime-time speech addressing the issue of race. In the speech, for the first time, Obama made it undeniably clear to the black voters that he embraces his blackness. For example, instead of dismissing Rev. Wright (a popular black preacher with a history of saying disparaging remarks about America) as a "crank or a demagogue" (Obama, March 18, 2008), Obama stated the following:

> He [Rev. Wright] contains within him the contradictions—the good and the bad—of the community that he has served diligently for so many years. I can no more disown him than I can disown the black community. I can no more disown him than I can my white grandmother—a woman who helped raise me, a woman who sacrificed again and again for me, a woman who loves me as much as she loves anything in this world, but a woman who once confessed her fear of black men who passed by her on the street, and who on more than one occasion has uttered racial or ethnic stereotypes that made me cringe. These people are a part of me. And they are a part of America, this country that I love (Obama, March 18, 2008).

This particular paragraph is a powerful declaration of neutrality—in that, Obama reveals that he is not going to choose a side, but be loyal to his "blackness" and his "whiteness", regardless of the faults that these individuals possess (Rev. Wright and his grandmother). The speech was also groundbreaking because, for the first time, Obama spoke at length about the policy issues that are important to the black electorate. It's interesting to point out that Obama blames these problems (which are confronted by blacks) on the social structure, instead of pointing the finger at blacks.

This recognition that race (more so than individual decision-making) negatively affects blacks' advancement in the U.S. is congruent to the dominant philosophy held by many in the black community.

> [W]e do need to remind ourselves that so many of the disparities that exist in the African-American community today can be directly traced to inequalities passed on from an earlier generation that suffered under the brutal legacy of slavery and Jim Crow. Segregated schools were, and are, inferior schools; we still haven't fixed them.... Legalized discrimination—where blacks were prevented, often through violence, from owning property, or loans were not granted to African-American business owners, or black homeowners could not access FHA mortgages, or blacks were excluded from unions, or the police force,

> or fire departments—meant that black families could not amass any meaningful wealth to bequeath to future generations. That history helps explain the wealth and income gap between black and white, and the concentrated pockets of poverty that persists in so many of today's urban and rural communities. A lack of economic opportunity among black men, and the shame and frustration that came from not being able to provide for one's family, contributed to the erosion of black families—a problem that welfare policies for many years may have worsened. And the lack of basic services in so many urban black neighborhoods—parks for kids to play in, police walking the beat, regular garbage pick-up and building code enforcement—all helped create a cycle of violence, blight and neglect that continue to haunt us (Obama, March 18, 2008).

Second, in addition to his groundbreaking race speech, Obama also sent a signal by getting endorsements from prominent black leaders and entertainers. For example, on the political side, Obama received the endorsements of Jesse Jackson, Al Sharpton, Louis Farrakhan, and the majority whip for the 110th Congress, James E. Clyburn (the third-ranking Democrat in the U.S. House of Representatives). On the entertainment side, he received the support of Will Smith, Halle Berry, Oprah Winfrey, Morgan Freeman, Cornel West, Toni Morrison—to name a few. Finally, Obama's victory in Iowa created a sense of hope that his success is connected to the success of the entire black community—in that, if Obama can be the first black president, then other members of the black community can reach the pinnacle of government and society. Even Bill Clinton made the comment that he knew when Obama won the Iowa caucuses that Obama would receive a great deal of black support. Specifically, Clinton, on ABC's *Good Morning America* stated, "Iowa happened. The minute it became possible that he could be the nominee, he was going to win the lion's share of the African-American vote." These are some of the ways Obama directly solidified his link to the black community.

Additionally, certain experiences Obama encountered during the primary election further solidified this link between him and the black community. Obama had experienced what "most blacks" experience in this country, and that is racism. For example, Hillary Clinton, on Fox News, stated that, "Dr. King's dream began to be realized when President Lyndon Johnson passed the Civil Rights Act of 1964. It took a president to get it done." Then President Clinton stated, "Jesse Jackson won in South Carolina twice, in '84 and '88, and he ran a good campaign. And Senator Obama is running a good campaign." Many interpreted Clinton's comparison of Obama's victory to that of Jackson's as an attempt to diminish Obama's victory. These two comments created uproar on black radio, Internet blogs, and cable television stations. A prominent black member of the U.S. House of Representatives (James Clyburn) expressed in an interview with CNN that Bill Clinton ought to "chill out." Witnessing Obama's encounter with racism, (a situation other blacks deal with on a day-to-day basis), the black electorate rallied around Obama and offered their overwhelming support. In the crucial South Carolina primaries (with a large black population), Obama received 55.4 percent of the vote to Senator Clinton's 26.5 percent. A huge black voter turnout helped Obama to victory. In the end, those candidates who don't publicly articulate their positions on race issues may be interpreted as not being "authentically black" or caring about black interests. The electoral implication is that among those blacks who feel that race defines the very nature of who they are may not support this type of candidate.

While the research findings are interesting, the limitation is that I would have preferred to use measures of black identity that were multidimensional in nature, instead of one-dimensional measures such as linked-fate and racial salience (which are used most prevalent in political science research). While these one-dimensional measures are appropriate, they don't take into account the complexities of black identity. In saying that, I use them in this research, because National Black Election Studies only ask questions regarding linked-fate and racial salience. Regardless of the measurement issues, the findings do provide a necessary glimpse into the effects of black identity in shaping political behavior.

References

Allen, Richard and Hatchett, Shirley. 1986. "The Media and Social Reality Effects: Self and System Orientations of Blacks." *Communication Research* (13): 97-123.

Allen, Richard; Dawson, Michael; and Brown, Ronald. 1989. "A Schema-Based Approach to Modeling an African-American Racial Belief System." *American Political Science Review* (83): 421-41.

Associated Press, September 20, 2007: 1.

Bacon, Perry Jr. "Can Obama Count on the Black Vote?" *Time Magazine*: 1.

Banks, James. 1981. "Stages of Ethnicity: Implications for Curriculum Reform. Pg. 129-139 in *Multiethnic Education: Theory and Practice*, edited by James A. Banks. Boston: Allyn and Bacon.

Bledsoe, Timothy; Welch, Susan; Sigelman, Lee; and Combs; Michael. 1995. "Residential Context and Racial Solidarity among African Americans." *American Journal of Political Science* (39): 434-458).

Bobo, Lawrence and Kluegel, James. 1993. "Opposition to Race-Targeting: Self-Interest, Stratification Ideology, or Racial Attitudes." *American Sociological Review* (58): 443-464.

Broman, Clifford; Neighbors, Harold; and Jackson, James. 1988. "Racial Group Identifications among Black Adults." *Social Forces* (67): 146-58.

Burke, Peter J. 1980. "The Self: Measurement Requirements from an Interactionist Perspective." *Social Psychology Quarterly* (43): 18-29.

Campbell, Angus; Converse, Phillip; Miller, Warren; and Stokes, Donald. 1960. *The American Voter*. Chicago: University of Chicago Press.

Condi, J. and Christiansen, James. 1977. "An Indirect Technique for the Measurement of Changes in Black Identity." *Phylon* (38): 46-54.

Conover, Pamela. 1984. "The Influence of Group Identification on Political Perception and Evaluation." *Journal of Politics* (46): 760-85.

Cornell, S. and Hartman, D. 1998. "*Ethnicity and Race: Making Identities in a Changing World*." Thousand Oaks, CA: Pine Forge Press.

Coser, Lewis. 1965. *The Functions of Social Conflict*. Glencoe, IL: Free Press.

Cross, William. 1971. "Discovering the Black Referent: The Psychology of Black Liberation." Pg. 95-110 in *Beyond Black and White: An Alternative America*, edited by Vernon J. Dixon and Badi G. Foster. Boston: Little, Brown and Company.

Cross, William. 1978. "The Thomas and Cross Models of Psychological Nigrescense: A Review." *Journal of Black Psychology* (5): 13-31.

Davis, Jessica and Gandy, Oscar. 1999. "Racial Identity and Media Orientations: Exploring the Nature of Constraint." *Journal of Black Studies* (29): 367-397.

Dawson, Michael. 1994. *Behind the Mule: Race and Class in African-American Politics*. Princeton, NJ: Princeton University Press.

Dawson, Michael. 1996. "Black Power and Demonization of African Americans." *PS: Political Science and Politics* (24): 456-61.

Dawson, Michael. 2001. *Black Vision: the Roots of Contemporary African-American Political Ideologies*. Chicago: University of Chicago Press.

Demo, David and Hughes, Michael. 1990. "Socialization and Racial Identity among Black Americans." *Social Psychology Quarterly* (53): 364-374.

Ellison, Christopher. 1991. "Identification and Separatism: Religious Involvement and Racial Orientations among Black Americans." *Sociological Quarterly* (32): 477-494.

Fletcher, Michael. January 25, 2007. "Obama's Appeal to Blacks Remains an Open Question." *The Washington Post*: 2.

Gay, Geneva. 1985. "Implications of Selected Models of Ethnic Identity Development for Educators." *Journal of Negro Education* (54): 43-55.

Gecas, Viktor. 1979. "The Influence of Social Class on Socialization." Pg. 365-404 in *Contemporary Theories about the Family*, edited by Wesley Burr, Reuben Hill, Ivan Nye, and Ira Reiss. New York: Free Press.

Gecas, Viktor. 1981. "Contexts of Socialization." Pg. 165-199 in *Social Psychology: Sociological Perspectives*, edited by Morris Rosenberg and Ralph Turner. New York: Basic Books.

Gecas, Viktor and Schwalbe, Michael. 1986. "Parental Behavior and Dimensions of Adolescent Self-Evaluation." *Journal of Marriage and Family* (48): 37-46.

Gecas, Viktor and Mortimer, Jeylan. 1987. "Stability and Change in the Self-Concept from Adolescence to Adulthood." Pg. 265-86 in *Self and Identity: Individual Change and Development*, edited by T.M. Hones, and K.M. Yardley. New York: Routledge and Kegan Paul.

Grills, C. and Longshore, D. 1996. "Africentrism: Psychometric Analysis of a Self-Report Measure." *Journal of Black Psychology* (22): 86-106.

Gurin, Patricia; Hatchett, Shirley; and Jackson, James. 1989. *Hope and Independence: Blacks' Response to Electoral Party Politics*. New York: Russell Sage Foundation.

Harris, David. 1995. "Exploring the Determents of Adult Black Identity." *Social Forces* (74): pg. 227-241.

Hecht, Michael and Ribeau, Sidney. 1991. "Socio structural Roots of Ethnic Identity: A Look at America." *Journal of Black Studies* (21): 501-513.

Herring, Mary; Jankowski, Thomas; and Brown, Ronald. 1999. "Pro-Black Doesn't Mean Anti-White: The Structure of African-American Group Identity." *Journal of Politics* (61): 363-386.

Hughes, Michael and Demo, David. 1989. "Self-Perceptions of Black Americans: Self-Esteem and Personal Efficacy." *American Journal of Sociology* (95): 132-159.

Jackson, Bryan. 1987. "The Effects of Racial Group Consciousness on Political Mobilization in American Cities." *Western Political Quarterly* (40): 631-646.

Jaret, Charles and Reitzes, Donald. 1999. "The Importance of Racial-Ethnic Identity and Social Setting for Blacks, Whites, and Multiracials." *Sociological Perspectives* (42): pg. 711-737.

Kinder, Donald and Winter, Nicholas. 2001. "Exploring the Racial Divide: Blacks, Whites, and Opinion on National Policy." *American Journal of Political Science* (45): 439-456.

Lau, Richard. 1989. Individual and Contextual Influences on Group Identification." *Social Psychology Quarterly* (52): 220-31.

McGuire, William; McGuire, Claire; Child, P.; and Fujioka, T. 1978. "Salience of Ethnicity in the Spontaneous Self-Concept as a Function of One's Ethnic Distinctiveness in the Social Environment." *Journal of Personality and Social Psychology* (36): 511-20.

Obama, Barack. March 18, 2008. "A More Perfect Union." Constitution Center Philadelphia, Pennsylvania.

Olsen, Marvin. 1970. "Social and Political Participation of Blacks." *American Sociological Review* (35): 682-96.

Olzak, Susan and Nagel, Joane. 1986. *Competitive Ethnic Relation*. Orlando, FL: Academic Press.

Phinney, Jean S. 1990. "Ethnic Identity in Adolescents and Adults: Review of Research." *Psychological Bulletin* (108): 500.

Porter, Judith and Washington, Robert. 1979. "Black Identity and Self-Esteem." *Annual Review of Sociology* (5): 53-74.

Rosenberg, Morris. 1975. "The Dissonant Context and the Adolescent Self-Concept. Pg. 97-116 in *Adolescence in the Life Cycle*, edited by Sigmund E. Dragastin Glen H. Elder. New York: Wiley Press.

Sellers, Robert; Shelton, J.; Smith, Mia; Shelton, J.; Rowley, Stephanie; and Chavous, Tabbye. 1998. "Multidimensional Model of Racial Identity: A Reconceptualization of African American Racial Identity." *Personality and Social Psychology* (2): 18-39.

Sellers, Robert; Caldwell, Cleopatra; Schmeelk-Cone, Karen; and Zimmerman, Marc. 2003. "Racial Identity, Racial Discrimination, Perceived Stress, and Psychological Distress among African American Young Adults." *Journal of Health and Social Behavior* (44): pg. 302-317.

Smith, E.M. 1989. "Black Racial Identity Development: Issues and Concerns. *The Counseling Psychologist* (17): 277-288.

Spencer, Margaret B. and Markstrom-Adams, Carol. 1990. "Identity Process among Racial and Ethnic Minority Children in America." *Child Development* (61): 290-310.

Swarns, Rachel. February 2, 2007. "So Far, Obama Can't Take Black Vote for Granted." *The New York Times*: 1.

Tate, Katherine. 1993. *From Protest to Politics: The New Black Voters in American Elections*. Cambridge, MA: Harvard University Press.

Tate, Katherine. 2003. *Black Faces in the Mirror: African Americans and Their Representatives in the U.S. Congress* (New Jersey: Princeton University Press).

Thomas, Charles. 1971. *Boys No More: A Black Psychologist's View of Community*. Beverly Hills: Glencoe Press.

Verba, Sidney and Nie, Norman. 1972. *Participation in America: Political Democracy and Social Equality*. New York: Harper and Row.

White, Clovis and Burke, Peter. 1987. "Ethnic Role Identity among Black and White College Students: An Interactionist Approach." *Sociological Perspectives* (30): 310-331.

White, Ismail. 2007. "When Race Matters and When it Doesn't: Racial Group Differences in Response to Racial Cues." *American Political Science Review* (101): 1-15.

Winant, Howard. 1995. "Dictatorship, Democracy, and Difference: The Historical Construction of Racial Identity. Pg. 31-49 in *The Bubbling Cauldron*, edited by M.P. Smith and J.R. Feagin. Minneapolis: University of Minnesota Press.

Learning to Participate: The Effects of Civic Education on Racial/Ethnic Minorities

Melissa Comber
Allegheny College

Introduction

Civic skills, or the abilities to understand one's polity and think critically about civic and political life, enable citizen participation in the democratic process. Civic skills originate from a number of sources, including one's home environment, participation in various groups, general education, and civic education. High school civic education courses are a potential source of civic skill development and acquisition.

Researchers hypothesize that higher education and professional employment provide an alternative to civic education for acquiring civic skills (Schwadel, 2002; Putnam, 1995; Verba et al., 1995). However, higher education and professional employment are often only selectively available, primarily to people of higher socioeconomic status. Citizens without access to professional employment, higher education, civic education, or other paths to civic skill development are politically disabled.

As a source of civic skill development, high school civic education may be more equally available than higher education and professional employment. I use propensity score matching methods in this paper to examine the effect of civics coursework and content on civic skill levels of American 14-year-olds. I conduct these same analyses on only African-American students and only Latino students. In turn, this chapter speaks to broader issues of inequality in cognitive civic skill development and the distribution of civics coursework. The chapter is guided by research previously done in the field of political socialization examining the effects of schooling on African-American children's political socialization.[1] The following sections outline theories of political participation, the current state of civic education, data and methods used, and results.

Theories of Political Participation

Rational choice theory is one of the oldest theories of individual behavior to be applied to political participation (Downs, 1957). Rational choice theory explains individual behavior as utility maximizing. Individuals make choices based on their preferences to maximize their personal objectives. Rationality is assumed to be consistent across all individuals (Green and Shapiro, 1994). With regards to voting, a primary measure of political participation, the individual rationally weighs the costs and benefits of voting when choosing whether to vote. Voting is seen through the perspective of a market transaction. Costs include the inconvenience of travel to the polls and the belief that one vote will not influence the outcome of the election. Benefits include the gratification of seeing one's preferred candidate win the election and the gratification of the act of voting. When viewed as a collective action problem, rational choice theory predicts that individuals will not vote. The theory also predicts that voter turnout rates decline as the projected margin of victory increases (Barzel and Silberberg, 1973).

Social-psychological theories explain political participation through psychological motivators. According to these theories, citizens' attitudes, feelings of political efficacy, beliefs about governmental responsiveness, and even threats of pending undesirable policy changes all motivate political participation and voter turnout (Abramson and Aldrich, 1982; Miller and Krosnick, 2004). According to these theories, market-like costs and benefits are not influential to participation. Instead, these theories focus on providing social and psychological explanations for political participation among citizens (Fitzgerald, 2001).

Other theories of individual political participation are resource-based. Rosenstone and Hansen (1993) document the importance of resources in promoting political participation. Resources include money, time, knowledge, skills, and self-confidence (ibid., 74). Political efficacy is included as a psychological resource valuable to participation. Verba et al. (1995) develop a resource-based theory in their civic voluntarism model. The civic voluntarism model maintains that political participation is a function of political engagement, recruitment through social networks, and resources. Resource-based models are the only theories to account for the contribution of civic skills and political abilities toward political participation.

While theories of political participation are numerous, theories of the origins of political abilities are scarce. Most theories of political participation explain why people want to participate, not whether they are able to participate. With the exception of resource-based theories, theories of participation do not consider the contribution of skills and abilities to political participation. Resource-based theories document the importance of resources such as money, time, knowledge, skills, self-confidence, and political efficacy in promoting political participation. Yet even resource-based theories do not explain the derivation of civic skills and abilities in individuals. For example, while Verba et al.'s model includes civic skills to explain the origin of political participation, the model does not explain the origin of civic skills themselves. Although incomplete, resource-based theories provide the best available framework for understanding a relationship between civic skills and political participation.

Some researchers hypothesize that education can be a source of civic skill development. Verba et al. (1995) correlate education to increased civic skills. They assert that primary skills such as reading and writing are necessary for political participation, and that increased education leads to greater political participation (ibid.). Campbell (2005) contends that a deliberative classroom enhances civic education. More common, however, are studies that catalog civic skills that should be taught in schools (Kirlin, 2003; Patrick, 2002). Yet these studies do not address whether schools are actually teaching these skills. This chapter explores the relationship between civics course taking and civic skill levels.

Civic Education

Not all American schools require civic education of their students; many citizens have never taken a civics course. Civics coursework or social studies is currently mandated in 41 states and the District of Columbia (CIRCLE 2004). State policies requiring civics coursework or examination vary widely. In general, over 70 percent of American ninth-grade students have studied a civics topic, according to the IEA/CivEd survey (Torney-Purta et al., 2001). According to Niemi and Junn (1998), 10 percent of students took no American government or civics coursework in grades 9 through 12 (66). The majority of states require a government or civics course for high school graduation, while fewer have a state statute requiring schools to offer government or civics courses (CIRCLE 2004). As of 2003, only five states required students to pass a social studies examination as a high-school graduation requirement (National Center for Learning and Citizenship 2003). State civic education policies are summarized in Table 1 below.

Civic Skills

In general, existing studies of civic skills employ qualitative and theoretical research methods. Studies that do employ quantitative methods view civic skills as an exogenous or given variable in explaining political participation and civic engagement. Both Verba et al. (1995) and Brady et al. (1995) provide bedrock studies by using civic skills and resources as predictors of political participation. Nie et al. (1996) include civic skills among the attributes of political engagement and democratic enlightenment in an examination of civic skills and formal education. Campbell (2001) and Schwadel (2002) consider civic skills as direct outcome measures in empirical settings. While these studies are noteworthy

Table 1
State Civic Education Policies

Course Requirement in Civics for at least 3 Credits of Social Studies / History	AL, AK, CA, DE, GA, HI, ID, IN, KS, KY, LA, MD, MN, MS, NC, ND, NM, OR, SD, TN, UT, VT, VA, WI, WV, WY
Course Requirement Specifically Mentions Constitution	AZ, GA, MA, ME, NM, ND, SC, WY
Course Requirement for Social Studies Includes Civics or American Government	AL, AR, CA, CO, CT, DC, FL, GA, HI, ID, IN, IA, KS, KY, LA, ME, MD, MA, MS, MN, MI, MO, NV, NH, NM, NY, NC, ND, OH, OK, OR, PA, SC, SD, TN, TX, UT, VA, WI, WA, WV, WY
State Assessment Includes Civics	CA, DE, GA, IL, IN, KS, KY, LA, MD, MI, MO, MT, MA, NC, NM, OH, OK, SC, TX, UT, VA, WI
State Evaluations of Schools Measure Civic Outcomes	CA, HI, GA, IL, IN, KY, LA, MD, MI, MS, NH, OH, SC, TX, VA

Source: Education Commission of the States, July, 2005, and the Center for Information and Research on Civic Learning and Engagement (CIRCLE).

for their empirical explanations of political participation, civic engagement, and citizenship, they do not contribute to a deeper understanding of the relationship between civic education and civic skills.

According to Torney-Purta (2002), correctly interpreting political information is a skill necessary for political participation. She argues that the abilities to interpret political communications (such as interpreting political leaflets and cartoons) are primary components of civic knowledge. Participatory behaviors, such as voting, require an ability to understand political communication. In this chapter, I examine the effect of civic education on political interpretation skills.

This chapter's contribution to understanding civic skill acquisition is twofold. Primarily, the analyses find that civic education positively influences civic skill levels, as the resource models assume. Second, this chapter employs robust quantitative methods to examine the relationship between political interpretation skills and civic education. Other quantitative studies of civic skills (Campbell, 2001 and Schwadel, 2002) have not examined civic education and have not applied a matching methods framework to the study of civic education. This chapter employs propensity score matching methods to examine civic skill presence and civics coursework.

Heterogeneous Effects of Civic Education

Specifically, I analyze the effect of civics coursework on cognitive civic skill levels for a sample of 14-year-olds from the International Association for the Evaluation of Educational Achievement Civic Education survey (Torney-Purta et al., 2001) (IEA/CivEd). I repeat the analyses to compare the same effect on only African-American students and only Latino students.

While little research has been done to examine the differences in civic education and civic skills between racial/ethnic minorities and non-Hispanic whites, much research has examined the gap in overall student performance between racial/ethnic minorities and non-Hispanic whites. Current research focuses particularly on the academic achievement gap between African-American students and non-Hispanic white students.

A significant gap exists between African-American and non-minority students' test scores in subjects such as reading and math (Jencks and Phillips 1998). Regardless of socioeconomic status, African-American children's academic achievement lags behind their non-Hispanic white counterparts. Although the racial achievement gap improved in the 1980s, it has worsened or remained constant from 1990 to the present (ibid.; Bok, 2003).

Studies reveal stronger effects of education treatments for minority students than for non-Hispanic white students. The field of political socialization originally had a minor focus on differences in socialization among minority children, particularly African-American students. In particular, Langton and Jennings (1968) found that African-American students showed greater effects from civic education than their white counterparts on their levels of political socialization, political knowledge, and political efficacy. More recently, Winfield (1990) documents a stronger effect of minimum competency tests on African-American students' academic achievement than non-Hispanic white students' academic achievement. Sanders and Rivers (1996) and Ascher and Fruchter (2001) find that high-quality teachers have a greater impact on the academic achievement of low-achieving students than of high-achieving students. These studies provide evidence that efforts to improve education can have stronger effects for lower achievers and minorities than for others. Civic education may be one such effort.

While current studies focus on the achievement gap between African-American and non-Hispanic white students, Latinos and inner-city residents also lag behind their non-Hispanic white counterparts. Although there is disagreement as to how the high school drop-out rate is calculated, it is clear that Latinos have a higher drop-out rate than their non-Hispanic white counterparts (Fry 2003; Barton 2005).

At best, current research on the academic achievement gap can be assumed to apply also to civic education and civic skills. It is clear that there is a consistent difference in academic achievement between racial/ethnic minorities and non-Hispanic whites. In this chapter I examine separately the effect of civic education on political interpretation skill levels for minority and non-minority students.

Data and Sample

To further explore the relationship between education and political participation, I examine the effect of civic education, specifically, on civic skill levels. I conduct separate analyses of African-Americans, Latinos, and non-Hispanic whites, to better examine racial/ethnic civic education effects.

This chapter employs data from the International Association for the Evaluation of Educational Achievement Civic Education survey (Torney-Purta et al., 2001) (IEA/CivEd). The IEA/CivEd survey was conducted to measure civic skills and civic education course content. The IEA/CivEd comprises data from surveys conducted in October of 1999 of ninth-graders in the U.S. as part of an international study of civics among fourteen-year-olds. This chapter uses only the U.S. data. U.S. schools were chosen for participation in the survey through a three-stage design. Random sampling within classrooms was not done; entire classrooms were administered the survey during their school day. Response rates within schools were at least 85 percent. The data is adjusted for missing values and weighted toward a nationally-representative sample. With these adjustments, the total sample size is 1,953.

Key Measures

Civic skills are measured as dichotomous dependent variables. The IEA/CivEd survey measures political interpretation skills as ability measures. In these analyses, political interpretation skill measures include the interpretation of political leaflets and a political cartoon. The IEA/CivEd survey measures political interpretation skills as correct or incorrect answers to multiple choice questions.

Civic education is measured as civics courses, government courses, and courses requiring students to pay attention to current events. Civic education measures are the primary independent variables of interest. The IEA/CivEd survey includes six measures of civic education; students were asked whether they have studied the Constitution, Congress, the Presidency, how laws are made, political parties and voting, and state and local governments.

According to Niemi and Junn (1998), approximately 60 percent of Americans took a civic education course most recently in twelfth grade (66). In this sense, the IEA/CivEd survey may be measuring civic education course taking too soon, as its respondents were ninth-graders. However, because the IEA/CivEd measures students at age fourteen, it fully captures a broad range of students, including those who do not complete high school.

The analyses control for various background factors. Analyses using IEA/CivEd data include controls for participation in student government and school activities, whether or not the student expects to complete a four-year college degree, classroom climate measures, and demographic factors such as age, sex, and household environment.

Sample Descriptive Statistics

Appendix A contains a means table of descriptive statistics for the IEA/CivEd survey. As evidenced by simple means, students who have studied civics and government topics are more likely to exhibit civic skills. For example, 85.5 percent of the full sample correctly interpreted which party issued a political leaflet, while at least 86.2 percent of students who have studied a civic education topic correctly interpreted which party issued a political leaflet. In contrast, less than 77 percent of students who have studied two or fewer civic education topics correctly interpreted which party issued a political leaflet.

Methods

This chapter's analyses determine whether a correlation exists between civic education and civic skill levels, and how such effects differ by racial/ethnic groups. To properly test this, it is necessary to isolate the effect of civic education on civic skill development. While many factors influence civic skill development in individuals, such as extracurricular activities, religious participation, and home environment, I focus on the influence of civic education. Furthermore, simple summary statistics show that civic skills are present when respondents have a history of civic education course taking. This suggests that civic education influences civic skill levels. I use propensity score matching methods to isolate the effect of civic education.

An ideal test of the relationship between civic education and cognitive civic skills would randomly assign students to take civics courses and then assess the impact of these courses on cognitive civic skills. Unfortunately, this is difficult and expensive to do. Because this chapter's analyses do not originate from a randomized experiment, endogeneity may exist. Acquiring cognitive civic skills and taking civic education courses may both be affected by an outside, unobservable factor. For example, students may select to take civic education courses based on their pre-existing interests, which may explain their levels of civic skills. Systematic self-selection may indicate the presence of an unobservable factor influencing civic education course taking and level of cognitive civic skill development.

In this chapter I use propensity score matching as a robust control for selection on the observable factors. Although matching strategies may not completely correct for endogeneity within the analyses, they will contribute to a more robust measure of civic skills and lessen bias.

Propensity Score Matching Methods

Propensity score calculations originate from probit estimations of separate civic skills. Specifically, these civic skills include:

- Ability to interpret two political leaflets, dichotomously measured (IEA/CivEd)
- Ability to interpret a political cartoon, dichotomously measured (IEA/CivEd)

Each analysis is executed for African-Americans, Latinos, and non-Hispanic whites only, resulting in numerous distinct models. Whether the student has a history of civics coursework is the primary independent variable.

For purposes of this chapter, the primary parameter of interest from the matching methods is the average treatment effect (ATE), measured in percentage points. The ATE indicates the magnitude of the influence of civic education for all respondents, regardless of whether they had civic education. In this sense, the ATE predicts the expected effect of civic education for all survey respondents. This is the most policy-relevant statistic, as it mirrors the effect of mandating civic education for everyone.

Results

Balance Across Comparison Groups

Prior to employing propensity score matching methods, the data was tested for a "balance" among the observed characteristics in the treatment group and the matched comparison group. For this chapter, F tests were calculated to test the balance between treated and matched comparison groups. Most of the p-values associated with the F tests were well above .05. Almost all p-values were above .01. This indicates that observed characteristics were fairly well-balanced between the treatment group and the matched comparison group.

The use of propensity score matching methods requires the assumption of common support. A lack of common support is not a concern with the IEA/CivEd survey. For the treated and untreated groups, the distributions where all observed characteristics are supported generously overlap. The similarity in propensity score values between the treated and untreated groups in the IEA/CivEd data indicates common background characteristics for the analysis.

Full Sample Results

Propensity score matching methods indicate the magnitude of the average treatment effect of studying civic education on political interpretation skills. According to the IEA/CivEd study, the average treatment effect of studying civic education topics on interpreting political communication material nears 8 percentage points. These results follow in Table 2. For example, the average effect of studying the presidency results in a 7.8 percentage point increase in the ability to interpret which party issued a political leaflet, and the effect is statistically significant (Table 2). The average treatment effect of studying other civics topics, such as political parties, however, is near zero at times. Also, all of the civic education topics yield significant effects on interpreting a cartoon about a political leader.

Different civic education topics affect civic skill levels differently. The analyses reveal that studying the Constitution and the presidency yield a greater effect on civic skill presence over other topics. Yet, studying state and local government often results in different effects on civic skill levels than studying other civic education topics. The differences between the effects of studying national-level government topics and local or state-level government topics should be further explored.

Table 2
Political Interpretation Skills: IEA/CivEd. Matching Methods[a]

	Leaflet 1[b] ATE[c] (1)	Leaflet 2 ATE (2)	Cartoon ATE (4)
Civic Education Variables:			
Studied Constitution	.039 (.023)	.039 (.020)	.050* (.020)
Studied Congress	.029 (.019)	.042* (.020)	.042* (.017)
Studied Presidency	.078* (.020)	.031 (.017)	.057* (.016)
Studied How Laws are Made	.046* (.023)	.030 (.022)	.063* (.019)
Studied Political Parties	.009 (.021)	-.005 (.019)	.048* (.020)
Studied State and Local Gov't.	.017 (.020)	.005 (.018)	.063* (.017)

a) Civic education variable is the treatment effect. Nearest-neighbor matching methods with replacement were employed. Individual matching analyses were conducted for each of the 6 treatment effects (civic education types).
b) Leaflet 1: Dependent variable = 1 if student correctly interpreted which political party issued the leaflet. Leaflet 2: Dependent variable = 1 if student correctly interpreted what leaflet issuers think about taxes. Cartoon: Dependent variable = 1 if students correctly interpreted a political cartoon about a political leader.
c) ATE = Average treatment effect in percentage points. Bootstrapped standard errors are in parentheses.
All calculations used the "total weight" as provided in the survey data. N=1,953.
Controls used in constructing the propensity scores include race/ethnicity and gender measures, classroom climate measures, immigrant status, student government participation, number of books in the home, expectation of completing a four-year college degree, group participation, and feelings of political efficacy.
* Statistically significant at .05 level.

Results by Race/Ethnicity

To determine the effects of civic education on African-American and Latino students, each group was analyzed separately. For example, propensity score matching methods were conducted for African-American students only and Latino students only. These results were compared to results for non-Hispanic whites. In this sense, it is simple to compare the effects of civics course-taking on the African-American and Latino sub-samples. The sizes of the African-American and Latino subgroups were 223 and 229, respectively. A sample size of 200 is generally the minimum needed for a robust regression, and is considered small, but not unusual, for propensity score matching methods.[2]

Simple means calculations show that African-Americans and Latinos receive less civic education than their non-Hispanic white counterparts. The subgroup analyses reveal that, overall, African-American and Latino students' civic skill levels are differently influenced by civic education than non-Hispanic whites' civic skill levels.

African-American Students

Overall, the effect of civic education on correctly interpreting political leaflets is stronger for African-American students than for non-Hispanic whites. However, the opposite holds for the interpretation of a political cartoon. These results follow in Table 3. For example, among African American students, the study of almost any civics topic leads to a greater average effect of correctly interpreting which political party issued a political leaflet than for non-Hispanic white students (Table 3). For some civics topics, the effect is very large. For example, studying the Constitution results in an over 25 percentage point increase in the ability to interpret which party issued a political leaflet for African-American students. For non-Hispanic white students, this same effect is approximately 3 percentage points (Table 3).

Other civics topics also strongly influence African-American students' correct interpretation of political communication material compared to non-Hispanic whites. Studying how laws are made provides a stronger average effect on the correct interpretation of the political leaflets for African-American students than for non-Hispanic white students (Table 3).

Potentially, the large effects of studying civic education topics for African-American students may signify that some African-American students do not come to the classroom with pre-existing civic skills, unlike some non-Hispanic white students. For example, if African-American students have had no exposure to alternative sources of civic skill development outside the classroom, the effect of civic education on their civic skill levels would be greater than this same effect on students who have had exposure to alternative sources of civic skill development. Similarly, if non-Hispanic white students have had previous exposure to numerous sources of civic skill development, once exposed to civic education, they may show a smaller improvement in their civic skill levels than African-American students. In other words, when alternative sources of civic skill development are present (such as religious group participation, student government participation, and home environment), civic education may have a smaller effect on civic skill presence than when these sources are absent.

Latino Students

As well, Latino students experience stronger effects from civic education on their ability to interpret political leaflets than non-Hispanic white students. Again, the opposite is true for the interpretation of a political cartoon. Overall, the results of the subgroup analyses are comparable for Latino and African-American students. Similar to African-American students, Latino students exhibit strong political interpretation skills when they study civic education topics. These results follow in Table 4.

For Latino students, studying the Constitution and political parties has strong effects on interpreting political leaflets and a political cartoon (Table 4). While the effect is positive, and sometimes significant, for non-Hispanic white students, it is not as strong.

Table 3
Political Interpretation Skills: IEA/CivEd
Matching Methods – African-Americans[a]

	Leaflet 1[b]		Leaflet 2		Cartoon	
	African-Americans	Non-Hispanic Whites	African-Americans	Non-Hispanic Whites	African-Americans	Non-Hispanic Whites
	ATE[c]	ATE	ATE	ATE	ATE[c]	ATE
	(1)	(2)	(3)	(4)	(1)	(2)
Civic Education Variables:						
Studied Constitution	.253* (.098)	.031 (.025)	.158* (.065)	.016 (.028)	.099 (.063)	.014 (.019)
Studied Congress	.106 (.070)	.01 (.024)	-.072 (.063)	.009 (.023)	-.049 (.045)	.053* (.024)
Studied Presidency	.045 (.065)	.063* (.029)	.011 (.065)	.024 (.024)	.003 (.054)	.04 (.022)
Studied How Laws are Made	.074 (.082)	.03 (.028)	.086 (.108)	.06 (.035)	-.004 (.098)	.084* (.026)
Studied Political Parties	.068 (.070)	-.019 (.028)	-.068 (.061)	.002 (.026)	.049 (.053)	.055 (.031)
Studied State and Local Gov't.	.124 (.094)	.02 (.025)	.073 (.102)	.011 (.023)	.054 (.074)	.057* (.023)

a) Civic education variable is the treatment effect. Nearest-neighbor matching methods with replacement were employed. Individual matching analyses were conducted for each of the 6 treatment effects (civic education types).
b) Leaflet 1: Dependent variable = 1 if student correctly interpreted which political party issued the leaflet. Leaflet 2: Dependent variable = 1 if student correctly interpreted what leaflet issuers think about taxes. Cartoon: Dependent variable = 1 if students correctly interpreted a political cartoon about a political leader.
c) ATE = Average treatment effect in percentage points. Bootstrapped standard errors are in parentheses.
All calculations used the "total weight" as provided in the survey data. N=223.
Controls used in constructing the propensity scores include measures of other races/ethnicities, gender, classroom climate measures, immigrant status, student government participation, number of books in the home, expectation of completing a four-year college degree, group participation, and feelings of political efficacy.
* Statistically significant at .05 level.

Table 4
Political Interpretation Skills: IEA/CivEd
Matching Methods - Latinos[a]

	Leaflet 1[b]		Leaflet 2		Cartoon	
	Latinos	Non-Hispanic Whites	Latinos	Non-Hispanic Whites	Latinos	Non-Hispanic Whites
	ATE[c]	ATE	ATE	ATE	ATE	ATE
	(1)	(2)	(3)	(4)	(5)	(6)
Civic Education Variables:						
Studied Constitution	.113 (.073)	.031 (.025)	.116 (.070)	.016 (.028)	.158* (.075)	.014 (.019)
Studied Congress	.101 (.089)	.01 (.024)	.157 (.096)	.009 (.023)	.078 (.046)	.053* (.024)
Studied Presidency	.156* (.063)	.063* (.029)	.122 (.064)	.024 (.024)	.076 (.048)	.04 (.022)
Studied How Laws are Made	.032 (.063)	.03 (.028)	-.008 (.064)	.06 (.035)	.069 (.055)	.084* (.026)
Studied Political Parties	.111 (.062)	-.01 (.028)	.061 (.057)	.002 (.026)	.153* (.070)	.055 (.031)
Studied State and Local Gov't.	.003 (.057)	.02 (.025)	.085 (.056)	.011 (.023)	.062 (.046)	.057* (.023)

a) Civic education variable is the treatment effect. Nearest-neighbor matching methods with replacement were employed. Individual matching analyses were conducted for each of the 6 treatment effects (civic education types).
b) Leaflet 1: Dependent variable = 1 if student correctly interpreted which political party issued the leaflet. Leaflet 2: Dependent variable = 1 if student correctly interpreted what leaflet issuers think about taxes. Cartoon: Dependent variable = 1 if students correctly interpreted a political cartoon about a political leader.
c) ATE = Average treatment effect in percentage points. Bootstrapped standard errors are in parentheses.
All calculations used the "total weight" as provided in the survey data. N=229.
Controls used in constructing the propensity scores include measures of other races/ethnicities, gender, classroom climate measures, immigrant status, student government participation, number of books in the home, expectation of completing a four-year college degree, group participation, and feelings of political efficacy.
* Statistically significant at .05 level.

For example, for Latino students, studying the Constitution or political parties has an over 11 percentage point effect on correctly interpreting which political party issued a leaflet. The same effect for non-Hispanic white students who study the Constitution is approximately 3 percentage points, while it is near zero for non-Hispanic white students who study political parties. The effects of these two civics topics on political cartoon interpretation skills are statistically significant for Latino students. However, interestingly, while studying Congress, how laws are made, and state and local government has significant effects on cartoon interpretation skills for non-Hispanic whites, none of these topics appear helpful for either African American or Latino students in the interpretation of a political cartoon.

Generally, these results mirror those found for African-American students, although the magnitudes of the effects are not as strong. These results may have similar explanations. Again, Latino students as a whole reflect a wide range of civic skill levels. Some Latino students may have had no exposure to civic skill development outside of civic education. This may explain the stronger influence of civic education on political interpretation skills for Latino students compared to non-Hispanic white students. Also, small effects of civic education on political interpretation skills may be a result of classroom climate or student feelings of alienation.

Overall, the effects of civic education on political leaflet interpretation for minority race/ethnicity students are stronger than the effects for non-minority students. The opposite was found in an examination of political cartoons. While political leaflets, or campaign material, require political knowledge to interpret, political cartoons require political knowledge coupled with a nuanced understanding of the current political environment. Potentially, civic education coursework teaches a skill level that is sufficient to affect non-Hispanic white students' cartoon interpretation abilities, but insufficient on minority students' cartoon interpretation abilities.

These findings are similar to those found previously by Langton and Jennings (1968) and others.[3] As mentioned earlier, other researchers also document strong effects of educational benefits for disadvantaged students. In particular, this chapter's analyses reveal strong effects of civic education on political interpretation skill levels.

Of note, this chapter examines civic skills that are necessary for political participation in the non-Hispanic white political system that dominates American democracy. Political and civic participation in minority communities may require other skills not measured in these analyses. Alternatively, different skills may be more effective for minority youth than for non-Hispanic whites to interpret political communication and effectuate policy change. For example, Rockeymoore (2004) encourages minority youth to use their artistic talents to perpetuate political change, to use cleverness to obtain internships and jobs with major political figures, and to use pure determination to lobby elected officials for political change. However, by judging minority youth on the political interpretation skills measured in this chapter, I may be perpetuating an evaluation of minority youth through an Anglo lens. This may be especially relevant in understanding the differences between leaflet and cartoon interpretation; the political cartoon measured may not resonate in a minority political community.

Conclusions

This chapter examines the correlation between civic education and political interpretation skills using propensity score matching methods. The effect of civics course taking for African-American and Latino students is explored separately. By examining civic skills, I focus on the ability to politically participate, not the willingness to participate. Both ability and willingness are necessary for successful political participation. The methods used simulate the effect of civics course taking for all students, regardless of their civics course taking history. By focusing on civic education as a source of civic skill development, this chapter provides evidence of a link between civics course taking in high school and civic skills. Civic skills are necessary for political participation, according to the resource model (Verba et al., 1995). Yet prior to this chapter's research, civic education has been assumed to contribute to civic skill development. This chapter provides evidence of that assumption.

As a resource, civic education is not distributed equally. Because some states and school districts do not mandate civic education, not every American student takes a civics course. Furthermore, students who drop out of school may miss their only opportunity for civic education if it is taught at a later grade. This chapter shows that civic education course taking is correlated with the presence of political interpretation skills in American fourteen-year-olds. This important policy implication speaks to mandating civic education in all states. As well, this chapter's research reveals that political interpretation skills are not equally distributed among different race and ethnicity populations.

The study of civics topics has a strong positive effect on political interpretation skill levels for African-American students. At times this effect is statistically significant. Often, this effect is greater than the same measured effect on non-Hispanic white students, particularly for the interpretation of political leaflets. A similar pattern of effects was found for Latino students. These results may be evidence that other sources of civic skill development, such as after-school curricular activities and jobs, religious group participation, and parents and families may be unavailable to minority students. In this sense, civic education may be the primary option for civic skill development.

While simple calculations of means from the IEA/CivEd data reveal that African-American and Latino students are less likely to take civics courses, this chapter's analyses establish the importance of civics course taking for minority race/ethnicity students. The findings parallel other researchers' findings that educational improvements have stronger positive effects for minority students than for non-Hispanic white students.

Historically, our nation's educational system has valued equity. Current standards require school resources to be distributed as equitably as possible. However, this chapter shows that African-American and Latino students' civic skill levels benefit more than non-Hispanic white students' from civic education. This suggests that focused attention on civic education for racial and ethnic minority students can contribute toward equalizing the participatory effects of civic education. Equalizing civic skill levels among all race/ethnic groups is essential for a healthy participatory democracy.

Finally, this chapter provides evidence that cognitive civic skills are correlated with civics course taking among American fourteen-year-olds. In turn, civic skills are a necessary component of political participation, according to the resource model (Verba et al., 1995). In this sense, civic education may be a means of equalizing the distribution of skills necessary for successful political participation.

Acknowledgements

I thank Mark Hugo Lopez, Peter Levine, Christopher Foreman, Jr., Jeff Smith, and Dan Shea for helpful comments on previous drafts of this chapter. Grant support from the Center for Information and Research on Civic Learning and Engagement (CIRCLE) at the University of Maryland School of Public Policy is gratefully acknowledged. Support from the Center for Political Participation at Allegheny College is also acknowledged. All errors in fact or interpretation are my own.

Appendix A
IEA/CivEd Study: Means

		Of Those who Studied…						
	Full Sample	Const-itution	Congress	Presidency	Laws	Political Parties	State / Local Gov't.	Studied 2 Or Fewer Topics[a]
	(1)	(2)	(3)	(4)	(5)	(6)	(7)	(8)
Studied:								
Constitution	81.1%	100%	94.9%	93.4%	90.7%	90.7%	90.8%	19.2%
Congress	77.7	91.0	100	93.0	89.8	89.4	89.7	9.0
Presidency	67.6	77.9	81.0	100	78.9	79.7	78.8	7.6
Laws	78.9	67.6	91.2	92.1	100	89.7	89.5	19.3
Political Parties	73.3	82.0	84.4	86.3	83.3	100	88.7	16.9
State/Local Gov't.	69.1	77.3	79.7	78.3	78.3	83.5	100	16.6
Civic Skills:								
Leaflet 1[b]	85.5	87.5	87.2	88.4	87.0	86.2	86.5	76.6
Leaflet 2	86.4	88.9	88.8	88.8	87.7	87.6	88.0	77.8
Cartoon	90.3	92.4	92.1	92.9	91.9	92.0	92.1	80.8
Demographics:								
African-American	11.4	10.8	10.1	10.2	10.7	11.3	11.7	14.1
Latino	11.7	11.0	11.0	10.5	12.2	11.3	10.2	13.4
White	74.3	75.8	76.5	77.4	75.5	75.1	75.5	67.1
Sample size:	1,953	1,559	1,493	1,312	1,520	1,427	1,355	361

a) Students who report studying 0, 1, or 2 of the six listed civic education topics.
b) Percent correctly interpreting political leaflets and political cartoons
Leaflet 1: Dependent variable = 1 if student correctly interpreted which political party issued the leaflet. Leaflet 2: Dependent variable = 1 if student correctly interpreted what leaflet issuers think about taxes. Cartoon: Dependent variable = 1 if students correctly interpreted a political cartoon about a political leader.

All calculations used the "total weight" as provided in the survey data.

Notes

1. See Langton and Jennings (1968), Ehman (1980), and Abramson (1977).
2. Jeffrey Smith, e-mail communication, January 31, 2005.
3. See, as well, Abramson (1977) and Ehman (1980).

References

Abramson, Paul R. 1977. *The Political Socialization of Black Americans*. New York: Free Press.

Abramson, Paul R. and Aldrich, John H. 1982. "The Decline of Electoral Participation in America." *American Political Science Review* 76, pp. 502-521.

Ascher, Carol and Fruchter, Norm. 2001. "Teacher Quality and Student Performance in New York City's Low-Performing Schools," *Journal of Education for Students Placed at Risk* 6 (3) pp. 199-214.

Barton, Paul. 2005. "One-Third of a Nation: Rising Dropout Rates and Declining Opportunities," Educational Testing Service Report, www.ets.org.

Barzel, Yoram and Silberberg, Eugune. 1973. "Is the Act of Voting Rational?" *Public Choice* 16, pp. 51-58.

Bok, Derek. 2003. "Closing the Nagging Gap in Minority Achievement." *Chronicle of Higher Education*, October 24, 2003.

Brady, Henry E., Verba, Sidney and Schlozman, Kay Lehman. 1995. "Beyond SES: A Resource Model of Political Participation." *American Political Science Review*, 89 (2) pp. 271-294.

Campbell, David E. 2001. "Bowling Together: Private Schools, Serving Public Ends." *Education Next*, Fall.

Campbell, David E. 2005. "Voice in the Classroom: How and Open Classroom Environment Facilitates Adolescents' Civic Development," Working Paper 28, Center for Information and Research on Civic Learning and Engagement (CIRCLE) www.civicyouth.org.

Center for Information and Research on Civic Learning and Engagement (CIRCLE). 2004. Around the CIRCLE – Research Roundup, 1 (3). http://www.civicyouth.org/PopUps/v1.i.3.pdf.

Center for Information and Research on Civic Learning and Engagement (CIRCLE) Staff. 2004. "Youth Voting in the 2004 Election," http://www.civicyouth.org.

Downs, Anthony. 1957. *An Economic Theory of Democracy*. New York: Harper and Row.

Ehman, Lee H. 1980. "The American School in the Political Socialization Process." *Review of Educational Research*. 50 (1) pp. 99-119.

Fitzgerald, Mary. 2001. Alternative Voting Techniques and Electoral Participation: Voting Reform in the American States, 1972-1998. Ph.D. diss., University of Maryland.

Fry, Richard. 2003. "Hispanic Youth Dropping Out of U.S. Schools: Measuring the Challenge," Pew Hispanic Center report, www.pewhispanic.org.

Green, Donald and Shapiro, Ian. 1994. *Pathologies of Rational Choice Theory, A Critique of Applications in Political Science*. New Haven: Yale University Press.

Jencks, Christopher and Phillips, Meredith. 1998. "The Black-White Test Score Gap: An Introduction." In *The Black-White Test Score Gap*, eds. Christopher Jencks and Meredith Phillips. Washington: Brookings Institution.

Kirlin, Mary. 2003. "The Role of Civic Skills in Fostering Civic Engagement." Center for Information and Research on Civic Learning and Engagement working paper 06, http://www.civicyouth.org/research/products/working_papers.htm.

Langton, Kenneth P. and Jennings, M. Kent. 1968. "Political Socialization and the High School Civics Curriculum in the United States." *American Political Science Review* 62 (3), pp. 852-867.

Miller, Joanne M. and Krosnick, Jon A. 2004. "Threat as a Motivator of Political Activism: A Field Experiment." *Political Psychology* 25 (4), pp. 507-523.

National Center for Learning and Citizenship. 2003. *Citizenship Education Policy Brief, State Policies to Support Citizenship Education*. November. www.ecs.org.

Nie, Norman H., Junn, Jane, and Stehlik-Barry, Kenneth. 1996. *Education and Democratic Citizenship in America*. Chicago: The University of Chicago Press.

Niemi, Richard G. and Junn, Jane. 1998. *Civic Education*. New Haven: Yale University Press.

Patrick, John J. 2002. "Defining, Delivering and Defending a Common Education for Citizenship in a Democracy." Paper presented at the *Summit on Civic Learning in Teacher Preparation*, Boston, MA May 15, 2002.

Putnam, Robert D. 1995. *Bowling Alone*. New York: Simon and Schuster.

Rockeymoore, Maya. 2004. *The Political Action Handbook*. Personal printing www.mayarockeymoore.com.

Rosenstone, Steven J. and Hansen, John M. 1993. *Mobilization, Participation, and Democracy in America.* New York: Macmillan Publishing Company.

Sanders, William and Rivers, June. 1996. "Cumulative and Residual Effects of Teachers on Future Student Academic Achievement," University of Tennessee Value-Added Research and Assessment Center, www.coe.ohio-state.edu/ahoy/Sanders%20and%20Rivers.pdf.

Schwadel, Philip. 2002. "Testing the Promise of the Churches: Income Inequality in the Opportunity to Learn Civic Skills in Christian Congregations." *Journal for the Scientific Study of Religion*, 41 (3) pp. 565-576.

Torney-Purta, Judith, Lehmann, Rainer, Oswald, H., Schultz, W. 2001. *Citizenship and Education in Twenty-Eight Countries: Civic Knowledge and Engagement at Age Fourteen.* Amsterdam: International Association for the Evaluation of Educational Achievement. http://www.wam.umd.edu/~iea.

Torney-Purta, Judith. 2002. "The School's Role in Developing Civic Engagement: A Study of Adolescents in Twenty-Eight Countries." *Applied Developmental Science*, 6 (4) pp. 203-212.

Verba, Sidney, Kay Lehman Schlozman, and Henry E. Brady. 1995. *Voice and Equality*. Cambridge: Harvard University Press.

Winfield, Linda. 1990. "School Competency Testing Reforms and Student Achievement: Exploring a National Perspective," *Educational Evaluation and Policy Analysis* 12 (2) pp. 157-173.

The Literature on Senator Barack Obama's 2008 Presidential Campaign

Hanes Walton, Jr.
University of Michigan

Josephine A.V. Allen
Cornell University and Binghamton University

Sherman C. Puckett
Wayne County

Donald R. Deskins, Jr.
University of Michigan

Leslie Burl McLemore
Jackson State University

The very first words about this candidate came from himself in the form of two autobiographies and later in an edited volume of his most important speeches. After his stellar keynote speech to the Democratic National Convention in 2004, words about this candidate and his possible candidacy flowed from numerous media commentators and pundits, journalists, and academics Since his announcement on February 10, 2007, the flow of words about his candidacy and possibility has come from nearly everywhere and everyone. The flow of words has been continuous and now threatens to overtake the total number of books written on all of the African American presidential candidates since the nomination of Frederick Douglass for vice president on the Equal Rights Party ticket of 1872. Douglass of course, declined the nomination, but since that day and time, African American candidates have appeared on numerous third-party tickets and black-party tickets, as well as candidates for major party nominations.

With the appearance of a slowly evolving and ever-meandering stream of candidates throughout American history, a slow and evolving stream of pamphlets and books on these pioneering women and men presidential candidates has been growing. The purpose of this chapter is to organize, structure, and analyze the current stream of books on the first African American candidate to achieve the presidential nomination of one the nation's two major parties. This candidate is Senator Barack Obama and his historic nomination on August 28, 2008 is currently generating so many books that attention to his story will soon eclipse that paid to all other blacks that have tried to capture a major party's nomination.

The Data and Methodology

The data for this chapter are the books written by Senator Barack on himself and the books written by others on him. This means that the coverage in this chapter will focus upon autobiographies, biographies, academic and scholarly studies, campaign attack books, children's books, legislative voting studies, photo-books, and works on his campaign speeches. Simply put, the data source for this chapter is every book and monograph written on Senator Obama up to this point in time. Since this chapter's aim is to cover both in a systematic and comprehensive manner the entire corpus of literature currently written on this new political trailblazer, literally every book will be covered.

In terms of methodology, this work seeks to analyze each and every book for its theme, thesis, interpretations, and points of view. To attain this information, a content analysis will be made of each book and the findings will be placed in context and evaluated in terms of their contributions to understanding the recent emergence of Obama in the American political process as well as their relationship to an older genre of books, known as "political campaign books." Thus, as in any book review-essay, the traditional methodology is a content analysis and critical reading of these books. But this chapter is not like the traditional book review-essays simply because of its conceptualization.

To be sure, each of the books will be organized and placed into specific categories that encapsulate it. This will allow the books to be separated and treated as individual works with merit or the lack thereof and later fitted into a unified whole. Also, this approach will permit the reader to see an entire portrait as well as the missing and/or non-functional parts. Gaps as well as linked parts will become clearer and exposed. In this approach, some notion of the motivations and forces behind some of the works hopefully will come to light and point to what some of the authors hoped to achieve with their works. Because of this categorization, it might help scholars and academics understand the role and function of "political campaign" books in presidential elections.

In nearly every one of America's presidential cycles, "political campaign" books have become staples, but because most of these books have only been seen as part and parcel of the campaign fodder, serious analysis of this genre of books is yet to take place. Much like campaign paraphernalia, "political campaign" books are tossed aside after, and sometimes before, the campaign is over. But because of the historical nature of both the candidacy of Obama and his campaign, the "political campaign" books arising around him and his historic campaign simply cry out for a much more serious analysis than has transpired in the past or to use this opportunity to only do a traditional book review-essay. Therefore, the purpose of this chapter on the books about Senator Barack Obama allows a new kind of scholarly case study to be undertaken so that we can learn not only about this presidential candidate and his campaign, but also generate insights into other "political campaign" books both in the past and future. Thus, the conceptualization in this chapter seeks to not only to review these books but also to develop an empirically based theoretical formulation about the nature and scope of "political campaign" books that is missing and underdeveloped in the current political science literature, despite the nearly innumerable books in this genre.

The Categories of the Book Literature on Senator Barack Obama

Table 1 offers both the categories and the books in each of the categories. With possible sole exception, i.e., Senator Obama's book on his father, all of the other books in the table are "political campaign" works. Thus, excluding this one work (and even it has some discussion of politics in the new paperback edition, particularly in the preface to the 2004 edition, and in the afterword section there is an excerpt from *The Audacity of Hope*), all of the other books in the table hang together making something of a nearly coherent whole because they all look at his presidential campaign. Such a unity of scope and perspective in this literature gives it a uniqueness and rare quality not always seen in this literature genre.

There are five distinct categories of studies on Senator Obama. The initial category, autobiographical studies, contains three books authored by Senator Obama himself. Written a year after he finished Harvard Law School, and a year a before he entered the Illinois State Senate, this book reflects upon "a personal, interior journey—a boy's search for his father, and through that search a workable meaning for life as a black American" (p. xvii). This work predates his political career and is more about the father he never really knew, his mother who was always with him, and his divided racial inheritance, than about politics. If it is anyway related to politics, it is about the politics of race in American society from a man with a white mother and an African father. In this way, of all of the literature on Senator Obama, this one volume is the one least reflective of his political journey and career in American politics. But because it has been used so much in this historic campaign by both the electronic and print media, it will be referenced here as one of the "political campaign" books, even though it does not completely fit that definition.

Beyond this single book, all of the others are essentially "political campaign" books because they were prepared by journalists, academics, critics, and opponents to satisfy the ever-growing demand for information about Obama, who came suddenly into national prominence via his keynote address to the 2004 Democratic National Convention. This followed his meteoric rise in the Democratic presidential primaries, including his victory in the initial Iowa Caucus over the presumed frontrunner, the former first lady, Senator Hillary Clinton. None of the works in Table 1 appeared before his presidential announcement in February, 2007.

Thus, besides the autobiographical category, the other seventeen books fall into four other categories. In the second category there are the biographical studies, books specifically by individuals to describe Obama's life and former political achievements to the reading public. The third category of works are those written primarily by academics and scholars that assesses and evaluates from different perspectives Obama's political chances and potential success in the presidential primaries and beyond. Each of these books attempts to follow traditional canons of academic research, analysis and interpretation. They seek to find the facts and use those facts for evidence in their narratives. After the academic research category comes the fourth category, which includes journalistic studies written by some individuals in the media and that do not strictly follow the canons of academic and scholarly works. Although they may pretend or declare some loose connections to aspects of academic work, they simply provide a narrative without careful documentation and well-researched evidence. The last and fifth category consists of the

Table 1
The Book Literature on Senator Barack Obama's Presidential Campaign

Category	%
Autobiographical Studies	**15%**
1 Dreams from My Father: A Story of Race and Inheritance.	
2 The Audacity of Hope: Thoughts on Reclaiming the American Dream.	
3 Change We Can Believe In: Barack Obama's Plan to Renew America's Promise.	
Biographical Studies	**20%**
1 Obama: From Promises to Power.	
2 Barack Obama for Beginners.	
3 Hopes and Dreams: The Story of Barack Obama.	
4 Barack Obama: Working to Make a Difference.	
Academic & Scholarly Studies	**30%**
1 Barack Obama: The Improbable Quest.	
2 Barack Obama: The New Face of American Politics.	
3 What's Wrong with Obamamania: Black America, Black Leadership and the Death of Political Imagination.	
4 Obama vs. McCain: Voting Records of Barack Obama and John McCain for the 109th and 110th Congresses.	
5 Obama Nomics: How Bottom Up Economic Prosperity Will Replace Trickle-Down Economics.	
6 Obama's Challenge: America's Economic Crisis and the Power of a Transformative Presidency.	
Journalistic Studies	**15%**
1 Barack Obama in His Own Words.	
2 Barack Obama and the Future of American Politics.	
3 The Dream Begins: How Hawaii Shaped Barack Obama.	
Campaign Attack Studies	**20%**
1 A Bound Man: Why We Are Excited About Obama and Why He Can't Win.	
2 Fleeced: How Barack Obama, Media Mockery of Terrorist Threats, Liberals Who Want to Kill Talk Radio, the Do-Nothing Congress, Companies That Help Iran, and Washington Lobbyists for Foreign Governments Are Scamming Us ... and What to Do About It.	
3 The Case Against Barack Obama: The Unlikely Rise and Unexamined Agenda of the Media's Favorite Candidate.	
4 The Obama Nation: Leftist Politics and the Cult of Personality.	
20 Total number of books	**100%**

opposition campaign attack studies. Books in this category may be written by trained academics and well regarded or fringe journalists. These works are designed to weaken, destroy, malign, or defeat the candidate. The works in this category that viciously attack Senator Obama come primarily from individuals on the political right, but not exclusively so, who are of various partisan persuasion.

To test the efficacy of these five categories or some parts of them we will delineate any thing from them that will give us new and meaningful insights and findings about the genre known as "political campaign" books.

The Autobiographical Studies Category

The second book of the autobiographies is Senator Obama's, *The Audacity of Hope* and it is unmistakably his campaign book. Although the book is bereft of any discussion of his three state senate campaigns, and how he campaigned and achieved victory in them or, for that matter, his losing congressional campaign, except for a few scattered remarks, the book does devote several sections and chapters to his U.S. Senate race. There are also discussions about his values, his view of the Constitution, his family, and foreign policy ideas and legislation. There are also discussions of race, opportunity in America, Republicans and Democrats, the 2004 speech at the Democratic National Convention, and the number of press and media opportunities that it generated for him. Of the nine chapters and epilogue in the book, one is devoted to his faith and how he views religion and politics. Eventually, it was in the promotion of this book that Obama settled on the idea of running for the Democratic Party's nomination in 2008.

The third book in this autographical category is truly a campaign book. This book, *Change We Can Believe In: Barack Obama's Plan to Renew America's Promise*, has a foreword written especially for this volume by Obama, seven key speeches from the 2008 primary campaign, and his entire campaign program contained in Part I. This book was released during the primaries and before the start of the general election campaign. All proceeds from this book are scheduled for charity.

The Biographical Studies

The *Chicago Tribune* journalist David Mendell, who had covered Obama from the beginning of his U.S. senator campaign through some of the early months of the pre-primary period authored the first biography of him, *Obama: From Promise to Power.* This book, which relied upon "exclusive interviews with Obama's closest aides, mentors, political adversaries and family and wife, Michelle, fills in all of the gaps, omissions and some details ignored in Obama's autobiographical studies. It is as of this writing the most complete and comprehensive work on the candidate. None of the other books in the table is as informative as this initial biography.

Another biography, *Barack Obama: Working to Make a Difference* was written for children. This forty-eight-page book is so brief and sketchy that it is superficial and overpriced. The only useful thing in this book is its beautiful color photographs of Obama and members of his family. However, the photographs set this book apart from *Barack Obama for Beginners: An Essential Guide*. Described as a documentary comic book, this one has hand drawn pictures in black and white, which makes them appear rather drab. For a comic documentary, it seems a bit silly. But in terms of photographs, the book *Hopes and Dreams: The Story of Barack Obama* overshadows the other two biographies. This oversized book is literally a photo-journalistic work that offers more pictures of Obama and his family (and his political career key moments) than the narrative in the book. It succeeds as a book that tries to provide a biography of Obama via photographs. The photographs in this work are not only in color, but also in black and whites as well.

The Academic and Scholarly Studies Category

Falling into this category is the work by one of Obama students from his constitutional law class at the University of Chicago. This book, *Barack Obama: This Improbable Quest* is not only a study of Obama's "legislative experience as well as his ideas about race, religion, and politics," but a careful analysis of how African American and whites who are on the right and the left of the political spectrum, and the media, both print and electronic, have reacted to Senator Obama's effort to acquire the presidential nomination of the Democratic party. This is the strength of the book. More than any other book, it pulls together in one place, the negative and positive reactions to his presidential ambitions. And it has the most beautiful black and white photographs seen of his political announcement, several campaign activities and his family. This one is worth its price.

Two white political scientists wrote, *Barack Obama, The New Face of American Politics*, which is essentially a study of his U.S. Senate race. It offers financial data, and an analysis of the aggregate election returns to describe and explain how he won the U.S. Senate seat. It does not analyze his state senate races or his congressional race. Although it briefly discusses the rise of African American statewide candidates in Illinois, there is no quantitative analysis of how the state's electorate voted for them or their relationship to Obama or, for that matter, each other. While this book uses a lot of newspapers and magazine articles and Internet sites as evidence and data, there is no use of any works on African American politics either on Chicago politics or elsewhere. Yet a few references from the *American Political Science Review* do surface. The book tries to conclude from this single case of that American politics is about to undergo a transformation.

An African American political scientist, Ricky L. Jones, in his *What's Wrong With Obamamania?: Black America, Black Leadership, and the Death of Political Imagination* raises the question of what the rise of Obama means for African American political leadership. He writes: "at a time when black people still face incredibly daunting problems on a number of fronts, many are highly disturbed that most politicians, including Obama, rarely speaks to these troubles.... However, he should also not expect blanket black support if he becomes viewed as a candidate who often takes the opportunity to distance his agenda from difficulties hampering black progress" (122). Using the definition of black leadership promulgated by W.E.B. DuBois and exemplified by Martin Luther King, Jr., Adam Clayton Powell, Charles Hamilton Houston, and Frederick Douglass, Professor Jones finds Obama in several ways wanting.

The book, *Obama vs McCain: Voting Records of Barack Obama & John McCain for the 109th and 110th Congress*, is not authored by anyone, but was pulled together and complied by the publishing company. There is not a word of narrative, just table after table of how these two candidates voted in the two sessions of Congress that they shared participation. On the very last page of the book, there is a summary table that puts all of the votes in a comprehensive and systematic fashion.

The rest of the books in this category look specifically at Obama's economic plans and proposals and what they mean for the nation. The first one: *Obama Nomics: How Bottom Up Economic Prosperity Will Replace Trickle-Down Economics* appeared before the September, 2008 Wall Street economic meltdown and is written by a former investment banker for Goldman Sachs. He includes a discussion of the housing and mortgage crises and argues that Obama plans will lead the nation back to prosperity. The second book, *Obama's Challenge: America's Economic Crisis and the Power of a Transformative Presidency* also appeared before the Wall Street meltdown and makes the argument that if Obama can solve the economic crises engulfing the nation, it will make him a great president like Franklin Delano Roosevelt and Abraham Lincoln. Both of these books are quite timely, very informative and written by men with impressive economic credentials.

The Journalistic Studies Category

The book, *Barack Obama: In His Own Words* is nothing more than a book of quotes taken from his speeches, talks, comments, and discussion. These quotes are placed into twenty-three different groups and preceded by a very brief introduction and even briefer bio-sketch that does little to tie the man and the context to the quotes. To say the least this is a troubling book.

A journalist with a progressive perspective and outlook wrote the next book, *Barack Obama and the Future of American Politics* and he raises questions about the Obama presidential candidacy in light of his perspectives. Looking for radical reforms and solutions, he finds that Obama is not really representative of the progressive tradition in American politics. He declares: "the simple facts of skin color and that early 'antiwar' position, I argue, have gone a very long way in helping Obama wrap his conservative, establishment-oriented politics and world-view in the 'rebel clothing' of progressive insurgency" (p. xiii). Like several other progressives who also criticized Jesse Jackson campaign from the left, this book is in that tradition.

Recently, two journalists in Hawaii penned a book, *The Dream Begins: How Hawai'i Shaped Barack Obama* , which describes in a comprehensive way, the life of Obama in this state. And they try to show how aspects of the Hawaiian culture and outlook have become a permanent party of his life and politics. The book has a foreword written by one of the congressman from the Island State, Neil Abercrombie.

The Campaign Attack Studies Category

If a few of the previous books represent an attack on Obama's presidential campaign from the left, all of the books of this category attack and harshly criticize Obama from the right. Unlike those on the left who see in African American presidential candidates like Obama some redeeming features and possibilities, those on the right see none and argue that individuals like Obama must be stopped in their tracks because they threaten their concept of American democracy.

One of the first of these works to appear is *The Case Against Barack Obama: The Unlikely Rise and Unexamined Agenda of the Media's Favorite Candidate.* Said book declares itself to be a true exposé of Obama. It declares that Obama is no reformer and the "least experienced politician in at least one hundred years to obtain a major party nomination for President of the United States." He adds: "This book contains some new and many buried stories that the media has mostly ignored. They puncture the image Obama has created for himself" (p. xiv). This book is designed to generate a "stop-Obama-movement."

Quickly following on the heels of this work was *The Obama Nation: Leftist Politics and the Cult of Personality*, written by the same author of the "Swift Boat" book that attacked 2004 Democratic Party nominee John Kerry. And since that sensationalist book destroyed Senator Kerry candidacy, this book was designed to repeat that success in 2008. It was quickly exposed by the Obama camp for what it is, a no holds barred negative attack work. Enough said.

Following in the shadow of these books, is the book by political consultant Dick Morris, *Fleeced.* Although it simply has Obama's name in its subtitle and a chapter devoted to attacking him and his ideas, the book mainly focuses upon the lobbyists and their congressional supporters that bend the system to their goals instead of those of the American people. Since blame is put upon left-wingers Obama is smeared along with these groups in guilt by association and by his own liberal ideology. During the primaries, in continual appearances on all of the Fox News shows, Morris slammed Senator Hillary Clinton and his former boss, President Bill Clinton, who fired him. After the primaries concluded, he has taken to slamming Obama and promoting McCain. A good bit of this aminus comes through in the book.

Of all of the critical books, the very first to appear was the one by African American conservative and professor of English, Shelby Steele entitled, *A Bound Man: Why We are Excited About Obama and Why He Can't Win*. The book appeared on December 4, 2007. Thus, this man declared that Obama could not win even before the initial caucus and primary elections took place due to this enduring idea that the African American community and its leaders have embraced a "victimhood and separatist" ideology. These beliefs and values ride on white guilt and there is a limit and weakness to this support that places a ceiling on how far African Americans can rise, especially in, the political system. A further consequence of this ideology is that if Obama wins, he will advance liberal programs like affirmative action and other social safety net governmental programs instead of those that emphasize individualism, self-help, and racial assimilation. The silly dichotomy of "challengers and "bargainers," which he creates to provide evidence for his thesis, reveals the limits of both his imagination and that of the theory.

The Political Campaign Books as Seen from the Literature on Senator Obama

Like Obama, John McCain has released three "political campaign" books (over two presidential attempts, 2000 and 2008). The first one, *Faith of My Fathers* appeared in 1999, just before his initial presidential race and its looks only at his exploits, survival tactics, and punishments in Vietnam. This work of heroism, courage, terrible suffering, and self-sacrifice got him only so far because he was badly beaten by a candidate who did not fight abroad, but served in the National Guard in a state with a huge number of military bases and personnel. Thus a second book appeared just prior to the 2004 presidential campaign in 2003 entitled, *Worth the Fighting For*. This book discusses the return of this candidate after more than five years of being a POW, his elections to the House of Representatives and the U.S. Senate, and the heroes who supposedly inspired him to fight for the best in America. Yet, as a campaign book, it did not engage others to encourage McCain to challenge the incumbent President George W. Bush in his reelection of 2004 that featured a campaign reacting to the 9/11 terrorist attacks on America three years earlier.

Thus, a year later in 2004, McCain released his third "political campaign" book, *Why Courage Matters: The Way to a Braver Life,* so as to position himself for his second presidential run. Altogether this collection of books has clearly primed him for the 2008 race by showing him as an authentic American hero. But they have also generated two books about McCain and these books. The first one by journalist Elizabeth Drew emerged in 2002, *Citizen McCain* declares that these books made McCain the darling of the media and garnered him almost the full backing of the mainstream media. Re-issued in 2008 with a new introduction, it describes how McCain has through sheer self-determination become the Republican frontrunner, this time without very much help from the media simply because the conservative media wanted Mitt Romney.

The second book, written by David Brock and Paul Waldman, *Free Ride: John McCain and the Media,* reveals in great detail how the media, largely because of McCain's campaign books and the image that they created and promoted, became part of his political base. This then ensured that the media would give his campaign a positive spin in each and every one of his national political challenges until he was knocked out by others and/or overshadowed by newcomers.

Summary and Conclusions

Therefore, in the end, we can declare that the "political campaign" books surrounding the Obama candidacy not only reveal the candidate, his background and family life, and motivations, they can also introduce the candidate to an interested and supportive public. They can create an electoral base that had not existed before.

Secondly, "political campaign" books can become a decision-making device. Obama indicated that because of the book tour for his second book, buyers urged him to run for the presidency, and these individuals helped him make up his mind to throw his hat into the political ring in 2008 instead of later. Former Secretary of State Colin Powell indicated that it was the book tour for his book that made him consider running for the presidency and provided him with the public exposure that got him in part his high governmental appointments.

Thirdly, "political campaign" books expand the potential candidate's public persona and place him in contact with other national political players that might provide various forms of political resources, particularly campaign contributions and technical support that one will need to mount a successful presidential campaign.

Fourthly, there is the matter of sharpening the candidate's vision and message and political positions due to the simple fact that these "political campaign" books bring out a host of critics and opposition. Some of these critics and opponents must be answered while others can be ignored. In the response to attackers, however, candidates must shore up their weak areas and grow into the statespersons that the American electorate might want. We are watching that in terms of the two vice-presidential candidates in 2008. Currently, the Democratic nominee, Senator Joseph Biden, has his own "political campaign" book, *Promises to Keep: On Life and Politics* written for his 2008 race. While he did not write one for his 1988 race, a journalistic account of him based on interviews did surface in a work on several others entitled: *What It Takes: The Way to the White House.*

A similar problem faces Biden's counterpart, Republican vice-presidential candidate Sarah Palin, who had little time to prepare a "political campaign" book, but nevertheless a work has surfaced any way: *Sarah: How a Hockey Mom Turned Alaska.* This book has little to say about her national realities because of her sudden rise to national politics.

Collectively, the literature on Obama attracted the work of two economists who have offered ideas to the candidate about national investment strategies, instead of spending strategies that might help him in raising the nation out of its economic crisis. Thus, the role and function of "political campaign" books can be both positive and negative, and they have significantly matured since the earlier works appeared on African American presidential candidates.[1]

Note

1. Hanes Walton, Jr., Josephine A.V. Allen, Sherman C. Puckett, Donald R. Deskins, Jr., and Billie Dee Tate, "The Literature on African American Presidential Candidates," *Journal of Race and Policy* vol. 4 (Spring/Summer, 2008).

Bibliography

Brill, M. (2006). Barack *Obama: Working to Make a Difference.* Minneapolis, MN: Millbrook Press.

Corsi, J. R. (2008). *The Obama nation: leftist politics and the cult of personality.* New York: Threshold Editions/Simon & Schuster.

Dougherty, S. (2007). *Hopes and Dreams: The Story of Barack Obama.* New York: Black Dog and Leventhal Publishers.

Dupuis, M., & Boeckelman, K. (2008). *Barack Obama, the New Face of American Politics. Women and Minorities in Politics.* Westport, Conn: Praeger.

Freddoso, D. (2008). *The Case against Barack Obama: The Unlikely Rise and Unexamined Agenda of the Media's Favorite Candidate.* Washington, DC: Regency Publishers.

Glauberman, S. and Burris, J. (2008). *The Dream Begins: How Hawaii Shaped Barack Obama.* Watermark Publishers.

Jones, R. (2008). *What's Wrong With Obamamania: Black America, Black Leadership and the Death of Political Imagination.* Albany: State University of New York Press.

Kuttner, R. (2008). *Obama's Challenge: America's Economic Crisis and the Power of a Transformative Presidency.* White River Junction, VT: Chelsea Green Publishers.

Obama, B. (1995). *Dreams from My Father: A Story of Race and Inheritance.* New York: Times Books.

Obama, B. (2006). *The Audacity of Hope: Thoughts on Reclaiming the American Dream.* New York: Crowne Publishers.

Obama, B., & Rogak, L. (2007). *Barack Obama in His Own Words.* New York: Carroll & Graf.

Obama, B. (2008). *Change We Can Believe In: Barack Obama's Plan to Renew America's Promise.* New York: Three Rivers Press.

Obama vs. McCain: voting records of Barack Obama & John McCain for the 109th and 110th Congress. (2008). Rockville, MD: Arc Manor.

Mendell, D. (2008). *Obama: From Promises to Power.* New York: HarperCollins Publishers.

Morris, D., & McGann, E. (2008). *Fleeced: How Barack Obama, Media Mockery of Terrorist Threats, Liberals Who Want to Kill Talk Radio, the Do-Nothing Congress, Companies That Help Iran, and Washington Lobbyists for Foreign Governments Are Scamming U s—and What to Do About It.* New York, NY: Harper.

Neer, B., & Lee, J. (2008). *Barack Obama for Beginners: An Essential Guide. A for Beginners Documentary Comic Book.* Danbury, CT: For Beginners.

Street, P. L. (2009). *Barack Obama and the Future of American Politics.* Boulder: Paradigm.

Steele, S. (2007). *A Bounded Man: Why We Are Excited About Obama and Why He Can't Win.* New York: Free Press.

Talbott, J. R. (2008). *Obamanomics: How Bottom-Up Economic Prosperity Will Replace Trickle-Down Economics.* New York: Seven Stories Press.

Wilson, J. (2008). *Barack Obama: The Improbable Quest.* Boulder, CO: Paradigm.

A Radical Critique of the Reparations Movement

Carter A. Wilson
University of Toledo

Reparations for the outrages of the past—the holocaust of the Atlantic slave trade, the atrocities of plantation slavery, the exploitation of the sharecropping system, the indignities of segregation and the horrors of over a century of lynchings—are long overdue. Over the past decade the movement for reparations has gained in visibility and popularity. Although the movement is stronger today than it has been in the past, as a movement for social justice it is most problematic. It is problematic because even the most symbolic reparations proposals are stalled and unlikely at this point to succeed. It is problematic because racial oppression persists and because the current, dominant racist culture and prevailing socioeconomic and political arrangements stand like a brick wall between the movement and the attainment of reparations. Moreover, there are problems endemic to the movement. It has failed to address the dominant racist culture, to construct an effective counterideology and to develop the type of coalition strong enough to challenge the dominant power arrangement.

At its best, this movement explains current patterns of racial inequality in terms of the past history of slavery. This explanation shifts public attention away from current problems of racial oppression. At its worse, this movement not only fails to confront present forms of racial oppression, it is tainted by the contemporary racist culture.

This movement has been gaining in popularity among African Americans and growing at the same time that civil and human rights violations against them have been increasing. The call for reparations today is like the odd cry of a slave who is being brutally whipped. Instead of crying out for the immediate cessation of the whipping, the slave demands compensated for the beatings that took place years ago. The beatings must stop first. That is, the current patterns of racial oppression and repression must stop before compensation can be paid.

Current patterns of racial inequality are not simple artifacts of the past. The facts that there are more African Americans on death row, more African American in prison and jail, and more African American teenagers serving life sentences without any chance of parole than ever before in U.S. history are not artifacts of past slavery. These facts are functions of current forms of state racial repression. The growth of concentrated poverty in the inner cities of Detroit, Chicago, Cleveland, and other older industrial areas is not a function of past slavery, but the results of current processes of racial oppression. Just as racist culture in the past legitimized the institution of slavery, racist culture today legitimizes and normalizes current patterns of racial oppression and repression. Before there can be any compensation for slavery in the past, racial oppression must end in the present. The beating of the slave must stop first, before the slave can realistically expect any compensation. The cry for reparations muffles the call for an immediate end to racial oppression.

This essay reexamines the reparations movement in the larger context of contemporary patterns of racial oppression and current forms of racist culture. It does this first by reporting on the status of the reparations movement. Second, it briefly outlines current patterns of racial oppression. That is, it associates these patterns with the emergence of advanced capitalism or post-Fordism, which explains the growth of concentrated poverty and the persistence of racial inequality. It outlines forms of state repression and briefly describes contemporary racist culture. Racist culture today, as it has been in the past, legitimizes racial oppression. Finally, this essay concludes with a reassessment of the reparations movement and makes recommendations for a redirection of this movement.

Status of the Reparations Movement

There have been many reparations proposals, ranging from the symbolic to the radical. Although there have been a few minor successes, most have faced insurmountable opposition. Successes have included local reporting ordinances, a state reparations payment, a private voluntary donation, and a few minor acknowledgements. Chicago, Detroit, Los Angeles, Richmond, and a few other local governments have passed ordinances requiring businesses contracting with the city to declare whether they had any past involvement with the slave trade. The state of Florida compensated the survivors of the Rosewood massacre in the amount of about $7 million. Three reparations lawsuits were filed against several businesses with financial ties to slavery. J.P. Morgan acknowledged that its original investors were involved in the slave trade and the bank set-aside $5 million for scholarships for African Americas. Aetna Insurance admitted to and apologized for providing insurance policies to slave owners for the loss of their slaves. Although Brown University admitted that it was founded by money earned through the slave trade, it has refused to pay reparations because its major contributors opposed any form of repayments.

Most reparations proposals are stalled, even though they are symbolic and well grounded in law. The most notable examples include the Tulsa, Oklahoma and John Conyers' proposals. Tulsa involved a race riot in the early 1920s, which destroyed an area of the city known as Black Wall Street. This area contained one of the largest concentrations of black businesses. Property loss included about 600 parcels of commercial land: about 30 grocery stores, 21 restaurants, 21 churches, several law offices, barber and beauty shops, a bank, and many more. The lost of life has been estimated from 100 to 3,000. The state of Oklahoma established a commission to investigate the facts surrounding the Tulsa riot and to make recommendations. Although the commission recommended reparations, the state legislature did not support a reparations bill. Reparations supporters sued the state. However, the state court rejected the suit on grounds that the statutory limit for filing had expired.

John Conyers' bill, HR 40, would acknowledge the harm done by slavery, recognize the role of the national government in allowing it, apologize to the descendents of slavery, and create a task force to examine the feasibility of monetary settlements to the descendents of slavery. This bill has been stuck in committee for about a decade and it is likely to die there.

Despite the fact that these modest proposals are stalled, national reparations groups call for even more radical plans. These national organizations include the Reparations Assessment Group (RAG) and the National Coalition of Blacks for Reparations in America (N'COBRA). The RAG was established by a number of attorneys, law professors and civil rights activists such as Charles Ogletree of Harvard University, the late Johnnie Cochran, Randall Robinson, Alexander Pires and others. Speaking for the RAG, Dr. Charles Ogletree insists that a political settlement is preferable, but not likely given the current political climate.

The N'COBRA demands a political settlement. It participated in the October 15, 2005 Million More March. It supports all reparations proposals and calls on the U.S. government to publicly acknowledge and apologize for its role in supporting the holocaust of slavery and to pay reparations.

A number of prominent African American scholars support N'COBRA's proposal and insist that reparations must be a cry for social reconstruction. Amiri Baraka says this:

> That is, Reparations must take the form of Social Reconstruction, which is Economic and Political and Cultural at base. For instance, any initial demand must include the demand for free education for the Afro American people, not as affirmative action, but as a constitutional amendment which by law would give Black Americans education to the highest sectors of the US without charge (Baraka, 2002: 123).

Political Scientists Lawrie Balfour published an article in the *American Political Science Review* in which he provided a brilliant discussion of how Du Bois would conceive reparations, making it clear that Du Bois would not argue for payments to individuals, but for the massive infusion of money for the economic development of the poorest African American communities.

> First, reparations could respond to both strands of Du Bois's claims about the economic requirements of a genuinely reconstructed democracy. Conceived as a massive investment in black communities, rather than a per capita payment, and targeted primarily at the poorest African Americans, reparations could create a basis for attacking the deep economic inequality Du Bois understands to be incompatible with democracy and thereby broadening the base of African Americans who can be said to enjoy the fruits of citizenship in a meaningful sense (Balfour, 2003: 41).

Balfour shows how Du Bois would argue for reparations as a precondition for a truly democratic and just society and as a way to deal with the current racial inequality and to compensate for the centuries of slavery and the years of state-mandated segregation. Despite his passionate advocacy for social reconstruction, Du Bois saw some fundamental problems with reparations, which Balfour acknowledges:

> This is not to say that Du Bois himself would endorse a campaign for reparations. Indeed, he might well dismiss it as a pipedream, much as he did in 1916, when a group of African Americans sought compensation from the U.S. Treasury for a share of the revenues from American cotton production. Of the vow by the group's attorney to seek $68 million, Du Bois scoffs, "Of course, he can claim it and anybody else can claim it and they may also claim the moon but the chance of getting the one is about as great as that of getting the other" (Balfour, 2003: 40-41; Du Bois, 1916).

Of course, Balfour insists that Du Bois eventually changed his position after World War II, as a delegation of civil rights leaders approached the United Nations with a reparations proposal. There is another interpretation. That is, Du Bois never changed his position. The reparation proposal presented to the UN after WWII was fundamentally different. It accused the United States of current human rights violations against African Americans and focused as much on the present as it did on the past.

Du Bois no doubt saw reparations as a pipedream for three major reasons. First, corporate leaders of the industrialized North formed a powerful alliance with the land aristocracy of the South to guarantee the protection of money-generating private property—land or production facilities—and to accelerate the exploitation of labor, whether in the industries or on the land. Northern industrial interests had played a major role in squashing the 40 acres and mule proposal in the first place, as they saw the proposal not only as an offense against the Southern land aristocracy, but as a threat to the sanctity of private property.

Second, the dominant racist culture not only justified slavery in the past, it legitimized the system of segregation, sharecropping, convict lease, lynching, and other aspects of racial oppression. W.E.B. Du Bois argued 100 years ago that the inability of a nation to acknowledge its past injustices is generally symptomatic of the presence of remnants of the cultural, political, and social mechanism responsible for the perpetration of the injustices in the first place (Balfour, 2003). So long as remnants of the dominant racist culture of the past remain in the current period, acceding to even symbolic reparations like an apology will be difficult to attain.

Third, the political isolation and powerlessness of African Americans was a major obstacle to a reparations movement. The dominant power arrangement, the culture of racism, and the political isolation and powerlessness of African Americans made reparations a pipedream.

The current reparations movement has made little progress today because it is faced with many of the same obstacles Du Bois recognized 100 years ago. Moreover, support for reparations is profoundly divided along the color line. One poll reports that 55 percent of African Americans support reparations, whereas 90 percent of whites oppose it (Balfour, 2003: 40).

The problem is that the movement is rising at a time when the nation is still divided along a color line, racist culture is expanding and racial oppression is intensifying. To make this point clear, it is necessary to briefly examine different types of racism and current patterns of racial oppression and contemporary racist culture. This examination would provide the context for a critical assessment of the reparations movement.

Different Types of Racism

Racism today operates much as it has over the centuries of U.S. history. Racism involves patterns of racial oppression, forms of racist culture and the mediating role of the state. Racism changes forms as patterns of racial oppression and racist culture changes. For a more detailed discussion, see *Racism from Slavery to Advanced Capitalism*. Racial oppression is related to the dominant mode of production and the prevailing methods of exploiting labor. Racist culture consists of images, stories, and ideologies that operate to legitimize racial oppression. Repression has to do with the method the state uses to control oppressed groups and preempt rebellion.

The literature identifies several types of racism, depending on different patterns of racial oppression and forms of racist culture. Three deserve brief mention: 1) dominative racism, 2) dominative/aversive racism, and 3) metaracism.

Dominative racism (colonial period up to 1865) was associated with slavery, the dominant mode of production and exploitation of labor in the Southern plantation economy, which existed up to 1865. The prevailing racist culture, which functioned to legitimize the institution of slavery, included images of African cannibals, happy slaves, and Little Black Sambo. It contained stories of how kidnapping people in Africa saved them from other barbarous and cannibalistic Africans and how slaves were happy and grateful for their good Christian masters. It consisted of ideologies of biologically and genetically superior and inferior races, which justified master-slave relations. The state and the U.S. Constitution protected the institution of slavery.

Dominative/aversive racism (1865-1964) was associated primarily the sharecropping system, the dominant mode of production and method of exploiting labor in the Southern economy. It was also associated with debt peonage and state-mandated segregation. The landowners in the South dominated the state and imposed segregation to keep African Americans on the land as sharecroppers. Segregation allowed landowners and industrialists to pit blacks and whites against each other in ways that enhanced the exploitation of both, and kept wages low in the industries and on the land. Its cultural form consisted of images of Steppin Fetchit, happy illiterate blacks, and bull-like crazed black male rapists, who terrorized white women and needed to be subdued by the Ku Klux Klan. It included stories of dirty, smelly, undesirable, intellectually inferior blacks endowed with impure blood and biologically predisposed to laziness and manual labor. It contained ideologies of blacks as biologically and culturally predisposed to immoral and criminal behavior. This culture operated to legitimize sharecropping, debt peonage, forced segregation and lynching. The Southern state governments mandated and promoted racial segregation up to the passage of the Civil Rights Act of 1964.

The civil rights movement exposed and de-legitimized many images and symbols of the older forms of racism. Today, we recognize slavery, state-mandated segregation and lynchings as outrageous representations of the old racism, with absolutely no legitimacy. However, as Toni Morrison and Margaret Burnham point out in an analysis of the Clarence Thomas hearings and the use of the expression high-tech lynching, most people recognize images and symbols of the old racism, but unthinkingly and unconsciously accept contemporary racial and gender stereotypes as normal and legitimate (Morrison, 1992; Burham, 1992). The major problem with the reparations movement is that it recognizes past racism, but does not understand contemporary racism.

Contemporary Racism: Metaracism

Contemporary racism is metaracism. Metaracism is associated with post-Fordism, the dominant mode of exploiting labor, which contributes to the growth of concentrated poverty in inner cities. The prevailing racist culture consists of images of welfare queens, dangerous drug-crazed black males, and dangerous teenaged street gangs. This culture transmits stories of welfare cheats, financially imprudent black families, and destructive teenage street gangs. It promotes an ideology that substitutes the culture of poverty ideology for biological racism. The state imposes heightened police control of inner-city residents, particularly black males, to preempt any chance of rebellion.

A fuller understanding of metaracism requires more discussion of changing modes of production and methods of exploiting labor, the growth of concentrated poverty, state repression, the weakening of black political power, the erosion of affirmative action, and contemporary racist culture.

Post-Fordism

Metaracism is associated with advanced capitalism or post-Fordism capitalism. Capitalism from the 1930s to the end of the 1970s involved what Gramsci calls Fordism. Gramsci sees Fordism as a compromise between capital and labor, or between the industrial corporation and its workers and local community. It emerged from the ideas and practices of Henry Ford. Fordism is based on the construction of huge, mammoth, multistory and labor-intensive production facilities, built on major railroad arteries with incredibly large initial capital investments. Capital was fixed. That is, production facilities were practically immobile, tied to the industrial city, and set in concrete near major railroad lines on which they depended. Fordism entailed concessions to labor and community. The corporation accepted labor unions, provided decent wages and security for its workers, and invested in local communities. Ford believed that by paying workers a decent wage, they could afford to purchase his automobiles. Thus, in exchange for these concessions to labor and community, Ford bought labor peace and stable markets.

With the rise of mobile capital and global markets, corporations can move beyond Fordism into the post-Fordist period; that is, they can rescind the concessions and increase the exploitation of labor. Post-Fordism is based on the construction of smaller, single story, automated production facilities. Under post-Fordism, capital or production facilities are more mobile. The corporation is less tied to the local community and it focuses on global markets to sell its products. The post-Fordist corporation increases the exploitation of labor by reducing wages. It does this several ways. First, with the dramatic increase in the mobility of capital, a corporation can easily close down a production facility in Detroit, where labor unions are strong and wages are high, and move around the world to find areas where unions are non-existent and wages low. Second, the corporation can close down an entire division, where wages are high, and subcontract with a smaller nonunion firm, where wages are lower. Third, the corporation can hire more part-time and temporary workers. Post-Fordism is characterized by weaker labor unions and lower wages.

Labor processes under post-Fordism have contributed to the creation of a large reservoir of unemployed workers or what Marx referred to as a reserve army of labor. This reservoir of unemployed workers also helps to suppress wages. Under post-Fordism, African Americans suffer super-exploitation and state repression as they form a large proportion of the members of this reserve army of labor, as they make up the bulk of the poor families concentrated in the inner cities of these older industrial cities, and as they become disproportionately overrepresented in America's prison system.

Post-Fordism and the Growth of Concentrated Poverty among African Americans

These post-Fordist economic changes had its most devastating impact on black industrial workers in older industrial cities, particularly Chicago, Cleveland, Detroit, Gary, New York, Newark, Philadelphia, Pittsburgh, St. Louis, and many other cities. For example, between the late 1960s and the early 1980s, Detroit lost over 70,000 jobs in the industrial sector, after a number of automobile production facilities closed and about 40,000 jobs in retail and wholesale, especially after the closing of major department stores like J.L. Hudson in the downtown area (Wilson, 1992). This massive loss of jobs in the industrial, retail, and wholesale areas contributed to rising rates of unemployment and poverty in Detroit. As African Americans were disproportionately overrepresented in the more vulnerable unskilled industrial jobs during the 1970s, the loss of these jobs impacted most severely on them, contributing to growing poverty and unemployment rates.

The second factor is the rise of the black middle class and their exodus from central cities. As the ranks of the black middle class increased, many moved out of the city, leaving the black poor more isolated and concentrated in the inner cities (Wilson, 1987). Even though the black middle class increased, black unemployment and poverty rates remained high compared to the rates of whites. Black unemployment rates remain twice the white rate today. Black poverty rates remain almost three times the white rate today, see tables 1 and 2. The concentration and isolation of the black poor in inner cities characterize the racial oppression of the post-civil rights period.

Although the economic expansion of the late 1990s ameliorated some of the concentrated poverty, African Americans continued to suffer much higher poverty and unemployment rates than whites and black poverty remained concentrated within inner cities. Today, white poverty tends to be broadly distributed and there are more poor whites. However, black poverty remains isolated and concentrated in inner cities.

Concentrated poverty had two major consequences. First, it created what Marx would call a reserve army of labor, which generates pressure to reduce wages and weakens the power of unions. In constant 2001 dollars, the minimum wage peaked at $7.10 in 1970, but declined to about $5.00 by 2005 (see *Statistical Abstract*, 2005). Moreover, the percentage of the workforce unionized peaked around 1970, but declined by 2005 to about what it was in the late 1930s.

Second, concentrated poverty contributed to growing social problems: High infant mortality rates, low-life expectancy rates, high morbidity and mortality rates. Many inner-city areas such as Detroit, Washington DC, Philadelphia, Saint Louis, Gary, etc. have infant mortality rates as high as third-world nations (Wilson, 2006).

Ordinarily, the creation of a reserve army of labor and the production of pockets of concentrated and isolated poverty would generate political opposition. However, the likelihood of a revolt is reduced by the racial composition of the people trapped in these pockets of poverty. This concentrated poverty defines contemporary racial oppression. Racist culture normalizes this oppression as it dehumanizes the poor, provokes contempt toward them and legitimizes racial repression. This repression becomes obvious in a glance at the criminal justice system.

Table 1
Black and White Unemployment Rates

Year	Black	White
1970		4.5
1973	9.4	
1980	14.3	6.3
1985	15.1	
1990	11.4	4.8
1995	10.4	4.9
2000	7.6	3.6
2003	10.8	5.2

Statistical Abstracts

Table 2
Black and White Poverty Rates

Year	Black	White
1973	31.4	7.5
1980	32.5	9.1
1985	31.3	9.7
1990	31.9	8.8
1995	29.3	8.5
2000	22.5	7.4
2004	24.7	8.6

State Repression

The state response to concentrated black poverty has been greater repression. Whereas the dominant culture promotes the illusion that the United States has a liberal criminal justice system, it has the most repressive system in the world. Americans incarcerate more people per population than any other country in the world. Several factors contributed to this horrendous incarceration rate: the Supreme Court gutting of the rights of those accused of crimes, and state legislatures and the U.S. Congress passing mandatory sentencing laws, eliminating of the discretion of judges and establishing three-strikes-you're-out laws. Willie Wisely summarizes some of the extreme cases:

> Larry Fisher, 35, was convicted of his third strike in Snohomish County superior court in Washington. He is in prison and will stay there for the rest of his life. Fisher was convicted of putting his finger in his pocket, pretending it was a gun, and robbing a sandwich shop of $151 dollars. An hour later police arrested him at a bar a block away while he was drinking a beer. Fisher's two prior strikes involved stealing $360 for his grandfather in 1986 and robbing a pizza parlor of $100.
>
> In March 1995, Jerry Dewayne Williams of Los Angeles got 25 years to life for stealing a slice of pizza from a group of children on a pier....
>
> In Monterey County, Joel Murillo faced a term of 35 years to life for stealing television sets (Wisely, 1998: 21-22).

The U.S. Supreme Court upheld the constitutionality of the three-strikes-you're-out law in *Ewing v. California* (2003). In this case, a man was sentenced to life in prison for stealing three golf clubs. Sentencing people to life for petty thief is a practice expected in some of the most repressive third-world countries, not in the United States. The increased incarceration rates have racial implications, especially since both the type of laws and style of enforcement target black males. Police often target poor black males in inner-city areas, particularly for possession of crack-cocaine. Moreover, sentencing for possession of five grams of crack is a mandatory five years. Possession of 99 grams of pure cocaine, a drug more commonly used among more affluent drug abusers, is just a misdemeanor. Almost 90 percent of the offenders sentenced to state prisons for drug offenses are black (Irwin and Austin, 1997: 4). Today, almost one-third of the black male population between 18 and 29 is in the system—in jail or prison, on parole or probation (Mauer, 1999).

The repression against African Americans has not gone unnoticed by international human rights organizations. Amnesty International and Human Rights Watch have cited the United States for several violations in addition to the incarceration crisis. An October 12, 2005 report by Amnesty International cited America's high proportion of teenagers sentenced to life imprisonment without any chance of parole, and its tendency to sentence black teenagers to life without parole at rates ten times greater than those of whites. The report adds, "The Convention on the Rights of the Child, ratified by every country in the world except the United States and Somalia, forbids this practice" (Amnesty International Press Release, October 12, 2005). The article cited cases in which teenagers in the United States were sentenced to life without parole on their first felony conviction. Apparently, they were accomplices in a botched robbery, which ended in a murder committed by an adult. The report concluded that the practice of sentencing children to life without parole is based on the presumption that the child cannot be salvaged or redeemed, a view too often applied to young black males. This view is promoted by the culture of poverty thesis, by racist images of young black males in the media and by other aspects of the dominant racist culture.

Other Amnesty International human rights citations include racial profiling and police violence. A 1998 Amnesty International news release concluded, "There is a widespread and persistent problem of police brutality across the USA.... Police officers have beaten and shot unresisting suspects; they have misused batons, chemical sprays and electro-shock weapons..." (Amnesty International, October 18, 1998). The report was written before the murder of Amadu Diallo in New York City in February 1999. After this case, Amnesty filed another report calling for a review of New York City police. This report adds, "The Diallo case is one of more than a dozen incidents in the past five years, in which black, Hispanic or other minorities have been shot in highly questionable and disputed circumstances.... Many shootings, including the Diallo case, appear to violate international standards set out under UN rules which provide that law enforcement officials shall, as far as possible apply non-violent means before resorting to the use of force and firearms..." (Amnesty International 2000). A police officer who shoots an unarmed suspect violates international law and the dignity and human rights of the individual.

The death penalty provides another example of a human rights violation and the racial implications of the repressive criminal justice system. There is substantial statistical evidence of racial biases in capital punishment. The U.S. Supreme Court acknowledged the bias, yet upheld the use of the death penalty (*McClesky v. Kemp*). Justice Brennan writes,

> The capital sentencing rate for all white-victim cases was almost 11 times greater than the rate for black-victims cases. Furthermore, blacks who kill whites are sentenced to death at nearly 22 times the rate of blacks who kill blacks, and more than 7 times the rate of whites who kill blacks. In addition, prosecutors seek the death penalty for 70% of black defendants with white victims, but for only 15% of black defendants with black victims, and only 19% of white defendants with black victims (*McClesky v. Kemp*).

The increase in state repression against blacks is related to the growth of concentrated poverty. With close over two million people in jail or prison, the official unemployment rate would be substantially higher. It is almost as if the growth in the incarceration rate is a way of warehousing the reserve army of labor. This is a form of super-exploitation and repression. It constitutes serious human right violations. It is exasperated by a 21st-century phenomenon: private exploitation of prison labor.

The convict lease system in which prisoners were leased to railroad companies or plantations ended in the early 20th century. The chain gangs ended in the mid-1950s. Up to the end of the 20th century, most convict labor was limited to making license plates or doing work exclusively for the prison, like washing cloths, cooking food, or cleaning the prison. Today, more than 30 states have passed laws allowing prisoners to work for private companies. Gordon Lafer adds:

> When most of us think of convicts at work we picture them banging out license plates or digging ditches. Those images, however, are now far too limited to encompass the great range of jobs that America's prison workforce is performing. If you book a flight on TWA, you'll likely be talking to a prisoner at a California correctional facility that the air line uses for its reservations service. Microsoft has used Washington State prisoners to pack and ship Windows software. AT&T has used prisoners for telemarketing; Honda, for manufacturing parts; and even Toys "R" Us, for cleaning and stocking shelves for the next day's customers (Lafer, 2002).

Lafer estimates that about 80,000 inmates work for private companies such as Honda, Toys "R" Us, Microsoft, TWA, Boeing Aircraft, and others. He adds, "Konica has hired prisoners to repair its copiers for less than 50 cents an hour.... And in Oregon, private companies can "lease prisoners for only $3 a day" (Lafer, 2002). Companies not only pay a faction of the cost of wages, they do not have to pay health insurance, unemployment insurance, workers' compensation, vacation time, sick leave, or overtime. Moreover, they do not have to bother with labor complaints, grievances, or unions. They end up with a compliant, captured and super-exploited workforce. Some states are beginning to experiment with prison workers to replace migrant labors. A March 2007, *New York Times* article reads: "As migrant laborers flee Colorado because of tough new immigration restrictions, worried farmers are looking to prisoners to fill their places in the fields" (Frosch, 2007).

Growing Political Powerlessness and the Erosion of Constitutional Protections

In addition to suffering super-exploitation and human rights violations, African Americans have lost considerable political power. This has occurred through both legal and extra-legal means. African Americans are being disenfranchised today through legal devices similar to those used over 100 years ago. One of the most common legal devices used today is the permanent expulsion of convicted felons from state voting rolls. According to Manning Marable,

> About 15 percent of all African American males nationally are either permanently or currently disenfranchised. In Mississippi, one-third of black men are unable to vote for the remainder of their lives. In Florida, 818,000 residents cannot vote for life (Marable, 2006: 6).

Most democratic nations disenfranchise convicted felons while they are incarcerated, but restore their right to vote once they are released. A few continue to disenfranchise them while they are on probation or parole, but restore their voting rights once they paid their debt to society. The United States in one of the few nations of the world that permanently disenfranchise convicted felons. Over 100 years ago, states were allowed to disenfranchise blacks because the denial of voting rights was based on character, rather than race. The states are now doing the same thing. The problem is that only a few civil rights organizations like the NAACP Legal Defense Fund are challenging these laws on grounds that they have the effect of denying black males the right to vote.

States use other devices to reduce the political involvement of convicted felons. Although Ohio does not permanently bar convicted felons from voting, the state prohibits them from signing official referendum petitions.

States have used a number of extra-legal means to reduce the black vote. The state of Florida is well known for purging not just the names of convicted felons, but all of the names that matched the names of convicted felons. This means that the state not only purged the names of all those with a felony conviction, but also purged the names of all those who were legitimately registered to vote and have no criminal records. They were purged simply because their names matched the name of a convicted felon. Close to 100,000 people who were legitimately registered to vote and had no criminal record in Florida lost the right to vote in the 2000 election. Of course, the Help America Vote Act of 2002 requires that states provide provisional ballots for those citizens who believe they are legally entitled to vote, but whose names were purged from the voter rolls.

Although the federal government provided grants to states under the Help America Vote Act to purchase voting machines, a number of states failed to purchase machines for predominantly black precincts. The state of Ohio was noted for this failure, as blacks in key precincts in the city of Cleveland had to wait on average for four and a half hours to vote in the 2004 presidential election. This excessive wait depressed the black vote in predominantly black precincts. Another device used in Ohio to depress the vote in predominantly Democratic precincts, which happened to also be predominantly black, was direct challenge to voter registration. Robert Kennedy, in a June 2006 *Rolling Stone* article, documented the practice of Republicans in the state of Ohio during the 2004 election aggressively challenging the registrations of Democrats, many of whom were African Americans. Kennedy says this:

> To stem the tide of new registrations, the Republican National Committee and the Ohio Republic Party attempted to knock tens of thousands of predominantly minority and urban voters off the rolls through illegal mailings know in electioneering jargon as "caging." During the Eighties, after the GOP used such mailings to disenfranchise nearly 76,000 black voters in New Jersey and Louisiana, it was forced to sign two separate court orders agreeing to abstain from caging. But during the summer of 2004, the GOP targeted minority voters in Ohio by zip code, sending registered letters to more than 200,000 newly registered voters in sixty-five counties. On October 22nd, a mere eleven days before the election, Ohio Republican Party Chairman Bob Bennett—who also chairs the board of elections in Cuyahoga County-sought to invalidate the registrations of 35,427 voters who had refused to sign for the letters or whose mail came back as undeliverable (Kennedy, 2006).

Just as Southern Dixiecrats over 100 years ago, in their efforts to eliminate the Southern Republican party, which then was the party that freed the slaves, also disenfranchised Southern blacks, the Republican party today in their efforts to eviscerate the Democratic party, disenfranchises blacks. Nationwide, African Americans have lost substantial political power within the electoral arena.

Although critics consider this measure a de facto poll tax and a tactic to reduce the voting rights of low-income voters, about 25 states now require voter identification to vote. Since the Supreme Court upheld the constitutionality of this requirement, a few states are considering requiring proof of citizenship.

Affirmative Action and Reparations

As blacks lose political power in the national electoral arena, they are also losing other forms of civil rights protections. The ironic thing is that as proponents of reparations promise substantially more to African Americans than they would get through affirmative action, affirmative action programs are being dismantled and the few gains won in the 1970s were lost in the 1980s. More was lost over the next two decades.

The term affirmative action can be traced back to the Kennedy administration. During the early 1960s, it became evident that African Americans were totally excluded from firms that were getting multi-million dollar contracts from the federal government. The federal government was supporting and rewarding firms that refused to hire African Americans. Kennedy issued an executive order requiring firms that received federal contracts to take affirmative steps to hire qualified minorities. After several years of frustration in pushing firms to stop excluding qualified minorities, the Equal Employment Opportunity Commission required firms to take more aggressive steps to recruit minorities. The EEOC also began to use statistical evidence, the low percentage of minorities hired as prima facie evidence of discrimination and required firms to demonstrate that their hiring practices were non-discriminatory. During the early 1970s, the Nixon administration introduced a pilot program, the Philadelphia plan, which set-aside a small percentage of federal money to stimulate the development of minority business enterprises. Around the same time, a number of universities established more aggressive programs to try to open the doors of opportunity to African Americans.

The first major Supreme Court case involving affirmative action was the 1978 *Regents v. Bakke* case. Bakke, a white male, claimed that a special admissions program of the University of California Medical School at Davis, which set aside 16 out of 100 seats for special admission students, constituted a form of reverse discrimination, as he was denied admissions to the program.

In his dissenting opinion in the *Bakke* decision, Justice Thurgood Marshall argued that those African Americans who applied to the University of California Medical College at Berkeley, where victims, not of a system of slavery that occurred in the distant past, but of a brutally oppressive system of apartheid and racial inequality during their grade school years. Many of the applicants who applied in the late 1960s and early 1970s had suffered the injustices of racially segregated and grossly underfunded public schools in the South during the 1950s and early 1960s. Marshall insisted that because state-mandated segregation had directly harmed them, the state had an obligation to remedy that harm by providing an affirmative action admission policy.

Rather than addressing Marshall directly, Justice Powell in his plurality decision ignored this argument and set-forth a bogus reparations argument. Powell redefined Marshall's argument as a call for compensating blacks for the past history of slavery. Powell then insisted that the argument for compensating blacks for slavery reached too far into the past to find the harm that needed to be remedied. It is ironic that the reparations movement ignores Marshall's argument and latches on to Powell's bogus reparations argument. After discrediting a reparations argument that no one made, Powell proceeded to accept a minimal affirmative action program. By the beginning of the 1980s, minimal affirmative action in admissions and government set-aside programs were established law. During the 1980s and 1990s, the Court hacked away at affirmative action.

In the *Richmond, Virginia v. Croson* (1989) decision the city had established a 30 percent set-aside after it discovered that less than one-tenth of one percent of city contracts went to minority contractors. In this decision, the Supreme Court struck down this set-aside. The reasoning was that set-aside programs could only be justified by substantially and clearly demonstrated discrimination, using appropriate data. The fact that less than one-tenth of one percent of the city contracts went to minority contractors was not sufficient to demonstrate discrimination. O'Connor insisted that this low figure could simply reflect the fact that there were no minority businesses that qualified for the city contracts. Later the Court struck down federal set-aside programs for minority contractors. Today, set-asides are generally considered illegal, unless discrimination can be demonstrated with relevant and substantial data.

A few years ago, the Supreme Court revised the issue of affirmative action in college admissions in the University of Michigan case. This case involved two separate opinions entailing two different admissions programs. In many ways, this decision reiterated *Bakke*.

The Court rejected the University of Michigan's undergraduate admissions affirmative action program as too expansive and as giving too much weight to race. The Court upheld the law school affirmative action program because it required admissions officers to look at each file separately and consider grade point average, test scores, letters of admission and many other factors, including race and gender. The Court agreed that diversity in student populations was a legitimate government purpose (*Grutter v. Bollinger* and *Gratz v. Bollinger*).

A national campaign against affirmative action had emerged during the early 1990s out of California. The campaign was spearheaded by Ward Connerly, an African American member of the University of California Board of Regents. Connerly was active in the American Civil Rights Institute, a non-profit organization committed to ending all forms of racial and gender preferences. Connerly campaigned in favor of the California Civil Rights Initiative, known also as Proposition 209. He came to Michigan in 2006 and successfully campaign for the passage of the Michigan Civil Rights Initiative, known also as Proposition 2. This initiative outlawed any form of affirmative action and has contributed to a substantial decline in black enrollment at several major universities throughout the state of Michigan during the fall 2008 enrollment.

Ward Connerly and the American Civil Rights Institute campaigns all over the country to oppose affirmative action. Connerly and the Institute ran into stiff opposition from the National Organization of Women. The Michigan chapter of NOW campaigned to preserve affirmative action. Pro-reparations organizations were conspicuous in their absence.

Contemporary Racist Culture

As we move close to the second decade of the 21st century in the post-9-11 era, racism persists in the United States. It is characterized by concentrated poverty, disproportionately high unemployment and poverty rates among African Americans. It is most noted by state repression, as about one-third of the black male population is in the criminal justice system. Indeed, the United States has been cited by several human rights organizations for violating the human rights of African Americans, for the racial discrimination in its justice system, for the continual use of the death penalty, for the disproportionately high rate of African Americans on death row, and for the incarceration of teenagers for life, without any chance of parole. In addition to these human rights violations, African Americans have suffered the gradual loss of civil rights and voting rights protections.

As noted earlier, contemporary racist culture legitimizes racial oppression, justifies state repression, and fosters contempt for young African American males living in concentrated poverty. While the world looks at the way this nation treats African Americans in horror, contemporary racist culture justifies it. Racist culture focuses attention, filters out information and uses images, stories and ideology ways that operate to legitimize racial oppression. It desensitizes the entire nation to the repression African Americans.

The contemporary racist cultural dumps the old genetic and biological racist ideas and focuses more on culture and immoral values and behavior. It contains images of welfare queens who collect welfare and drive Cadillacs—large black women who have more children to get more welfare money (Collins, 2000; Gilens,1999); and large, crazed, bull-like black males who are duped up on crack cocaine, highly excitable, endowed with enormous strength and threatening to the general public. The presence of these images of threatening black males explain the behavior of four New York City police officers who in 1999 shot Amadu Diallo 41 times, although he was unarmed. These images also explain the behavior of the jurors who acquitted the four officers. Racist images are major features of contemporary racist culture or metaracism. These images dehumanize African Americans, desensitize the larger population to their suffering and provoke contempt and fear toward them.

Martin Gilens (1999) shows how almost all of the negative images of welfare recipients in the major newspapers and magazines he examined were pictures of black people and most of the positive images of poor people were pictures of whites (Gilens 1999). These images explain why most Americans support the government helping poor people, but hate welfare. Americans hate welfare because the media portrays images of welfare queens and welfare cheats and promotes welfare as a black program, exploited by blacks. These images provoke contempt for poor black women and hatred for welfare. Whereas most people on welfare at the time of Gilens' study were white, most Americans believed it to be a black program.

Metaracism contains stories of excessively liberal governments that coddle criminals and give huge sums of money to undeserving poor blacks. David Horowitz provides a good example of metaracism in his racist diatribe against reparations. Drawing from the old racism, he maintains that slavery was good for African Americans. Reflecting current metaracism, Horowitz insists that the U.S. government already paid reparations to blacks, particularly in the form of welfare payments and preferential treatment during the 1960s and 70s:

> Since the passage of the Civil Rights Acts and the advent of the Great Society in 1965, trillions of dollars in transfer payments have been made to African Americans in the form of welfare benefits and racial preferences (in contracts, job placements and educational admissions)—all under the rationale of redressing historic racial grievances.... If trillion dollar restitutions and a wholesale rewriting of American law (in order to accommodate racial preferences) for African-Americans is not enough to achieve a "healing," what will (Horowitz, 2001)?

Horowitz's view reflects the current racist culture. This culture filters out the fact that African Americans were systematically excluded from welfare up to the mid-1960s (Neubeck and Cazenave, 2001). Aid for Dependent Children, the so-called welfare program established by the Social Security Act of 1935 was never a problem when the Southern states systematically excluded black women under provisions disqualifying any recipient in domestic or agricultural employment and for amorphous morality grounds. This stingy program became a problem the moment it could no longer exclude black women. Racist culture filters out the fact that welfare programs, Great Society programs, and trillions of dollars of federal money went mostly to whites, not blacks, although blacks paid taxes just like whites. It filters out the fact that tax dollars left Northern industrial cities and stimulated the economic development of Southern cities, as multibillion dollar defense contracts went to industries located in these areas (Watkins and Perry, 1977) and that federal grants such as the Community Development Black Grants were distributed more broadly during the 1980s to more affluent areas (Mollenkopf, 1983: 97). These omissions are common in contemporary metaracism. Horowitz's diatribe illustrates the point that a great deal of the opposition against reparations, even the most harmless, symbolic proposal like apologizing for slavery is symptomatic of the presence of both old and new racism.

Culture of Poverty Ideology

The ideology of metaracism is grounded in the culture of poverty thesis. Steinberg sees this thesis as a myth that arises from academics' attempt to explain black subordination in a country presumed to offer equal opportunity and success to anyone who works hard enough (Steinberg, 1989). This thesis also results from a methodological error of leaping to conclusions about values and attitudes based on superficial knowledge about behavior. Like older forms of racism, it dehumanizes poor blacks and it defines them in terms opposite of middle class whites, except that it rejects genetics. The culture of poverty defines the middle class as constrained, rational, responsible, and future-oriented. Conversely, it defines poor blacks as impulsive, irrational, irresponsible, and present-oriented.

The underclass literature is a more contemporary form of the culture of poverty thesis. As with the culture of poverty, contemporary scholars often define the black urban underclass as the antithesis of the white middle-class. For example, Ken Auletta defines the underclass as that proportion of the poor which will not assimilate into the mainstream of American society: the long-term welfare recipients, the hostile street criminals, high-school drop-outs, drug addicts, hustlers, drifters, and the homeless (Auletta, 1983). Charles Murray, the co-author of *The Bell Curve,* argues in another book, *Losing Ground*, "blacks widely rejected the legitimacy of white norms and white laws" (Murray, 1984: 118).

Some liberal and Afrocentric scholars ascribe to some aspect of the culture of poverty thesis, suggesting that both structural factors and cultural traits explain poverty. They assume that poor people have values and attitudes that are self-defeating, self-destructive and self-perpetuating; that is, they take on a life of their own, apart from structure. This self-defeating culture includes poor black girls who have babies to get on welfare and to feel important; poor black boys who become thugs and see time spent in jail as a badge of honor; young black children who see working hard and getting an education as acting white.

These scholars see within poor black communities high rates of black-on-black violence, teen pregnancy, drug dealing and abuse, welfare dependency, single-parent families, and other forms of self-destructive behavior. Without direct empirical data they leap to conclusions about values and attitudes and draw firm conclusions about a culture presumed to be independent of structure. Worst, they ignore the wealth of research on behavior, values and attitudes that contradict their assertions about culture.

For example, aggregate and statistical research demonstrates that rates of violence, welfare dependency, and female-headed households, vary strongly with economic indicators: rates of unemployment, concentrated poverty and community resources (Peterson and Jencks, 1991; Sampson and Wilson, 1995; Tienda and Stier, 1991).

Ethnographic, survey, and aggregate studies demonstrate that poor inner-city blacks are no different than anyone else, with the same values, hopes, and dreams as middle-class whites. Scholars have demonstrated that when opportunities for normal channels of economic advancement are blocked for any racial or ethnic group, their members often turn to illicit means. Some young black males turn to selling drugs, not as a function of values different from those of the middle class, but as a function of middle-class values played out in a social context devoid of legitimate opportunities (Kotlowitz, 1992; Liebow, 1967; Ladner, 1973; Stenberg, 1989).

Kristin Luker demonstrates that although pregnancy rates are higher among African American teenagers, rates of sexual activity among blacks and whites are roughly the same. The higher rate of pregnancy among poor black teenagers is not a function of a culture of poverty or immoral values, but of lower rates of exposure to contraceptives and health care. Luker and others also point to statutory rape and child sexual abuse as other contributing factors (Luker, 1996).

John Ogbu is noted for his research on education and his assertion that lower educational performance among blacks is a function of the self-defeating cultural attitude that working hard and getting a good education is undesirable because it is acting white. Research involving aggregate data contradicts Ogbu's conclusion. The best example of this research is the works of Ronald Ferguson, a Harvard Kennedy Center senior research associate. He collected survey data on 40,000 middle- and high-school students from 15 different school districts including Shaker Heights, the district examined by Ogbu. Ferguson's study demonstrated that blacks work just as hard and value education just as much as white students, although their teachers do not provide them with as much encouragement (Ferguson, 2002a, 2002b). Another study conducted by the National Center for Education Statistics surveyed about 17,000 students and found that black students have a more favorable attitude toward education than whites (Lee, 2002). Focus group interviews showed that the expression "acting white" referred to people who had an arrogant, condensing disposition and lacked empathy, rhythm, and soul (Bergin and Cooks, 2002).

The case of Stanley Tookie Williams, the founder of the Crips and four-time Nobel Prize nominee, further illustrates the problems with the gross oversimplifications of the culture of poverty ideology. Characterizing Williams as ascribing to a culture that valorizes gangterism or thug life is not only inaccurate, it dehumanizes Williams. It made it easier for the state to execute him, even though there was much doubt over his guilt.

Contemporary racist culture—with its images, stories and ideology—operates to portray oppressed racial groups as essentially different from the dominant group and in ways that provoke contempt toward the oppressed and legitimize repression. Consider the following statement:

> Ladies and gentlemen, the lower economic people are not holding up their end in this deal. These people are not parenting. They are buying things for kids—$500 sneakers, for what?...
>
> They're standing on the corner and they can't speak English....
>
> These are not political criminals. These are people going around stealing Coca-Cola. People getting shot in the back of the head over a piece of pound cake and then we are outraged, (saying) the cops shouldn't have shot him. What the hell was he doing with the pound cake in his hand (Bill Cosby quoted in the press).

This statement must be viewed apart from the person of Bill Cosby and must be understood in the context of a society that is becoming increasingly hostile to poor blacks and increasing tolerant of the repression against black males. The image of poor blacks purchasing $500 sneakers for their children provokes hostility against them. Justifying police killing of an unarmed person who stole a piece of cake is a profound expression of contempt for young black males. It denies their humanity and dignity. This type of contempt for black males is reminiscent of racism in the Deep South 100 years ago. This point is not to attack or demonize Bill Cosby, but to identify his statement as a reflection of the dominant racist culture, which legitimizes police shootings of unarmed young black males and state repression against blacks.

Critical Strategic Problems with the Reparations Movement

Now that I have provided a brief analysis of metaracism, current patterns of racial oppression and repression, and contemporary racist culture, I can return to an analysis of the reparations movement. This movement is occurring at the same time that racial oppression and repression are intensifying and racist culture is expanding. The success of any political movement depends on its ability to construct a counterideology, effective enough to undermine the legitimacy of the dominant culture/ideology and its ability to build a coalition strong enough to challenge the dominant power arrangement.

Counterideology

In developing a counterideology, the reparations movement suffers from two critical flaws: it focuses too little attention on current oppression and it is tainted by the very dominant culture it is attempting to oppose.

Focus Too Much on the Past

Most scholars writing on reparations emphasize not just the horrors of slavery past, but the effects of slavery on the present. The following passage from Robinson's book on reparations illustrates this point:

> Well before the birth of our country, Europe and the eventual United States perpetrated a heinous wrong against the peoples of Africa.... In 1965, after nearly 350 years of legal racial suppression, the United States enacted the Voting Rights Act and, virtually simultaneously, began to walk away from the social wreckage that centuries of white hegemony had wrought....
>
> But when the black living suffer real and current consequences as a result of wrongs committed by a younger America, then contemporary America must be caused to shoulder responsibility for those wrongs until such wrongs have been adequately compensated and righted... (Robinson, 2001: 230).

Robinson's book provides one of the most thoughtful and persuasive arguments for reparations. He focuses not just on African Americans and past slavery, but also on Africa and the rape of this continent during the Atlantic slave trade and the era of colonialism. He elaborates on the continual exploitation of this continent today. He discusses how racial inequality today is rooted in the past of slavery and segregation. He adds,

> American capitalism, which starts each child where its parents left off is not a fair system. This is particularly the case for African Americans, whose general economic starting points have been rearmost in our society because of slavery and its long racialist aftermath. American slaves for two and a half centuries saw taken from them not just their freedom but the inestimable economic value of their labor as well... (Randall 2001: 231).

Randall Robinson expresses bewilderment over his former Harvard Law professor's (Derrick Bell's) view of reparations. He quotes Bell, "Short of a revolution, the likelihood that blacks today will obtain direct payments in compensation for their subjugation as slaves ... is no better today than it was in 1866 ..." (Bell quoted in Robinson, 2001: 203-204). No doubt Bell understood the problems as clearly as Du Bois: Racism is still deeply imbedded in American culture. Robinson largely ignores current patterns of racial oppression and contemporary racist culture.

A Movement Tainted by the Dominant Culture

The perspective of a few leaders of the reparation movement has been tainted by contemporary racist culture. This point is evident in two areas: the Million Man and Million More Marches and the reparations literature.

The theme of the Million Man March of 1995 was the atonement of the black male. The whole premise of the march was that black men had not been responsible as individuals, fathers or community leaders, and that the black community was plagued with drug abuse, gang violence, welfare dependency, and other pathological behavior. Black men were urged to reassert themselves as men, as heads of their families and as leaders of their communities. Most speakers acknowledged racism. A few, most notably Jesse Jackson and Hadi Madhubuti, discussed specific aspects of contemporary racial oppression: racial discrimination in drug laws, racial profiling, targeted enforcement, cuts in anti-poverty programs, inadequate health care, and others. However, most speakers focused on the sins and shortcomings of black men and their need to rise up and assume responsibility for their families and communities.

The leaders of the Million Man March were disconnected from the members of the Congressional Black Caucus (CBC). The leaders of the Million Man March were struggling for the atonement of black men. The members of the CBC were fighting against new drug laws that would target black males and contribute to the dramatic increases in their incarceration rates and against the efforts to substantially cut welfare and other social programs that benefited low-income families, particularly African American families. The leaders of the Million Man March were successful in getting black males to confess their shortcomings, seek atonement and pledge to be more responsible. The members of the CBC failed, as more repressive laws were passed and anti-poverty programs cut.

The Million More March of October 15, 2005 had a broader coalition and a more extensive agenda. The organizers of this second March invited women, civil rights leaders, and others. Many speakers talked about the racist response to Katrina. Some leaders demanded reparations. The march was successful in terms of the large number of people who attended. However, it had little impact on the efforts to cut Medicaid, food stamps, and other anti-poverty programs.

Like some of the leaders of the march, a few prominent black scholars who advocate reparations reflect aspects of the dominant culture. For example, scholars offer a compelling case for reparations, with passionate and moving descriptions of the horrors of the past, the brutality of the slave trade and slavery, and the atrocities of the colonial era, but then proceed to describe African Americans today as having negative attitudes toward work, being disrespectful toward property, and having the propensity to clown. Professor Nuruddin provides this summary:

> Psychologist Na'im Akbar adds to Karenga's litany of negative cultural values when he states that black people possess a set of pathological attitudes that are a legacy of slavery. Included among the eight attitudes which Akbar lists are negative attitudes toward work and property, and a propensity to play the clown role.... Note that both Karenga and Akbar attribute these values to the black community in general, not to any specific underclass (Nuruddin, 2002: 103).

Akbar and Karenga are brilliant social scientists and strong supporters of reparations. However, the characterization of blacks as having negative attitudes toward work and property and having a propensity to play the clown, with absolutely no empirical data, is not much different than saying that everyone knows that blacks are lazy, don't respect property, and act like clowns. Advocates of reparations reflected aspects of the dominant culture's negative characterization of blacks, except that they attribute these characteristics to the impacts of slavery. For these impacts they ask for reparations.

The Future of the Movement

The reparations movement has been successful in exposing and attacking old racism, in mobilizing large numbers and in establishing a coalition of nationalist organizations. It has attracted some support from a few religious and traditional civil rights organizations. A small white organization supports it, Caucasians United for Reparations and Emancipation (CURE). The legal arguments for reparations are compelling (see Corlett, 2003). Nevertheless, the movement suffers from several serious and interrelated problems.

The first problem is a matter of priority. It is like the analogy of a man who is being beaten to death, asking for compensation for his injuries. He deserves compensation, but the beating must stop first, not as an aftermath, but as an immediate moral imperative. There is something almost perverse about the call for compensation at a time when human rights violations against African Americans are mounting, racist repression intensifying, racial oppression expanding and civil rights violations growing.

The demand for reparations is overshadowing the mangling of the black body and the call for ending the beatings. It has practically muted the utter outrage over the executions, especially the execution of Stanley Tookie Williams, the institutionalization of about a third of the black male population, the disproportionate sentencing of black teenagers to life without chance of parole, the unjustified police shootings and beatings, the dilution of the black vote, the growth of concentrated black poverty, the high infant mortality rates, the low life-expectancy, the blocked access to health care, the cuts in anti-poverty programs, the low minimum wage, and other aspects of oppression.

The second problem is that the reparations movement is growing at the same time the color line is widening and racist culture expanding. Under these circumstances, the movement has a choice. It can continue to push forward for reparations and fight for something that is opposed by 90 percent of whites in this country, partially because of the expansion of the racist culture, or it can launch a direct assault on that culture and on racial oppression. The former is doomed to begin with and the later requires a radical redirection of the movement into a true movement for social reconstruction and social justice.

Redirecting the reparations movement into a movement for social reconstruction requires a deeper understanding of the dynamics of racist culture and the extent to which this culture dehumanizes poor blacks, legitimizes oppression, and normalizes repression. Social reconstruction can only come from an assault on the dominant racist culture and an attack on the prevailing patterns of racial oppression. The problem is that the reparations movement has failed to adequately address contemporary racist culture. This failure has made leaders of the movement susceptible to aspects of this culture and has impeded their ability to confront current human rights violations.

The third problem is the weak reparations coalition. Even with its ties to CURE and a few traditional civil rights organizations, the movement is politically isolated. It has few ties with anti-poverty organizations, weak ties with labor, and few connections to the larger liberal religious community that made up the old civil rights coalition. It is almost as if the movement is lead by middle-class black nationalists who are cut off from the black poor. A connection with the black poor and the so-called black lumpenproletariat is necessary in order to develop a truly radical social movement.

The final problem is the growth of the power of the dominant corporate class. This class has increased and consolidated its power through a strong alliance with the religious right. It now dominates both the political and ideological arenas. Thomas Frank provides an excellent discussion of how this alliance dominates the political arena and explains the rapid growth in policies benefiting major corporations and hurting the poor (Frank, 2005). David Brock offers a most insightful and well-documented discussion of how this alliance dominates the media and the construction of contemporary political culture (Brock, 2004).

As Du Bois observed 100 years ago, the dominant power arrangements, the culture of racism, and the political isolation and powerlessness of African Americans make reparations a pipedream. Although reparations are justifiable, there are more immediate moral imperatives: the expansion of racist culture that promotes contempt toward the black poor; the growth of concentrated black poverty; the shifting of public resources from the poor to the rich and to major corporations; the intensification of state repression and human rights violations; the erosion of civil rights and civil liberties. Just as reconciliation came in South Africa after the fall of the apartheid regime, reparations must come after the end of the racially oppressive regime in the United States.

References

Amnesty International. 1998. Police Brutality, USA: Systematic and Widespread.

Amnesty International. 2005. USA: Thousands of Children Sentenced to Life Without Parole. AMR 51/160/2005.

Amnesty International. USA: Racist Police Brutality Remains Endemic in Many Areas.

Baraka, Amiri. 2002. "Plenary Address to Conference on Reparations." *Socialism and Democracy*. Vol. 16, no.1.

Belfour, Lawrie. 2003. "Unreconstructed Democracy: W.E. B. DuBois and the Case for Reparations." *American Political Science Review*. Vol. 97, no. 1 February, 33-44.

Bergin, David and Helen Cooks. 2002. "High School Students of Color Talk about Accusations of 'Acting White.'" *The Urban Review*, vol. 34, no.2.

Brock, David. 2004. *The Republican Noise Machine: Right-Wing Media and How It Corrupts Democracy*. New York: Crown Publishers.

Burnham, Margaret. 1992. "The Supreme Court Appointment Process and the Politics of Race and Sex." In Toni Morrison edited, *Race-ing Justice, En-gendering Power: Essays on Anita Hill, Clarence Thomas and the Construction of Social Reality*. New York: Pantheon Books.

Collins, Patricia. 2000. *Black Feminist Thought: Knowledge, Consciousness, and the Politics of Empowerment*. New York: Routledge.

Corlett, Angelo. 2003. *Race, Racism and Reparations*. Ithaca, NY: Cornell University Press.

Cruikshank, Barbara. 1997. "Welfare Queens: Policing by the Numbers." In Sanford Schram and Philip Neiser edited, *Tales of the State: Narrative in Contemporary U.S. Politics and Public Policy*. Lanham, MD: Rowman & Littlefield.

Ferguson, Ronald. 2002A. "Responses from Middle School, Junior High and High School Students in Districts of Minority Student Achievement Network (MSAN)." Wiener Center for Social Policy, John F. Kennedy School of Government, Harvard University.

Ferguson, Ronald 2002. "What Doesn't Meet the Eye: Understanding and Addressing Racial Disparities in High-Achieving Suburban Schools." Wiener Center for Social Policy, John F. Kennedy School of Government, Harvard University.

Frank, Thomas. 2005. *What's the Matter with Kansas: How Conservatives Won the Heart of America*. New York: A Metropolitan/Owl Book.

Frosch, Dan. 2007. "Inmates Will Replace Migrants in Colorado Fields." *The New York Times*.

Gilens, Martin. 1999. *Why Americans Hate Welfare: Race, Media, and the Politics of Antipoverty Policy*. Chicago: University of Chicago Press.
Goldberg, David Theo. *Racist Culture: Philosophy and the Politics of Meaning*. Oxford, UK Blackwell.
Horowitz, David. 2001. "Ten Reasons Why Reparations for Blacks is a Bad Idea for Blacks—and Racist Too." *FrontPageMagazine*.com. January 3.
Howell, Ricardo. 2001. "Slavery, The Brown Family of Providence and Brown University." Brown University News Service. Providence, Rhode Island.
Irwin, Hohn, and James Austin. 1997. *It's About Time: America's Imprisonment Binge*. Belmont, CA: Wadsworth.
Kirschenman, Joleen and Kathryn Neckerman. 1991. "We've Love to Hire Them, But." In Peterson and Jencks edited, *The Urban Underclass*. Washington DC: The Brookings Institution.
Kovel, Joel. 1984. *White Racism: A Psychohistory*. New York: Columbia University Press.
Ladner, Joyce, ed. 1973. *The Death of White Sociology*. New York: Random House.
Lee, Felicia. 2002. "Why Are Black Students Lagging?" *The New York Times*, November 30.
Lafer, Gordon. 2002. "Captive Lobor: America's Prisoners As Corporate Workforce." In *The American Prospect*. November 30.
Liebow, Elliot. 1967. *Tally's Corner*. Boston: Little, Brown and Company.
Luker, Kristin. 1996. *Dubious Conceptions: The Politics of Teenage Pregnancy*. Cambridge, Mass.: Harvard University Press.
Marable, Manning. 2006. "Empire, Racism and Resistance: Global Apartheid and Prospects for a Democratic Future." In *The Black Commentator*. December 21, 2006. Issue 211. http://www.blackcommentator.com.
Mauer, Marc. 1999. *Race to Incarcerate*. New York: New Press.
Mollenkopf, John. 1983. *The Contested City*. Princeton, NJ: Princeton University Press.
Morrison, Toni. 1992. "Introduction: Friday on the Potomac." In Toni Morrison edited, *Race-ing Justice, En-gendering Power: Essays on Anita Hill, Clarence Thomas and the Construction of Social Reality*. New York: Pantheon Books.
Neubeck, Kenneth and Noel Cazenave. *Welfare Racism: Playing the Race Card against America's Poor*. New York: Routledge.
Nuruddin, Yusuf. 2002. "Promises and Pitfalls of Reparations." *Socialism and Democracy*. Vol. 16, no.1.
Peterson, Paul and Christopher Jencks. 1991. *The Urban Underclass*. Washington DC: The Brookings Institute.
Ripley, Randall. *1984. CETA: Politics and Policy, 1973-1982*. Knoxville, TN: University of Tennessee Press.
Robinson, Randall. 2001. *The Debt: What America Owes to Blacks*. New York: Plume.
Sampson, Robert and William J. Wilson. 1995. "Toward a Theory of Race, Crime, and Urban Inequality." In Johan Hagan and Ruth Peterson edited, *Crime and Inequality*. Stanford, CA: Stanford University Press.
Shepard, Paul. 2000. "Lawyers Plan Slave Reparations Suit." AP November, 4, 2000.
Steinberg, Steven. 1989. *The Ethnic Myth: Race, Ethnicity, and Class in America*. Boston: Beacon Press.
Tienda, Marta and Haya Stier. 1991. "Joblessness and Shiftlessness: Labor Force Activity in Chicago's Inner City." In Peterson and Jencks edited. *The Urban Underclass*. Washington, DC: The Brookings Institute.
Watkins, Alfred and David Perry. 1977. "Regional Change and the Impact of Uneven Urban Development. In Perry and Watkins edited, *The Rise of the Sunbelt Cities*. Beverly Hills, CA: Sage Publications.
Williams, Brandt. 2000. "The Case for Slavery Reparations."
Wilson, Carter 1992. "Restructuring and the Growth of Concentrated Poverty in Detroit." *Urban Affairs Quarterly*, vol. 28, no. 2. December.
Wilson, Carter. 1996. *Racism: From Slavery to Advanced Capitalism*. Thousand Oaks, CA: Sage Publications.
Wilson, Carter. 2006. *Public Policy: Continuity and Change*. Boston: McGraw-Hill.
Wilson, Carter and Mitchell Rice. 1988. "From CETA to JTPA: Administrative and Distributional Impacts of Federal Job Training Policy Changes in the State of Ohio." *State and Local Government Review*. volume 20, number 2, Spring,
Wilson, William J. 1987. *The Truly Disadvantaged*. Chicago: University of Chicago Press.
Wisely, Willie. 1998. "Who Goes to Prison?" In *The Celling of America: An Inside Look at the U.S. Prison Industry. Edited by Daniel Burton-Rose*. Monroe, ME. Common Courage Press.
Young, Iris. *Justice and the Politics of Difference*. Princeton, NJ: Princeton University Press.

Cases

Ewing v. California. 538 U.S. 11 (2003)
Gratz v. Bollinger. 539 U.S. 309 (2003).
Grutter v. Bollinger. 539 U.S. 244 (2003).
McClesky v. Kemp. 481 U.S. 279 (1987)
Regents v. Bakke. 438 U.S. 265 (1978)

Creating a Transnational Network of Black Representation in the Americas: A Profile of the Legislators at the First Meeting of Black Parliamentarians in Latin America

Michael Mitchell
Arizona State University

Minion K.C. Morrison
University of Missouri

Ollie Johnson, III
Wayne State University

The Brasília Conference

In November of 2003, black legislators from several Latin American countries, including Brazil, Colombia, Costa Rica, Ecuador, Peru, and Uruguay, met over a three-day period to discuss a list of topics related to their roles as blacks in the legislative process. Convened under the auspices of the office of Deputy Luiz Alberto Silva Dos Santos of the Brazilian Chamber of Deputies, the meetings also attracted, in addition to the black legislators, scores of observers from non-governmental organizations with interests in racial justice issues.

Members in attendance clearly understood the gathering to be an historic one. No less an astute observer than Ronald Walters, of the University of Maryland, described the meeting in those terms. Recalling an earlier visit to Brazil, Walters remarked about the long road black politics had traveled since the days when he could count the small number of black representatives in the Brazilian Congress, figuratively, on the fingers of a single hand. In Walters' estimation, the dramatically increased presence of blacks in the politics of Latin America was evidenced by having assembled fifteen or more parliamentarians from the Latin American region with openly declared sympathies to their black communities (Walters, 2003). Beyond numbers and place, there were other confirmations of the meeting's significance. It was an event which signaled the move of black politics in Latin America into the halls of power. The meeting demonstrated that blacks in Latin America had arrived at a stage in their political development not unlike the transition from movement politics to institutional politics experienced by black Americans four decades ago. The black legislators of Latin America were approaching from the inside the sources of power where law and policy were made.

The black legislators also found themselves at the confluence of politics in a globalizing age. Globalization most frequently refers to economic change. However, it also encompasses the kinds of social and political changes in which transnational networks have acquired a growing presence in civil society and in the politics of citizens' groups. Just as NGOs have discovered the utility and effectiveness of transnational networks (Chalmers, 1997) so the legislators looked to establish a transnational link to push the struggles against racism and discrimination into the parliamentary institutions of the region. They were beginning to experiment with ways to convert a resource like racial solidarity into a transnational vehicle of struggle. They were searching for new forums for commanding attention for the grievances and demands of communities that had been traditionally excluded from the formal institutions of government and politics.

The Brasília meeting fit neatly into a new trend in the politics of Latin America in which the claims of racial and ethnic minorities are becoming increasingly salient. Indigenous groups, for example, have made their presence felt in the politics of the Andean nations and were instrumental in the presidential resignations of Gonzalo Sanchez de Losada of Bolivia and Lucio Gutierrez of Ecuador. As Donna Lee Van Cott (2000) has pointed out, claims of minorities in Latin America have triggered calls for the implementation of constitutional reforms, whose purpose has been to strengthen the democratic regimes of the region. This new assertiveness, moreover, grows out of a decades old process of democratization which the conferees were ready to assert their presence in.

The black Latin American legislators were also tapping into a rich tradition of Pan-African mobilization begun by W.E.B. Du Bois and others at the beginning of the twentieth century. Even though, as Elisa Larkin Nascimento (1981) has pointed out, Pan-Africanism has not resonated historically with the same force in Latin America as has been the case in the United State, Africa, or the Caribbean, its current emergence, in the form of the meeting in Brasília, reaffirms the continuing vitality of Pan-African inspirations in forging links among blacks throughout the African diaspora (Morrison, 2005). In a genuine sense, the Brasília meeting represented a maturing and expansion of the Pan-African inspiration into the Latin American region.

At the end of the meeting the conferees drafted a document called the "Declaration of Brasília." This Declaration captured both the sense and the concrete objectives of the gathering. Two of the center pieces of the Declaration were statements on the state of Latin American democracy and regional economic pacts. In the first instance, the Declaration explicitly asserted that any democratic consolidation could not be complete without greater attention being given to the historically excluded groups, such as blacks, in Latin American society. This statement dovetailed neatly into another concern, that for affirmative action. On this issue the legislators gave their broad transnational support for the measure's adoption in their respective countries. In the second instance, the declaration contained an insistence that regional economic pacts, such as the proposed Free Trade Area of the Americas in particular, include formal protocols outlining guarantees that the historically excluded groups not be adversely affected by these new economic arrangements. Implicitly this statement acknowledged the manner in which foreign competition had contributed to painful labor market adjustments that ordinary citizens and blacks in particular had to suffer through.

The Survey

The core of the analysis contained in this paper is derived from a survey of the elected officials present at the meeting in Brasília. The survey questionnaire was constructed to tap into several areas of theoretical concern, including the relevance of socio-economic characteristics in determining both the cross-national similarities among the legislators as well as their perceptions of their links to their constituencies, and the manner in which their institutional environments, i.e., their performance in their respective influences the ways in which they articulate the issues affecting black communities. In all, the questionnaire comprised 47 items divided into five sections. These sections covered: the personal backgrounds of the respondents (age, gender, occupation, education, income, parents' background, etc.); party affiliation, description of the respondent's constituency, and length of time in office; legislative agenda, and positions in the legislature; perceptions of the social and economic conditions of blacks in general and of the respondent's own constituency; and the manner in which the respondent conducts his or her election campaigns. Taken together these 47 items yields information for constructing a social and economic profile of the legislators. It also allows for gauging how the legislator feels about his or her role as a "black legislator" and the extent to which this perceived role shapes his or her relationship with constituents.

Overall general attendance at the meeting was high. Guest observers, drawn mainly from labor unions and NGOs, added to the 200 people who were in attendance. However, the actual number of legislators at the meting was considerably lower than this. Of the approximately twenty legislators attending the meeting, thirteen completed the survey questionnaire. This produced rather modest survey size. Nevertheless, despite the relatively small number of respondents in the survey, its results can be regarded as significant for a couple of reasons. First, the results can be read as representing a benchmark or starting point, from a first meeting of black legislators to subsequent meetings, where results may be compared. With the starting point of the first meeting at hand further research may note either consistencies or changes in the patterns reported on here. Second, the survey was conducted in an opportune moment when black legislators from across the vast region of Latin America were situated in a central location. This circumstance reduced considerably the logistical problems of conducting the survey in a single country manner. For these reasons, this analysis constitutes a fair starting point and a beginning of discussion regarding the emergence of black electoral politics in Latin America.

The Issue of Representation

The development of this survey instrument was informed by the issues raised in the literature on black representation. It is from this literature that we constructed our questionnaire around three general rubrics: 1) background characteristics, such as social class standing, national origin, gender, religion, and age; 2) racial identity and the related subject of descriptive representation; and 3) the institutional environment, including factors such as group cohesion, voting orientations, and party discipline. A brief sketch of this literature follows in order to provide the theoretical context on which our discussion is based.

One of the starting points of this analysis is, therefore, to explore the issue of representation. In the case of the conferees at the Brasília meeting, whose presence at the meeting was premised on their self-perceptions as "black legislators," an appropriate place to begin would be to look at the concept of descriptive representation. Descriptive representation denotes a type of representation in which an elected official shares common physical, cultural, racial, ethnic, or gender characteristics with his or her constituents. In studies of African American representation, it refers to the situation, simply put, of "blacks representing blacks" in legislative assemblies.

The term also serves to focus discussions on the benefits which accrue to racial, ethnic and gender constituents where elected officials and constituencies share status characteristics. Jane Mansbridge (1999) has made a normative argument for claiming that the racial affinities between elected officials and constituencies do indeed afford benefits to racial, ethnic, and gender minorities. According to Mansbridge, the racial similarities in representation serve several important purposes, such as, increasing communications and trust between representative and constituent and validating the legitimacy of minority members as possessing the capacity to govern. Others have concurred with Mansbridge's positive assessment of descriptive representation. Katherine Tate (2003), for example, has discovered that blacks are likely to say that black elected officials would represent them better than others. Kenneth Whitby (1998) has noted that black members of the U.S. Congress are more likely to concern themselves with racial issues than their institutional counterparts.

Nevertheless, descriptive representation has arguable limitations. Carol Swain (1993) has proposed looking strictly at the material benefits of representation to assess how effective any particular style of representation would be. According to Swain, black members of the U.S. Congress may not necessarily represent black interests any more meaningfully than do whites. Swain uses this proposition to make a distinction between descriptive and substantive representation where substantive representation refers a representative's ability to "deliver the goods." Swain proposes that blacks may gain more materially from moderate white representation which is more congenial to the compromise necessary for gaining substantive material benefits.

Whether substantive representation should be preferred over descriptive representation is a matter of continuing debate (for a review of this debate see Dovi, 2002). Katherine Tate's (2003: 96-110) contribution to this debate is in pointing out that by focusing solely on the material benefits derived from substantive representation, some of the important functions of representation are left ignored. Tate observes that symbolic legislation, in fact, consumes more time and energy of members of Congress than so-called substantive legislation. And in this regard, producing symbolic legislation is a key component of descriptive representation. It serves to link representatives and constituents together in acknowledgement of the particular characteristics of the representatives' constituencies. For African Americans the symbolic legislation of black representatives can affirm a presence in American politics that would otherwise be neglected. Measures such as the passage of the Martin Luther King holiday or the congressional medal awarded to Rosa Parks elevate the place of African Americans to levels of distinction in American society. Proposals such as these tend to counterbalance the marginalization that African Americans experience in other spheres of American life. Moreover, if constituent satisfaction is any indication of the validity of descriptive representation, then its value is substantial when considering the greater satisfaction that blacks express with blacks representing them over others. And, high constituent satisfaction reinforces governmental legitimacy. Tate observes that, "[d]escriptive representation ... may still affect citizens' perceptions of the [political] system's legitimacy and their commitment to the political system" (Tate 2003: 152). In the end, Tate concludes that descriptive representation cannot be discarded in favor of substantive representation, or vice versa. On the contrary, a complete narrative of representation must include both dimensions: descriptive and substantive.

However rich the debate over descriptive representation may be, the formal usage of the term in our analysis is somewhat restricted for the two reasons. First, our survey does not include indicators directly measuring constituent sentiment. Without such a source of data we cannot fully assess the interactions of both elements of descriptive representation, that of the representatives' as well as the constituents' perceptions of the representational relationship, that is, whether they both are looking at "Black faces in the mirror," to use Katherine Tate's expression. Second, we cannot presume in the Latin American context that similarities in physical characteristics alone define a situation of descriptive representation. There still exists in Latin America, even if in significantly diminished form, a domain of racial ambiguity in which an individual may opt for an identity that does not place him or her within the category of Afro-descendent. While this situation is less the case today than it may have been a generation ago, racial identity in the Latin American context can be adopted in certain cases in a fluid manner in which individuals with the physical characteristics of persons of African descent may not self-identify as belonging to a "black" racial group. Nor do "black" representatives necessarily regard themselves as representing black constituencies. This situation led Ollie Johnson (1998) to conclude that in the Brazilian case, when using descriptive representation as a criterion, blacks were significantly underrepresented in the Brazilian Congress, since some members of the Brazilian Congress who could otherwise be identified as black did not openly declare their own racial identities in the political arena. Our analysis, therefore, may be skewed somewhat in favor of those representatives who have implicitly declared their racial identity by attending a gathering of "Black Legislators." Nevertheless, we make no assumptions about the self-declared racial identities of the respondents in our survey. We have included an item specifically asking the respondents to choose their preferred racial label to identify themselves.

While the concept of descriptive representation significantly informs our analysis, in light of the debates surrounding the concept, we ought to clarify how the concept will be used in our subsequent discussion. We will use a modified form of descriptive representation, which we call coherent representation. We make this modification for two reasons. First, since our survey is limited to the realm of legislators, we do not have at our disposal any empirical basis for making claims about the legislators' respective constituents. In effect, we are dealing with strictly one component of the representational relationship. And, second, our research concern focuses primarily on the legislators in this sense. We wish to the perceptions of the legislators as the basis for continued cooperation among them. Specifically, we are looking for uniformities among them with regard to the manner in which they carry out their roles as legislators. One tack to take would be to see just how the legislators perceive their legislative styles as falling within the framework of descriptive representation. In other words, we are looking for an abbreviated form of descriptive representation, or coherent representation.

Coherent representation is a subset or derivative of the more encompassing term, descriptive representation. Even though coherent representation incorporates essential features of descriptive representation, the term implies no claim about the actual impact of such representation on constituents. It does assume, however, that there is a logic in the convergence of culture, racial, ethnic, or gender identity between representative and constituency, which the representative openly proclaims. What is implied by the use of the term is that representatives feel an obligation to deal with their constituencies in some way that is grounded in the perception of a shared culture or group identity.

With this discussion in mind, our analysis proceeds in the following fashion. First, we draw a socio-economic profile of the legislator attendees at the Brasília meeting. We describe their social class backgrounds as well as their religious affiliations and genders. We next describe the contours of the attendees' racial identification and look at the ways in which their declared racial identities shape the perception of their legislative roles. Here we wish to determine whether the legislators possess some sense of descriptive or coherent representation. We move on to discuss the institutional environments in which the legislators function to determine the levels of satisfaction and support they have with their respective legislative institutions. Finally, we examine the national contexts of the various legislative attendees. Our aim is to probe the manner in which national situations may engender obstacles to cooperation among the black legislators.

Race, Class and Descriptive/Coherent Representation

One question that is bound to surface when discussing descriptive or coherent representation, particularly with regards to black representation, is this: how do the class characteristics of black representatives coincide with or deviate from the class characteristics of their constituents? In other words, to what degree might discernible class differences shape or determine the context of descriptive representation for blacks?

This is a significant question to ask for this reason. The interactions of socio-economic factors among African Americans remain one of the central themes in the overall study of African American politics. In his seminal work on black politics, Michael Dawson (1994) lays out as his point of departure the existence of a tension between the forces of race and class as they exert their mutual influences on African American attitudes and behavior. According to Dawson, class should exercise a strong influence in its own right on the political behavior and attitudes of black Americans. Instead, race exerts a stronger influence than class. African American experiences with, and the collective memory of, white supremacy have served to mold their attitudes as the racialized constructions of their political environment. Class cleavage, in Dawson's analysis, is not to be ignored. In fact, Dawson has found significant class differences among African Americans with respect to public policy preferences and the outlook toward assimilation. For example, poor blacks are more prone to assert preferences for redistributive public policies and the ideals of black nationalism than are affluent blacks. In any case, despite these class differences, Dawson concludes that racial experiences and the collective memory of racial exclusion override intra-group class differences to produce a group logic rooted in a collective racial identity that displays itself in the political arena.

Taking Dawson's argument a bit further, scholars of black representation have indicated that class differences may, in fact, be consonant with the preference of black representatives to frame the issues they articulate and advance in racial terms. With regard to social background characteristics, Robert Smith (1981) discovered that the black members of Congress generally held middle-class standing. This finding led Smith to speculate about the link between middle-class standing and political leadership. Smith concluded that his data did suggest a link between social class and leadership within the black community with regard to black members of Congress. In this regard, Smith was echoing a well established conclusion about black leadership. Higher income and education are commonly associated with leadership characteristics within the black community (on this issue of black leadership, see Walters and Smith, 1999).

Katherine Tate (2003: 27-34) provides an extended discussion of this issue. Tate points to an historical pattern of an existing socio-economic status gap within the arrangements of descriptive representation among African Americans. Tate notes that during Reconstruction (1863-1877), the period of classic descriptive representation among blacks, black members of Congress, while being ex-slaves for the most part, came from a professional class of lawyers, teachers, businessmen, and ministers. They were far from the stereotypical images of illiterate peasants which generations of revisionist literature on Reconstruction wrongly portrayed them to be. In more contemporary times, black members of Congress tend to possess the socio-economic characteristics typical of middle class standing. In other words, black members of Congress approximate their White counterparts in this regard. However, they find common ground with their constituents in the shared immediacy of their encounters with racial discrimination.

With this discussion in mind, our analysis proceeds in the following fashion. First, we draw a socio-economic profile of the legislator attendees at the Brasília meeting. We describe their social class backgrounds as well as their religious affiliations and genders. We next describe the contours of the attendees' racial identification and look at the ways in which their declared racial identities shape the perception of their legislative roles. Here we wish to determine whether the legislators possess some sense of descriptive or coherent representation. We move on to discuss the institutional environments in which the legislators function to determine the levels of satisfaction and support they have with their respective legislative institutions. Finally, we examine the national contexts of the various legislative attendees. Our aim is to probe the manner in which national situations may engender obstacles to cooperation among the black legislators.

A Socio-Economic Profile of the Brasília Meeting Legislators

With regards to class standing, our survey indicates that all of the respondents, except for two, should be appropriately described as belonging to the middle class. One measure which indicates this class standing are the occupations which the respondents held prior to assuming office. In eleven cases, the respondents selected occupational categories that would place them solidly within the middle class. Among the categories selected were "professional," "executive," or "white collar worker." The remaining two respondents selected occupational categories that would classify them as belonging to the working class (i.e., "skilled worker," and "unskilled worker"). The educational attainments of the respondents reinforced the pattern of the respondents' belonging to the middle class. All of the respondents had acquired at least some level of post-secondary education. Eight respondents declared that they had university or professional degrees, while four indicated that they had not finished completing their university degrees (there was one no-response to this item). The family backgrounds of the respondents indicate that they either belong to a second generation cohort of the middle class, or are the products of social mobility. The evidence for this is the fathers' occupations. Five of the respondents declared their fathers to have had middle-class occupations, while six of the respondents said that their fathers held occupations such as skilled or unskilled worker.

However, the social background portraits of the respondents did not place them in the upper reaches of the middle class or as members of an economic elite. None of the respondents indicated that categories such as owners of large business enterprises were characteristic of their current circumstances or their family backgrounds. By way of contrast, the national legislatures of Latin America contain members with markedly elite characteristics. For example, Timothy Powers (2000), in his work on the conservative parties in the Brazilian Chamber of Deputies, found that the vast majority of conservative party members were also members of Brazil's economic elite. In any case, their class standings were at a level that made them susceptible to the vicissitudes and shocks of economic forces, consequences in many cases of the neo-liberal economic reforms adopted by many Latin American nations in the 1990s.

Social and economic characteristics remain pertinent in discussions Latin American race relations. These discussions continue to be overshadowed by the debates regarding the determinants that shape the position of blacks in Latin American societies. One perspective in this debate holds that blacks are primarily the of victims economic inequalities. Their sociological disabilities stem more so from class rather than from race. The competing perspective takes the opposite tact. It maintains that racial exclusion through mechanisms of discrimination deserves a primacy over class (on the evolution of the class v. race debate, see Wade, 1997).

The kinds of relationships which the legislators forge with their constituents may, hypothetically, be shaped as much by their socio-economic characteristics as by their racial identities. These characteristics may determine just how the legislators perceive their public personae. Do the legislators assume the roles that they choose for themselves by virtue of their approximation to their constituents' social class? Or, do the legislators stand apart from their constituents with regards to their class standing? If the latter is the case, would their different class standing imbue them with sense of mission which is pegged to their higher class status and which accentuates their own sense of racial identity?

The class standing of the respondents turns out to be a poor predictor of the way that they describe the constituencies which they represent. We ran cross-tabulations of the respondents' educational levels with the respondents' description of their constituencies, and, contrary to any expectations that might be based on class assumptions, the respondents with relatively high educational attainment were as likely as those with relatively modest educational attainment to describe their constituencies in the same terms of their constituents' economic levels. In other words, the respondents were not given to suggest that class standing was a characteristic that they were likely to share with their constituents. Respondents with high educational achievements were not necessarily likely to describe their constituencies as possessing some middle-class characteristics. Nor were the respondents with relatively modest educational attainment levels likelier to describe their constituencies as simply poor or very poor than the respondents with higher educational attainments. This finding leads to the inference that class standing and class identity are not pronounced cleavages as the respondents described their constituencies. In fact, class standing may be overridden by other considerations.

Table 1
Perceptions of the Economic Level of Constituencies
By Respondent's Educational Level

Respondent's Educational Level	*Economic Level of Constituency*		
	"Very poor/poor" n=	"Poor" n=	"Poor/middle class" n=
High School	1	1	1
Some or Complete University	2	0	3
Post Graduate Level	0	2	2
TOTAL	3	3	6

Source: Black Legislators in the Americas Survey, Race and Democracy in the Americas Project, 2003

With regard to other social characteristics, the respondents looked like a homogeneous group in one respect. Most, ten in all, were male. This suggests that even within a group, such as blacks, whose citizenship has been circumscribed, there still exists a gender bias common in Latin American societies. With respect to religious affiliation there was greater variety. Six of the respondents described themselves as Catholic, two claimed to be Protestants, and three declared no religious affiliation at all. Just one respondent affirmed adherence to an African-based religion. In any case, our respondents can be described as fitting well within the mainstream of Latin American society

There is one more background factor which bears on our discussion. This factor may explain in a direct way, in the context of our analysis, who the respondents are. While social and economic characteristics are, of course, interesting in their own right, we would want to know in a more direct way, other than SES factors, why the respondents settled on their careers in electoral politics. Why did they choose this route over others in satisfying their ambitions?

Unanimously, the respondents' answers suggested that the idea of a political career was something that had evolved out of preexisting experiences associated with community activism or other similar experiences in civil society. In other words, the respondents regarded their electoral careers as extensions of prior work and commitments. By contrast, none of the respondents chose replies from the survey instrument which would have suggested any long-term plans to enter electoral politics. None, for example, chose, "I've always been interested in politics," or "I was encouraged by family and friends." Effectively, the respondents are the creatures of civil society.

The Scope of Racial Identity

Our discussion now turns to the issue of racial identity. In this discussion we will assess the extent to which racial identity figures into the legislators' orientations towards representation and towards their institutions.

As expected, there was considerable agreement among the parliamentarians with respect to the label of racial identity that they prefer. The finding should come as little surprise since the respondents had chosen to participate openly in an encounter designated as a meeting of *black* legislators. On this score, all but one of the thirteen respondents chose the term "Afro-descendent" as the label that identified them. [1] (One of the parliamentarians described him/herself as "mestizo.") This label was more than a subjective descriptive identity, however. The parliamentarians also specified that they projected their identities into their campaigns. Ten respondents affirmed that it was very important for them to highlight their racial identities in their campaigns; the remaining three respondents said it was somewhat important to do so. Taken together, these two items indicate that racial identity is an essential element in the parliamentarians' political profiles as well in their subjective identities.

Their affirmations of racial identity, however, were qualified by their own sense of their political realities. This is reflected in the parliamentarians' assessments of the payoffs of declaring one's racial identity in the electoral arena. One of our questionnaire items asked the legislators to make an assessment of generally injecting racial identities into electoral campaigns. We presented them with a set of responses ranging from "positive," "neutral," and "negative." Of the thirteen respondents, just four chose the "positive" option, while six chose the "neutral" option. One respondent indicated the "negative" response (and the remaining respondents either did not respond to this item or said "don't know.

In other words, the parliamentarians seemed cautious about the overall benefit of racial identity as an electoral resource, even if they had chosen to adopt an explicit one for themselves. This would suggest that for a significant number of the black legislators asserting their racial identities might be going against the grain of the accepted conventions of electoral politics. While they embraced their own racial identities, they expressed reservations about the utility of this embrace for others.

There emerged some interesting results when probing how the legislators perceived the manner in which their racial identities carried over into their institutional behavior. Legislators comprise groups or blocks for the purpose of voting on a legislative agenda. Whether making up majority, a governing coalition, or in opposition, legislators, in exercising this function, must affirm loyalty, to some degree, to a larger entity which serves to organize their votes. In some instances, such as in the classic British parliamentary model, the vehicle for organizing votes is the party, which exercises near rigid discipline over a legislator's individual vote. In other cases such as in the U.S. Congress, the party serves simply as a point of reference and exercises less control over legislators. With this in mind, one question that seems reasonable to ask is whether the reach of racial identity conforms to or extends beyond that of the political party. To answer this question we asked the respondents to choose their preference for either voting as a racial block, that is, as blacks, or upholding loyalty to their respective parties. For the legislators that were surveyed, the answer to this question was somewhat revealing.

Nine of the thirteen respondents chose voting as a racial block over party loyalty. This finding suggests a tendency in which the black legislators do convert their racial identities into actual institutional behavior. That is, the black legislators see their racial identities as a vehicle for organizing their votes more so than the conventional means of the political party. Ordinarily, one would expect a legislator to be mindful of party loyalty, especially in light of its rewards (favorable committee assignments, reciprocal support for the legislator's own agenda, etc.). These rewards might even be more crucial to minority legislators who may not have achieved seniority in their legislatures, or senior standing in their own parties. Nevertheless, in our survey, of those who declared themselves to be

"Afro-descendents," nine indicated that blacks should vote as a block, while three of the Afro-descendents chose party loyalty.

One inference to be drawn from this finding is that the racial identity of the legislators surveyed had crystallized in ways that transcend the normal course of doing business. The legislators appear ready to assert their presence in the legislative process in a distinctive way, one which places racial identification on a par with the political party. In other words, racial identification can potentially affect the legislators' institutional outlook and behavior.

The next step in our discussion is to examine racial identity in the context of representation. This is a matter that has found its place in the literature on black politics since the inception of the Congressional Black Caucus in the U.S. House of Representatives in the 1970s. The questions raised in this literature focus on the extent to which racial identities genuinely reflect the interests of the constituencies which legislators represent. In basic terms, the question posed in this literature can be boiled down to this. Do legislators who insist on articulating their identities do so in ways that are materially beneficial for their constituents? In other words, is representation "descriptive," or "substantive," or a combination of the two? We pose this question to raise another. Is representation "coherent," that is, is there an actual match in the first place between a legislator's declaration of identity and the racial characteristics of his or her own consistency?

To some extent, our survey allows us to discuss these questions. In our survey, we asked the respondents to answer several questions regarding their constituencies. The most pertinent questions were these. We asked for the respondents to assess the proportion of blacks in their constituencies. This item gives us some basis for determining the measure of fit between the respondents' racial outlooks and the character of the constituency which they represent. We determine the measure of fit in the following way. In our analysis we adjudge the representation to be "coherent," that is, that the respondents' own racial outlook is effectively consistent with the racial contours of his or her constituency. If the proportion of blacks in the constituency is small, then, correspondingly, we expect that the respondents would not be inclined to act with a strong racial orientation. However, if there is no match either way, then we may conclude that the structure of representation is either inconsistent or perhaps even dysfunctional.

To come to terms with this matter, we ran cross-tabulations between both the concentration of blacks in the constituency with the preference for "voting black" over loyalty to party as a measure of racial orientation. These are the results. A burgeoning pattern does emerge from our cross-tabulations. Those who are racially inclined, with respect to their voting black, as opposed to doing so on the grounds of party loyalty, do share common constituency characteristics. They tend to report their constituencies as having more than more than a 30 percent concentration of blacks. Moreover, there is a greater tendency among those reporting overwhelmingly black constituencies to prefer voting black. The responses with constituencies made up of more than 70 percent of blacks opted for this preference.

On another dimension of representation, we asked the respondents about their electoral strength, or the approximate margin of victory in their last election. Electoral strength tells us the extent to which the respondents' racial orientation is anchored in his or her constituency. Our cross-tabulations suggest a hint that the legislators adopt racially ori-

Table 2
Black Concentration in Constituency and Voting Black/Party Loyalty

Percent Blacks in Constituency	*Vote Black*	*Remain Loyal to Party*
Under 30%	2	2
Over 30%	6	2
Total	8	4

Source: Black Legislators in the Americas Survey, Race and Democracy in the Americas Project, 2003

ented institutional postures, that is, their preference for voting black over party loyalty, despite their electoral strength. The cross tabulation between Electoral Strength (margin of Victory) and Voting Black over Party shows that even when the margin of victory is reported to be simply "sufficient", that is at a minimum threshold for victory, six of the eight respondents in this category still chose a racially oriented option of institutional behavior, i.e., voting black over party loyalty.

The legislators opted for a racial profile over and above what their constituencies might be able to support for them to win elections decisively. This finding suggests, moreover, that the legislators are expressing a measure of independence from conventional structures of representation such as the political party in favor of representing their own representatives as they see fit.

Another pattern which reinforces this observation has to do with combining the concentration of blacks in the constituency with electoral strength. When the concentration of blacks in the constituency is relatively large (30 percent or more), coupled with a modest electoral strength, would signify that the legislator is expressing a racial outlook despite the small electoral payoff for doing so. In this sense, the legislator can be regarded as shaping the structure of representation in ways that the legislator regards as in the better interest of a constituency that has not quite realized the electoral importance of affirming a collective racial identity.

Taken as a whole, these findings on representation point to a tendency for the legislators to appear to be leaders in articulating a racial perspective beyond what their constituencies might consider to be important in electoral politics.

Table 3
Margin of Electoral Victory and Voting For A Black Agenda or Voting Party Loyalty

	Vote a Black Agenda	*Vote by Party Loyalty*
Margin of Electoral Victory		
Twice the Necessary Number for Election	1	0
Sufficient for election	6	2
Total	7	2

Note: Alternates or Suplentes are not included in this table.
Source: Black Legislators in the Americas Survey, Race and Democracy in the Americas

The Institutional Environment

What kind of reception do the legislatures receive in their respective institutions and how conducive are their institutions to accommodating black representation? Do the legislators encounter support or hostility? Do they believe that their institutional settings offer the promise of allowing them to achieve their goals? Our survey allows us to tap into some of these questions. We asked whether the legislators thought that the legislative process was important, whether they found support from their colleagues for their work, and whether they would find it useful to work in coalitions.

Generally speaking, the respondents expressed satisfaction with their legislative roles and with their presence in their respective assemblies. When asked whether the legislative process was important for blacks, virtually all of the respondents said yes. Only one respondent dissented from this view. In addition, most of the respondents replied that they felt that they experienced some measure of support from their colleagues. The perception of this support corresponded to various facets of institutional structure in interesting ways. More of the respondents were ready to say that they received support from the leadership of their parties. Slightly fewer respondents claimed to receive support for other party members, and fewer still felt that their other colleagues supported them.

Our findings suggest that, despite their positions as being representatives of a racial minority, the legislators do not feel any appreciable sense of institutional isolation as a result. They regard themselves to be integral members of their legislative bodies, sufficiently enough so as to indicate receiving some measure of support for their work. A further indication of this institutional satisfaction is the fact that a large proportion of our respondents indicated that they held positions of leadership in their respective legislatures or party caucuses (nine of the thirteen said so).

The findings are also consistent with the trends in the process of Latin American democratization that have been unfolding over the past decade. During this time, ethnic and racial minorities have assumed a greater presence in the region's politics. Indigenous groups, especially, have begun to exert an influence in politics that flies against centuries of subservience. This new assertiveness has manifested itself in the role played by indigenous groups in the resignation of Ecuador's president in the mid-1990s, and in the election of an indigenous leader, Evo Morales, as president of Bolivia, as well as in the election of Alejandro Toledo as the first Peruvian president of indigenous heritage. Also, racial issues have assumed increasing salience in Brazil with the appointment of a number of blacks to the cabinet of President Luiz Ignacio Lula da Silva.

The respondents also displayed a sense of institutional identity with respect to the design of the state's powers, and in particular with regard to two of the branches of government: the legislature and the executive. Traditionally in Latin America, legislatures have played a secondary role to the power of the presidency. This is a situation in which Latin America legislatures have attempted to assert an institutional identity as an agent of curbing the hidden authoritarian tendencies of concentrated executive power. With regard to this issue, our respondents fit somewhat fairly into this array of institutional power by expressing negative sentiments regarding the national executive. In our survey, a substantial number of the respondents picked the executive branch as the major obstacle to their legislative success. Five of the respondents indicated this (three of the respondents said the legislatures were the main obstacle, two cited political parties, and one indicated that the obstacles were various). In any case, even though by a small margin, the respondents appear to fall within a commonly recognized pattern in Latin American politics. It is a pattern in which institutional identity has some significance regarding their place and role in the institutions of the state (on the recent scholarship on Latin American legislatures, see Morgenstern and Nacif, 2002).

Over and above their satisfaction with their institutional environments, the legislators approach their respective assemblies with perspectives that differentiate them from their other colleagues. As representatives of unique communities that are marked by distinctive disabilities of citizens' exclusion, they would be expected to hold notions of their elective functions which reflect this distinctiveness.

This difference is expressed, for example, in response to the question about their most important tasks. The majority of the respondents chose "maintaining the confidence of their constituencies" above other tasks such as "maintaining the support of the party," and "assuring one's legislative capacities." This set of responses suggests that the legislators are more attuned to how their institutions function as a form of mirror reflection that projects their standing within their respective communities. This standing appears to hold a higher priority than those tasks and obligations that would benefit in more concrete ways their own legislative careers. In other words, the respondents see legislative politics more as a field of representation than an arena of career advancement or a venue for plying expertise in any given field of public policy.

Country Background

There is one more consideration that should be included in our discussion. This deals with the set of factors against which the legislators at the Brasília meeting were attempting to define themselves as a transnational network. The attendees came from a diverse range of countries with their own distinct social, economic and political circumstances. However, the aim of the attendees was to close the gap of nationalities in order to create a genuinely transnational entity. National differences among the conferees were dramatic in some cases. National demographic factors posed the greatest potential division within the group. The attendees from Brazil, the largest country in the region, sat along side those from Costa Rica, the smallest country. Moreover, the demographic situation of the Afro-descendent populations varied widely. Brazil and Colombia possess significant numbers of people of African descent, while in Costa Rica their numbers are small. And, there are situations, such as Ecuador and Peru, where Afro-descendent populations exist along side of more politically active Indigenous communities.

Bridging these national differences was one of the unspoken challenges of the conference, and it remains to be seen whether this regional gathering of black legislators could generate the kinds of common outlooks and agendas that would permit them to transcend their national differences. In any case, even though these national differences were seldom alluded to during the Brasília meeting, it would be useful to sketch out some of them out before concluding our discussion.

Demographic Differences. The demographic concentrations of the legislators' individual national populations were spread across a broad spectrum. In two instances, the demographic concentrations were pronounced, such as in the cases of Brazil and Colombia, where blacks made up as much as 45 percent and 26 percent of the population, respectively. At the other end of the scale were countries such as Costa Rica and Uruguay, where blacks were less than 5 percent of those national populations (Inter-American Dialogue, 2003).

Differences in Social Development. There is little doubt that blacks in Latin America suffer a common plight. Generally, their communities record substantially lower levels of social development than those of their white fellow citizens. David Ferranti, the vice-president of the World Bank, alluded to these disparities in a presentation to the Inter-Agency Consultation on Race in Latin America in 2002 (Ferranti, 2002). In his presentation, Ferranti made reference to the fact that throughout Latin America, blacks suffered from significantly lower life expectancies, higher incidents of infant mortality, lower levels of educational achievement, and lower levels of poverty than the national averages. Multilateral institutions such as the World Bank and the Inter-American Development Bank have used the terms, "economic exclusion," and "racial exclusion," to refer to the situation described by Ferranti (Stubbs and Reyes, 2006). However, notwithstanding the pervasive nature of racial exclusion, the degree of exclusion, nevertheless, differs from country to country. In Brazil, for example, the degree of racial exclusion is substantially greater than it is in Costa Rica.

To provide a sense of these differences, we offer the tabular counts of the University of Maryland's Minorities at Risk (MAR) Project on this topic. The MAR Project comprises a database that contains numerical evaluations of the position of minority groups in their respective societies. It includes in its dataset evaluations of the situation of blacks in almost every country in the Americas.[2] The MAR project assesses such situations as a minority community's extent of economic discrimination, disparities in education, income, life chances, and the like. Based on the MAR indexes, we can compare the situation of blacks in the countries that the legislators come from.

The MAR dataset contains an index of racial exclusion, called the aggregate economic difference index. This index is constructed on the basis of scores on eighteen dimensions of group difference, including cultural differences such as language and religion, economic inequality and discrimination, and political discrimination, that is, the extent to which the groups may enjoy full citizens rights or otherwise. The higher scores on this index denote a greater aggregate ethnic difference. The maximum score is 18. Table 4 lays out the wide variation among the countries regarding racial exclusion and racial discrimination.

Brazil and Colombia receive the highest scores, indicating that racial exclusion is more pronounced in those two countries than in the others in the table. Ecuador and Costa Rica

Table 4
Minorities at Risk (MAR): Aggregate Ethnic Difference Index
Intra-Regional Comparisons of Blacks in Selected Countries

Country	*MAR Index*
Brazil	11
Colombia	10
Ecuador	8.5
Costa Rica	8
Peru	4

Source: Minorities at Risk Project, University of Maryland, 2000

receive relatively high scores as well. Peru, on the other hand gets assigned a smaller score (data on blacks in Uruguay, the country of origin of one of our respondents, was not included in the MAR dataset). Comparing these scores suggest that there may be a reason to suppose that the representatives of these countries may differ in the strategies they pursue to deal with this exclusion. For example, we may expect that the Brazilians as well as Colombians might emphasize the strictly racial dimensions of their legislative programs, while the Peruvians might tend to fold their formulations of constituency issues into broader platforms, since racial exclusion is a less salient or sharply drawn issue there.

Differences in the Political Environment. The national political environments also varied among the attendees. Costa Rica and Uruguay, for example, enjoy long-standing reputation as showcases of democracy in Latin America. Brazil has a more mixed reputation. Brazil, which is in its twentieth year of democratic consolidation, for the first time in its history saw a person of decidedly working-class background assume its presidency in 2002. On the other hand, Brazil continues to hold an ambiguous record on human rights, primarily because of the extralegal conduct of its police forces. Colombia is perhaps an extreme case. It is a democracy surviving under severe stress as a consequence of both a decades old civil war and the corrosive effects of an illicit drug economy. Black Colombians particularly have been among the worst victims of Colombia's endemic violence.

The conditions of democracy vary across the legislators' countries. To determine these differences we look at one of the latest report of the respected Latinobarómetro polling firm. The report which we rely on focuses particularly on the levels of acceptance and support for democracy in the region.

The Latinobarómetro Summary Report of 2003 lays out the extent of the challenges facing any of the legislators of the region, and not just black legislators. As the report makes clear, Latin American legislators operate in environments in which mass publics hold a complex set of views about their democracies. Overall, while there appears to be little prospect for a dissolution of the region's democratic regimes, there is a significant erosion of satisfaction with democracy, and disillusionment with the failure of democratic regimes to deliver on promises of improvements in the daily lives of citizens. Such is the extent of this erosion of satisfaction with democracy that the Latinobarómetro report characterizes it as one of the few constant patterns in Latin American politics. Sadly, Latin Americans have come to view their political systems as being run by the few and for the few. Latin Americans are disenchanted with their democracies, but they do no show any inclination to replace them with any other form of government (Latinobarómetro 2003).

The range of support for democracy varies considerably across the nations in our study. At one end of the spectrum are Uruguay and Costa Rica, where public opinion support reaches relatively high levels. In both countries, public opinion support was a little more than three-fourths of the respective national samples. By way of contrast, the percentages of support in Peru, Ecuador, and Colombia fell to 50 percent or less. Brazil reached the lowest point, with just 35 percent of the national sample declaring support for democracy. Even in the countries where support was high, satisfaction was pointedly low. For example, the level of satisfaction in Costa Rica and Uruguay hardly reached the 50-percent mark (47 percent and 43 percent, respectively). Brazil, Ecuador, and Colombia hovered in the range of 20-30 percent, and Peru fell to a dismal 11 percent.

Table 5
Public Opinion Support for Democracy in Selected Latin American Countries

Country	*% of Latin Barometer Sample Expressing Support for Democracy*
Uruguay	78
Costa Rica	77
Peru	51
Ecuador	46
Colombia	46
Brazil	35

Source: Latinobarómetro, *Summary Report: Democracy and Economy,* Santiago, 2003, p.41

Table 6
Public Opinion Satisfaction with Democracy in Selected Latin American Countries

Country	*% of Latin Barometer Sample Expressing Satisfaction with democracy*
Costa Rica	47
Uruguay	43
Brazil	28
Ecuador	23
Colombia	22
Peru	11

Source: Latinobarómetro, Summary Report: Democracy and Economy, Santiago, 2003, p. 42.

The Latinobarómetro findings provide little comfort to Latin American legislators as a whole. The findings, moreover, point to the daunting task, for black legislators in particular, of convincing their constituencies with long-standing grievances to stay in the game of politics. Embedded in this portrait of dissatisfaction are the national differences among the black legislators themselves. How and by what means the black legislators respond collectively to the dissatisfaction with democracy, and how they will go about bridging the national gaps among them, are questions that represent a particular challenge to the black legislators of the Americas.

Overall, however, we found reasons for optimism. Our analysis indicates that on every significant item discussed thus far there was virtually no difference that distinguished any one nationality from the others with respect to their profiles or outlooks. When we ran cross-tabulations between nationality on the one hand and the racial identity and institutional environment factors on the other we found no significant results. This is an encouraging sign. It suggests that the legislators in our study do, in fact, have a common ground to work from. Race identity represents that common ground. Building on this, their first efforts at this meeting may certainly draw them closer to fulfilling the promises of widening their constituents' economic and political inclusion that was the objective of the Brasília encounter.

Conclusion

Several limitations in our study require us to be cautious about making generalizations. Our evidentiary base is somewhat limited. Moreover, our focus on racial identity is restricted by the self-selected nature of our sample. Nevertheless, we make these concluding comments in an effort to draw implications that might lead to further study.

At the outset of our discussion we offered an encapsulated version of "The Declaration of Brasília," the document which the legislators released at the conclusion of the Brasília meeting. The declaration outlined two aims, which the legislators affirmed to be their guiding principles. These were the goals of continuing a collective struggle against racism and exclusion, and of promoting the ongoing democratic projects of their respective nations. Our analysis shows that these principles are highly consistent with the racial, social, and political profiles that we have sketched.

We briefly restate the major features of the profiles in order to illustrate the extent of this consistency.

* The legislators openly declared their racial identities in the form of being consciously black;
* They possess middle-class characteristics and cultural traits common to Latin American societies. These are the ingredients of an emerging leadership pool;
* They launched their careers from their activism in civil society, which suggests a tendency toward a preferred attachment to civil society over loyalty to their legislative institutions;
* They peg their legislative behaviors and strategies to promoting black causes over institutional considerations such as party loyalty;
* They indicate confidence in the legislative process and of receiving at least some level of support from their legislative colleagues, suggesting a degree of satisfaction with their legislative roles;
* They display a uniformity in their profiles which transcended whatever national differences that exist among them.

We may infer from these profiles that the legislators share a commitment both to their racial communities as well as to an ongoing democratic project. In other words, there is a consistency between their words as expressed in the "Declaration of Brasília," and their profiles. That is, they say who they actually are. What implications may we draw from this observation?

The black legislators are not mere "parochials" in the sense of their narrowly defining their communal commitments. They appear to define their commitments both inwardly toward their racial group, and outwardly toward the broader reaches of their societies. They are both "black" and "democrats." We might call their perspective "cosmopolitan."

As "cosmopolitans," they may be carving out a distinctive place for themselves in the politics of their respective countries. In the process, they are taking on two kinds of obligations: one is in improving the material quality of life for their communities; the other is in reinforcing the foundations of democracy, particularly with regards to the incorporation of their excluded communities into the mainstream of politics, and with respect to the rule of law and political participation.

These goals, of combating exclusion and defending democracy, are, undoubtedly, noble ones. And, the legislators may find them satisfying in their own right in embracing them.

However, the legislators must also deliver the goods for their constituencies. They must provide tangible benefits that their constituencies can see as evidence that the legislators do, in fact, play an important part in their lives. This latter task is an especially difficult challenge in political environments, such as Latin America's, where social and redistributive policies frequently become enmeshed in bureaucratic inertia and corruption, or where such policies face the daunting power of the privileged to abort them.[3]

The challenges faced by the legislators may be daunting to the point of imposing tempting but counterproductive choices on them. On the one hand, the idealism of fighting racism and exclusion, and of affirming democratic principles may entice them to engage in purely symbolic politics. As a consequence, they may be inclined to pursue symbolic politics at the expense of delivering the goods. On the other hand, they may be prompted to seek any means for furnishing tangible and material rewards for their constituencies. Such an option would surely lure them into the old-fashioned patronage and clientelist politics that have traditionally vitiated the ideals of genuinely participatory democracy in Latin America. Either way these choices could certainly be seen as an abdication of leadership. In any case, the mark of leadership, which their profiles reflect, would be for the legislators to search for ways to hold these obligations together as complementary ones, rather viewing them as "zero-sum" choices.

Notes

1. The significance here is that "Afro-descendent" is, in its current usage, the term denoting one who consciously assumes a black identity over other more ambiguous terms that have been part of the conventional racial lexicon of Latin America. On the usage of racial terms in Brazil, see Nobles, 2000; see also Htun, 2004.
2. For more information on the Minority at Risk Project see the website at www. Cidcm.umd.edu/inscr/mat.home.htm.
3. Larry Rohter of *The New York Times* reported recently on the mismanagement of Pres. Luiz Ignacio Lula da Silva's poverty program a year after his inauguration as the most progressive president in recent Brazilian history. Such mishandlings, as Rohter reports, has dramatically frustrated the expectations of Lula's natural constituency among the working class and the poor. See Larry Rohter, "In a Slum of Shanties on Slits, Help Isn't Always Helpful," *The New York Times*, March 19, 2004, online edition).

References

Chalmers Douglas, et al., 1997. "Associative Networks: New Structures of Representation for the Popular Sectors?" in Douglas A. Chalmers, et al., (eds.), *The New Politics of Inequality in Latin America*, New York, Oxford University Press, 543-582.

Dawson, Michael C. *Behind the Mule: Race and Class in African-American Politics*. Princeton, N.J.: Princeton University Press.

Dovi, Suzanne 2002. "Preferable Descriptive Representation: Will Just Any Woman, Black, or Latino Do?" *American Political Science Review* 96:4 (December): 729-743.

Ferranti, David. 2002. "Remarks at the Inter-Agency Consortium on Race in Latin America." Washington D.C.: Inter-American Dialogue.

Htun, Mala. 2004. "From 'Racial Democracy' to Affirmative Action: Changing State Policy on Race in Brazil," *Latin American Research Review*, vol. 39 no.1.

Inter-American Dialogue. 2003. *Race Report*. Washington D.C.: Inter-American Dialogue.

Johnson III, Ollie 1998. "Racial Representation and Brazilian Politics: Black Members of the National Congress, 1983-1999," *Journal of Inter-American Studies and World Affairs*, 40:4 (Winter): 97-118.

Latinobarómetro 2003. *Summary Report: Democracy and Economy*. Santiago: Latinobarómetro (available from www.latinobaróetro.org).

Mansbridge, Jane 1999. "Should Blacks Represent Blacks and Women Represent Women? A Contingent Yes," *Journal of Politics*, vol. 61 no. 3 (August): 628-657.

Morgenstern, Scott and Benito Nacif (eds.). 2002. *Legislative Politics in Latin America*. Cambridge, U.K.: Cambridge University Press.

Morrison, Minion K.C. 2005. "The Emergence of a Legislative Caucus of Afro-Descendant Legislators in the Americas: Context, Progress, and Agenda Setting," paper presented at the Annual Meeting of the National Conference of Black Political Scientists (NCOBPS), Washington, D.C., March.

Nascimento, Elisa Larkin. 1981. *Pan-Africanismo na América do Sul*. Petrópolis, Editôra Vozes.

Nobles, Melisa. 2000. *Shades of Citizenship: Race and the Census in Modern Politics*, Stanford, CA: Stanford University Press.

Powers Timothy. 2000. *The Political Right in Post Authoritarian Brazil*. University Park, PA: Penn State University Press: 85-87.

Smith, Robert C. 1981. "The Black Congressional Delegation," *The Western Political Quarterly*, vol. 34 no. 2 (June): 203-221.

Stubbs, Josefina and Hiska N. Reyes (eds.). 2006. Más Allá de los Promedios: Afrodesciendentes en América Latina. Washington, D.C.: The World Bank.

Swain Carole. 1993. *Black Faces, Black Interests: The Representation of African Americans in Congress*. Cambridge, MA.: Harvard University Press.

Tate, Katherine. 2003. *Black Faces in the Mirror: African Americans and Their Representatives in the U.S. Congress*. Princeton, N.J.: Princeton University Press.

Van Cott, Donna Lee. *The Friendly Liquidation of the Past: The Politics of Diversity in Latin America*. Pittsburgh, PA: University of Pittsburgh Press.

Wade, Peter. 1997. *Race and Ethnicity in Latin America*. London: Pluto Press.

Walters, Ronald W. 2003. "Black Power in Brazil." *The Sacramento Observer*, online at www.Sacobserver.com/news/commentary/120803/Brazil_black_power.shtml.

Walters, Ronald W. and Robert C. Smith. 1999. *African American Leadership*, Albany, NY: State University of New York Press: 12-15, 38-39.

Whitby Kenneth. *The Color of Representation*, Ann Arbor: University of Michigan Press.

Introductory Political Science Textbooks: Are They Inclusive of African American Politics?

Sherri L. Wallace
University of Louisville

Dewey M. Clayton
University of Louisville

Introduction

"Introduction to American Government" is a standard course for college freshmen. Most of the major textbooks used for these courses utilize the institutional and behavioral approach to the study of American government. Historically, these textbooks have treated African American politics as separate from mainstream American politics, and, as such, have usually relegated its discussion to a separate chapter on civil rights or equal rights in most traditional textbooks.

Stroup and Garriott (1997) argued that little had changed since the publication of the classic Ogg and Ray "Introduction to American Government" in 1922, in which the general focus was on institutions and processes. We acknowledge also that little has changed in ten years. Although most introductory American Government/Politics textbooks have substantially more coverage of African American politics in the form of historical analysis, the civil rights struggle, and contemporary political actors and a few textbooks are now include photographs of African Americans and/or separate narratives, we argue that the majority of introductory American government textbooks still fail to portray African American politics as an integral part of the study of American politics but rather as a minor subset relegated to one or two chapters.

To test our thesis, we conducted a content analysis of the top-selling introductory American government textbooks to examine to what extent African American politics is integrated into the study of American politics. Our qualitative analysis begins with a literature review which provides the contextual framework. We then review each textbook separately for extent of coverage and integration of African American politics. To our knowledge, there have been very few studies that have examined this research question directly in the field of political science.

Literature Review

Clawson and Kegler (2000) examined images in 27 American Government college textbooks for a racial bias in the portrayal of poverty. They found that African Americans are portrayed as poor in these images at a disproportionately higher rate than whites and other minorities. The intersection of race and poverty as portrayed in these textbooks "perpetuate racist constructions of reality" and is likely "to reinforce existing (erroneous and insidious) beliefs regarding Black citizens in our society" (184). Replicating the Clawson and Kegler study for economics textbooks, Clawson (2003) found that these introductory texts "reinforce stereotypes and marginalize the experiences of minorities (and women) and downplay the impact of discrimination in our society" (358).

In an analysis of the development of history textbooks and their treatment of ethnic groups, Foster (1999) identified three "enduring and essentially conservative themes" (267). The textbooks were found to perpetuate and promote nationalist views of American history and institutions, avoid issues of conflict and controversy, particularly in the realm of institutionalized racism and contemporary issues, and what Foster describes as "mentioning." Mentioning is the phenomenon in which a textbook will add content, such as a sidebar on ethnic groups, without incorporating the information into the central message of the text. (271). The central message of history textbooks, while incorporating more diversity through their 'mentioning,' has remained relatively unchanged for two centuries (272).

Stone (1996) examined introductory sociology texts both for their overall coverage of issues of race and gender and the amount to which that coverage was concentrated, or in the author's term, "ghettoized," in a single chapter. Using a methodology that counts both unique and total citations, the author concludes that despite an "absolute yardstick for judging how much coverage is adequate," there is a substantial amount of coverage of both, but it is largely confined to a single chapter (361). "These findings give the impression that people of color are relevant to the discussion of only a limited number of social institutions or processes' in effect they are marginalized from many of the major concerns of the course" (Stone, 1996: 361).

Manza and Schyndel (2000) used a content analysis of introductory sociology texts to examine the "nonproblematic" sociological representation of race, class and gender. Their study replicated Ferree and Hall (1996), which proposed examining textbooks on the basis that "textbooks are time-lagged measures of the state of the disciple," and that they are representative of the mainstream of the discipline (930–931). While Ferree and Hall (1996) found a disproportionate amount of coverage for class and race compared with gender, Manza and Schyndel (2000) found that coverage of gender issues had improved, suggesting that in newer research gender issues had moved more into the mainstream in sociology.

The importance of incorporating new research into classroom materials is echoed by Prestage (1994). The author examined the mainstreaming of gender and race in American Government texts and found that the traditional approach of most textbooks of focusing on American institutions often excluded women and minorities as active participants in the political process. "One major problem … is that the experience of women and racial minorities did not fit easily into the major frames of reference or organizational schemes of the standard textbooks used in American Government courses" (720). Because of "limited participation" of many minorities in the institutions that were the focus of researchers and the relative lack of minorities in the profession, information on race and gender often had to be pulled from outside political science for classroom use. "Inclusion of information on gender and race required not only supplementing the textbook information, but reinterpreting essential concepts and offering new frames of reference, sometimes diametrically opposed to that of the textbook" (720).

Wilson (1985) contended that political science as a discipline has largely ignored questions of black politics. The reasons for this trend, in Wilson's account, is that on one hand, minority recruitment into the discipline has been poor, and on the other hand the dominant paradigms and research focuses of political science largely excluded the most interesting aspects of African American politics. Most of political science is concerned with political elites and political power, and since African Americans have been historically excluded from institutional power and rely on informal channels, they are largely unrepresented in scholarship (Wilson, 1985: 604; Jones, 1992). The focus on formal institutions and prevailing research questions that are dominant in mainstream political science often exclude analyses of historically excluded minorities.

Jones (1992) attributed this institutional and elite focus, and corresponding disinterest in African American issues, to "basic epistemological and paradigmatic assumptions of American political science" (26). Jones locates political science as a discipline as originating from and in service to dominant, that is white, social groups (27). The absence of African American issues is not an aberration, but a persistent feature of the dominant political paradigm reflected in political science. For Jones, the epistemological position of mainstream political science, and its corresponding focus on institutions and elites, disguises and furthers the exclusion of African-Americans from political analysis. For some scholars it is imperative to increase the participation of black scholars in order to counter the exclusionary focus of the discipline (Pinderhughes, 1990; Wilson, 1985). Jones (1997) argued that black political scientists should challenge the dominant paradigm by advancing a black perspective in the discipline.

The focus on formal institutions is mirrored in most introductory texts. Stroup and Garriott (1997), in their presentation of an alternative model for introductory American Government courses, claimed that the format of introductory textbooks suggested that these courses follow "the same format almost everywhere" (73). Introductory textbooks, the authors contend, have changed little since the publication of the classic Ogg and Ray *Introduction to American Government* in 1922, and generally focus on institutions and processes studied sequentially. Stroup and Garriott (1997) hold that this format presents a compartmentalized view of the American political process, ignores the cultural and economic context of American politics, and presents an essentially static picture of American politics in their piecemeal representation of history. This has important repercussions for the perceptions of minorities that are advanced in these texts. Sleeter and Grant (1991), in their analysis of secondary education texts, linked the representation of minorities with wider issues of the perception of legitimate political actors. In effect, the underrepresentation of minority groups as active participants undermines their symbolic representation as such (Sleeter and Grant, 1991: 79-80).

Methodology

Our analysis of 17 top-selling American Government/Politics textbooks printed between 2004 and 2006 (see Appendix: Introductory American Government/Politics Textbooks Reviewed) is modeled after the recent published report submitted to the American Political Science Association's Standing Committee on the Status of Lesbians, Gays, Bisexuals, and Transgendered in the Profession (Novkov and Gossett, 2007). We used the index in each textbook to search for key terms: African Americans, affirmative action, civil rights, minority, race, race discrimination, redistricting (or "racial gerrymandering"), segregation, slavery, and voting to locate as many African Americans as possible. Next, we examined the content of the texts to discern how African Americans were being portrayed throughout the texts: whether confined to one or two chapters on civil rights and equality, or significantly integrated throughout the entire textbook.

Understanding that political science American government introductory texts typically focus on institutions and elites as decision makers, we found as Wilson (1985) observed,

> Blacks have historically been deprived of elite status and hence, rarely are involved in authoritative decisions, they are more frequently the objects or victims of the use of power; politics, as such often involves the creative design of adaptation to disenfranchisement and economic domination through reliance on … 'nonformal' or multi-purpose institutions like the [black] church or voluntary associations like the National Association for the Advancement of Colored People (NAACP) (604).

Moreover, according to Wilson, the dominant political experience of blacks has been one of responding to manifold attempts at political domination, expressed through political and non-political channels (Wilson, 1985: 604). Given this context and the overall themes that the textbook authors employ as our framework, we offer brief summaries that seek to highlight the best or worst aspects of each textbook reviewed.

The Text Reviews

Burns, James MacGregor, Peltason, J.W., Cronin, Thomas, Magleby, David, O'Brien, David, and Light, Paul. *Government by the People.* (National Version) 21st edition. Upper Saddle River, NJ: Prentice Hall, 2006.

The main discussion on African Americans is found in Chapter 17: "Equal Rights Under the Law" (430–457) where the context highlights all disempowered groups in American society and their struggle for equality and equal rights. The roughly two-page discussion on African Americans as a social group (433–436) gives little agency to African Americans as actors (aside from Rosa Parks and Martin Luther King, Jr.), but is written from a dominant Eurocentric voice that is rife with overgeneralization, trivialization, and victimization of the African American political experience. The same is true for the discussion on "Voting Rights" (445–446) and "Education Rights" (447–449), "Rights of Association, Accommodations, Jobs and Homes" (449–451); however, "The Affirmative Action Controversy" is a more balanced (451–455).

Dye, Thomas. *Politics in America.* 6th edition. New York: Pearson Prentice Hall, 2005.

By using Harold Lasswell's (1938) classic definition of politics as the unifying framework, this text strives to present a clear, concise, and stimulating introduction to the American political system (xvii). In Chapter 2: "Political Culture: Ideas in Conflict" the author accurately discusses the concept of political equality, but with a slight error of mentioning "Neither women nor slaves could vote anywhere," failing to note that American Indians, white males with no property, or free blacks in the North were disenfranchised as well. The one-paragraph discussion of African Americans as a racial/social group gives some agency to the African American struggle with references to more integrated discussions on each topic in other chapters of the text. The short discussion on the institution of slavery in Chapter 3: "The Constitution: Limiting Governmental Power" is historically refreshing in that it does not shy away from the real conflicts between northern and southern delegates, but clearly delineates the issues in the Constitution. It also refers to slaves as "African slaves." In Chapter 5: "Opinion and Participation: Thinking and Acting in Politics" the discussions on "Race and Opinion" and the "Securing the Right to Vote" are balanced. Most of the discussion on African American politics is found in Chapter 15: "Politics and Civil Rights," which begins with the struggle from slavery to affirmative action (537–556). The discussion highlights civil rights political actors like Martin Luther King, Jr., debates between Booker T. Washington and W.E.B. Du Bois, and organizations like the NAACP and SCLC. Unfortunately, the discussion on women is based on the history of white middle-class women and says little about the active participation of African American women.

Dye, Thomas, and Zeigler, Harmon. *The Irony of Democracy: An Uncommon Introduction to American Politics*. 13th edition, Belmont, CA: Thomson Wadsworth, 2006.

The theme of the text is based around the concept of "elitism," which holds that "a tiny handful of people make decisions that shape the lives of all of us, and, despite the elaborate rituals of parties, elections, and interest-group activity, we have little direct influence over these decisions" (xv). Given this perspective, the concise text is written to reflect the worldview of elites in American politics.

Most of the discussion on African Americans struggle is found in Chapter 15: "Elite Response to Mass Protest," where the authors basically argue that elites responded either positively or negatively to protest movements designed and/or orchestrated by protest organizations seeking political redress or responses regarding their issues. The agents of change for the masses of African Americans in this discussion are through organizations like the NAACP and the National Urban League, with brief mentions of civil rights icons like Rosa Parks, Martin Luther King, Jr. and the SCLC. Interestingly, there were very few photographic images in the text. The visuals were primarily graphs, tables, and cartoon illustrations.

Edwards, George III, Wattenberg, Martin, and Lineberry, Robert. *Government in America: People, Politics, and Policy*. 12th edition. New York: Pearson Longman, 2006.

The theme for this text is "politics and government matter" (2). This text seeks to help students understand why politics and government are necessary in our society. Although discussions on African American political involvement can be found throughout the text in other chapters, most of the discussion on African American politics is found in Chapter 5: "Civil Rights and Public Policy" (138–173), which opens with the recount of Rosa Parks as a member of the NAACP who refused to give up her seat on a bus in Montgomery, Alabama, in 1955, thus sparking the civil rights movement. The narrative also highlights the leadership/legacy of Martin Luther King, Jr. The chapter frames the discussion on African Americans as the struggle for racial equality spanning two centuries. The discussion on slavery opens with the recognition that the first African immigrants were kidnapped (143) and "most" African Americans lived in slavery for the first 250 years of American settlement (143), which is an accurate depiction that recognizes those African descendants who were never enslaved.

There were some factual, yet controversial statements made in text that can be viewed as offensive such as the discussion on AIDS: "the issue thus remained a low priority on the government's policy agenda until infections started to spread to the general population, including celebrities like basketball star Magic Johnson" (15), and a remark that refers to Justice Thurgood Marshall's excitement over weekly reviewing of pornographic movies for the Supreme Court (113).

The visuals throughout the text were not universally integrated. African Americans were used most often when issues pertaining to them were discussed. Almost all of the images of African Americans were of men, most often in stereotypical roles such as athletes and rap stars and less often in positions of leadership and power.

Fiorina, Morris, Peterson, Paul, and Voss, Stephen. *America's New Democracy*. 4th edition. New York: Pearson Education, Inc., 2005.

The theme of this text is elections and their repercussions, emphasizing the research backgrounds and interests of the authors (xxi). As a result, most of the discussions are framed in the context of majorities vs. "numerical" minorities and special interest groups. Specific racial/ethnic social groups are discussed under "Social Diversity" (89) in Chapter 4: American Political Culture. Given the focus on elections and voting, the discussion on "Voting Rights in the Amendment Process" (150) is rather simplistic, with little agency given to the struggles of different social groups in obtaining the right to vote. African American electoral participation is highlighted throughout other chapters of the text when making comparisons between voters/citizens on key issues and concerns. The authors use an awkward phrase "affirmative action redistricting" (302)—to describe the process of drawing district lines to maximize the number of majority-minority districts, which again highlights the need for a new language that accurately describes the diversity among social groups and that is not centered on a European worldview. Interestingly, Chapter 17: "Civil Rights" (463–496) opens with the controversy over affirmative action and a discussion on "Origins of Civil Rights" that is thorough with respect to the African American struggle for freedom and universal rights. Although most of the political actors are associated with institutions like the NAACP, SCLC, CORE, and SNCC, the authors also note black elected officials as well as Martin Luther King, Jr., Rosa Parks, and Malcolm X as political actors. The discussion culminates with affirmative action—"programs designed to enhance opportunities for groups that have suffered discrimination in the past" (477)—before moving on to "Civil Rights of Other Minorities" (479). There were relatively few photographs of African Americans aside from those of Rosa Parks, Martin Luther King, Jr., and members of the Congressional Black Caucus.

Janda, Kenneth, Berry, Jeffrey, and Goldman, Jerry. *The Challenge of Democracy: Government in America*. 8th edition. New York: Houghton Mifflin, 2005.

There are two themes in this text. The first is the "clash among the values of freedom, order, and equality; and the second focuses on the tensions between pluralist and majoritarian visions of democracy" (xviii). Using a western-dominated approach to American government, the authors show how America evolved from influences from other western nations and cultures. In Chapter 5: "Public Opinion and Political Socialization" (132–165), the discussion on race and ethnicity is situated in an overall discussion of social groups and political values beginning with "*major* ethnic minorities… immigrants from Ireland, Germany, Poland and other European countries" (154, emphasis mine) to "racial minorities" (154). The entire discussion is only four paragraphs (one page) and is situated in the simplistic and trivialized context of how each of these social groups vote and their overall political attitudes.

When speaking of political participation of African Americans in Chapter 7: "Participation and Voting," the authors make a controversial observation that "Black protest activity—both violent and nonviolent—has been credited with increased welfare support of blacks in the South" (204), which begs clarification. Most of the discussions are chopped up and distributed throughout the text and chapters with the only groups receiving substantive attention being African Americans and women. Other groups are lumped under the term "minority," which can be confusing. Chapter 16: "Equality and Civil Rights" (510–546) situates the struggle for civil rights in the context of two conceptions of equality "equality of opportunity" and "equality of outcome." The authors inappropriately state: "The struggle of blacks has been a beacon lighting the way for Native Americans, Hispanic Americans, women, the disabled and homosexuals," suggesting that these groups owe their struggles and gains to African Americans, which is arguably not totally accurate (513). The political actors representing African American involvement include the NAACP, Rosa Parks, and Martin Luther King, Jr. Notably, there is a brief discussion on "Racial Violence and Black Nationalism," in which the violence of the era ends in the election of Carl Stokes, Cleveland's first black mayor, in 1967 and the formation of the Congressional Black Caucus in 1969 (525). The discussion then turns to "Civil Rights for Other Minorities" (525). The chapter ends with affirmative action framed in the context of equal opportunity vs. equal outcome (538). Interestingly, the authors showcase how other nations such as India, Canada, and Australia struggle with affirmative action (540–541) or "preferential treatment/positive discrimination" policies.

Kernell, Samuel and Jacobson, Gary. *The Logic of American Politics*. 3rd edition. Washington, DC: CQ Press, 2006.

The goal of this text is to "help students discern the rationale embedded in the extraordinary and complex array of American political institutions and practices that we observe today" (xxiii) emphasizing "the strategic dimension of political action, from the Framers' trade-offs in crafting the Constitution to the efforts of contemporary officeholders to shape policy, for [the authors] want students to understand current institutions as the products of, as well as venues for resolving, political conflicts (xxiii). The authors admit that the text has an "unorthodox structure" (xxiv) in that it covers "the rules of the game and formal institutions of government before discussing the input side of the political process ... because [the] emphasis is on the way rules and institutions structure the actions and choices of citizens and politicians alike" (xxiv). Given this institutional perspective, the issue of slavery is dealt with as one of a few "Substantive Issues" along with foreign policy and interstate commerce in framing the Constitution (60). There is a brief case study on the issue of slavery as "Strategy and Choice: Logrolling a Constitution" between Northerners and Southerners (62–63) in which the authors use a formula to demonstrate the range of choices and solutions available to both sides in reaching compromise. In Chapter 4: "Civil Rights," the authors seek to define civil rights within its different historic context, but situated within a "Madisonian" perspective of democracy as articulated in *Federalist* #10. They begin with the heading "the Civil Rights of African Americans" followed by the heading "The Politics of Black Civil Rights" (116–117), which is a bit confusing. A great deal of space is given to the discussion of the historical and institutional debates and struggles in eras of slavery, reconstruction, Jim Crow and segregation, Democratic party sponsorship of civil rights, emergence of civil rights coalitions, and remedial action; affirmative action is briefly discussed up to the legacy of the civil rights movement (116–143). Unfortunately, in this otherwise very comprehensive survey, African Americans receive little recognition as political actors.

Landy, Marc, and Sidney M. Milkis. *American Government: Balancing Democracy and Rights*. Boston, MA: McGraw Hill, 2004.

This text frames the "tension between liberalism and democracy by focusing on the political importance of two key features of American political life that contemporary political science often neglects: religion and localism" (xviii). The authors' goal is to "show how the centrality of local self-rule to the idea of American democracy, rooted in the relationship between size and democracy, has created greater resistance to the centralization of power in the United States" (xviii). This textbook is unique in that it offers "separate chapters on immensely important and interesting subjects that are rarely treated comprehensively in other textbooks".... [and] contains no separate chapters about civil rights, civil liberties, and public policy because these subjects are so integral to American politics that [the authors] wanted them to permeate the entire book" (xix). Instead, the authors incorporate extensive discussions of all three topics in the chapter narratives, and "every chapter devotes one box each to a contemporary civil rights, civil liberties, and public policy issue" (xix). In "Part One: the Formative Experience," Chapter 2: "Political Culture: The Foundation of the American Republic" (21–28) opens with Martin Luther King, Jr.'s "I Have a Dream Speech" and the March on Washington, which is used to set the context for understanding American political culture and America's political creed. "The Declaration and Slavery" (42–45), where slavery is described as the "dreadful compromise" (84–87) provides a full discussion of how some notable historical political actors, white and black, dealt with what this issue would mean for American society. In Chapter 5: "Federalism," "Slavery and National Supremacy" (164–167) are discussed and their impact in relation to the "civil rights legacy" (174 -176). *Dred Scott v. Sandford* is used to teach the power of judicial review (349–351), as are other landmark cases, *Plessy v. Ferguson, Brown v. Board, Smith v. Allwright,* found in Chapter 9: "The Courts" (358–360). Affirmative Action is found in Chapter 10: "The Bureaucracy" (418–419). The Voting Rights Act of 1965 is integrated in Chapter 11: "Political Parties" (452–453), and in Chapter 12: "Social Movements, Public Opinion and the Media" (481–512), which highlights an excellent discussion on the history of voting. By integrating African American scholars and columnists with extensive quotes from African American political actors, readers get a rare opportunity to read the political expressions of actors such as Frederick Douglass, James Baldwin, Martin Luther King, Jr., Malcolm X, A. Philip Randolph, and Rosa Parks. Unfortunately, Condoleezza Rice is the only African American female pictured with a brief highlight in the entire text; however, there were very few photographs in the text overall.

Lowi, Theodore, Ginsberg, Benjamin, and Shepsle, Kenneth. *American Government: Power and Purpose*. 8th edition. New York: W.W. Norton & Co., 2004.

This text is based on the idea that "the best way to teach students is to expose them to repeated applications of a small number of the core ideas [or "five fundamental principles of politics"] of the discipline" (xx). The authors seek to integrate the historical-institutional and the rational-choice perspectives to help faculty and students develop a way of thinking about and analyzing politics (xx). Thus, the discussion over the question of slavery is analyzed from the historical-institutional perspective where the framers preferred compromise between the North and South as opposed to the breakup of the Union (49). The discussion on African American political involvement is found in Chapter 4: "The Constitutional Framework and the Individual: Civil Liberties and Civil Rights" (118–159). The civil rights discussion begins with the adoption of the Fourteenth Amendment in 1868 and ends with school desegregation cases as late as 1995. Because the focus is mainly a historical-institutional approach with a rational-choice motive, African American-dominated organizations like the NAACP and the SCLC with Martin Luther King, Jr. are the major political actors. Affirmative action is dealt with separately in the chapter as a "policy program designed to redress historic injustices committed against specific groups," accurately expanding the discussion beyond African Americans (149). The text evenly distributes African American political involvement mostly as a collective group throughout the text in the other chapters under the appropriate topics/issues. Interestingly, this text has no photographic images (which are not missed), but includes excellent tables, charts, and graphs to illustrate significant context and data.

O'Connor, Karen, Sabato, Larry, Haag, Stefan, and Keith, Gary. *American Government: Continuity and Change*. 8th edition. New York: Pearson Longman 2006.

This text seeks to understand how the United States is governed today by understanding how it exists and how it evolved over time from the framers' intentions (xxiii-xxiv). The authors seek to integrate African American political involvement evenly throughout the text in every chapter, utilizing historical examples in the African American political struggle to validate points and arguments. Data were gathered from diverse scholars and think-tanks in the discipline. The main discussion on the African American political experience is found in Chapter 6: "Civil Rights" (196–235), which combines the struggles of African Americans and women under the heading of "Slavery, Abolition, and Winning the Right to Vote, 1800–1890." It begins with era of slavery from 1800 and ends with the 1964 Civil Rights Act (199–217). In this innovative, integrated discussion, African American activists like Frederick Douglass are mentioned along with notable white women; however, there is no mention of prominent African American female activists of the period. The NAACP is characterized as an organization that grew out of "a handful of individuals active in a variety of progressive causes, including women's suffrage and the fight for better working conditions for women and children, [who] met to discuss the idea of a group devoted to the problems of the Negro."

Patterson, Thomas. *The American Democracy*. 7th edition. Boston, MA: McGraw Hill, 2005.

This text takes a narrative approach that "weaves together theory, information, and examples in order to bring out key facts and ideas" (xix) with a "heighten emphasis on liberty, equality, and self-government as the three great principles of American Democracy" (xxi). In the first chapter, "American Political Culture: Seeking a More Perfect Union," a very brief synopsis of the African American historical political struggle is highlighted, but framed in the context of blacks' relation to whites: "There have always been at least two Americas, one for whites and one for blacks" (15). African Americans are presented as a collective and how the government responds to the collective in all other chapters as well. At most times, African Americans are combined in the phrase "women and minorities" throughout the text. Chapter 5: "Equal Rights: Struggling Toward Fairness" (142–179) articulates the history of the African American political experience. The discussion is framed in the context of "disadvantaged groups" in American democracy such as "African Americans, women, Native Americans, Hispanic Americans, Asian Americans and other groups" listed respectively (144). The narrative under "African Americans" (145–147) is concise beginning with the transport from Africa to America and ending with the election of black officials since the 1960s. Linda Carole Brown, (daughter of the plaintiff in *Brown v. Board of Education*), and Martin Luther King, Jr. are the only two African American political actors mentioned.

Schmidt, Steffen, Shelley, Mack, and Bardes, Barbara. *American Government and Politics Today*. 2006-07 edition. Belmont, CA: Thomson Higher Education, 2006.

The theme of this text emphasizes that "politics is not an abstract process but a very human enterprise" by highlighting "how different outcomes can affect students' civil rights and liberties, employment opportunities, and economic welfare" (xxiii). In Chapter 2: "The Constitution," the authors' presentation of the "three-fifths compromise" is taken from a historical-institutional perspective that centers on the framers' dilemma in creating a united democracy. Curiously, the authors seek to highlight the fact in their "Did You Know" box that "During the four centuries of slave trading, an estimated ten million to eleven million Africans were transported to North and South America and only 6 percent of these slaves were imported into the United States" (42)—without any explanation. The authors also challenge students to consider "Could the Founders Have Banned Slavery Outright?" (43) in their "Politics and Diversity Discussion," with a rather tame cartoon showing an enslaved African male fully clothed with hat in hand standing on the auction block. Again, the rationale for these highlights is unclear to the reader. The main discussion on African American political involvement takes place in Chapter 5: "Civil Rights" (149–187). The comprehensive and balanced survey begins in 1863, covering the constitutional amendments, early civil rights acts and their ineffectiveness, voting barriers, *Brown v. Board of Education* and school integration policies, up to the civil rights movement and its consequences. The African American political actors mentioned are Frederick Douglass (quoted), Jesse Jackson, Rosa Parks, Martin Luther King, Jr., and A. Philip Randolph, and Bayard Rustin (mentioned as the architects of the March on Washington for Jobs and Freedom 1963), and Malcolm X as an alternative approach to Black Power. The major institutional agents are the NAACP, SCLC, and the Urban League. Affirmative Action is dealt with separately under "Civil Rights: Extending Equal Protection" (170–171) as a policy "in educational admissions or job hiring that gives special attention or compensatory treatment to traditionally disadvantaged groups in an effort to overcome present effects of past discrimination" (170). African Americans are integrated throughout the remainder of the text as collective political actors generally.

Sidlow, Edward & Henschen, Beth. *America at Odds*. 5th edition. Belmont, CA: Thomson Learning, 2006.

This text looks at "government and politics in this country as a series of conflicts that have led to compromises" (xxv). Slavery is framed within a historical institutional perspective as a compromise over representation and importation (33). The main discussion on African American political involvement is found in Chapter 5: "Civil Rights" (101–126). The discussion begins with the Equal Protection Clause and various levels of classification with respect to how it is applied to different social groups in society. The condensed and concise survey of African American political involvement centers on major Supreme Court cases and how different laws in different eras affect African Americans as a collective (105–109). The dominant political actors are Rosa Parks and Martin Luther King, Jr., with mention of Malcolm X and Stokely Carmichael. The main institutional agents are the NAACP, SCLC, CORE, and SNCC.

Spitzer, Robert, Ginsberg, Benjamin, Lowi, Theodore J. & Weir, Margaret. *Essentials of American Politics*. 2nd edition. New York: W.W. Norton & Co., 2006.

The focus on this text is on the "relationship between the citizen and the government. Every important question raised in the book stems from the key issue of how people relate to their government, and in turn, how the government reacts, regulates, and responds to the people" from a historical institutional perspective (xix). In Chapter 4: "Civil Liberties and Civil Rights" (79-122), African American political involvement is highlighted in "Civil Rights" beginning with a discussion of the Fourteenth Amendment, then a progression of major cases that dealt with government protection of African Americans as a collective from the Civil Rights Acts of 1875 to 1965 (103-112). The major political actor mentioned is Martin Luther King, Jr., along with the NAACP and SCLC.

Stephenson, Jr. D. Grier, Bresler, Robert J., Friedrich, Robert J., Karlesky, Joseph J., and Turner, Charles C. *Introduction to American Government.* 3rd edition. Reno, Nevada: Best Value Textbooks, 2005.

This text highlights the importance of economics and ideology in the context of American government, and "how these forces shape the perennial pursuit of power in a democracy" (xix). The major narrative surrounding the political involvement and participation of African Americans is found in Chapter 3: "Civil Liberties and Civil Rights," (71-105).

The civil rights discussion in situated within the context of equality defined as "equality of opportunity" vs. "equality of condition" vs. "equality of result." The African American political experience begins with the passage of the Thirteenth Amendment and all the subsequent civil rights legislation that affected African Americans as a collective (91-96). Interestingly, the major political actors were Thurgood Marshall—as the lead attorney in *Brown v. Board of Education*—and Martin Luther King, Jr. with the NAACP. Affirmative Action is highlighted twice in the chapter as a case study: "Contemporary Controversies: How Much Affirmative Action" (85) and briefly wedged between a discussion on the continuing effects of *Brown* and voting rights (95-96). The predominantly black and white visuals were historical and well-known images in general. There were relatively few photographs of African Americans aside from the civil rights eras and one each of U.S. Congresswoman Shirley Chisholm and Professor Anita Hill in other chapters.

Volkomer, Walter. *American Government*. 11th edition. Upper Saddle River, NJ: Prentice Hall, 2006.

The text is based around the Constitution and its provisions as the theme that runs through each chapter (xvii). Although African American political involvement is integrated in the chapters throughout the text, the main narrative is found in Chapter 12: "Civil Rights" (303-327) with a comprehensive summary on racial relations in the U.S. It begins with Europeans and the treatment of American Indians and progresses through history with the influx into cities of blacks and Hispanics in the cities up to about the 1970s. The major African American political actors are Frederick Douglass, W.E.B. Du Bois, and the NAACP, Martin Luther King, Jr., the Urban League, and a very brief mention of Minister Louis Farrakhan (erroneously referred to as "Reverend") as representing "more militant black nationalist groups."

Welch, Susan, Gruhl, John, Comer, John & Rigdon, Susan. *Understanding American Government* (Brief Edition). 8th edition. Belmont, CA: Wadsworth, 2006.

This text centers on the "impact of government: how individual features of government affect its responsiveness to different groups (in Lasswell's terms, "Who gets what and why?") (xiii). This textbook integrates African American political involvement—with box highlights or case studies in almost every chapter—throughout the entire text evenly and comprehensively giving political agency to African Americans as political actors throughout the development of the American political system. At the same time, it recognizes that "race" in and of itself is a social construct that has evolved over the centuries of America's existence. In discussing the "three-fifths compromise," the authors are careful to highlight the issues and concerns of the framers, while at the same time recognizing the humanity of the Africans in bondage (35-36). Instead of dispersing the entire narrative on African American political involvement in the "Civil Rights" chapter, the authors integrate African American political involvement progressively in appropriate chapters. For example, the narrative on "Blacks and the Right to Vote" is found in Chapter 8: "Elections" (237–241)—a very logical location. Chapter 12: "Civil Rights" begins in 1619 when the first Africans were transported to America for human bondage and ends with the current status of African Americans, raising the issue of "Improving Conditions of African Americans" (528-530). Although the longest narrative, spanning

23 pages (508–531), deals with African Americans as a collective, it is comprehensive and historically accurate, giving agency to African American political leaders/activists like W.E.B. Du Bois as one of the founders of the NAACP; Thurgood Marshall and Legal Defense Fund of the NAACP; Black fraternities and sororities; Dorothy Counts; Martin Luther King, Jr. and SCLC; the black and white students of the sit-ins; James Farmer and CORE.

Findings

Although a few texts sought to integrate the African American political experience in each chapter on topics such as the "three-fifths compromise" or "slavery" in the Constitution, the history of the "Voting Rights Acts" in political participation or voting, and/or the perceptions of African Americans in public opinion overall, a majority of the reviewed texts situate their discussions of African Americans in the chapter on civil rights or equality. These discussions generally frame the African American struggle for universal freedom/inclusion as "the most" or "the primary" disempowered group that "other" disempowered groups have learned to emulate in their struggles.

African Americans receive the most substantive discussion in all reviewed texts in depth and page length in relation to other social and racial/ethnic groups, but

> The worldview of a people conditions the nature and content of its social science knowledge and that two peoples' or cultures' social sciences will differ to the extent that they have different worldviews. However, when there is an adversarial relationship between two peoples' who share a common territory, as is the case with white and black Americans, the worldview of the dominant group will be used to give meaning to social reality and to generate social science knowledge. Knowledge so generated conveys only a caricature of the oppressed or dominated people and hence has little prescriptive utility for their struggle to end their domination (Mack Jones, 1992: 25).

Most of narratives utilize a historical-institutional approach that focus on historical cases like *Dred Scott v. Sandford, Plessy v. Ferguson,* and *Brown v. Board of Education* with agents of change emerging via "nonformal" or multipurpose institutions like the NAACP with Rosa Parks, SCLC with Martin Luther King, Jr., and occasionally CORE, SNCC, the Urban League, and the mention of a few other African American political actors. Many of the discussions begin their narratives after the Civil War and end with the affirmative action debate, sometimes immediately following or at the end of the chapter. The discussions on affirmative action are usually framed in a dichotomous relationship between equal opportunity versus equal outcome and/or equality of opportunity versus equality of results, outcome or condition. This is noteworthy because in texts where affirmative action follows directly from the historical narrative on African American political involvement, it is most often portrayed as a policy that is used to eliminate discrimination against "minorities and women." Moreover, much of the focus typically is on the controversy over the use of race as opposed to gender, and the discussion highlights the dilemma of "reverse discrimination" toward white males.

A majority of the reviewed texts incorporate visuals like photographs and brief commentary/highlights on significant historical or contemporary issues. Overall, the visuals in some reviewed texts were more universally integrated and balanced, showing African Americans in positive, nonstereotypical postures. Images of African Americans were used most often when issues alluded or pertained to race such as the images of African slaves in the chapters on the "Founding" or pictorial images from the civil rights era.

Almost all of the images in the reviewed texts were overwhelmingly those of African American men. The few images of African American women were overly represented in photographs dealing with domestic policy or social issues such as poverty, welfare, and single parenthood. It should be noted as well that the discussions on women and women's political involvement are based on the historical worldview of white middle-class women, with no mention of the active participation of African American women—aside from Condoleezza Rice— in the American political experience.

A quick glance of the "Notes" pages for the corresponding chapters in most of the reviewed textbooks revealed very little research taken from works by African American political scientists, scholars, journalists, and commentators. Contributions by noted and respected African American scholars across the disciplines are necessary if we want to continue to broaden our understanding and raise critical questions regarding the African American political experience. As Dianne Pinderhughes (1990), the first African American woman elected as president of the American Political Science Association, surmised:

> If we do not transmit these rich memories, interests and understanding of how the discipline has functioned in a highly discriminatory fashion, and how American institutions have organized political life according to the racist preferences of American slave owners and their descendants in the present, the new generations of Black political scientists will enter the field and either be absorbed along in an uncritical manner, or find themselves unwelcome but unable to understand the whys and wherefores. New White political scientists will be unsocialized by our influence. And generations of American students, Black as well as White, will have no knowledge or understanding of the politics of race that we have worked so carefully to understand and to publish because it will have gone untransmitted" (17).

We found that the terms "African American" and "black" are used interchangeably and almost exclusively to describe or discuss African Americans as a collective often with very little analysis of the political variation within the group. Although most textbooks employ minimal use of the convoluted misnomer "minorities," many resort to its use when speaking in generalized terms, often combining the terms "women and minorities," which continues to trivialize the profound differences in political experiences for these groups as well as ignoring the politics surrounding the intersection of race, gender, and class in political participation.

Of the texts reviewed, we believe the lesser known Landy/Milkis, *American Government: Balancing Democracy and Rights,* (2004), was the most comprehensive and integrated textbook on African Americans as decision makers and political actors in the American political system. This was an intentional goal of the authors, who explained, "The book offers separate chapters on immensely important and interesting subjects that are rarely treated comprehensively in other textbooks.... [It] contains no separate chapters about civil rights, civil liberties and public policy because these subjects are so integral to American politics that we wanted them to permeate the entire book" (xix). In addition, the authors make generous inclusion of works by African American authors. Welch/Gruhl/ Comer/Rigdon, *American Government* (2006), was the most balanced, integrated top circulating textbook on African American political involvement and issues for some of the same reasons as Landy/Milkis (2004). Also, Dye, *Politics in America* (2005), O'Connor/Sabato/Haag/Keith, *American Government: Continuity and Change* (2006), and Schmidt/Shelley/Bardes, *American Government and Politics Today* (2006) offer notable discussions on African American political involvement, with some agency given to African Americans as political actors. Finally, Kernell/Jacobson's *The Logic of American Politics*

(2006) is noteworthy for its very comprehensive historical review of African American political history from 1808 through the 1990s, spanning 27 pages, but it lacks a substantive discussion of African Americans as decision makers and political actors.

Cursory qualitative appraisals of each text in three areas are reflected in Table 1. The degree to which discussions of African Americans is concentrated in the text is listed under the heading of "Concentration." As most texts reserve discussion of African Americans to a single chapter, this category lists how many chapters contain significant discussions of African Americans. This variable is coded by three variables, 1 chapter, 2 chapters, or 3 or more chapters (1; 2; 3+). The category of "Integration" lists whether African Americans are included outside of chapter concentrations. Though most texts concentrate discussions to a single chapter, some also include reference throughout the text. This "Integration" is coded as Low, Medium or High (Low; Med; High). The final category is an assessment of whether African American politics is discussed in a way that highlights political agency. This category considers the degree to which African American political agency is highlighted across issue areas, not just in discussions of civil rights. Listed under the category "Agency," this variable is coded as Low, Medium, or High (Low, Med, High).

A summary of the Concentration, Integration, and Agency of all 17 textbooks selected for our analysis is shown in Table 2. It reveals that 76 percent (slightly more than three-fourths) of the text reviews concentrate discussions on African American politics to a single chapter. However, the texts in general do tend to mention African Americans throughout their discussion, with 53 percent in the High Integration category, and 35 percent in the

Table 1
Textbook Comparisons

Text	Concentration	Integration	Agency
Burns, et al.	1	Med	Low
Dye	1	High	Med
Dye and Zeigler	1	Low	Low
Edwards et al.	1	High	Med
Fiorina et al.	2	Med	Med
Janda et al.	3+	Med	Med
Kernell and Jacobson	1	Med	Low
Landy and Milkis	3+	High	High
Lowi et al.	1	High	Med
O'Connor et al	1	High	High
Patterson 2005	1	Med	Low
Schmidt et al.	1	High	High
Sidlow and Henschen	1	Med	Med
Spitzer et al.	1	High	Med
Stephenson et al.	1	Low	Low
Volkomer	1	High	Med
Welch et al.	3+	High	High

Medium category. The coding of the Integration category does not measure how well African American politics is integrated into the main narrative of the text, but the inclusion of references throughout. The final category, Agency, has a more center weighted distribution, with 29 percent in the Low category, 47 percent in the Medium category, and 24 percent in the High category.

Conclusion

For the most part, introductory textbooks in American government/politics still focus on the institutional and behavioral approach. This approach examines institutions and processes from a majoritarian perspective, with emphasis on the political actors who dominate these institutions. In employing this approach, we found that the majority of the textbooks we examined tended to parcel African American politics into a single chapter on civil rights or equal rights. Relegating African American politics to minority status and condensing the discussion to primarily one or two chapters we believe, sends a clear message to the reader: African American politics does not merit thorough integration throughout the text because it is only a subset of American politics and not an integral part of it. However, it is precisely our contention that African American politics is not only integral, but essential to the study of American politics. The struggle of African Americans, originally locked out of the political process, denied the right to vote and to hold political office, is crucial to the study and meaning of democracy in America. This country was born in revolution and throughout our history; African Americans—originally enslaved and stripped of citizenship—have struggled successfully against injustice to force this country to be true to its democratic promise.

Because many of the textbooks are written from a largely Eurocentric point of view with rare mention of African Americans outside of the well-known figures of the modern civil rights movement such as Thurgood Marshall, Rosa Parks, and Martin Luther King, Jr., we frequently found factual inaccuracies in the discussion of African American politics. Often major historical events are not mentioned, such as the Reconstruction Period following the Civil War, the years between 1870 and 1901, where African Americans were active participants in the political process and held elective office from the local level to the national legislature. For example, we know that 22 blacks were elected to both the U.S. Senate and House of Representatives where important democratic legislation was passed to help all citizens. The failure to include such important information may leave most college students totally unaware of these events and their significance.

Also, we observed that a majority of the texts analyzed failed to discuss the significance of race in American politics. There is very little mention that race is a social and political construct that has very little meaning in the scientific community today. Additionally, there is little to no discussion about the role of the electronic and print media

Table 2
Summary of Textbook Comparisons

Concentration			Integration			Agency		
1 Chapter	2 Chapters	3+ Chapters	Low	Medium	High	Low	Medium	High
13	1	3	2	6	9	5	8	4

in reinforcing negative stereotypes of African Americans in society. Almost all of these textbooks have a chapter on "the media" but there is little discussion of how the media informs and shapes our consciousness about politics overall as well as issues in popular culture, which is a very powerful role in shaping perceptions and perpetuating negative stereotypes, thus undermining positive perceptions of African Americans.

Our study is by no means exhaustive, and we recognize that introductory textbooks are published within the political and economic constraints driven by markets, resources, and power; however, our findings suggest an increased need for improvement in the content of introductory textbooks that actively and wholly integrates African American politics into the mainstream of American politics.

Acknowledgments

The authors wish to acknowledge that the textbook reviews, methodology, and findings reflected in this chapter derive from a study commissioned by the American Political Science Association's Standing Committee on the Status of Blacks in the Profession.

Appendix
Introductory American Government/Politics Textbooks Reviewed

Burns, James MacGregor, J.W. Peltason, Thomas Cronin, David Magleby, David O'Brien, and Paul Light. *Government by the People.* 21st edition. Upper Saddle River, NJ: Prentice Hall, 2006.

Dye, Thomas. *Politics in America.* 6th edition. New York: Pearson Prentice Hall, 2005.

Dye, Thomas and Zeigler, Harmon. *The Irony of Democracy: An Uncommon Introduction to American Politics* 13th edition, Belmont, CA: Thomson Wadsworth, 2006.

Edwards, George III, Martin Wattenberg, Robert Lineberry. *Government in America: People, Politics, and Policy.* 12th edition. New York: Pearson Longman, 2006 (Brief 8th Edition, 2006).

Fiorina, Morris, Paul Peterson, and Stephen Voss, Stephen. *America's New Democracy.* 4th edition. New York: Pearson Education, Inc., 2005.

Janda, Kenneth, Jeffrey Berry, and Jerry Goldman. *The Challenge of Democracy: Government in America.* 8th edition. New York: Houghton Mifflin, 2005.

Kernell, Samuel and Gary Jacobson. *The Logic of American Politics.* 3rd edition. Washington, DC: CQ Press, 2006.

Landy, Marc, and Sidney M. Milkis. *American Government: Balancing Democracy and Rights.* Boston, MA: McGraw Hill, 2004.

Lowi, Theodore, Benjamin Ginsberg, and Kenneth Shepsle. *American Government: Power and Purpose.* 8th edition. New York: W.W. Norton & Co., 2004.

O'Connor, Karen, Larry Sabato, Stefan Haag, and Gary Keith. *American Government: Continuity and Change.* 8th edition. New York: Pearson Longman 2006.

Patterson, Thomas. *The American Democracy.* 7th edition. Boston, MA: McGraw Hill, 2005.

Patterson, Thomas. *We the People: A Concise Introduction to American Politics.* 6th edition. Boston, MA: McGraw Hill, 2006.

Schmidt, Steffen, Mack Shelley, and Barbara Bardes. *American Government and Politics Today.* 2006-07 edition. Belmont, CA: Thomson Higher Education, 2006.

Sidlow, Edward and Beth Henschen. *America at Odds.* 5th edition. Belmont, CA: Thomson Learning, 2006.

Stephenson, D. Grier, Jr., Robert J. Bresler, Robert J. Friedrich, Joseph J. Karlesky, and Charles C. Turner. *Introduction to American Government.* 3rd edition. Reno, Nevada: Best Value Textbooks, 2005.

Volkomer, Walter. *American Government.* 11th edition. Upper Saddle River, NJ: Prentice Hall, 2006.

Welch, Susan, John Gruhl, John Comer, and Susan Rigdon. *American Government.* 10th edition. Belmont, CA: Wadsworth, 2006.

References

Apple, Michael W. and Linda K. Christian-Smith (eds.) 1991. *The Politics of the Textbook.* New York and London: Routledge.

Clawson, Rosalee A. 2003 "Poor People, Black Faces: The Portrayal of Poverty in Economics Textbooks." *Journal of Black Studies* 32(3), 352-361.

Clawson, Rosalee A. and Elizabeth R. Kegler. 2000. "The 'Race Coding' of Poverty in American Government College Textbooks." *The Howard Journal of Communications* 11, 179-188.

Ferree, Myra Marx and Elaine J. Hall. 1996. Rethinking Stratification from a Feminist Perspective: Gender, Race, and Class in Mainstream Textbooks."

Foster, Stuart J. "The Struggle for American Identity: Treatment of Ethnic Groups in United States History Textbooks." *History of Education* 28(3), 251-278.

Jones, Mack H. 1992. "Political Science and the Black Political Experience: Issues in Epistemology and Relevance." *National Political Science Review: Ethnic Politics and Civil Liberties* 3, 25-39.

Jones, Mack H. 1977. "Responsibility of Black Political Scientists to the Black Community." In Shelby Lewis (ed.) 1977. *Essays in Honor of A Black Scholar*. Detroit: Balamp Publications.

Manza, Jeff and Debbie Van Schyndel. 2000. Still the Missing Feminist Revolution? Inequalities of Race, Class, and Gender in Introductory Sociology textbooks. *American Sociological Review* 65(3), 468-475.

Novkov, Julie and Charles Gosset. 2007. "Survey of Textbooks for Teaching Introduction to U.S. Politics: (How) Do They See Us?" *PS: Political Science and Politics* 40(2), 393-398.

Pinderhughes, Dianne M. 1990. "NCOBPS: Observations on the State of the Organization." *National Political Science Review* 2, 13-21.

Prestage, Jewel Limar. 1994. "The Case of African American Women and Politics." *PS: Political Science and Politics* 27(4), 720-721.

Sleeter, Christine E. and Carl A. Grant. 1991. "Race, Class, Gender and Disability in Current Textbooks." In Apple and Christian-Smith 1991. *The Politics of the Textbook*. New York: Routledge: 1991.

Stone, Pamela. 1996. "Ghettoized and Marginalized: The Coverage of Racial and Ethnic Groups in Introductory Sociology Texts." *Teaching Sociology* 24(October), 356-363.

Stroup, Daniel G. and William Garriott. 1997. Teaching American Government: An Alternative to Ogg ad Ray. PS: Political Science and Politics 30(1), 73-77.

Wallace, Sherri L. 2006. "A Review of Introductory American Government/Politics Textbooks: Integration of African Americans in the American Political Experience" an unpublished report/project of the American Political Science Association's Standing Committee on the Status of Blacks in the Profession (September).

Wilson, Ernest J. 1985. "Why Political Scientists Don't Study Black Politics, But Historians and Sociologists Do." *PS: Political Science and Politics* 18(3), 600–607.

Part III

Book Forum

African American Politics in Third Parties and Urban Affairs: A Review Essay

Omar H. Ali. *The Balance of Power: Independent Black Politics and Third-Party Movements in the United States* (Athens, Ohio: Ohio University Press, 2008), xii + 244 pp.: ISBN 978-0-8214-1806-2 (cloth) / 978-0-8214-1807-9 (paper).

Charles L. Lumpkins. *American Pogrom: The East St. Louis Race Riot and Black Politics* (Athens, Ohio: Ohio University Press, 2008), xiii + 312 pp.; ISBN 978-0-8214-1802-4 (paper).

In the bright political glow and glare of the electronic and print media coverage of the historic 2008 presidential campaign—with its nomination of the first African American candidate, Senator Barack Obama, by one of the major political parties, the Democratic party—very limited attention is being given to those African American candidates running on third- and independent-party tickets. Throughout history, these African American candidates of minor parties and independent movements have had to struggle in near or total obscurity, except for brief notices in fringe and small newspapers and pamphlets.

The historic 2008 election threatened to not only continue this tradition of the media rendering these African American candidates and their political vehicles as nonentities, but also, due to the singular nature and scope of their focus on Senator Obama's pioneering political achievement, to end up declaring that he represents the death of African Americans politics as we know it. Thus, nothing could be further from the truth in the light of the fact that as he was securing the Democratic party's nomination, African American Republican Alan Keyes, also running in 2008, lost his bid and the Green Party nominated former Atlanta congresswoman Cynthia McKinney. Thus, this third-party candidate, McKinney, will be running against Democratic nominee Obama, creating another historic first in this 2008 campaign of numerous rare electoral realities.

Professor Omar H. Ali of Vanderbilt University has written a very fine scholarly, topical, and timely book. Writing in the foreword, historian Eric Foner, the advisor of Professor Ali's dissertation at Columbia University, says that he "traces the history of black participation in third parties and in other forms of political activism. His narrative … reveals the complex dynamics that have shaped the sometimes problematic relationships between African Americans and third party movements"(x). Professor Foner concludes with this thought about his students insightful and carefully reflective scholarship: "Whether independent political action or operating within one of the two major parties offers the best hope for improving the condition of black Americans … Ali shows … (that at) …

many points … (these third party and independent efforts have) … energized the black community and helped to make America a better place for all its people" (xii).

In his introduction, Professor Ali noted that it has been "over thirty-five years ago … (since) … a book-length work been devoted to the subject of African Americans and third parties" (7). Therefore, he began in Chapter One of this six chapter work with an epigraph describing the innumerable problems that have faced African Americans from slavery to the rise of the anti-slavery movement, and the poor response of the fledging political party system and process to develop solutions for these problems. As a consequence of the failure of the political system to response, African American leaders in this era laid the groundwork for an independent and alternative course of political action to solve their own problems.

Chapter Two focuses upon the community problem of Abolitionism, and the role and function of the anti-slavery third-parties, as well as how African American leaders in this period kept and continued the option of political independence. Chapter Three analyzes the Republican party in the Reconstruction era and how its strategies addressed and resolved community problems. About the options in this era, Professor Ali writes: "the development of independent black politics in the post-Reconstruction period shifted largely to the South, where 90 percent of the black population worked and lived.… African Americans responded to their growing political and economic marginalization in two principal ways" (68)—either exodus or black and white coalitions in progressive movements. Needless to say, because of southern white racism, difficulties abounded with these black and white coalitions.

Chapter Four follows the movement of African American independents and partisans in the late 1880s and 1890s into the agricultural movement of white farmers that eventuated into the Populist party. When this movement and party discounted and disregarded African American populism, "independent black politics, which had shifted from the North to the South after Reconstruction, would once again largely shift back to the North" (99). One of the main reasons for this new shift is that with the decline of populism is the rise of disenfranchisement in the eleven states of the old Confederacy. In the urban milieu of northern cities, the assertions of African American political independence would form linkages and coalitions with the newly transplanted European ideological parties.

The narrative in Chapter Five concentrates its attention and analysis on black communists, socialists, and nationalists. Emerging along with the rise of Garvey's Back-to-Africa Movement and a great decline of the major parties' interest in the problems of African Americans, political independence moved to the left. This occurred by joining and forming electoral coalitions with the Socialist party, the early Progressive parties of 1912 and 1924, and later the Communist party, as well as the Progressive party of 1948 and 1952. In Professor Ali's captivating analysis, one sees all of the problems and difficulties and potentials with the African American independents in these movements.

Finally, in Chapter Six, the book brings the African American political independents and third-party activists into the 1960s with the civil rights and black power movements. In this era, we watch the rise of African American third parties, interracial third parties, and numerous nominations of African Americans on third-party tickets. We also see attempts by African American independents, like Fannie Lou Hamer and the Mississippi Freedom Democrats (MFDP), and later the National Democrats of the Party of Alabama

(NDPA), as well as the Freedom Now Party, the Black Panther Party, the Peace and Freedom Party, and the United Citizens Party to try to reform the two major parties. Also covered in this chapter are the National Black Political Conventions, the two presidential nomination races of Reverend Jesse Jackson and the 1988 campaign of Dr. Lenora Fulani. By 1992, African American political independents were flirting with the Perot third-party movement.

This comprehensive and systematic book closes with an epilogue that looks at the state of African American political independents and third-party activists in 2008. In this chapter, one sees the variety and diversity of these two groups and their relationship to the current Democratic presidential nominee, Senator Barack Obama. Professor Ali, with this chapter brings his brilliant book full circle.

Overall, this is this first full-length scholarly work on African American political independents and their sometime allies, African American third-party activists. No other historical work has ever undertaken such a longitudinal study of this group of unattached partisans over the entire sweep of American history. Minority political independents and third-party activists are voters that are in constant motion—aligning, realigning, and dealigning—fluid in their alliances and electoral support. Professor Ali's profound scholarship has finally given the disciplines of political science, history, sociology, and African American studies a holistic political portrait. It is a landmark work.

Professor Charles Lumpkins, a historian at Pennsylvania State University, has written a book that could be read in conjunction with that of Professor Ali, simply because it analyzes African American political independents and partisans and their interaction and relationship in a single urban area, East St. Louis, Illinois. This book can be read, quite beneficially, and very rewardingly, alone. This book, which defines systematic violence against an African American community as a pogrom or ethnic cleansing, instead of being a race riot, breaks out of the genre of race-riot books and offers a scholarly innovation.

Heretofore, this concept or terminology, pogrom, has been applied to ethnic violence perpetrated "against Jews in czarist Russia and against Armenians in Ottoman Turkey" (xii). As defined by Professor Lumpkins in this book, a pogrom is "an assault, condoned by officials, to destroy a community defined by ethnicity, race, or some other social identity," which results in "ethnic cleansing" campaigns (xi). Instead of seeing anti-black violence as defined in most scholarly and academic books as merely being a series of race riots, Professor Lumpkins notes that the July, 1917 race riot in East St. Louis came after "nearly three decades of an unbroken series of mass antiblack attacks" (8). Therefore, he adds: "the most dramatic and best-known of these episodes occurred in 1898 in Wilmington, North Carolina; in 1900 in New Orleans and New York City; in 1906 in Atlanta; and in 1908 in Springfield, Illinois" (8). After the July, 1917 race riot in Illinois, the second one in the state in less than a decade, they continued in the nation, occurring in "August, 1917 in Houston, Texas; in 1918 in Philadelphia; in 1919 in Elaine, Arkansas; and in 1921 in Tulsa, Oklahoma" (8). Thus, in terms of Lumpkins conceptualization, there is a linkage, connection, and relationship between these terrible and horrifying events. While others have treated and analyzed them as unrelated and isolated events except by name, Lumpkins' bold and unique approach declares that they should been seen and analyzed as parts of a whole, despite their differences in geographical sites and locations.

What connects and links them? African American political empowerment. They were designed, argues Lumpkins, to "oust black politicians from office; to neutralize, if not eliminate, African American influence in electoral politics; to reconstruct city government; and to institute a rigorous de facto residential segregation" (8). This is a fresh and creative approach, a new way to theorize about race riots and a new empirical way to measure and evaluate and assess this social fury in the political context of local politics and the political process. This ingenious approach moves the knowledge base away from the numbers of individuals, black and white, who were murdered, maimed, and harmed, to the new roads and venues that the African American community had to take to empowerment or in the case of East St. Louis, re-empowerment.

Chapter One of this six chapter book with a postscript provides the background data on how the African American community began. The next chapter gives data on how the African American community initially empowered itself between 1898 and 1915. Then Chapter Three reveals that the race riot in the city was designed to end African American political and electoral power in the city. Chapter Four tells the reader that the pogrom re-established East St. Louis as a "White Man's Town." According to Professor Lumpkins' findings, "the violence dramatized the limitations imposed upon any attempt by black Americans to build a political structure that advocated African American interests in a manner equal to and independent of white-dominated political institutions" (8).

What the rest of the chapters show, in great and nuanced detail, is how African Americans in the city—via partisan, third-party, and political independent activism—regained some aspects of their former political empowerment, and a degree of their civil rights, just before the civil rights and black power movements began in the 1960s and 1970s. Yet, when they did take over the city, deindustrialization by white leadership left them without the employment and economic resources to make the city once again a viable reality. Thus, the pogrom had long-run consequences.

However, the brilliant nature and intellectual contribution of this exceptional work is not just in its conceptualization and theorizing, or in its new findings of political facts and leaders in the city, but in its political analysis that is so rare or non-existent in other race-riot books. Political scientists have much to learn from this new work.

These two historical studies of African American politics are highly recommended to students of race and politics and African American politics. They complement each other. And most importantly, both works are breakthrough studies by any intellectual yardstick.

Hanes Walton, Jr.
University of Michigan

Invitation to the Scholarly Community

The National Political Science Review (NPSR), a refereed publication of the National Conference of Black Political Scientists is seeking to expand its contributor and subscriber base.

The NPSR was conceived with emphasis particularly on theoretical and empirical research on politics and policies that advantage or disadvantage groups by reason of race, ethnicity, or gender, or other such factors. However, as a journal designed to serve a broad audience of social scientists, the NPSR welcomes contributions on any important problem or subject that has significant political and social dimensions.

The NPSR seeks to embrace the socio-political dimensions of all disciplines within the social sciences and humanities, broadly defined. Generally, the NPSR seeks to incorporate analyses of the full range of human activities that undergird and impinge upon political and social life. Thus, in addition to contributions from political scientists, the NPSR seeks relevant contributions from historians, sociologists, anthropologists, theologians, economists, ethicists, and others. The NPSR strives to be at the forefront of lively scholarly discourse on domestic and global political life, particularly as disadvantaged groups are affected. While not meant to be exhaustive, the listing below is illustrative of the different areas of scholarly inquiry that the NPSR wishes to draw upon:

Public policy
Health policy
Domestic, and Comparative Social Policy
Educational policy
Science and technology policy
Policy history
Communications, media, and new media
History
Sociology
Philosophy
African studies
American Government
Global studies
Economics and Political economy
Criminology and Criminal Justice
Race and ethnicity
Gender politics and policy
Anthropology and ethnography
Public management
Ethics
Language and communication
Religion and public affairs
Law and Legal studies
Leadership studies

The NPSR welcomes conventional manuscripts, as well as research notes, on important issues. The NPSR is particularly interested in contributions that set forth research agendas in critical scholarly areas within the context of past scholarship and ongoing contemporary developments. The Editor encourages collaborative efforts by two or more contributors as well as contributions by single authors.

For the initial review, manuscripts may be submitted in two formats: (1) Manuscripts may be submitted electronically as an email attachment, preferably a Word document. This will greatly facilitate timely review. However, *it is the author's responsibility to ensure that the electronic attachment contains one version that does NOT carry the author's name.* In addition to an electronic format, two hardcopies of manuscripts must be submitted, with one copy bearing the author's name, academic institution, and email address on the cover page. (2) Authors may choose to submit only hardcopies for the initial review, in which case four (4) hardcopies are required, only one of which should carry the author's name, institutional address, email and telephone number.

Manuscripts should not exceed thirty (30) typewritten pages double-spaced, inclusive of notes and references, and must be prepared in accordance with standard APA style, or consistent use of another standard style system. Specifically, manuscripts should NOT carry footnotes at the bottom of manuscript pages. All tables and figures must be numbered, with a clear title/heading, and source and date of data. Tables, figures, and graphs must be submitted in camera-ready condition for publication. For tables, use a uniform typeface (preferably Times Roman).

Correspondence, manuscripts, and book review inquiries and submissions should be sent to:

Dr. Georgia A. Persons, Editor
National Political Science Review
School of Public Policy (0345)
Georgia Institute of Technology
Atlanta, GA 30332-0345

Phone: (404) 894-6510. FAX (404) 894-0535
Email: Georgia.persons@pubpolicy.gatech.edu

Inquiries regarding reprinting or other usages and copyright matters should be directed to the website of Transaction Publishers (www.transactionpub.com). Clicking on the contact button will bring up contact information for the Permissions Department.

www.ingramcontent.com/pod-product-compliance
Lightning Source LLC
Chambersburg PA
CBHW081431270326
41932CB00019B/3160

* 9 7 8 1 4 1 2 8 1 0 4 8 7 *